SAP PRESS e-books

Print or e-book, Kindle or iPad, workplace or airplane: Choose where and how to read your SAP PRESS books! You can now get all our titles as e-books, too:

- By download and online access
- For all popular devices
- And, of course, DRM-free

Convinced? Then go to www.sap-press.com and get your e-book today.

SAP® on Microsoft® Azure®

SAP PRESS is a joint initiative of SAP and Rheinwerk Publishing. The know-how offered by SAP specialists combined with the expertise of Rheinwerk Publishing offers the reader expert books in the field. SAP PRESS features first-hand information and expert advice, and provides useful skills for professional decision-making.

SAP PRESS offers a variety of books on technical and business-related topics for the SAP user. For further information, please visit our website: *www.sap-press.com*.

Bilay, Gutsche, Krimmel, Stiehl
SAP Cloud Platform Integration: The Comprehensive Guide (3rd Edition)
2020, 906 pages, hardcover and e-book
www.sap-press.com/5077

Denys van Kempen
SAP HANA 2.0: An Introduction
2019, 438 pages, hardcover and e-book
www.sap-press.com/4884

Mark Mergaerts, Bert Vanstechelman
SAP S/4HANA System Conversion Guide
2020, 537 pages, hardcover and e-book
www.sap-press.com/5035

Saueressig, Stein, Boeder, Kleis
SAP S/4HANA Architecture
2021, 520 pages, hardcover and e-book
www.sap-press.com/5189

Bardhan, Baumgartl, Choi, Dudgeon, Lahiri, Meijerink, Worsley-Tonks
SAP S/4HANA: An Introduction (3rd Edition)
2019, 647 pages, hardcover and e-book
www.sap-press.com/4782

Ravi Kashyap

SAP® on Microsoft® Azure®

Architecture and Administration

Editor Will Jobst
Acquisitions Editor Hareem Shafi
Copyeditor Julie McNamee
Cover Design Graham Geary
Photo Credit iStockphoto.com: 170094749/© mf-guddyx
Layout Design Vera Brauner
Production Graham Geary
Typesetting III-satz, Husby (Germany)
Printed and bound in the United States of America, on paper from sustainable sources

ISBN 978-1-4932-2017-5

© 2021 by Rheinwerk Publishing, Inc., Boston (MA)
1st edition 2021

Library of Congress Cataloging-in-Publication Data
Names: Kashyap, Ravi, author.
Title: SAP on Microsoft Azure : architecture and administration / Ravi Kashyap.
Description: 1st edition. | Boston : Rheinwerk Publishing, Inc. 2020. | Includes index.
Identifiers: LCCN 2020043889 (print) | LCCN 2020043890 (ebook) | ISBN 9781493220175 (hardcover) | ISBN 9781493220182 (ebook)
Subjects: LCSH: Cloud computing. | Microsoft Azure. | SAP ERP.
Classification: LCC QA76.585 .K37 2020 (print) | LCC QA76.585 (ebook) | DDC 004.67/82--dc23
LC record available at https://lccn.loc.gov/2020043889
LC ebook record available at https://lccn.loc.gov/2020043890

All rights reserved. Neither this publication nor any part of it may be copied or reproduced in any form or by any means or translated into another language, without the prior consent of Rheinwerk Publishing, 2 Heritage Drive, Suite 305, Quincy, MA 02171.

Rheinwerk Publishing makes no warranties or representations with respect to the content hereof and specifically disclaims any implied warranties of merchantability or fitness for any particular purpose. Rheinwerk Publishing assumes no responsibility for any errors that may appear in this publication.

"Rheinwerk Publishing" and the Rheinwerk Publishing logo are registered trademarks of Rheinwerk Verlag GmbH, Bonn, Germany. SAP PRESS is an imprint of Rheinwerk Verlag GmbH and Rheinwerk Publishing, Inc.

All of the screenshots and graphics reproduced in this book are subject to copyright © SAP SE, Dietmar-Hopp-Allee 16, 69190 Walldorf, Germany.

SAP, ABAP, ASAP, Concur Hipmunk, Duet, Duet Enterprise, Expenselt, SAP ActiveAttention, SAP Adaptive Server Enterprise, SAP Advantage Database Server, SAP ArchiveLink, SAP Ariba, SAP Business ByDesign, SAP Business Explorer (SAP BEx), SAP BusinessObjects, SAP BusinessObjects Explorer, SAP BusinessObjects Web Intelligence, SAP Business One, SAP Business Workflow, SAP BW/4HANA, SAP C/4HANA, SAP Concur, SAP Crystal Reports, SAP EarlyWatch, SAP Fieldglass, SAP Fiori, SAP Global Trade Services (SAP GTS), SAP GoingLive, SAP HANA, SAP Jam, SAP Leonardo, SAP Lumira, SAP MaxDB, SAP NetWeaver, SAP PartnerEdge, SAPPHIRE NOW, SAP PowerBuilder, SAP PowerDesigner, SAP R/2, SAP R/3, SAP Replication Server, SAP Roambi, SAP S/4HANA, SAP S/4HANA Cloud, SAP SQL Anywhere, SAP Strategic Enterprise Management (SAP SEM), SAP SuccessFactors, SAP Vora, TripIt, and Qualtrics are registered or unregistered trademarks of SAP SE, Walldorf, Germany.

All other products mentioned in this book are registered or unregistered trademarks of their respective companies.

Contents at a Glance

1	Introduction to Microsoft Azure	21
2	SAP on Microsoft Azure	35
3	Microsoft Azure Infrastructure Offerings for SAP	59
4	System Design Framework	85
5	Governance and Compliance	115
6	Infrastructure Architecture Guidance	129
7	Resiliency	141
8	Backup Architecture and Mechanisms	175
9	Automation	193
10	Encryption	207
11	Migrating SAP to Microsoft Azure	213
12	Operations	239
13	Case Study	277
14	Outlook	287

Dear Reader,

Beginning a new project is exciting. This is the "expansive" phase of design—everything is an option, and the mind can run wild with possibilities. Like the renaissance master Michelangelo staring at a blank marble slab and visualizing his art, we take this moment in the design process to reach the edges of possibility—and then comes the first knock of the chisel and hammer.

SAP on Microsoft Azure first shows you the expanse, and then provides you with your chisel and hammer. As you consider the possibilities and begin to visualize your SAP public cloud landscape, this book will help shape your vision into a fully-functioning architecture. With author Ravi Kashyap's years of expertise to guide you, you'll be running in the cloud in no time.

What did you think about *SAP on Microsoft Azure: Architecture and Administration*? Your comments and suggestions are the most useful tools to help us make our books the best they can be. Please feel free to contact me and share any praise or criticism you may have.

Thank you for purchasing a book from SAP PRESS!

Will Jobst
Editor, SAP PRESS

willj@rheinwerk-publishing.com
www.sap-press.com
Rheinwerk Publishing · Boston, MA

Contents

Preface 17

1   Introduction to Microsoft Azure   21

1.1	What Is Microsoft Azure?	21
1.2	**Cloud Deployment Options**	22
	1.2.1 Public Cloud versus Private Cloud	22
	1.2.2 Hybrid Cloud	22
1.3	**Cloud Models: Comparing IaaS, PaaS, and SaaS**	23
	1.3.1 Infrastructure as a Service	25
	1.3.2 Platform as a Service	25
	1.3.3 Software as a Service	26
1.4	**Cloud Adoption Framework**	26
1.5	**Service Availability and Preview Features**	28
1.6	**Understanding Microsoft Azure's SLAs**	29
	1.6.1 Service Level Agreement Percentages	30
	1.6.2 When Microsoft Can't Meet the SLA	30
	1.6.3 Composite SLA	31
1.7	**Why Move to Microsoft Azure?**	32
	1.7.1 Benefits of Moving an Enterprise Infrastructure	32
	1.7.2 Event-Based Triggers	33
1.8	**Summary**	34

2   SAP on Microsoft Azure   35

2.1	The Unique SAP Architecture on Microsoft Azure	35
2.2	SAP on Microsoft Azure Support Prerequisites	36
2.3	**Supported SAP Products, Databases, and Operating Systems**	37
	2.3.1 Supported Operating Systems	38
	2.3.2 Supported Databases	38
	2.3.3 Supported SAP Products	38
	2.3.4 SAP HANA-Certified Hardware Directory	39

2.4		SAP Technology Stacks and Architecture	40
	2.4.1	Distributed versus Standard Systems	40
	2.4.2	SAP Technology Stacks	40
2.5		SAP on Microsoft Azure Reference Architecture	42
2.6		Deployment Models	43
	2.6.1	All SAP on Microsoft Azure	43
	2.6.2	Hybrid	44
	2.6.3	Multi-Cloud	44
2.7		Paths to Microsoft Azure	45
	2.7.1	Cloud Rationalization and the Five Rs of Migration	45
	2.7.2	SAP Migrations versus New Implementations	48
	2.7.3	Third-Party Systems	49
2.8		SAP Cloud Appliance Library	49
2.9		Relevant SAP Notes	56
2.10		Summary	57

3   Microsoft Azure Infrastructure Offerings for SAP   59

3.1		Microsoft Azure Enterprise Enrollment Hierarchy	59
3.2		Connectivity to Microsoft Azure	60
	3.2.1	ExpressRoute	61
	3.2.2	Site-to-Site Virtual Private Network	62
	3.2.3	Point-to-Site Virtual Private Network	62
3.3		Microsoft Azure Pricing Calculator and Total Cost of Ownership Calculator	62
3.4		Infrastructure Foundation Pillars	64
	3.4.1	Compute	64
	3.4.2	Storage	68
	3.4.3	Network	70
3.5		Shared Storage	73
	3.5.1	Microsoft Azure Shared Storage	73
	3.5.2	Microsoft Azure Shared Disks	74
	3.5.3	Microsoft Azure NetApp Files	74
3.6		Operating System Licenses in Microsoft Azure	75
3.7		Platform Maintenance and Notifications	77
3.8		Microsoft Azure Dedicated Host	78
	3.8.1	Virtual Machine Provisioning and Tracking Capacity	78

		3.8.2	Cost	80
3.9	**SAP HANA on Azure (Large Instances)**			80
		3.9.1	SAP HANA on Azure (Large Instances) Revision 4	81
		3.9.2	Deployment Timeline and Communication	81
3.10	**Key Vault**			82
3.11	**Microsoft Azure Landing Zone**			82
3.12	**Summary**			83

4 System Design Framework — 85

4.1	**Security**			85
		4.1.1	Identity	87
		4.1.2	Network Security	89
		4.1.3	Infrastructure Security	90
		4.1.4	Application and Data Security	92
4.2	**Performance**			93
		4.2.1	Compute	94
		4.2.2	Storage	96
		4.2.3	Network	98
		4.2.4	Database and Application	100
		4.2.5	Scalability	100
4.3	**Resiliency**			101
		4.3.1	Platform Resiliency	101
		4.3.2	Availability Set	102
		4.3.3	Availability Zone	103
		4.3.4	Region Resiliency	105
		4.3.5	Microsoft Azure Site Recovery	105
		4.3.6	Microsoft Azure Backup Service	107
		4.3.7	Microsoft Azure Storage Resiliency	107
		4.3.8	Microsoft Azure Load Balancer	108
4.4	**Operational Efficiency**			109
		4.4.1	Operational Use Cases	110
		4.4.2	Monitoring	111
		4.4.3	Governance	111
		4.4.4	Cost Optimization	112
		4.4.5	Automation	112
4.5	**Summary**			113

5   Governance and Compliance — 115

5.1	Policies	116
5.2	Management Groups	117
5.3	Resource Groups	118
5.4	Role-Based Access Control	119
	5.4.1 How to Use Role-Based Access Control	119
	5.4.2 Role-Based Access Control Scope	120
	5.4.3 Role-Based Access Control versus Policy	120
5.5	Naming Conventions	121
5.6	Resource Locks	122
5.7	Tagging	123
5.8	Microsoft Azure Blueprint	124
5.9	Regulatory and Audit Compliance	125
	5.9.1 Regulatory Compliance	126
	5.9.2 Microsoft Azure Logs	126
	5.9.3 Reporting	127
5.10	Summary	128

6   Infrastructure Architecture Guidance — 129

6.1	Microsoft Azure Regions	129
6.2	Subscription Design	130
6.3	Connectivity and Network Design	131
	6.3.1 Connectivity to Microsoft Azure	131
	6.3.2 Network Design	131
	6.3.3 Subnet Sizes for Gateway, Bastion, and Microsoft Azure NetApp Files	133
	6.3.4 SAP HANA Network Zones	134
	6.3.5 Database App Connectivity and Management Network	135
	6.3.6 Perimeter Network	135
6.4	Compute	136
6.5	Storage	139
6.6	Summary	140

7 Resiliency — 141

7.1 High Availability — 141
- 7.1.1 Shared Storage Using Platform as a Service — 143
- 7.1.2 SAP Application Server — 143
- 7.1.3 SAP Central Services and Database — 144
- 7.1.4 SAP Central Services on Windows Operating System — 150
- 7.1.5 SQL Server Database on Windows Operating System — 152
- 7.1.6 High Availability on the Linux Operating System — 153
- 7.1.7 IBM DB2 — 158
- 7.1.8 Oracle Database — 158
- 7.1.9 SAP Adaptive Server Enterprise Database — 159
- 7.1.10 SAP BusinessObjects Business Intelligence — 159
- 7.1.11 Standalone Enqueue Server 2 — 160
- 7.1.12 Multi-SAP System ID for SAP Central Services — 161

7.2 Disaster Recovery — 162
- 7.2.1 Recovery Time Objective and Recovery Point Object — 163
- 7.2.2 Microsoft Azure Paired Regions — 163
- 7.2.3 Disaster Recovery for SAP — 164
- 7.2.4 Disaster Recovery of SAP Components — 165
- 7.2.5 Application Disaster Recover — 166
- 7.2.6 Shared Storage in the Secondary Region — 169
- 7.2.7 Test and Drills — 170

7.3 Reference Architecture — 171

7.4 Summary — 173

8 Backup Architecture and Mechanisms — 175

8.1 Backup and Restore Overview — 175

8.2 Backup Classifications — 177

8.3 Microsoft Azure Backup and Recovery Vault — 178

8.4 Virtual Machine Backup — 178

8.5 Database Backup — 180
- 8.5.1 Microsoft Azure Backup for SQL Server and SAP HANA — 180
- 8.5.2 Virtual Machine Backup with and without Database File Systems — 183
- 8.5.3 Disk-Based Database Backup — 183
- 8.5.4 Storage Snapshot — 184

8.6 Shared Disk Backup — 185

Contents

8.7	**Third-Party Tools**	185
8.8	**Backup and Retention Policy**	186
8.9	**Restore and Recovery**	187
	8.9.1 Virtual Machine Restore	187
	8.9.2 SQL Server and SAP HANA	189
	8.9.3 Testing for all Use Cases	189
8.10	**Management and Reporting**	190
8.11	**Summary**	191

9   Automation 193

9.1	**Infrastructure as Code**	194
9.2	**Automation Use Cases**	195
	9.2.1 Infrastructure Deployment	195
	9.2.2 Application Deployment	196
	9.2.3 Infrastructure and Application Lifecycle	197
9.3	**Automation Tools**	197
	9.3.1 Microsoft Azure Cloud Shell	197
	9.3.2 Microsoft Azure Resource Manager Template	198
	9.3.3 Terraform	200
	9.3.4 Orchestration versus Configuration Management	201
	9.3.5 SAP Landscape Management	202
9.4	**DevOps Integration**	203
9.5	**Quickstart Templates**	203
9.6	**Disadvantages of Using Automation**	204
9.7	**Automation Recommend Practices**	205
9.8	**Summary**	206

10   Encryption 207

10.1	**Encryption at Rest**	207
	10.1.1 Storage Service Encryption	209
	10.1.2 Microsoft Azure Disk Encryption	209
	10.1.3 Database Encryption	209
	10.1.4 Backup Encryption	210

	10.1.5	Microsoft Azure NetApp Files	210
	10.1.6	Third-Party Software	210
10.2	**Encryption in Transit**		211
10.3	**Key Management**		212
10.4	**Summary**		212

11 Migrating SAP to Microsoft Azure   213

11.1	**Planning and Readiness**		213
	11.1.1	Readiness Evaluation	214
	11.1.2	Archiving and Cleanup	215
11.2	**Migration Paths and Methodologies**		215
	11.2.1	Database Migration Methodologies	217
	11.2.2	Homogeneous Migration	218
	11.2.3	Heterogenous Migration	220
	11.2.4	Application Server and SAP Central Services Migration	224
	11.2.5	Third-Party Solutions for Migration	225
	11.2.6	Migration Options Trade-Offs	225
11.3	**Large Databases and Migration Optimizations**		226
	11.3.1	Large Database Challenges	226
	11.3.2	Downtime Optimization Techniques	227
11.4	**SAP Landscape Migration Phases**		231
	11.4.1	Pilot	232
	11.4.2	Nonproduction	233
	11.4.3	Production Rehearsal	234
	11.4.4	Production Cutover	234
	11.4.5	Large Landscape Migration	235
11.5	**Lessons Learned**		236
11.6	**Summary**		238

12 Operations   239

12.1	**Cloud Operating Model**		239
12.2	**Operational Efficiency**		240
	12.2.1	SAP Snoozing	240
	12.2.2	Autoscaling	242

		12.2.3	Operating System and SAP Patching	244
		12.2.4	Rightsizing and Virtual Machine Resizing	249
		12.2.5	System Clone, Copy, and Refresh	250
		12.2.6	Microsoft Azure Backup	251
		12.2.7	Microsoft Azure NetApp Files and Disks Snapshot	251
		12.2.8	SAP Landscape Management Integration	251
		12.2.9	SAP HANA on Azure (Large Instances) to Virtual Machine Migration	251
		12.2.10	SAP Licensing and Hardware Key	253
		12.2.11	Operational Learning	254
	12.3	Monitoring		257
		12.3.1	SAP Solution Manager	258
		12.3.2	Microsoft Azure Monitor	259
		12.3.3	Dashboards	262
		12.3.4	Alerts	264
		12.3.5	Microsoft Azure Monitor for SAP Solutions	265
	12.4	Cost Management		268
		12.4.1	Understand the Cost Structure	268
		12.4.2	Plan with Focus on Cost	269
		12.4.3	Optimize for Cost Regularly	269
		12.4.4	Microsoft Azure Cost Management	269
		12.4.5	Cost Projections	274
	12.5	Summary		275

13 Case Study   277

	13.1	New Implementation Planning		277
		13.1.1	Milestone #1: Sizing and Total Cost of Ownership Calculation	277
		13.1.2	Milestone #2: Architecture Components	278
		13.1.3	Milestone #3: Infrastructure and SAP Deployment	281
	13.2	Migration Planning		282
		13.2.1	Shared Architecture on Microsoft Azure	283
		13.2.2	Resiliency Design (High Availability/Disaster Recovery)	283
		13.2.3	Migration Methodology and Sequence	284
		13.2.4	Phased Go-Live and Hybrid System Maintenance	284
		13.2.5	Data Center Exit and Future Optimizations	284
	13.3	Summary		285

14 Outlook — 287

14.1	Marching towards SAP S/4HANA	287
14.2	Integration to Cloud Native Tools	287
14.3	SAP Innovations	288
14.4	Evolution of Microsoft Azure	289
14.5	Containers for SAP?	290
14.6	Summary	291

The Author	293
Index	295

Preface

How is this book different from the myriad information available online (often free)? Why read a book when, given the velocity of the cloud, the content may be out of date?

These questions had a profound effect in shaping this book, and we often thought about these issues from a reader's point of view. How many times have you read an article online on a specific topic that doesn't explain how it fits in the bigger picture, or, even worse, there is a confusing diagram in the content that the article doesn't refer to or explain? A picture is worth a thousand words only if it's simple enough to understand and ties together with the article.

Another common problem we run into when reading something in bits and pieces is that there isn't enough foundational information to build on. For example, it may assume that you know certain things rather than explaining or providing context.

These issues, combined with the overwhelming amount of information out there, make the case for reading a book when you're trying to grasp not only new technology but also how it applies to the work you currently do or intend to perform.

Objective of This Book

This book builds your base knowledge first and then add the other different and flexible pieces as you understand how they work. The objective here is to start from the introductory level content and showcase how to use frameworks and design principles to successfully architect, deploy, and manage the SAP landscape in Microsoft Azure. It acts as a decision guide and shows what questions to ask rather than providing all the answers. For example, we've seen a lot of conversations about high availability (HA) without first asking what the uptime requirements are and disaster recovery (DR) conversations without knowing the recovery time objective (RTO) and recovery point objective (RPO). This book enables you to ask the right questions and make informed decisions.

If after reading a chapter, you feel that you've understood the concepts and decide to explore further by doing things yourself in Microsoft Azure portal or in some other form, that chapter has served its purpose. This book also highlights the importance of working together as a team because SAP on Microsoft Azure isn't just SAP, isn't just Microsoft Azure, nor just infrastructure as a service (IaaS); rather, it's a combination that works together.

Target Audience

The book is primarily geared toward folks who want to learn how SAP on Microsoft Azure is architected and managed, but it's also helpful for those trying to learn Microsoft

Azure and decision makers who want to understand how pieces fit together and use optimizations for cost and architecture. In terms of roles, this book will be helpful for SAP Basis administrators, SAP technical architects, Microsoft Azure administrators, and Microsoft Azure architects who are currently working or expect to work on SAP on Microsoft Azure deployments/migrations. Folks with operating system, storage, and network backgrounds will also learn how the work they do fits into the overall deployment.

Because things in Microsoft Azure change quickly, the book focuses more on concepts and working knowledge rather than all the specific restrictions and limitations that a service has primarily because the limitations change over time. Even if you're familiar with certain areas, we recommend for the first time, to read the whole book, rather than skipping contents, and from there use it as a reference. There is a good chance that something you were looking for exists in some other chapter under that context.

Structure of the Book

The book touches on a lot of topics from the introduction level to architectural details, deployment, and operations using automation. It starts with an introduction of Microsoft Azure and defining terms that are used frequently for cloud processes, and then discusses how to think about SAP architectural components to be mapped to Microsoft Azure services along the design principles. It goes on to explain Microsoft Azure–specific topics, such as technical services and governance, and SAP topics, such as technical architecture, HA/DR, migrations, and backup/restore.

Other topics, such as automation and operations, are discussed that complement the technical design and provides use cases from real-life SAP on Microsoft Azure deployments.

More information on each chapter follows:

- **Chapter 1: Introduction to Microsoft Azure**
  This chapter introduces Microsoft Azure and talks about cloud adoption framework, cloud models, available services and features, and Microsoft Azure's service levels. It also explores the benefits of moving an enterprise to Microsoft Azure.

- **Chapter 2: SAP on Microsoft Azure**
  This chapter introduces SAP on Microsoft Azure and discusses the importance of application-specific architecture. In addition, you'll learn about supported SAP products, prerequisites of SAP deployment to Microsoft Azure, and deployment and migration paths.

- **Chapter 3: Microsoft Azure Infrastructure Offerings for SAP**
  This chapter describes Microsoft Azure service offerings for SAP and trade-offs of decisions when choosing one service over other.

- **Chapter 4: System Design Framework**
  This chapter discusses the aspects that organizations need to consider when architecting SAP solutions in Microsoft Azure, such as performance, availability, and resiliency. It also discusses recommended practices for architecture design and service configuration.
- **Chapter 5: Governance and Compliance**
  This chapter talks about essential elements of governance and compliance and discusses options available in Microsoft Azure.
- **Chapter 6: Infrastructure Architecture Guidance**
  This chapter provides prescriptive guidance about the services and configurations to use for SAP on Microsoft Azure deployments based on architectural principles and the design framework.
- **Chapter 7: Resiliency**
  Reliability and resiliency go hand in hand, and this chapter talks about resiliency as a core aspect of Microsoft Azure reliability in terms of HA and DR. It discusses the important business metrics to consider for resiliency and how to architect the solution to meet those metrics.
- **Chapter 8: Backup Architecture and Mechanisms**
  This chapter talks about backup and recovery as a part of business continuity; it discusses services and mechanisms available in Microsoft Azure out of the box as well as using third-party solutions.
- **Chapter 9: Automation**
  This chapter introduces the automation aspects of deploying solutions in a cloud environment. It discusses Infrastructure as Code (IaC) for Microsoft Azure service deployments and the capabilities SAP provides to automate application deployment as well.
- **Chapter 10: Encryption**
  This chapter talks about the encryption mechanisms available in Microsoft Azure as it relates to each service and those provided by SAP. In addition, the chapter discusses encryption at rest and in transit.
- **Chapter 11: Migrating SAP to Microsoft Azure**
  This chapter talks about mechanisms to migrate existing SAP systems to Microsoft Azure, including planning, execution, and optimization. It also discusses lessons learned from past migrations.
- **Chapter 12: Operations**
  This chapter talks about the operations aspects of SAP on Microsoft Azure, such as monitoring, optimizing, and patching. It also discusses cost management, alerts, and budgeting.
- **Chapter 13: Case Study**
  This chapter showcases the decision-making steps for migrations and new implementations in case study format.

- **Chapter 14: Outlook**
  This chapter explores what SAP on Microsoft Azure may look like in coming years, including how the evolution of both Microsoft Azure and SAP impacts the architecture and effort required.

Acknowledgments

I had always wanted to write a book, but I just didn't know when and about what. This changed when I talked to Hareem Shafi from SAP PRESS, and I'll always be thankful to her for that. She guided me when I had no clue how to think about a book and why people would read it. When I started writing more, it turned out more difficult than I had initially thought, but Will Jobst (editor) was there to help keep me on schedule, give me tips to make the content clear to the audience, and recommend changes to make the writing style better! Thanks to Will for helping me through the process and the copyeditor for her review.

When I mentioned writing this book to one of my previous colleague (now friend), he asked whether I was the right person to write about SAP on Microsoft Azure (or whether I am considered a subject matter expert [SME]). That made me think again and determine that I didn't have to know everything because a book is more than just facts; it's also experience and the ability to convey things in a simple manner. I am happy that I have friends who ask me these difficult questions.

I am also thankful to my colleagues for being a part of my learning journey and inspiration for so many things that I've done professionally.

Finally, I couldn't have done this without the support of my wife, Katie, who was there not only when I needed help but also when I needed her and our daughter away from my office so I could concentrate on writing!

Chapter 1
Introduction to Microsoft Azure

Cloud computing is more important than ever in this fast-changing world where businesses need to adapt quickly to changes in demand and customer preferences. Cloud computing comes in several shapes and forms, and Microsoft has become one of the leading providers with its extensive cloud service portfolio.

The term *cloud* has become synonymous with IT infrastructure, and a few older terminologies have been rephrased to take advantage of the cloud movement. What used to be called *hosting* is now called *private cloud*, making way for the term *public cloud* to refer to the computing services available over the Internet.

This chapter will walk you through various cloud models, the advantages of adopting the cloud service, and how services and service level agreements (SLAs) work in the context of the cloud service known as Microsoft Azure.

1.1 What Is Microsoft Azure?

Microsoft Azure, originally called Windows Azure, is a *public cloud* computing platform by Microsoft that provides hundreds of services for creating or hosting applications that range from simple websites to enterprise applications such as SAP. These services can be accessed either via the Microsoft Azure portal (using a web browser or desktop app) or an application programming interface (API).

For application folks, the location or connectivity to the data center traditionally hasn't been as important, but if you're an infrastructure person or just curious, imagine a remote location with several buildings hosting a massive number of servers with interconnected networks. Now think about being able to access these servers or services from anywhere in the world on demand and paying only for what you use. Now that's powerful!

Throughout the book, we'll talk about how this infrastructure and these buildings translate into Microsoft Azure services, that is, virtual machines (VMs) that are used to deploy and scale applications at the speed of the cloud.

1.2 Cloud Deployment Options

We mentioned that Microsoft Azure is a public cloud, but what does that mean: Is there a private cloud too? Can both public and private clouds be used together? This section discusses the deployment options of cloud services and addresses these questions.

1.2.1 Public Cloud versus Private Cloud

A public cloud makes IT infrastructure available over the Internet in the form of self-service, often in a pay-as-you-go model as opposed to a private cloud, where a long-term contract must be in place with a service provider furnishing the infrastructure.

Table 1.1 shows some of the common differences between a private cloud and a public cloud.

Public Cloud	Private Cloud
Billed per second (pay-as-you-go)	Monthly or yearly contract
Highly scalable on demand	Scale often comes with large lead times
Instant provisioning	No instant provisioning
Services configured by end user	Service configured by service provider
Use of multiple programming languages	Fewer or no programming languages available
Open-source tools integration widely used	Fewer integration with open-source tools
Service management and monitoring by organization	Service management and monitoring by service provider

Table 1.1 Public versus Private Cloud

1.2.2 Hybrid Cloud

Hybrid cloud is an architecture where IT infrastructure (and workloads) span more than one environment. It may be a public cloud (e.g., Microsoft Azure) and on-premise, public cloud and private cloud, or two public clouds (sometimes also called multi-cloud).

Hybrid cloud has several use cases such as the following:

- Production system on-premise and nonproduction system in cloud
- Disaster recovery (DR) systems in cloud and primary systems on-premise, as shown in Figure 1.1
- SAP systems in private cloud and non-SAP systems in public cloud, such as Microsoft Azure

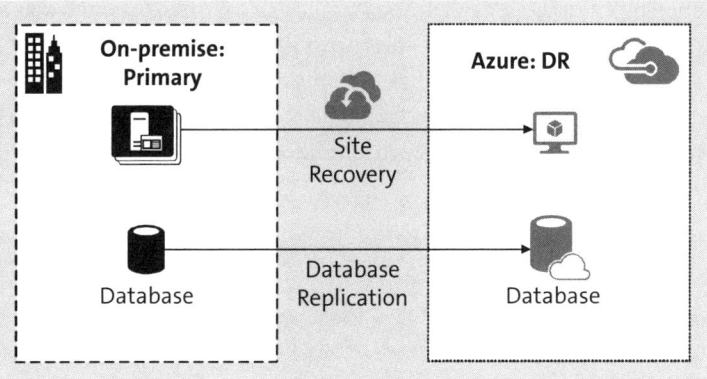

Figure 1.1 Hybrid Cloud Showing Primary Systems On-Premises and DR on Microsoft Azure

These kinds of setups provide flexibility and add to the deployment options; these setups are not uncommon with large and complex IT estates. In addition, having the DR system in the cloud serves as a test bed for running things in the cloud.

1.3 Cloud Models: Comparing IaaS, PaaS, and SaaS

Cloud services are broadly divided into three pillars as shown in Figure 1.2:

- Infrastructure as a service (IaaS), such as servers
- Platform as a service (PaaS), such as development tools and frameworks
- Software as a service (SaaS), such as websites

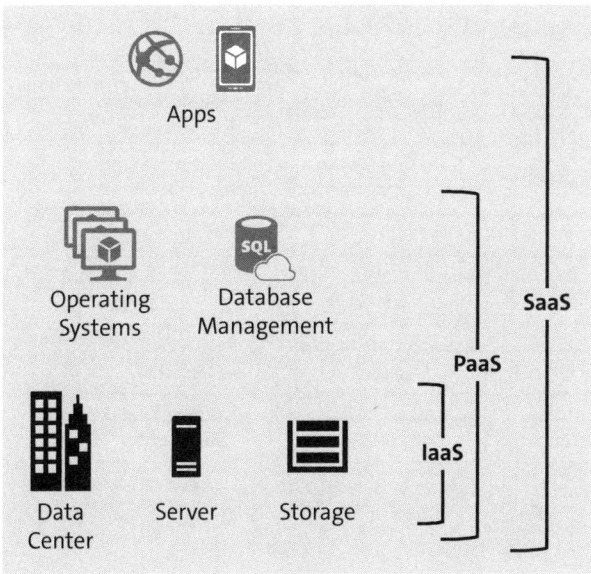

Figure 1.2 Overview of Cloud Services: IaaS, PaaS, and SaaS

1 Introduction to Microsoft Azure

From the user experience point of view, everything in Microsoft Azure is provided as a service, meaning whether you need a VM for enterprise applications or .NET framework for the custom application, you'll either click buttons in the Microsoft Azure portal or write code for it. Most of the services are available with a pay-as-you-go model (billed per second), which provides the flexibility to shut down the service when not in use as a way to optimize cost.

> **Note**
>
> The categorization should be read in the context of users; even though users don't need to worry about servers and networking for, say, a website, Microsoft still provides the underlying infrastructure.

Most of the Microsoft Azure services can be provisioned and accessed from the Microsoft Azure portal (a few services, e.g., SAP HANA on Azure [Large Instances], can't be provisioned from the portal as of this writing), so it's a good idea to broadly understand how the services are consumed and what you can control and configure.

Figure 1.3 shows a comparison between traditional on-premise systems, where all the infrastructure parts are self-managed, and cloud service models, where a service provider manages one or more of the underlying parts.

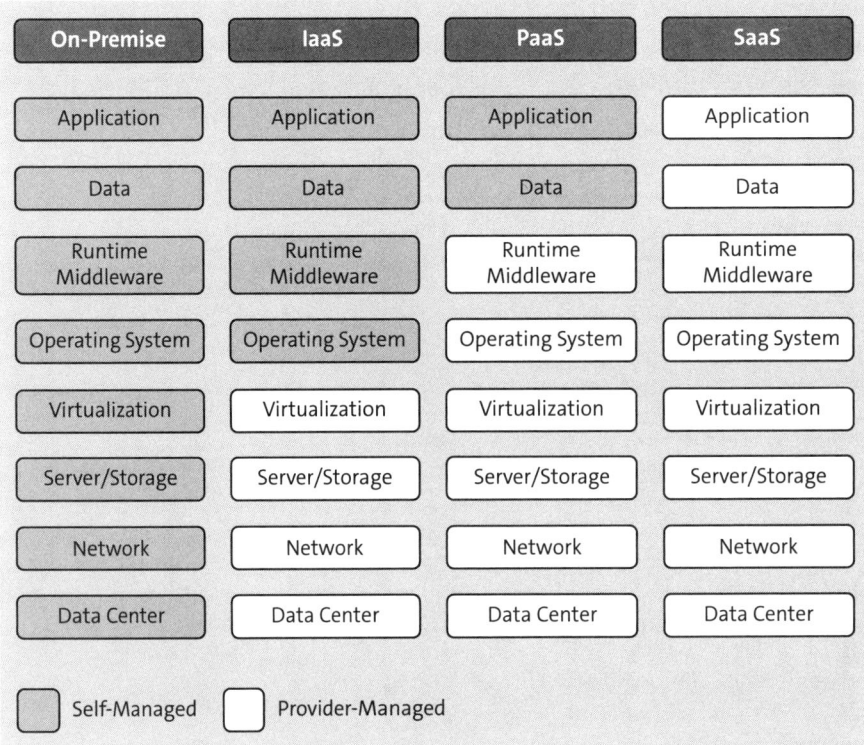

Figure 1.3 Cloud Models Compared with Traditional On-Premise Management

1.3.1 Infrastructure as a Service

Infrastructure as a service (IaaS) gives you quick access to compute VMs along with associated components such as network and storage without having to worry about managing physical building, power, security, and virtualization technologies. You can still install, configure, and optimize operating systems (OSs), databases, and applications.

IaaS can be scaled up and down on demand with short notice to meet business demands.

You should choose IaaS in the following situations:

- Control of the OS is required for configuration and parameter optimization, or OS patching needs to be controlled with specific patch levels for an application.
- Specific OS packages must be added for an application such as SUSE high availability (HA).
- A certification is required, such as for SAP products. SAP needs to certify every VM that will run production instances.
- Control over storage size, backups, and recovery is required.
- Application-specific HA and DR configuration needs to be implemented.
- Use cases include high-performance computing and Big Data analysis.

1.3.2 Platform as a Service

For some applications, including SAP, that require customization and optimization at the OS level and middleware configuration, IaaS is an obvious choice. What about the use cases where you can work on standard middleware and development tools, and don't want to worry about configuration and licensing of those tools to develop and deploy services? Say the application just needs the .NET framework on any kind of hardware. Enter the world of platform as a service (PaaS), which removes the need to manage the OS and other middleware and uses precoded application components to get to business results faster.

You should choose PaaS in the following situations:

- The underlying OS and/or middleware program isn't an important factor in building the application and is available as a service.
- Cloud providers have built-in frameworks or tools that can be developed or customized.
- PaaS services can integrate with applications on IaaS to enhance the functionality.

1.3.3 Software as a Service

The software as a service (SaaS) model makes the application available to users and organizations as a subscription, which includes licensing and all the maintenance and most of the configurations.

SaaS is available in consumer applications such as the Microsoft Office suite as well as enterprise applications such as SAP SuccessFactors and SAP Ariba.

You should choose SaaS in the following situations:

- Ready-to-use applications (or available customizations), such as document management or file editing software, meet the requirements.
- No customization is required and out-of-the-box features work for the use cases.
- You need to get the application up and running quickly, such as websites.

> **Note**
> Keep in mind that when you don't have to manage something, you also lose control of the component. For example, when using PaaS, you won't have access to the OS and can't control patching, maintenance, and configuration. Cloud providers ensure that the availability is considered when doing any maintenance.

With the popularity of cloud services, several other "as a service" models have popped up, such as database as a service (DBaaS), security as a service, and so on. This book doesn't go into the details of those models, and some of them can be easily categorized into the models discussed; for example, DBaaS can also be considered PaaS.

1.4 Cloud Adoption Framework

Every organization has its own unique journey to the cloud, and a framework allows you to follow an adoption path while keeping unique aspects of the company. Microsoft released its own version of a cloud adoption framework in 2019 that you can use for guidance, which includes the journey tracker as well.

Figure 1.4 shows an example cloud adoption framework that can be used as a model for cloud adoption.

Consider the framework as documentation and experience from the field to enable faster adoption. Following are the broad categories of the framework:

- **Discover**
  This includes not only the technical capabilities but also business outcomes. Fully automated provisioning may be the technical success metric, but does it align with the business outcome of, say, saving money? It's important to look at cloud adoption holistically.

- Plan

  Planning should include IT assets as well as people and skills; for example, you may need to plan trainings to acquire new skills. In addition, create a list of applications to move to the cloud and the order in which to move them, depending on business criticality and timelines.

- Operate

  Managing an IT infrastructure in the cloud requires a different operating model than on-premise management. There is no keeping track of additional capacity anymore, and if you need extra storage to additional backup, it can be done in minutes. After you get hang of how to manage the infrastructure the "cloud way," you can work on optimization and further increasing reliability. Use cloud-native tools and pay attention to systems not being used so they can either be decommissioned or snoozed when not in use.

- Execute

  We all are inherently biased toward action, so you'll likely tend to fast-forward to this step because building something tangible brings more joy then scribbling on whiteboards or sticking post-it notes around. However, it's important to understand the business requirements and execution plan before jumping into creating VMs and installing databases. As you start moving applications, you'll also learn the optimal methods and how to create checks and balances to avoid rework.

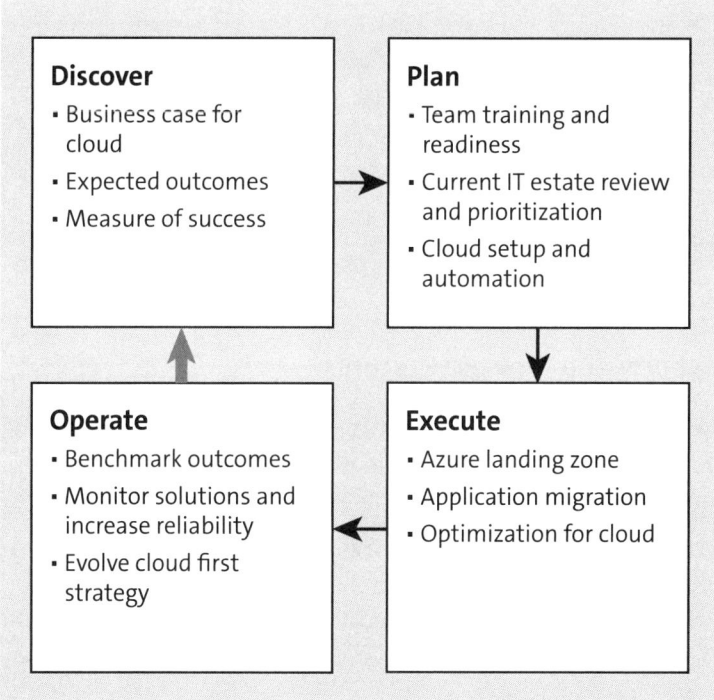

Figure 1.4 Elements of a Cloud Adoption Framework Model

1   Introduction to Microsoft Azure

In an ever-changing cloud world, these steps aren't one-time activities; therefore, it's important to incorporate a feedback loop, which not only goes to the previous step but also to the original discover stage if required. For example, if one of the outcomes was to automate provisioning of everything, and you don't meet that in the first round of execution, the feedback look would help better analyze and better plan the migrations that follow.

The feedback loop need not be at the end of a cycle; it can be a continuous improvement cycle as well when steps are running in sprints. Figure 1.5 shows the feedback loop cycle for this kind of adoption.

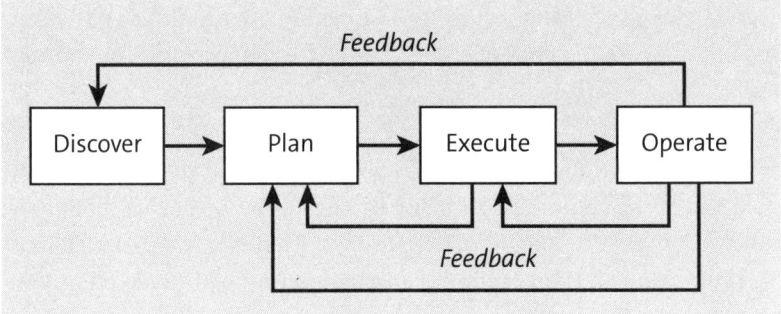

Figure 1.5 Feedback Loop for a Cloud Adoption Framework

Tools and Resources
At each stage, we'll be using a set of resources (e.g., documentation) and tools. It can be as simple as a template, or it may be a little more involved tool such as Movere (now part of Microsoft) to determine the readiness of moving systems to Microsoft Azure. The output from one stage acts as input for the next, and the feedback loop ensures that all the learning is captured.

1.5 Service Availability and Preview Features

As of writing this book, Microsoft Azure has more than 60 available regions worldwide (available in 140 countries); however, not all regions are created equal as we'll explore in the context of SAP.

Not all products (and services) are available in each region (as shown for M series VM in Figure 1.6), and the pricing differs based on the region (even within the same geography). It's important to keep this in mind when choosing the primary region because changing a region after you've already deployed systems can be expensive and labor intensive.

Products	nal	Canada Central	Canada East	Central US	East US	East US 2
M-series		✓	✓	🕒	✓	✓
Mv2-series					✓	✓

Figure 1.6 Microsoft Azure Product Availability for M Series VM

Before a service is generally available (GA), it goes through several testing phases and improvements based on feedback. To evaluate and better understand product features, Microsoft Azure rolls out services in previews as follows:

- **Private preview**
  This is invitation-only early access available to select Microsoft customers to test concepts and features. There is no formal support for items in private preview.

- **Public preview**
  At this phase, all customers are eligible to test the new service or feature. Microsoft provides support services but there is no SLA associated with it; therefore, these services aren't recommended to be used in production.

In Microsoft Azure portal, when a service is in public preview, it shows next to the service name, as shown in Figure 1.7.

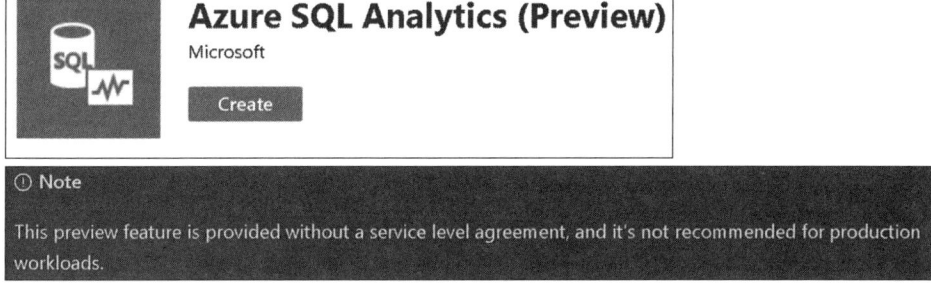

Figure 1.7 Example of Preview Feature from Microsoft Azure Portal and Note for SLA

1.6 Understanding Microsoft Azure's SLAs

When you don't control the data center infrastructure, you may be wondering how you measure reliability and availability. Microsoft does of a lot of things in the background such as redundancy configuration, proactive maintenance, failure prediction (using machine learning algorithms), platform update, and hardware replacement. With all the processes and technologies in place, they're certain that Microsoft Azure meets the availability and connectivity requirements of all organizations; to that extent,

Microsoft Azure provides legally bound, money-backed SLAs for each GA service, which can be found at *https://azure.microsoft.com/en-us/support/legal/sla/*.

Figure 1.8 shows the Microsoft Azure SLA for a VM in different configurations.

> LEGAL: SERVICE LEVEL AGREEMENTS / Virtual Machines
>
> # SLA for Virtual Machines
>
> Last updated: January 2020
>
> - For all Virtual Machines that have two or more instances deployed across two or more Availability Zones in the same Azure region, we guarantee you will have Virtual Machine Connectivity to at least one instance at least 99.99% of the time.
> - For all Virtual Machines that have two or more instances deployed in the same Availability Set or in the same Dedicated Host Group, we guarantee you will have Virtual Machine Connectivity to at least one instance at least 99.95% of the time.
> - For any Single Instance Virtual Machine using Premium SSD or Ultra Disk for all Operating System Disks and Data Disks, we guarantee you will have Virtual Machine Connectivity of at least 99.9%.

Figure 1.8 SLA for Microsoft Azure Virtual Machine

1.6.1 Service Level Agreement Percentages

Availability is often measured in the number of 9s: three 9s is 99.9%, four 9s is 99.99%, and so on. It reflects the total time, in percentage, that Microsoft guarantees the infrastructure to be available and connected.

While it's a good measure, it can come across as abstract; downtime in number of minutes provides better sense than 9s, as shown in Table 1.2.

Service Level Agreement Percentage	Potential Monthly Downtime	Potential Yearly Downtime
99.99%	4.32 mins	52.56 mins
99.95%	21.6 mins	262.8 mins (4.38 hrs)
99.9%	43.2 mins	525.6 mins (8.76 hrs)

Table 1.2 SLA Percentages with Corresponding Downtime in Minutes/Hours

Knowing the SLA, and thus the impact on downtime, is important because a lot of design decisions (as we'll discuss in later chapters) are based on the SLAs.

1.6.2 When Microsoft Can't Meet the SLA

These numbers are financial penalty based, meaning Microsoft will issue a service credit. An example of a service credit for a single VM is shown in Figure 1.9.

1.6 Understanding Microsoft Azure's SLAs

MONTHLY UPTIME PERCENTAGE	SERVICE CREDIT
< 99.9%	10%
< 99%	25%
< 95%	100%

Figure 1.9 Uptime Percentage and Service Credit for a Microsoft Azure Single VM SLA

> **Note**
> The downtime numbers are shown to illustrate the system impact, and it doesn't necessarily mean that a service will be down for 21.6 minutes every month if there's an SLA of 99.95%. To organizations, the numbers describe Microsoft's commitment for availability and connectivity; to lawyers, they mean that Microsoft will incur a financial penalty; and to IT architects, it means that the design decisions on Microsoft Azure should consider the potential disruption for business continuity and disaster recovery (BCDR).

1.6.3 Composite SLA

All the Microsoft Azure GA services are backed by SLAs, and different services have different SLAs. So, what happens to an SLA when different services are combined to support an application architecture?

The quest for an answer may take us back to probability class. Consider the example of an infrastructure HA setup for SAP Central Services in Microsoft Azure, as shown in Figure 1.10. It also shows the SLA for individual components at the time of this writing: internal load balancer = 99.99%; VMs in availability set = 99.95%; Microsoft Azure NetApp Files = 99.99%.

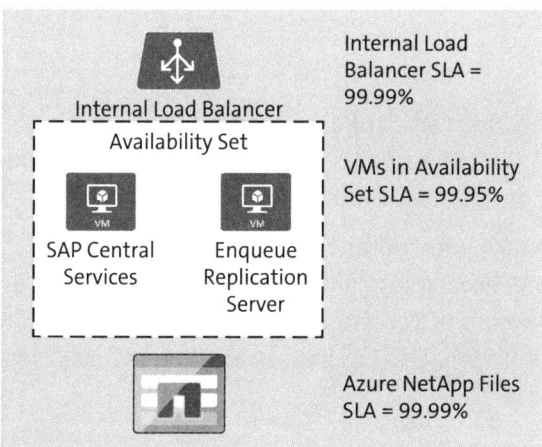

Figure 1.10 SAP Central Services Infrastructure HA Setup with Individual Component SLAs

In this HA setup, if any of the services fail (internal load balancer, both VMs, Microsoft Azure NetApp Files), the application will be unavailable to users. Because the probability of failing for each service is independent from the others, the composite SLA is as follows:

$99.99\% \times 99.95\% \times 99.99\% = 99.93\%$

Note that the composite SLA is lower than individual SLAs, which may sound surprising at first, but it makes sense because the system as a whole has more potential failure points.

1.7 Why Move to Microsoft Azure?

There are several reasons to move to a public cloud and specifically to Microsoft Azure:

- Microsoft realized the value of hybrid cloud early and provided the capability to extend Microsoft Azure services to private data centers using Microsoft Azure Stack.
- Microsoft has more than 90 compliance offerings (as of this writing) spanning across the globe as well as industries such as healthcare, finance, and so on.
- Microsoft has been an enterprise service provider for a long time, and a lot of SAP customers are also Microsoft customers. Because Microsoft also owns Windows Server, combining licensing with Microsoft Azure is easy and cost effective.
- Microsoft is the first global cloud provider to join hands with SAP to accelerate organizations' journey to the public cloud, as a part of the Embrace program.

1.7.1 Benefits of Moving an Enterprise Infrastructure

The popularity of the cloud may have started with cost savings, but as the cloud model matured, things such as agility, automation, and operational efficiency became instrumental in successful deployments.

Agility

In the traditional on-premise or private cloud environment, provisioning a simple VM can take days, if not weeks, and there isn't an easy way to quickly dispose of the VM when you're done with it.

In a public cloud such as Microsoft Azure, a server can be provisioned in less than an hour using automation; a lot of the SAP installation can be automated too. SAP installation automation isn't new and can be done in a private cloud and on-premise too, but public cloud automation brought SAP automation into the limelight. So, agility is a big part of the business case for cloud computing.

Operational Efficiency

Consider the following scenarios:

- The SAP upgrade process takes double the time it should because the necessary backups before and during the upgrade take several hours.
- During month-end close, a critical job that needs to run within a certain time takes so much priority that often everything else has to be halted because the job consumes a lot of resources.
- Having a technical sandbox environment to test new SAP processes is cost- and effort intensive because it would be used only for a few months per year, and buying hardware that would be sitting idle for months isn't a good use of the budget.

All of the preceding and many other operational activities are a breeze in Microsoft Azure thanks to the automation capabilities, on-demand resources, and a better pricing model.

Cost

No discussion of a move-to-cloud case would be complete without talking about cost benefits. Cost can be defined in several different ways:

- Cost of the hardware
- Cost of overprovisioning
- Incremental cost to set up a parallel SAP landscape
- Cost of the DR infrastructure
- Cost of downtime because the server wouldn't come up after a crash and took several hours to fix
- Cost of IT personnel because things need to be fixed in the middle of the night

All these costs can be optimized in Microsoft Azure because of the provided resiliency, pay-as-you-go model, snoozing the system when not in use, and automation.

1.7.2 Event-Based Triggers

Even if you're not looking to move to the cloud proactively, certain events may nudge you in that direction:

- The current data center is at capacity, and for the new project, you may have to get an entirely new data center.
- Current hardware is old, and you need to move all systems to new hardware in the next few years.
- You've heard about infrastructure-as-code (IaC), but you can't achieve the same level of automation on-premise as in the public cloud, which is required for a new business initiative to go live on the IT infrastructure.

- The primary data center just survived a hurricane, which led to the realization that the DR data center is just a few miles away, and both could be damaged by the same disaster in the future.

Events such as these often accelerate the journey to the cloud, so it's better to start exploring early before you absolutely need to.

1.8 Summary

While *cloud computing* has become ubiquitous in the past decade, the concept itself has existed for much longer than that; consumer emails and social media websites have always been SaaS products. It's not until the IT services became a commodity that a new common term was coined to symbolize the movement, which also happens to serve as a great marketing term!

Microsoft Azure is a leading cloud computing provider for IaaS, PaaS, and SaaS solutions backed by financial SLAs. Even though Microsoft Azure services are resilient by design, it's important to architect the solutions correctly to meet your organization's performance and availability requirements; you'll learn more about that in detail in later chapters. In the next chapter, we'll introduce SAP on Microsoft Azure, discuss requirements for SAP deployments in Microsoft Azure, and cover migration paths.

Chapter 2
SAP on Microsoft Azure

The reliability and scalability offered by Microsoft Azure for large companies is evident when you consider that Microsoft runs its SAP systems in Microsoft Azure, and SAP runs its applications in Microsoft Azure.

This chapter introduces the concepts of SAP on Microsoft Azure and the importance of application-specific architecture, along with Microsoft Azure support requirements and SAP-supported components. It explores SAP technology stacks and deployment models in Microsoft Azure; we also discuss the migration paths to Microsoft Azure and how to use SAP Cloud Appliance Library to provision preconfigured solutions in Microsoft Azure for demos and proofs of concept.

2.1 The Unique SAP Architecture on Microsoft Azure

If you're wondering why there is so much emphasis on SAP architecture if Microsoft Azure is supposed to be resilient and why there are service level agreements (SLAs) for availability and connectivity, you're asking the right questions. Throughout the book, we evaluate why we're doing what we're doing, and whenever Microsoft Azure allows multiple ways of doing something, we try to figure out the best choice.

The following explore some of these reasons and highlights the importance of the right architecture:

- Business-critical systems
  SAP estimates that 76% of the world's transactions touch an SAP system. With most of the organizations using SAP for the heart of their business, such as finance or supply chain, availability and performance are crucial. SLAs of 99.99% isn't uncommon, which leaves very little room for error.

- Network performance
  SAP Note 1100926 talks about recommendations for SAP-specific performance and deems a good round-trip value for networking between application and database to be <= 0.3 ms (milliseconds, as shown in Figure 2.1).

```
◦ Good value: Roundtrip time <= 0.3 ms

◦ Moderate value: 0.3 ms < roundtrip time <= 0.7 ms

◦ Below average value: Roundtrip time > 0.7 ms
```

Figure 2.1 SAP Recommendation for Network Round Trip between Application and Database from SAP Note 1100926

That value is lower than that of most other applications you may use, which highlights the importance of good architecture.

- **Certification requirement**
  SAP certifies most, if not all, the components to be used for infrastructure along with application/database versions and patches; these components are combined with what Microsoft Azure supports and certifies in collaboration with SAP.

  You don't want to risk running uncertified configuration for production environments. Requirements for nonproduction systems aren't as stringent, and any supported configuration may work.

> **Certified versus Supported**
>
> Supported and certified configurations don't mean the same thing. For example, an "L series" virtual machine (VM) is supported by Microsoft, but it's not certified for SAP. Similarly, SAP may support certain database and kernel versions that aren't certified to run on Microsoft Azure. Sometimes these two terms are used interchangeably, so if you're not sure, it's always a good idea to verify.

2.2 SAP on Microsoft Azure Support Prerequisites

SAP and Microsoft together set the minimum requirements that you need to meet before installing or migrating any SAP system. A full list of prerequisites is available from SAP Note, but following are a few salient ones:

- **Support contract**
  Microsoft provides five different support options for Microsoft Azure, as shown in Table 2.1. Professional direct is the minimum requirement, but premier support is recommended for SAP environments in Microsoft Azure.

Basic	Developer	Standard	Professional Direct	Premier
Request support	Purchase support	Purchase support	Purchase support	Contact Premier

Table 2.1 Microsoft Support Plans

- **Microsoft Azure enhanced monitoring extension**
  This extension enables SAP to collect performance (via SAP Host Agent) data from Microsoft Azure VMs to display at the SAP level in Transactions ST06/OS07, so it must be installed and configured correctly. Figure 2.2 shows the flow of data from Microsoft Azure to SAP via the extension.

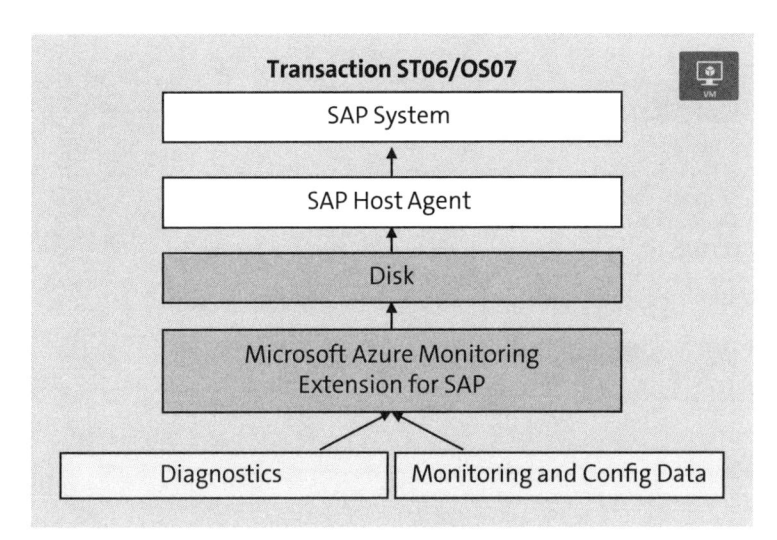

Figure 2.2 Microsoft Azure Enhanced Monitoring Extension for SAP

- **Splitting SAP (application) and database**
  Splitting the application and database between on-premise and Microsoft Azure or between different Microsoft Azure regions isn't supported. Each individual system (SAP Central Services, application, and database) must be in the same region (in Microsoft Azure) or on-premise.

2.3 Supported SAP Products, Databases, and Operating Systems

For a product version or feature to be supported on Microsoft Azure, Microsoft teams do additional due diligence and testing to ensure it works as intended. So, you'll find that even though some combination is in the supported list on the Product Availability Matrix (PAM) in SAP, it may not be supported on Microsoft Azure. SUSE Linux Enterprise Server (SLES) 15 is one example: it was supported by SAP (on-premise) before it became so on Microsoft Azure.

SAP Note 1928533 - SAP Applications on Microsoft Azure: Supported Products and Microsoft Azure VM Types is the central point to figure out what is and isn't supported on Microsoft Azure.

2.3.1 Supported Operating Systems

Microsoft Azure supports the following operating systems (OSs):

- Microsoft Windows
- SLES
- Red Hat Enterprise Linux (RHEL)
- Oracle Linux

> **Note**
> None of the Unix OSs, such as Solaris, HP-UX, and so on, are supported on Microsoft Azure.

2.3.2 Supported Databases

Table 2.2 shows the databases supported for each OS in Microsoft Azure.

Windows	SLES and RHEL	Oracle Linux
Microsoft SQL Server	SAP HANA	Oracle
SAP Adaptive Server Enterprise (SAP ASE)	SAP ASE	
IBM DB2	IBM DB2	
SAP MaxDB	SAP MaxDB	
Oracle		

Table 2.2 Database Support Matrix on Microsoft Azure

2.3.3 Supported SAP Products

Table 2.3 shows SAP products that are supported in Windows and Linux OSs.

Windows OS	Linux OS
■ SAP NetWeaver AS ABAP/ SAP NetWeaver AS Java ■ ABAP platform (SAP S/4HANA) ■ SAP Business Planning and Consolidation, version for SAP NetWeaver ■ SAP BusinessObjects BI Platform ■ Business Objects Data Services (BODS) ■ Search and classification engine (TREX) ■ Content Server ■ Financial Consolidation	■ SAP NetWeaver AS ABAP/ SAP NetWeaver AS Java ■ ABAP platform (SAP S/4HANA) ■ SAP BusinessObjects BI Platform ■ Business Objects Data Services (BODS) ■ TREX (SLES and RHEL) ■ Content Server

Table 2.3 Supported SAP Products on Microsoft Azure in Windows and Linux OSs

> **Note**
>
> Supported versions, support pack levels, and restrictions change often, so refer to SAP Note 1928533 for the latest information.

2.3.4 SAP HANA-Certified Hardware Directory

SAP also publishes the hardware and OS that are certified to run SAP HANA at *www.sap.com/dmc/exp/2014-09-02-hana-hardware/enEN/iaas.html#categories=Microsoft%20Azure*.

For SAP HANA-certified infrastructure as a service (IaaS) and OS version information, the hardware directory serves as a single point of truth, detailing the certified configuration and restrictions, as shown in Figure 2.3 and Figure 2.4.

Instance Type	M416ms_v2
Certification released	2019-10-17
Certification scenario	HANA-IAAS 2.0
CPU Architecture	Intel Skylake SP
RAM	11.4 TiB
Scale-Out	Yes
Application Type	OLTP
Sockets - virtual/logical CPUs	8 - 416
Sizing	Standard Sizing

Figure 2.3 Example of Certified Microsoft Azure VM for SAP HANA from the Hardware Directory

Restrictions & Comments	Workload (Single node): - OLTP (up to 11.4 TiB, incl. S/4 HANA & SoH) Workload (Scale-out up to 4 nodes: 1 master, 3 worker) - OLTP (incl. S/4 HANA) - For information about S/4 scale-out see SAP Note 2408419 and referenced SAP Notes. Options for storing performance critical /hana/data and /hana/log volumes: 1) Premium Disk with Write Accelerator for /hana/log. No shared storage and no standby node support for SAP HANA OLTP Scale-out configuration 2) Ultra Disk. No shared storage and no standby node support for SAP HANA OLTP Scale-out configuration 3) NFS v4.1 on top of Azure NetApp Files (ANF). Shared storage including standby node support n+m for SAP HANA OLTP Scale-out configuration Recommendations can be found at https://docs.microsoft.com/en-us/azure/virtual-machines/workloads/sap/hana-vm-operations-storage
Operating System	RHEL* 7.6 for SAP Solutions, SLES* 12 SP4

Figure 2.4 Example of Supported Configuration Information and Restriction for SAP HANA from the Hardware Directory

> **Tip**
> Mark SAP Notes as favorites in SAP Support Portal to receive emails whenever the note is updated and stay up to date with the latest information.

> **Note**
> SAP supports a lot more configurations on-premise than on Microsoft Azure. Therefore, always look at Microsoft documentation for what's supported or not in Microsoft Azure; a solution that appears in the support list in SAP Notes or documentation doesn't guarantee its support on Microsoft Azure.

2.4 SAP Technology Stacks and Architecture

This section introduces the most common architecture and technology stack that SAP applications use. It will be referred to in later chapters when we discuss high availability (HA), disaster recovery (DR) and other architectural decisions on Microsoft Azure.

2.4.1 Distributed versus Standard Systems

A standard system has all instances (group of processes that work together to make a system) running on the same host or VM; this was also known as a central- or two-tier architecture. In a distributed system, each instance resides on a different host or VM; this was also known as a three-tier architecture.

Figure 2.5 shows a representation of standard and distributed SAP systems.

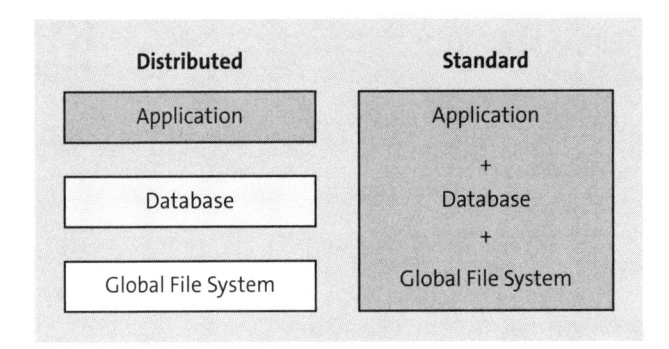

Figure 2.5 Illustration of Distributed and Standard SAP System Architectures

2.4.2 SAP Technology Stacks

SAP offers a huge list of products so it's difficult to generalize the architecture given that some of the companies that SAP has bought over the years had their own architecture

2.4 SAP Technology Stacks and Architecture

and technologies (e.g., Business Objects and Hybris) that were different from those used by SAP. Having said that, the majority of SAP's commonly-used products (not counting software as a service [SaaS] products) fall under the ABAP, Java, or dual stack.

Over the years, with product improvements and innovations, names have changed, with the most recent shift from SAP NetWeaver to the ABAP platform:

- The ABAP stack provides a platform for developing ABAP-based applications. SAP ERP 6.0 is an example of an ABAP system.
- The Java stack provides the Java Enterprise Edition (Java EE) platform to run and develop programs. SAP Portal is an example of a Java-based system.
- Dual stack combines both ABAP and Java application in one system. SAP Solution Manager is a dual-stack system.
- Architecture of systems such as SAP BusinessObjects and SAP Customer Experience (replaced the Hybris name) differ and use web-based technologies such as Apache.

Figure 2.6 shows the architecture of ABAP, Java, and dual-stack systems. Central Services for the Java stack is referred to as SAP Central Services and ABAP is called ABAP SAP Central Services. In a dual stack, there is an instance of SAP Central Services and another instance of ABAP SAP Central Services.

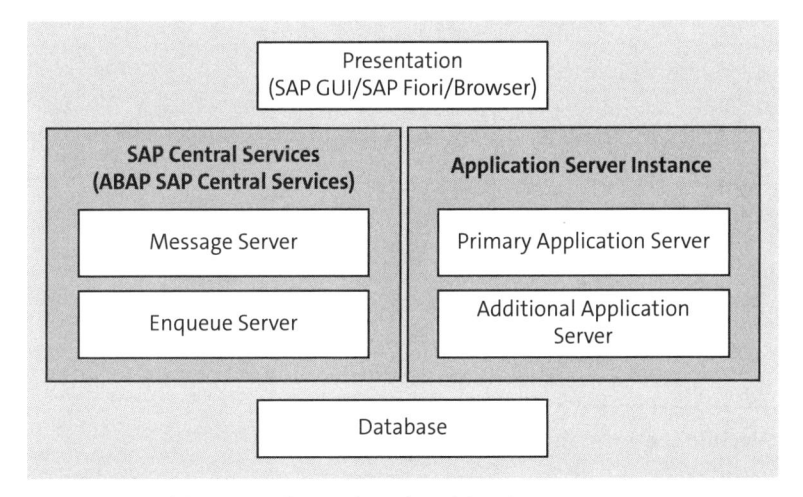

Figure 2.6 Architecture of ABAP/Java/Dual Stack

> **ABAP Platform**
> When SAP started to utilize all the in-memory features of SAP HANA for new innovations, SAP focused on the ABAP codebase optimized for SAP HANA. The new foundation was called ABAP platform.

2   SAP on Microsoft Azure

> **ABAP Platform versus SAP NetWeaver AS ABAP**
>
> The difference between SAP NetWeaver and ABAP platform lies in the fact that SAP NetWeaver AS ABAP provides support for all databases via a common codebase whereas ABAP platform code is optimized for SAP HANA. The SAP S/4HANA product line is built on ABAP platform.

2.5 SAP on Microsoft Azure Reference Architecture

Let's say you're very good at picking vegetables—you know exactly how to pick the freshest ones and how long they'll last in the refrigerator. But does that mean you're a good cook as well? To cook the vegetables, you need to know how to cut them, add other ingredients in the correct ratio, operate the stove, and so on. Similarly, to create an application architecture, say SAP, in Microsoft Azure, you need to know how individual Microsoft Azure services work together and how to configure them correctly with other components.

Microsoft has done a good job of creating a reference architecture for a lot of use cases, including for different SAP scenarios such as SAP S/4HANA, SAP on SQL Server, and SAP HANA on Azure (Large Instances), as shown in Figure 2.7, which can be found at the Microsoft Azure Architecture Center (*https://docs.microsoft.com/en-us/azure/architecture/*).

SAP
- SAP HANA on Azure Large Instances
- SAP NetWeaver for AnyDB
- SAP S/4HANA
- SAP for dev/test
- SAP for production

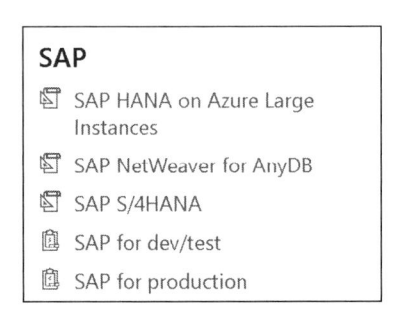

Figure 2.7 SAP Architecture Use Cases at the Microsoft Azure Architecture Center

Figure 2.8 shows a reference architecture for SAP on Microsoft Azure that we'll follow along for this book. In later chapters we'll discuss each section and decisions around each component. You'll learn how to stitch Microsoft Azure services together and create an architecture tailored to your organization.

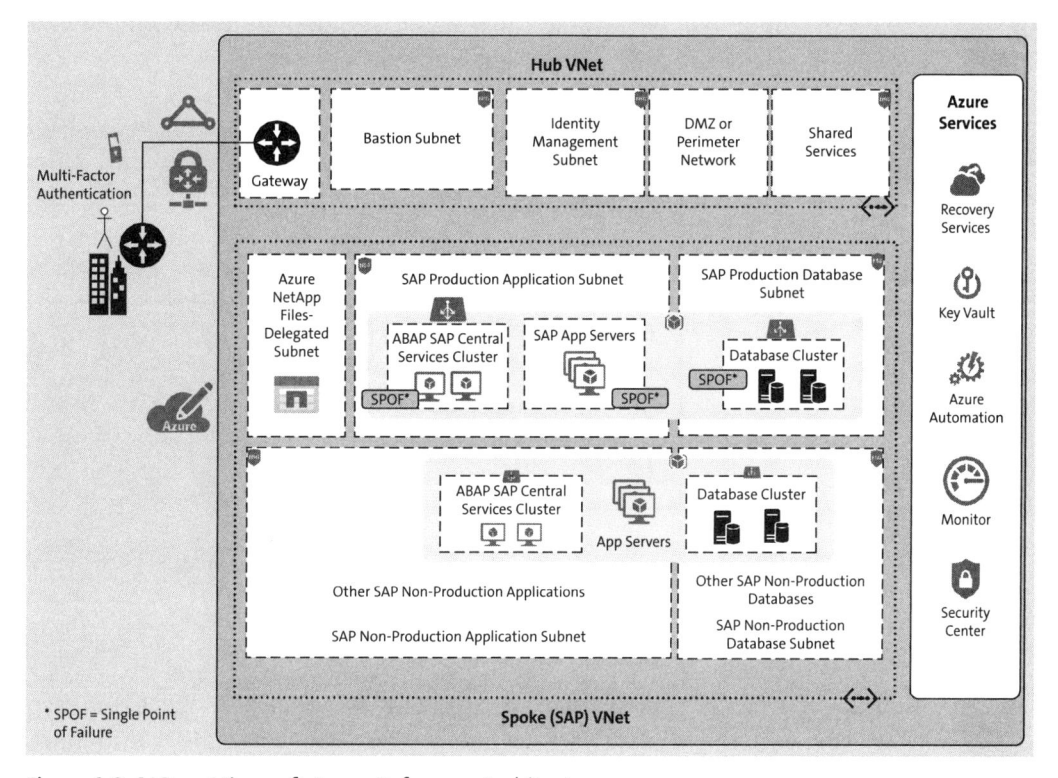

Figure 2.8 SAP on Microsoft Azure Reference Architecture

> **Note**
>
> The reference architecture shows most of the important components that decisions are based on. However, there are more things that happen in the background, which you'll learn about in later chapters, that aren't explicitly represented here.

2.6 Deployment Models

Moving the SAP landscape to Microsoft Azure is no small feat—a lot of decisions must be made, sometimes without fully knowing the effect. This section talks about one of the first decisions you're going to make: how the SAP landscape should be distributed among on-premise, Microsoft Azure, and potentially other cloud services.

2.6.1 All SAP on Microsoft Azure

This is the simplest approach where you move all SAP systems and related bolt-on, third-party systems to Microsoft Azure as illustrated in Figure 2.9. This book covers the possible scenarios, if you go this route, including SAP system copy, DR, parallel SAP landscape build for project, and so on.

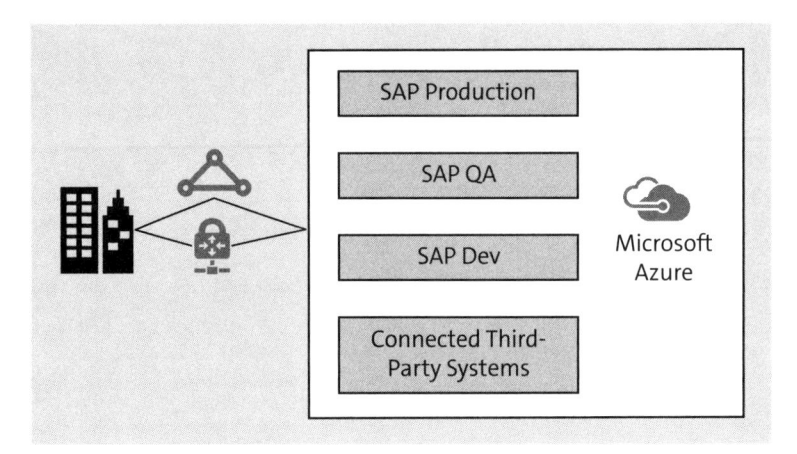

Figure 2.9 All SAP and Related Systems in the Microsoft Azure Deployment Model

2.6.2 Hybrid

If you're not ready to move production systems to the cloud yet but would like to save costs or experience the flexibility and features of the cloud, you may want to move nonproduction and/or DR systems as a hybrid system (see Figure 2.10).

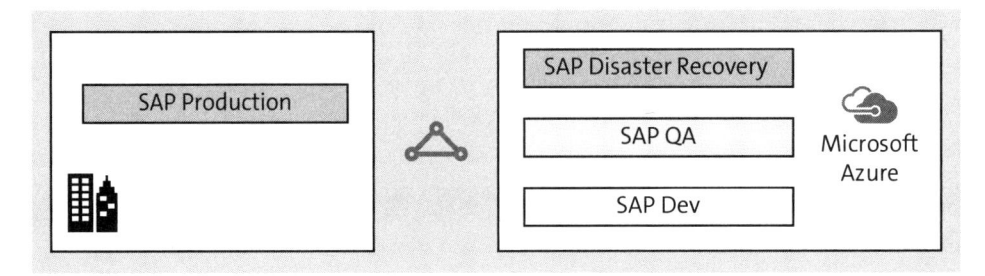

Figure 2.10 Example of Hybrid Scenario for the Move to Microsoft Azure

> **Note**
> Review the network latency, Microsoft Azure egress charges, and shared file system architecture for this setup.

2.6.3 Multi-Cloud

A multi-cloud strategy refers to working with multiple cloud providers in any of the following scenarios:

- Part of the SAP landscape is on one cloud, and the rest is on a different one.
- If there are multiple implementations of SAP according to business group, they are split in different clouds.
- SAP landscape is on one cloud, and specialized platform as a service (PaaS) or software as a service (SaaS) products are used from a different cloud.

> **Challenges**
>
> Besides the network latency and performance challenges, a multi-cloud system adds the complexities of governance, security, user access, and so on.

> **SAP HANA Enterprise Cloud on Microsoft Azure**
>
> If you're looking into the SAP HANA Enterprise Cloud offering, Microsoft Azure can still play a part there because Microsoft Azure is a public cloud partner for the SAP HANA Enterprise Cloud program as well.

2.7 Paths to Microsoft Azure

If you were moving to a new house, it's likely that you'd review what's important to take with you versus what can be donated, tossed, or left behind. Moving SAP environments to Microsoft Azure requires similar considerations and preparation. This section talks about the rationalization process and walks you through the decision framework.

2.7.1 Cloud Rationalization and the Five Rs of Migration

In the planning step of the cloud adoption framework, one of the goals is to review current systems to determine fit for migration. So, what are the options for migration? Gartner Research popularized the notion of the five Rs of migration, namely, rehost, refactor, revise, rebuild, and replace. It refers to the process that must be undergone to get to a future state—either through migration or modernization.

For SAP, it starts with gathering which business processes are using the systems, that is, mapping of business processes to the SAP system. That tells which systems are crucial for business and reveals those that have less dependency. This process helps not only with the migration approach but also with the DR approach, which we'll discuss during DR architecture. Figure 2.11 shows an example of this exercise.

The output of business processes to SAP system mapping feeds the rationalization decision. This can sometimes be an iterative process so you shouldn't get stuck on getting this 100% right; you can always reevaluate and refine later.

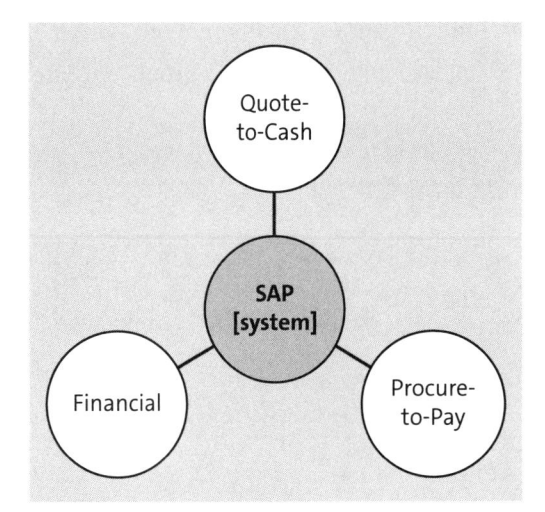

Figure 2.11 Business Process to SAP Mapping Illustration

Bringing the SAP context to the cloud rationalization process, first you need to figure out whether the systems need to be *retained*, can be *replaced*, or is ready to *retire*. Those in the retain list can be either *rehosted* on the cloud as is (lift-and-shift) or be *rearchitected* (modernized). Figure 2.12 shows these five Rs of the cloud rationalization process.

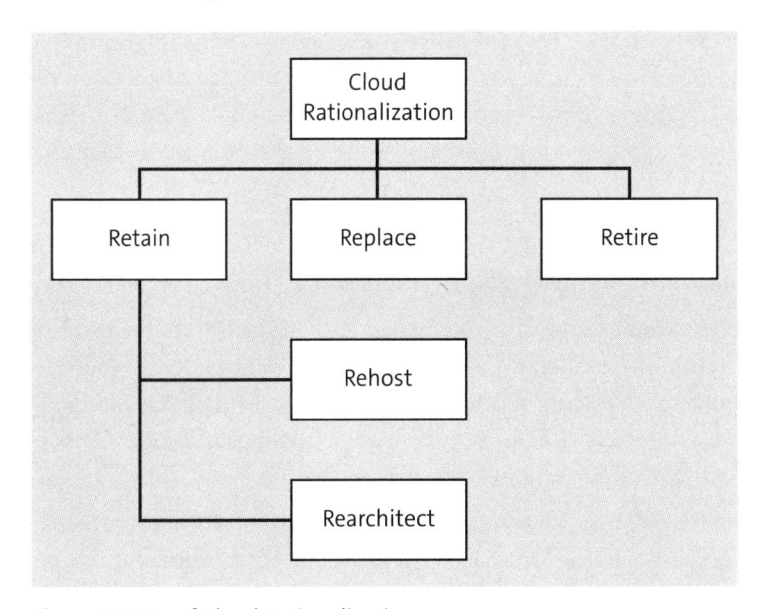

Figure 2.12 Rs of Cloud Rationalization

- **Retain**

    This is the most migration effort-intensive part because it brings in the complexity of moving the systems as well as testing the business processes on the new platform. Retain can be subdivided into the following:

- Rehost

  Also known as lift-and-shift, this process is achieved mostly through IaaS and focuses on moving the system to the cloud with minimal to no architectural changes. The overarching idea is to get to the cloud before you try to change anything.

- Rearchitect

  Also known as modernization of an application, this process can be either IaaS or PaaS and realizes the idea that the system is needed but not necessarily in the current form. For example, a business process can be merged into another system, or a PaaS service integrating with another system can perform the same function. This serves as a basis for application modernization.

- **Replace**

  If there is an old version of the system that is difficult to maintain or upgrade, a SaaS product may be a better fit if it provides the necessary functionalities. SAP SuccessFactors is an example of a SaaS product that provides a human resources (HR) and payroll solution, which can be a replacement for SAP ERP Human Capital Management (SAP ERP HCM).

  In addition, sometimes installing a new SAP product and moving the data may work better where there is no upgrade or migration path for older systems.

- **Retire**

  Traditionally in an on-premise environment, the variable cost of hosting small applications is low, and, over time, you may have accumulated a lot of those applications. Eventually, the evolution of business processes or system upgrades bringing more functionalities removes the need for those applications, but they are seldom decommissioned either due to lack of time or analysis.

  A good way to analyze these systems is by asking the question, "why not"—as in why can't this sytem be retired instead of why should this system be retired. This rephrasing triggers the analytical part of our brains to help figure out whether the functionality provided by the application is really being used and, if so, whether it can be done by any other system or cloud native solution.

  It's not uncommon for an organization to retire anywhere between 10% and 20% of the applications when moving to the cloud.

Figure 2.13 shows the decision flow for the cloud rationalization process leading to a decision regarding rehost, replace, or retire.

> **SAP System Certification as IaaS**
>
> For SAP systems, it's also important to note how the systems are certified on the cloud. Most of the ABAP/Java systems are certified only as IaaS solutions; thus, the decision about possible modernization also has a certification requirement built into it.

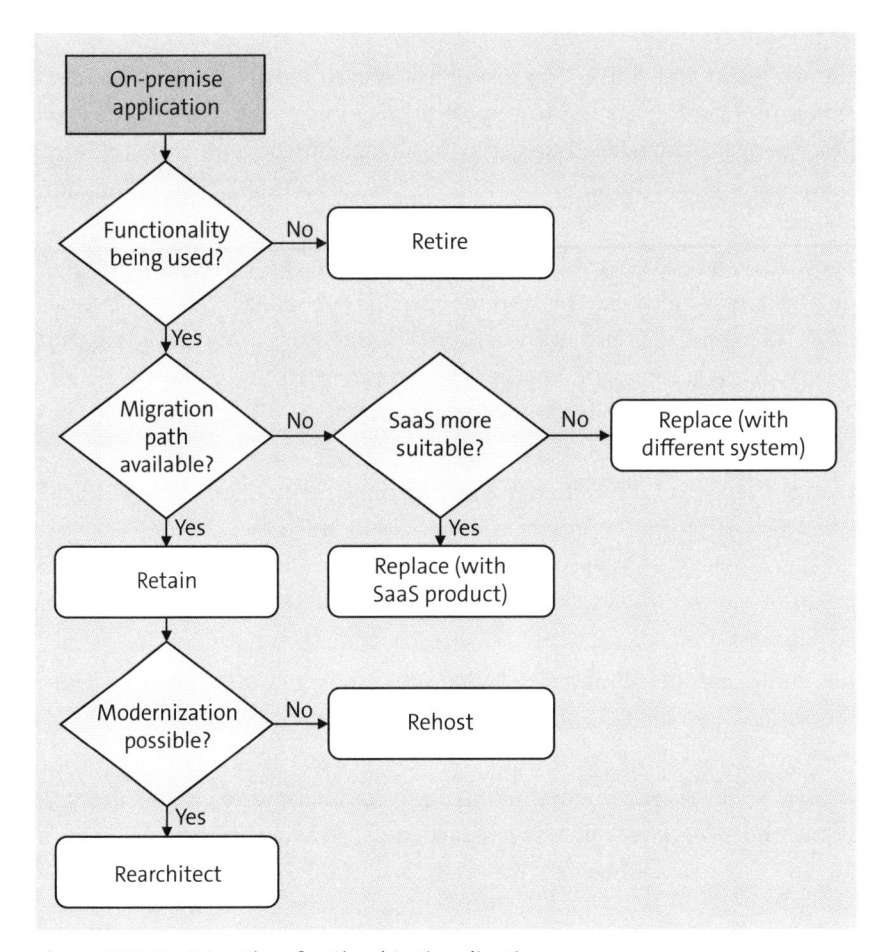

Figure 2.13 Decision Flow for Cloud Rationalization

2.7.2 SAP Migrations versus New Implementations

SAP provides several different migration paths, which can be a combination of as-is, upgrade and migration, SAP HANA conversion, and migration. As-is migration is probably the simplest among the available options, but you also need to make sure the application minimum requirement for certification on Microsoft Azure is met. In some cases, you may need to upgrade either the application or database (or both) before it can be migrated. For backward-compliant versions, you can do a new installation on Microsoft Azure and move the data or files to the newly installed system. For example, newer SAP HANA versions are often backward compliant (with few exceptions), and it's a good idea to install the latest version and patch on Microsoft Azure. With migration, you can often bring in a new SAP kernel as well.

Moving to the SAP S/4HANA new implementation in Microsoft Azure is also an option with data loading from the on-premise system, specifically when the current system is very old and/or has complex customizations.

Details of these paths are discussed in the migration section of the book, but we wanted to highlight that migration versus new implementation (or installation) isn't mutually exclusive and often cross paths.

2.7.3 Third-Party Systems

SAP systems are connected to several other applications, commonly called third-party systems or bolt-ons. These often have less stringent support requirements and are easier to either replace or rearchitect; you can follow the same decision path for retain, replace, and retire, keeping in mind that moving to Microsoft Azure may provide easier integration and better options.

For example, an on-premise Simple Mail Transfer Protocol (SMTP) solution can easily be replaced by something similar on Microsoft Azure without much consideration about compatibility or certification. Another example is the Vertex tax solution, which can be used as a SaaS solution integrating with SAP systems on Microsoft Azure.

2.8 SAP Cloud Appliance Library

SAP Cloud Appliance Library is a self-service platform by SAP with preconfigured solutions that can be deployed to the public cloud quickly for trials, proofs of concepts (POCs), and demos. You'll need an SAP ID to log in to SAP Cloud Appliance Library (*https://cal.sap.com*); from there, everything is web based, meaning you don't need to know any coding or configuration for provisioning, everything is done with clicks.

> **Note**
> These solutions also come with a temporary license installed, so it's a good way to explore product features without performing detailed configurations. SAP Cloud Appliance Library isn't intended to be used for production deployment.

This section walks through the process of provisioning a system from SAP Cloud Appliance Library on Microsoft Azure. In this example, we'll demo an instance of SAP NetWeaver AS ABAP 7.52 SP 01 on SAP ASE 16.0 database:

1. After you log in to SAP Cloud Appliance Library, go to the **Accounts** tab (left side menu) to create a new account connecting to your Microsoft Azure subscription, as shown in Figure 2.14.
2. Click on the **Create Account** button, and enter the details of the **Cloud Provider** (Microsoft Azure, in this case) and **Subscription ID**, which can be located from the Microsoft Azure portal, as shown in Figure 2.15.

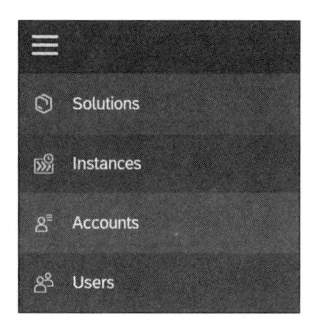

Figure 2.14 SAP Cloud Appliance Library Accounts Tab

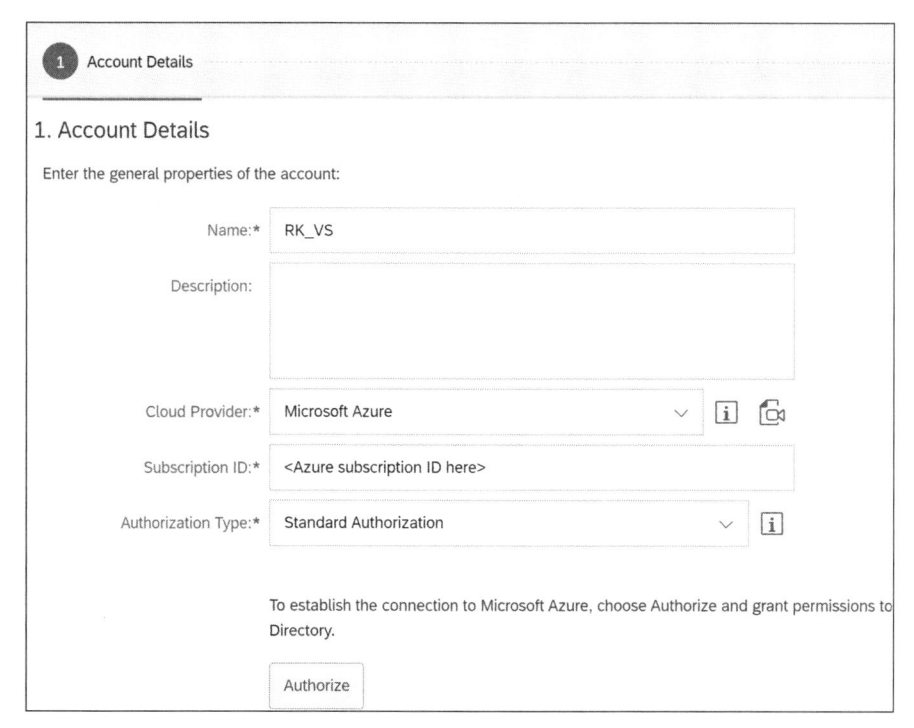

Figure 2.15 Account Details to Connect SAP Cloud Appliance Library to Microsoft Azure

3. Click the **Authorize** button to let SAP Cloud Appliance Library use your Microsoft Azure subscription.

   Once connected, the subscription appears in the **Accounts** tab, as shown in Figure 2.16.

Accounts : All (1)		Search		
Name	Cloud Provider	Cloud Provider ID	Instances	Status
RK_VS	Microsoft Azure	Visual Studio Enterprise Subscription	0	● Active

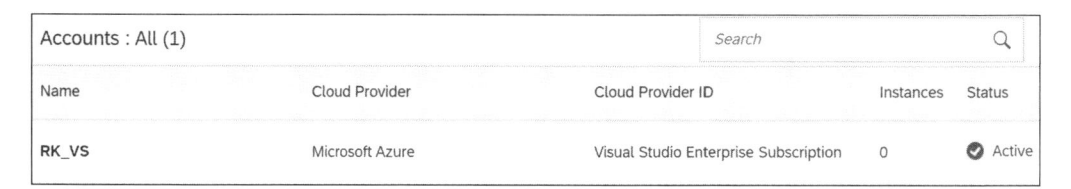

Figure 2.16 SAP Cloud Appliance Library Account Connected to Microsoft Azure

2.8 SAP Cloud Appliance Library

4. At this point, you're ready to deploy an SAP Cloud Appliance Library solution to Microsoft Azure. Locate the solution from the **Solutions** tab, and click on the **Create Instance** button, as shown in Figure 2.17.

SAP NetWeaver AS ABAP 7.52 SP01 on SAP ASE 16.0 TRIAL	Google Cloud Platform, Amazon Web Services, Microsoft Azure	● Available	Create Instance	○○○
SAP SE | Aug 29, 2018				

Figure 2.17 SAP NetWeaver Solution to Be Installed from SAP Cloud Appliance Library

5. Read in full (Figure 2.18) and accept the terms and conditions of the solution using the **I Accept** button on the bottom right.

Terms and Conditions

SAP NetWeaver AS ABAP 7.52 SP01 on SAP ASE 16.0

Read the terms and conditions of the solution. Use the scroll bar or press the Page Dow

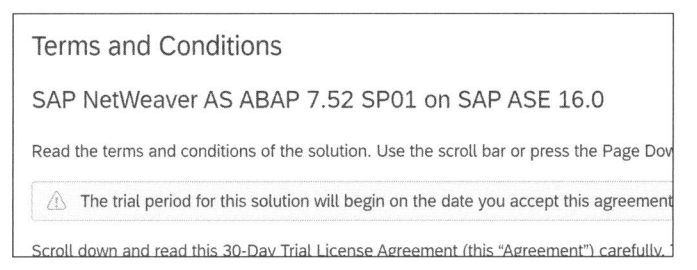

⚠ The trial period for this solution will begin on the date you accept this agreement

Scroll down and read this 30-Day Trial License Agreement (this "Agreement") carefully.

Figure 2.18 SAP Cloud Appliance Library Terms and Conditions Showing the Trial Period and Beginning Date

> **Tip**
>
> The trial period of the solution that you're going to install begins as soon as you accept the terms and conditions of the solution and lasts 30 days. Therefore, if you don't provision the system for, say, 10 days, you'll be left with only 20 days to explore the solution.

6. When creating the instance, click on the **Advanced Mode** button on the bottom right to get more options to customize. Select **Account** and instance details as shown in Figure 2.19.

> **Note**
>
> You may notice that certain fields such as **Region**, **Network**, and so on don't have many options in the dropdown menu. This is one of the restrictions of the SAP Cloud Appliance Library trial installation; therefore, the system may not be available in the region you like.

7. Select Microsoft Azure VM stock-keeping unit and storage options, as shown in Figure 2.20.

2   SAP on Microsoft Azure

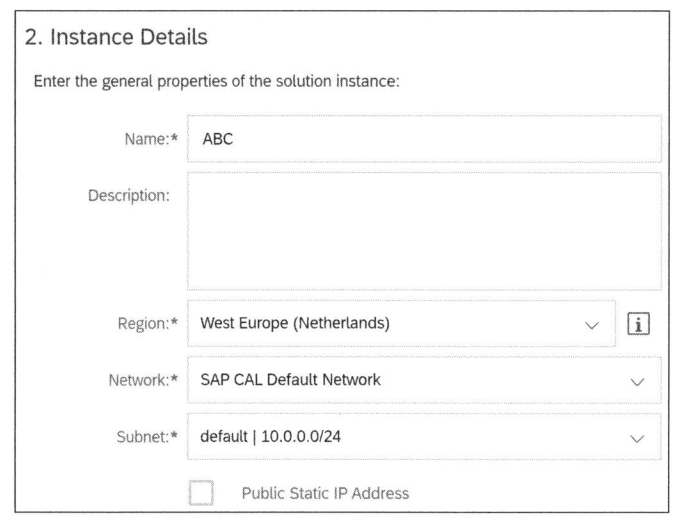

```
2. Instance Details
Enter the general properties of the solution instance:

           Name:*  ABC
    Description:

         Region:*  West Europe (Netherlands)          ⓘ
        Network:*  SAP CAL Default Network
         Subnet:*  default | 10.0.0.0/24

                   ☐  Public Static IP Address
```

Figure 2.19 SAP Cloud Appliance Library Instance Details

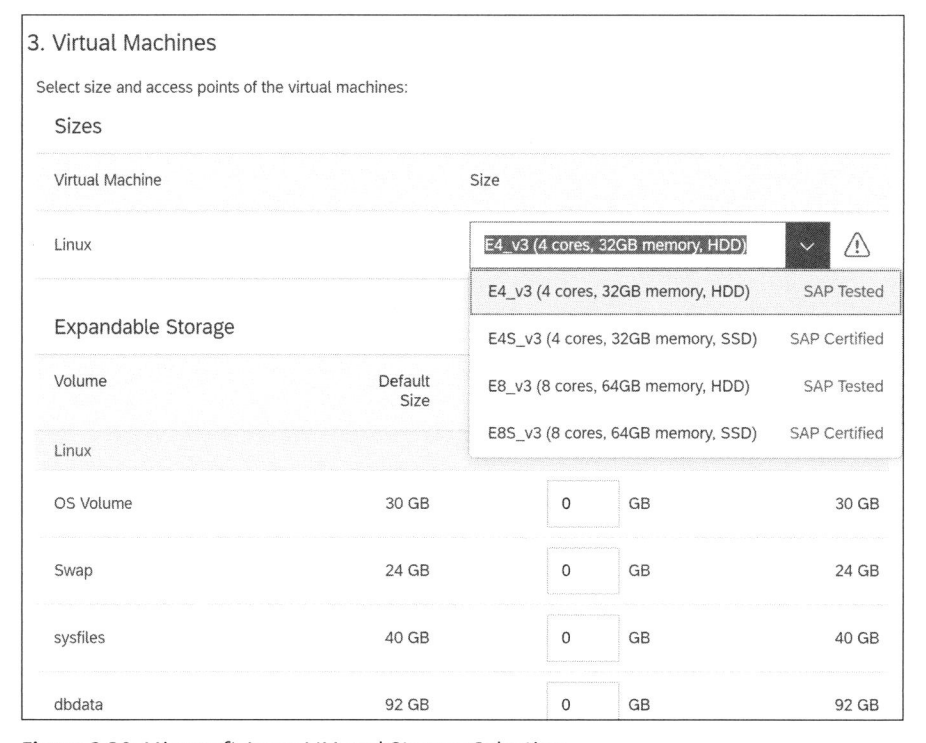

```
3. Virtual Machines
Select size and access points of the virtual machines:

Sizes

Virtual Machine                  Size

Linux                            E4_v3 (4 cores, 32GB memory, HDD)    ⚠

                                 E4_v3  (4 cores, 32GB memory, HDD)   SAP Tested
Expandable Storage
                                 E4S_v3 (4 cores, 32GB memory, SSD)   SAP Certified
Volume            Default        E8_v3  (8 cores, 64GB memory, HDD)   SAP Tested
                   Size
                                 E8S_v3 (8 cores, 64GB memory, SSD)   SAP Certified
Linux

OS Volume          30 GB          0     GB                             30 GB

Swap               24 GB          0     GB                             24 GB

sysfiles           40 GB          0     GB                             40 GB

dbdata             92 GB          0     GB                             92 GB
```

Figure 2.20 Microsoft Azure VM and Storage Selection

> **Note**
>
> A lot of these options go to the default selection if you choose the basic configuration instead of advanced mode. Also notice the options for **SAP Tested** versus **SAP Certified**

> configuration. You can read details for each by clicking ⚠. Because SAP Cloud Appliance Library isn't intended for a production instance, choosing any VM from the list is fine.

8. You can also customize ports and the IP range at this step.
9. Provide the master password.

    On the right side, SAP Cloud Appliance Library also forecasts the cost of the solution that you're going to incur in Microsoft Azure based on the selected VM and other configurations, as shown in Figure 2.21.

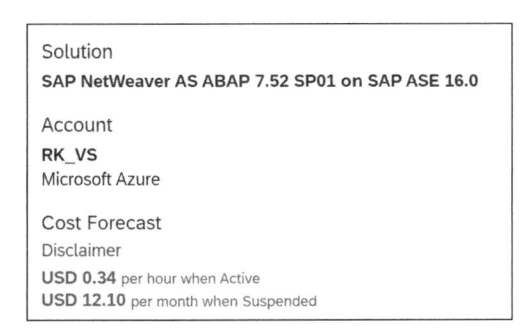

```
Solution
SAP NetWeaver AS ABAP 7.52 SP01 on SAP ASE 16.0

Account
RK_VS
Microsoft Azure

Cost Forecast
Disclaimer
USD 0.34 per hour when Active
USD 12.10 per month when Suspended
```

Figure 2.21 SAP Cloud Appliance Library Solution Cost Forecast

10. Configure the suspend and terminate options, as shown in Figure 2.22, for the infrastructure to control Microsoft Azure costs.

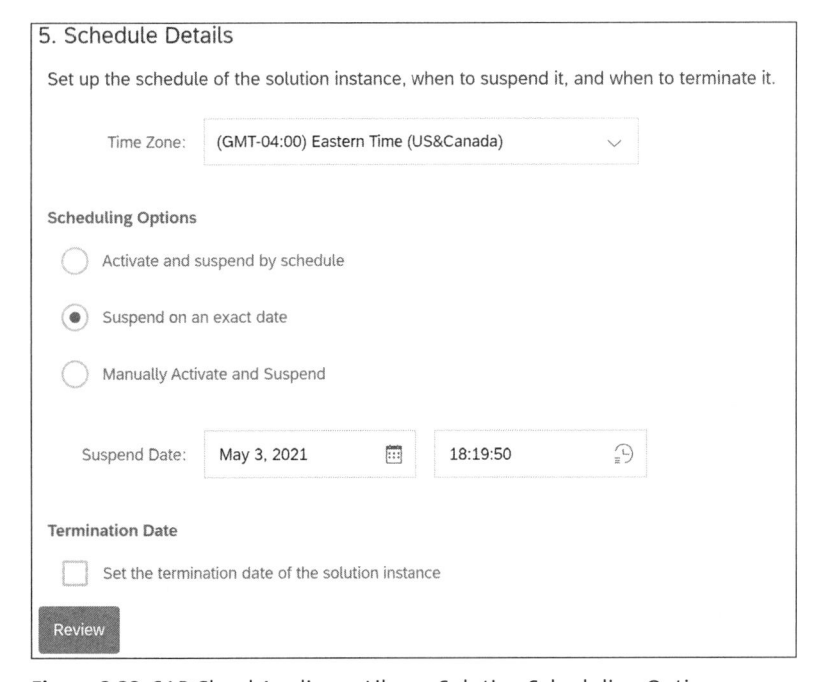

```
5. Schedule Details
Set up the schedule of the solution instance, when to suspend it, and when to terminate it.

    Time Zone:  (GMT-04:00) Eastern Time (US&Canada)

Scheduling Options
    ○ Activate and suspend by schedule
    ● Suspend on an exact date
    ○ Manually Activate and Suspend

    Suspend Date:  May 3, 2021    18:19:50

Termination Date
    ☐ Set the termination date of the solution instance

[Review]
```

Figure 2.22 SAP Cloud Appliance Library Solution Scheduling Options

2   SAP on Microsoft Azure

11. Click **Review** to look over the configuration, and then click **Create** to deploy the solution in the Microsoft Azure subscription.

12. Download the private key for the solution by clicking the **Download** button, in the next step as shown in Figure 2.23.

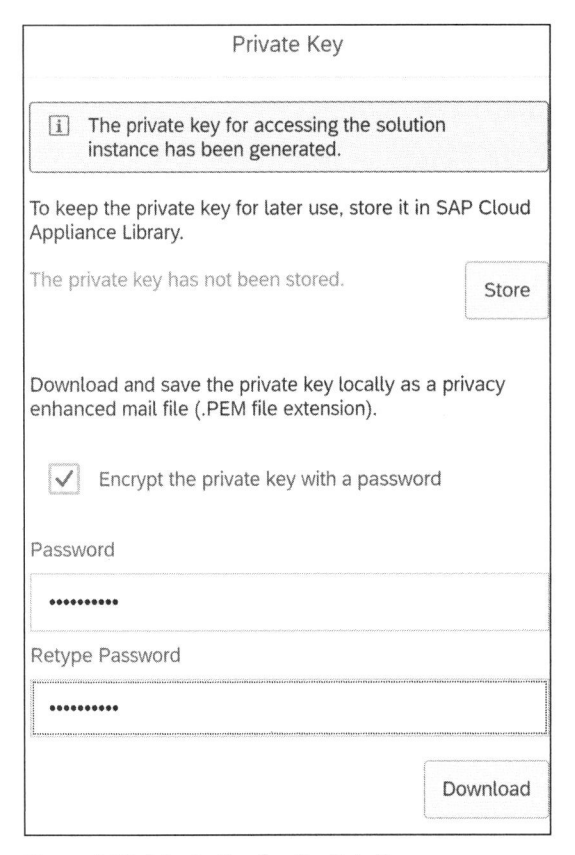

Figure 2.23 Private Key for the Solution

> **Warning!**
> Don't try to connect to the instance while the solution is being deployed. When it's finished deploying, the instance will appear in the **Instance** tab in SAP Cloud Appliance Library with a few operations options.

13. After the system is deployed, you can head over to **Instance** tab (in SAP Cloud Appliance Library) to view the allowed operations for that instance, as shown in Figure 2.24.

2.8 SAP Cloud Appliance Library

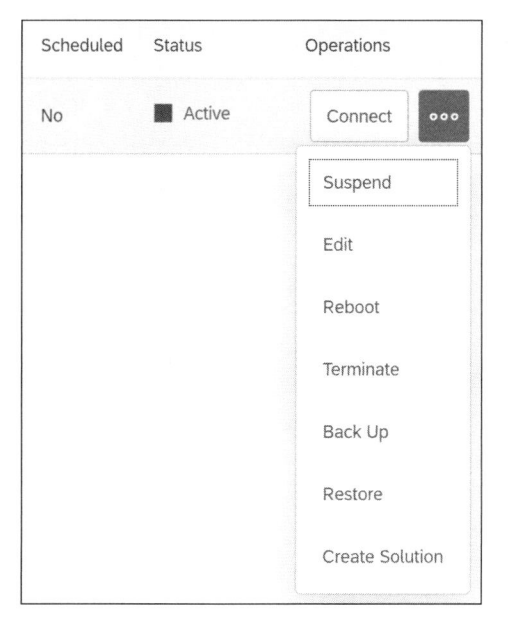

Scheduled	Status	Operations
No	■ Active	Connect •••
		Suspend
		Edit
		Reboot
		Terminate
		Back Up
		Restore
		Create Solution

Figure 2.24 Active SAP Solution and Operations Options

14. After the solution in provisioned and activated, the resources appear in your Microsoft Azure subscription, as shown in Figure 2.25.

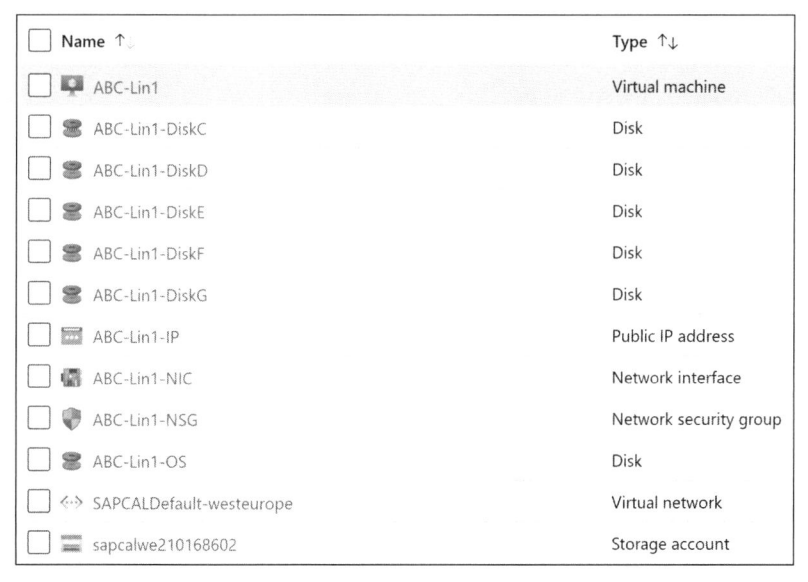

Name ↑	Type ↑↓
ABC-Lin1	Virtual machine
ABC-Lin1-DiskC	Disk
ABC-Lin1-DiskD	Disk
ABC-Lin1-DiskE	Disk
ABC-Lin1-DiskF	Disk
ABC-Lin1-DiskG	Disk
ABC-Lin1-IP	Public IP address
ABC-Lin1-NIC	Network interface
ABC-Lin1-NSG	Network security group
ABC-Lin1-OS	Disk
SAPCALDefault-westeurope	Virtual network
sapcalwe210168602	Storage account

Figure 2.25 Microsoft Azure Subscription Showing the Deployed Resources via SAP Cloud Appliance Library

55

At this point, you can connect to the SAP solution using SAP GUI or the browser and infrastructure layer at Microsoft Azure, and there is no dependency on SAP Cloud Appliance Library (except the license restriction). Proceed with the demo or POC within the license validity window. You can also perform maintenance activities such as backup, shutdown, reboot, and so on directly from the Microsoft Azure portal instead of the SAP Cloud Appliance Library portal.

2.9 Relevant SAP Notes

This chapter mentioned a few of the SAP Notes related to Microsoft Azure; it's crucial to follow the recommendations from those notes when deploying SAP on Microsoft Azure. Here's a list of key notes (including the ones already mentioned) for SAP on Microsoft Azure:

- SAP Note 1380654: SAP Support in IaaS Environments
- SAP Note 2015553: SAP on Microsoft Azure: Support Prerequisites
- SAP Note 1928533: SAP Applications on Microsoft Azure: Supported Products and Microsoft Azure VM Types
- SAP Note 2035875: Windows on Microsoft Azure: Adaption of Your SAP License
- SAP Note 2327159: SAP NetWeaver License Behavior in Virtual and Cloud Environments
- SAP Note 1999351: Troubleshooting Microsoft Azure Enhanced Monitoring for SAP
- SAP Note 2316233: SAP HANA on Azure (Large Instances)
- SAP Note 2243692: Linux on Microsoft Azure (IaaS) VM: SAP License Issues
- SAP Note 2367194: Use of Microsoft Azure Premium SSD Storage for SAP DBMS Instance
- SAP Note 2039619: SAP Applications on Microsoft Azure Using the Oracle Database: Supported Products and Versions
- SAP Note 2145537: Support of SAP BusinessObjects BI platform on Microsoft Azure
- SAP Note 2288344: EIM Applications on Microsoft Azure
- SAP Note 2555629: SAP HANA 2.0 Dynamic Tiering – Hypervisor and Cloud Support
- SAP Note 2729475: HWCCT Failed with Error "Hypervisor Is Not Supported" on Microsoft Azure VMs Certified for SAP HANA

> **Note**
>
> SAP Support Portal access is required to view these notes in the preceding list; note that this is a collection of commonly used notes but not an exhaustive list.

2.10 Summary

This chapter introduced SAP on Microsoft Azure and the importance of application-specific architecture, along with Microsoft Azure support requirements and SAP supported components. You also learned about the prerequisites for moving SAP to Microsoft Azure, deployment models, and cloud rationalization. The chapter talked about SAP Cloud Appliance Library and gave step-by-step instructions for deploying an SAP solution in Microsoft Azure via SAP Cloud Appliance Library.

Now that you understand the basics of SAP on Microsoft Azure, let's review the Microsoft Azure services that are applicable for SAP, including IaaS and some PaaS. In the next chapter, we'll discuss the infrastructure offerings for SAP and how to think about those in the context of SAP.

Chapter 3
Microsoft Azure Infrastructure Offerings for SAP

Cloud services need to be generic enough for wider use cases and at the same time customized for business-critical workloads such as SAP. The combination is where we harness the power of Microsoft Azure for SAP.

Microsoft Azure offers hundreds of different services, and there are also variances in service level, performance, and cost within a service group. While SAP runs mostly on infrastructure as a service (IaaS), there are some platform as a service (PaaS) components that are instrumental as well.

In this chapter, we'll talk about Microsoft Azure service offerings that are used for SAP deployments, which ones are certified or supported, and their performance and cost aspects.

3.1 Microsoft Azure Enterprise Enrollment Hierarchy

Microsoft Azure is managed mainly via the Microsoft Azure portal (*http://portal.azure.com*) and Enterprise Agreement (EA) portal (*http://ea.azure.com*). The Microsoft Azure portal is used to manage the technical aspects of the infrastructure, that is, deployment and maintenance of resources such as virtual machines (VMs), storage, network, application services, and so on (Microsoft Azure subscription and below; you're likely familiar with this if you've had a trial subscription), whereas the EA portal layer resides on top of the subscription and allows you to manage multiple accounts, departments, and subscriptions throughout the organization. You can also track cost and usage from the EA portal.

Figure 3.1 shows the enrollment hierarchy for Microsoft Azure EA customers. Let's take a look at the components:

- **Enrollment**
  Enrollment is the EA between an organization and Microsoft. It can be thought of as billing account where invoices are managed.
- **Department**
  Department is an optional layer in the hierarchy that helps set the budget at the department level, for example, finance, IT, or supply chain departments.

- Account

  Account enables you to manage subscription and service administrators; you can also access reports at the account level.

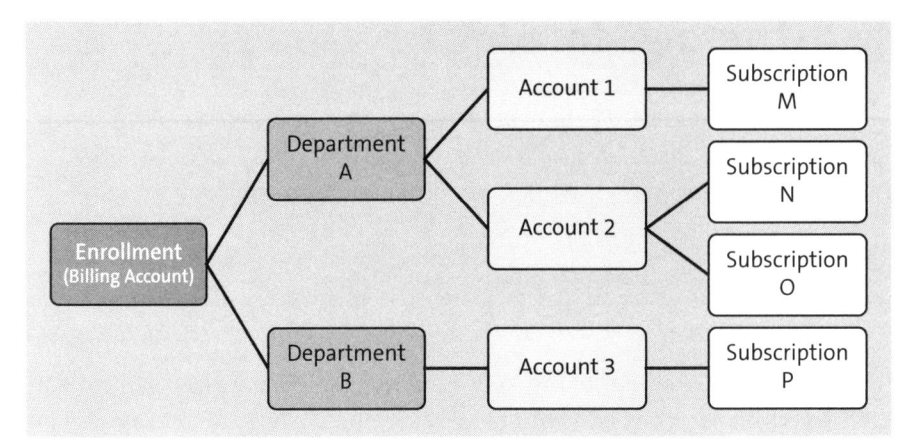

Figure 3.1 Microsoft Azure EA Enrollment Hierarchy

- Subscription

  Subscription is a logical container for technical services and resources in Microsoft Azure and acts as the administrative boundary. In Microsoft Azure, all the resources reside within a subscription. There are several subscription types, such as EA, pay-as-you-go, and Visual Studio, and some of those may not follow the hierarchy.

> **Microsoft Azure from Microsoft Partner**
>
> You can also get Microsoft Azure as part of a managed service from a partner, often called a Cloud Solution Provider subscription, which enables you to combine Microsoft Azure services and bills, as well as receive Microsoft Azure support from the Cloud Solution Provider.

> **Enterprise Agreement to Microsoft Customer Agreement**
>
> Microsoft is changing the structure to streamline the contract and billing process. Microsoft Customer Agreement is replacing EA, and billing is moving to Microsoft Azure portal. For more details, refer to the Microsoft Azure documentation at *https://docs.microsoft.com/en-us/azure/cost-management-billing/manage/mca-setup-account*.

3.2 Connectivity to Microsoft Azure

The Microsoft Azure portal can be accessed online using a browser or desktop app, but most of the resources and services are designed to be used from a private network.

Think of Microsoft Azure as a virtual data center, and to make it work with the current infrastructure, you need to connect it with on-premise systems and grant all the employees access to the new resources. Figure 3.2 shows connectivity options from on-premise systems (or other remote locations) to Microsoft Azure: ExpressRoute, Site-to-Site (S2S) Virtual Private Network (VPN), and Point-to-Site (P2S) VPN.

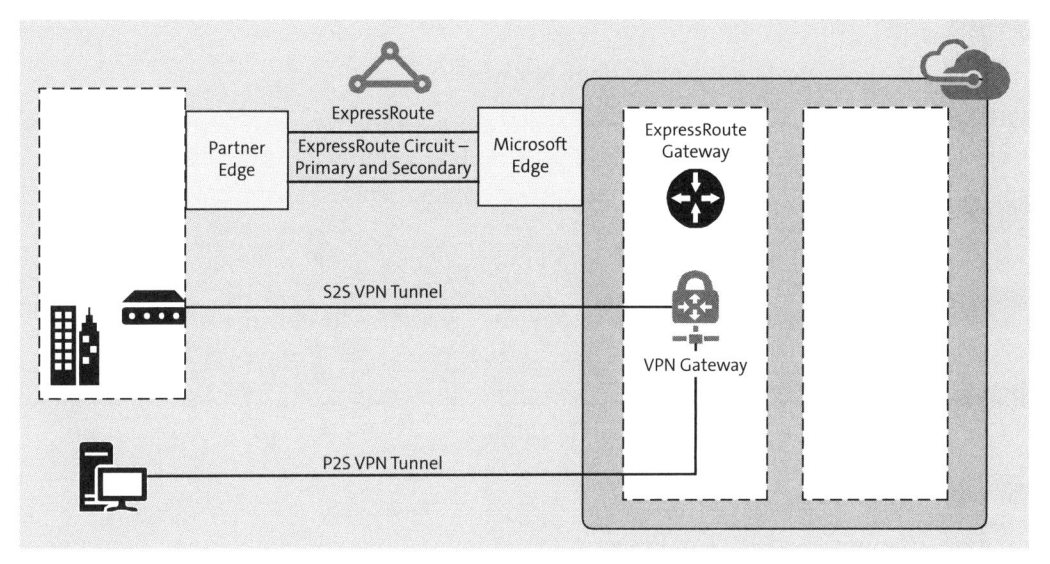

Figure 3.2 On-Premises/Remote to Microsoft Azure Connectivity Options

3.2.1 ExpressRoute

ExpressRoute is used to create a high-speed (up to 100 Gbps), private, and dedicated connection between on-premise systems and Microsoft Azure using third-party network partners such as Comcast or Verizon. This is suitable for applications with high speed/low latency requirements such as SAP.

ExpressRoute doesn't go over the public Internet (unlike VPNs), is more reliable, and comes with a 99.95% service-level agreement (SLA). It consists of two connections, so there is built-in redundancy:

- **ExpressRoute Premium**
  By default, the ExpressRoute connection circuit is limited to a single geopolitical region, but if you need cross-region connectivity, the premium feature (to be enabled) lets you do that.
- **ExpressRoute Global Reach**
  If your organization has multiple locations connected to Microsoft Azure via ExpressRoute, enabling Global Reach allows the traffic between those data centers to go through Microsoft's network.

3.2.2 Site-to-Site Virtual Private Network

S2S uses IP security (IPSec) to create a secure connection between your site and Microsoft Azure. This is good for doing proof of concepts (POCs) or development/sandbox environments because the bandwidth is typically lower (up to 100 Mbps). S2S can also be used as a backup or disaster recovery (DR) option for ExpressRoute

3.2.3 Point-to-Site Virtual Private Network

This is the simplest mechanism with limited use cases. It lets you connect your laptop or desktop to Microsoft Azure using a VPN, such as a corporate VPN configuration. It's a good option to get up and running quickly for some pilot work or for remote employees.

> **Connectivity Trade-Offs**
>
> Each option has its own pros and cons and different use case. ExpressRoute is private and dedicated, but it's also expensive and complex to set up. Similarly, P2S is easy and fast but not scalable.
>
> For connectivity to SAP in Microsoft Azure, ExpressRoute is the recommended option.

> **Microsoft Azure Virtual WAN**
>
> Microsoft Azure virtual wide area network (WAN) is like an umbrella service that brings a lot of services together, such as branch connectivity, P2S, S2S, ExpressRoute, firewall, encryption, and so on. You can start with one or some of the use cases and add more as the network evolves.

3.3 Microsoft Azure Pricing Calculator and Total Cost of Ownership Calculator

The *Microsoft Azure pricing calculator* provides a way to estimate the cost of Microsoft Azure products, and because SAP landscapes can be large with multiple components, this tool is a good starting point to visualize the cost for not only the initial systems but also ongoing and new project costs. You can access the pricing calculator at *https://azure.microsoft.com/en-us/pricing/calculator*.

As shown in Figure 3.3, the screen is pretty intuitive: you select the services you're looking to price, and the web page starts an estimate section that takes further configuration details such as Microsoft Azure region, storage size, VM stock-keeping unit, and so on.

> **Note**
>
> Whenever this book discusses costs for a specific service, the Microsoft Azure pricing calculator is used for the estimate.

3.3 Microsoft Azure Pricing Calculator and Total Cost of Ownership Calculator

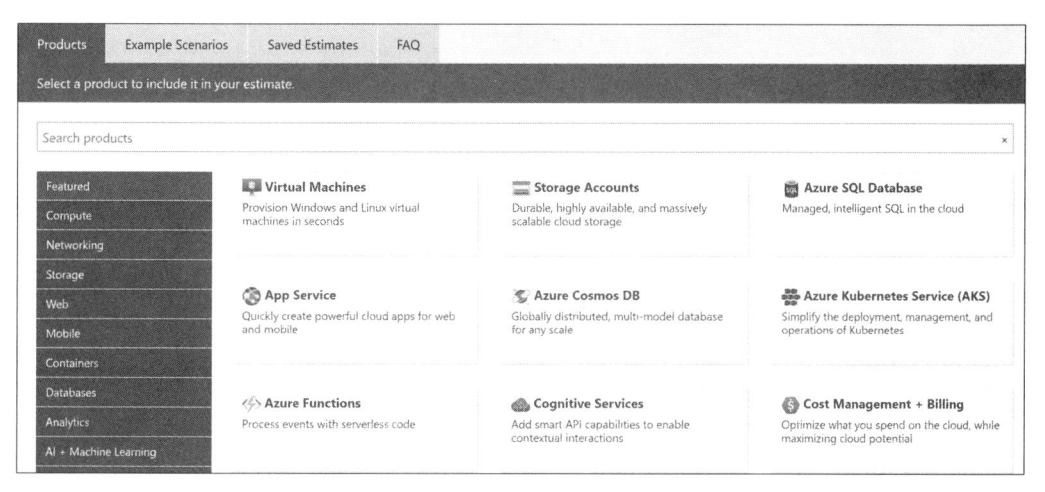

Figure 3.3 Microsoft Azure Pricing Calculator Screen

The Microsoft Azure total cost of ownership (TCO) calculator, which can be accessed at *https://azure.microsoft.com/en-us/pricing/tco/calculator/* goes a step further and provides a TCO graph, as shown in Figure 3.4, based on some assumptions such as electricity cost, virtualization cost, data center cost, and so on.

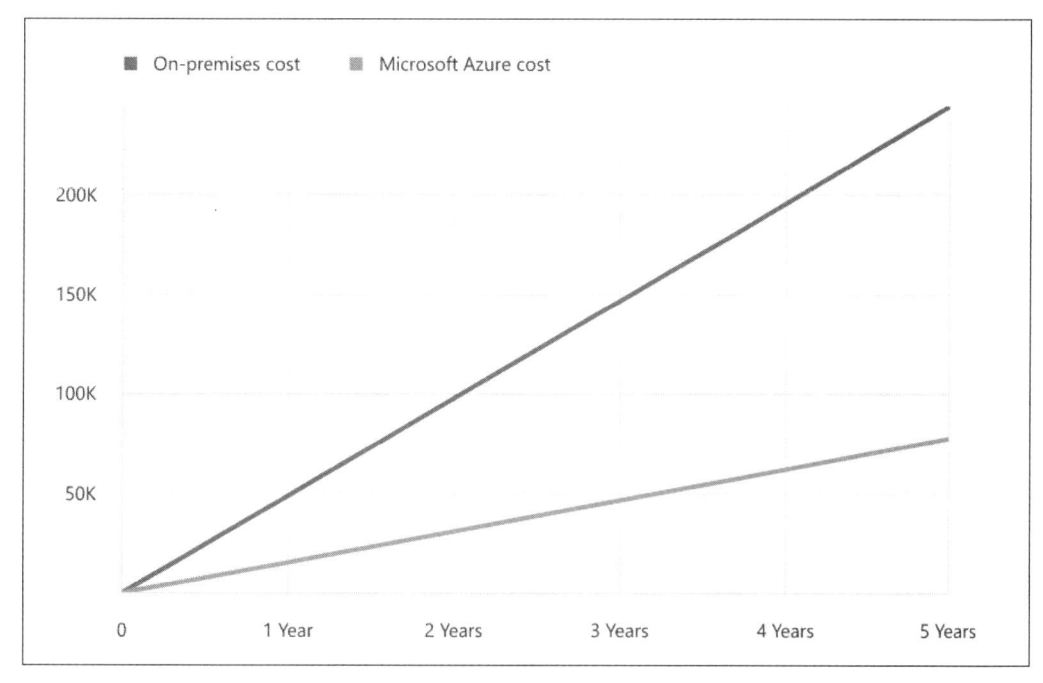

Figure 3.4 Microsoft Azure TCO Comparison with On-Premises TCO

3 Microsoft Azure Infrastructure Offerings for SAP

3.4 Infrastructure Foundation Pillars

Compute, network, and storage (Figure 3.5) are foundational components for any cloud computing platform, and we'll explore various related options available in Microsoft Azure.

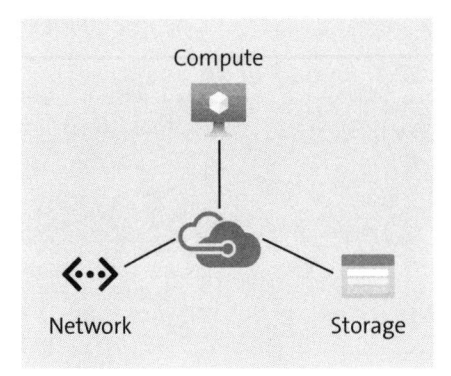

Figure 3.5 Cloud Infrastructure Foundation Pillars

3.4.1 Compute

Building or deploying any application starts with the compute option, which comes in several forms such as VM, bare metal, and containers (not supported for SAP). Microsoft Azure provides a variety of options in each area as illustrated in Figure 3.6; compute options certified for SAP, per SAP Note 1928533, are highlighted in yellow boxes.

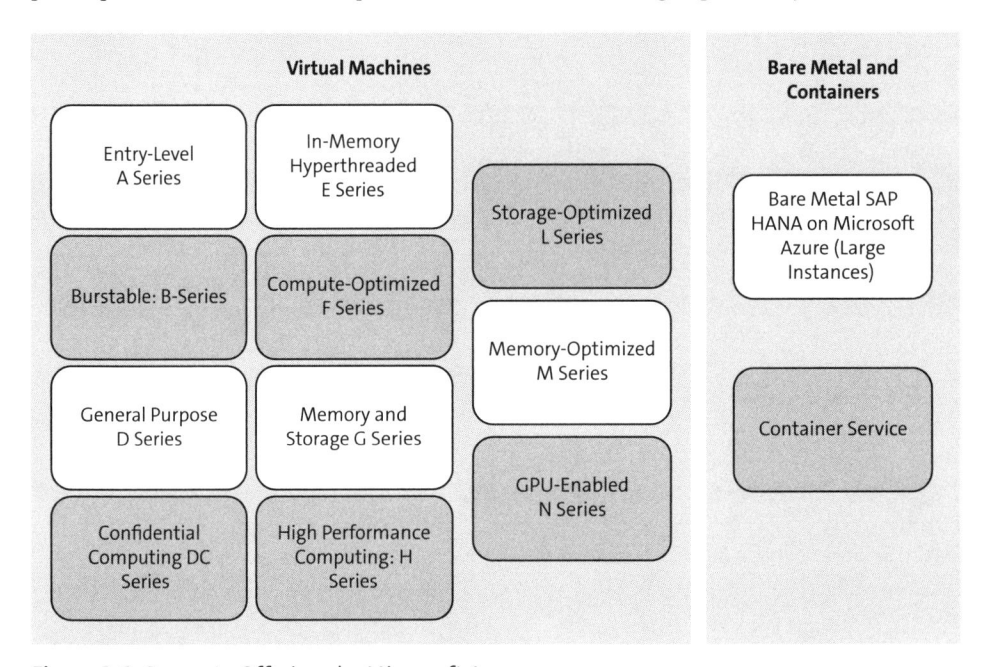

Figure 3.6 Compute Offerings by Microsoft Azure

3.4 Infrastructure Foundation Pillars

Following are the cost, performance, and constraints aspects for the compute offering.

Cost

This may not sound obvious, but the cost of VMs are region dependent (even within the same geography); while there may be many reasons for this, one explanation is the cost of operating the data center in the region (building, power, people, etc.).

Figure 3.7 shows the yearly pay-as-you-go cost for an SAP-certified VM (M64s) in three different North American regions, illustrating the regional price differences for the same machine.

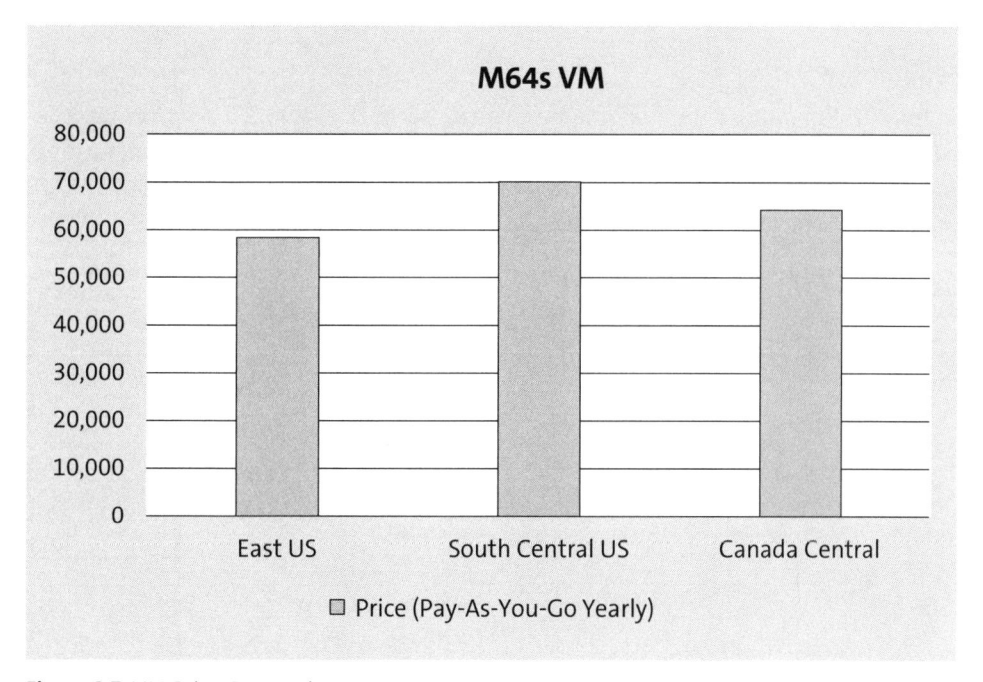

Figure 3.7 VM Price Comparison

Microsoft Azure offers several pricing models for VMs, including pay-as-you-go, reserved instances, and spot pricing, as compared in Table 3.1.

Pay-As-You-Go	Reserved Instances	Spot Pricing
Pay only when in use	Pay for whole commit duration (monthly payment option exists)	Paying for unused capacity
No commitment	One- or three-year commitment	No commitment
Good for flexible use	Good for large steady-state application such as SAP	Good for applications that can be interrupted

Table 3.1 Comparison of Microsoft Azure VM Pricing Models

Pay-As-You-Go	Reserved Instances	Spot Pricing
Cost optimization by shutting down	Budget predictability with upfront discount	Cheaper but can be evicted without much notice

Table 3.1 Comparison of Microsoft Azure VM Pricing Models (Cont.)

Container instances are charged by the gigabyte and virtual central processing unit (vCPU) second, whereas the bare metal service, also known as SAP HANA on Azure (Large Instances) is charged for the commitment period, with a monthly payment option introduced recently (not pay-as-you-go).

Performance

Several CPU-memory combinations are available so you can adjust the performance by going to a bigger or smaller VM. Because SAP employs hardware-independent measures for performance sizing called SAP Application Performance Standard (SAPS), SAP-certified VMs have the SAPS listed in SAP Note 1928533, as shown in Figure 3.8.

VM Series	VM Type	VM Size	2-Tier SAPS
A-series	Standard_A5	2 vCPU, 14 GiB	1,500
	Standard_A6	4 vCPU, 28 GiB	3,000
	Standard_A7	8 vCPU, 56 GiB	6,000
	Standard_A8 / Standard_A10	8 vCPU, 56 GiB	11,000
	Standard_A9 / Standard_A11	16 vCPU, 112 GiB	22,000

Figure 3.8 SAP Note 1928533 Listing SAPS for Certified Microsoft Azure VMs

> **Virtual Machine Size and Throughput**
>
> Network throughput (or bandwidth) is a function of VM size in Microsoft Azure. Because the VMs are on a shared environment, the throughput is allocated according to the size, leading to more bandwidth allocation for larger VMs.

Because SAP HANA on Azure (Large Instances) is a purpose-built bare metal offering, sizing is done in consultation with the customer while taking performance into account.

Constraints and Considerations

With all the flexibility that the Microsoft Azure compute offering provides, there are certain constraints as well:

- Not all VMs or SAP HANA on Azure (Large Instances) are available in all regions. Keep this in mind when selecting the region for your SAP deployment.
- Microsoft Azure provides off-the-shelf experience for VMs providing preconfigured CPU/memory ratios. Therefore, if you need to increase either CPU or memory, you can just resize to a bigger VM.
- Even within an SAP-certified VM series (e.g., D series), not all VMs are certified, so always refer to SAP Note 1928533 for choosing SAP VMs.
- VM scale sets, which let you create multiple identical VMs in a load balanced configuration, spot VMs, and containers, aren't supported for SAP.
- VMs have other restrictions as well, such as maximum number of network interface controllers (NICs), disks, input/output operations per second (IOPS) threshold (adjusted by Microsoft periodically with technological advances), so always refer to the Microsoft Azure documentation for the latest information.
- Some VM SKUs don't support Microsoft Azure premium disks, so those aren't supported for SAP databases.

Other Compute Offerings

Microsoft Azure offers some other compute offerings such as constrained VMs, isolated VMs, Microsoft Azure Dedicated Host, and VM scale sets:

- **Constrained vCPU VMs**
  In this offering, vCPU can be restricted to a half or quarter of the original VM specifications and are best fit for applications or workloads that aren't CPU intensive but require more memory, storage, or bandwidth. It may also help with product licenses that are CPU based.

  According to SAP Note 1928533, if a constrained VM is derived from an SAP-certified VM, it can be used for an SAP workload if SAPS is adjusted to take the new CPU configuration into account.

- **Isolated VMs**
  These VMs are dedicated to a single customer and are isolated to a specific hardware type. Not all VM SKUs are offered as isolated.

- **Microsoft Azure Dedicated Host**
  This is a physical server offering dedicated to your organization that can host multiple VMs. Microsoft Azure Dedicated Host is supported for SAP, and the Microsoft Azure documentation indicates that it will replace isolated VMs.

Generation 1 versus Generation 2 Virtual Machine

Microsoft Azure offers two different generations of VMs: generation 1 VMs have basic input/output system (BIOS)–based architecture, and generation 2 VMs come with a Unified Extensible Firmware Interface (UEFI)–based boot architecture. Besides the boot

> architecture difference, generation 2 also supports increased memory and persistent memory. VMs created with generation 1 architecture can't be changed to generation 2 just by restarting and selecting a different size; application migration will be required, so take this into consideration when choosing a VM generation.

3.4.2 Storage

Microsoft Azure offers a variety of storage types for different use cases, such as managed and unmanaged disks for VM, messaging platform, shared file, and so on, as shown in Figure 3.9. We'll discuss details of the most relevant ones for SAP.

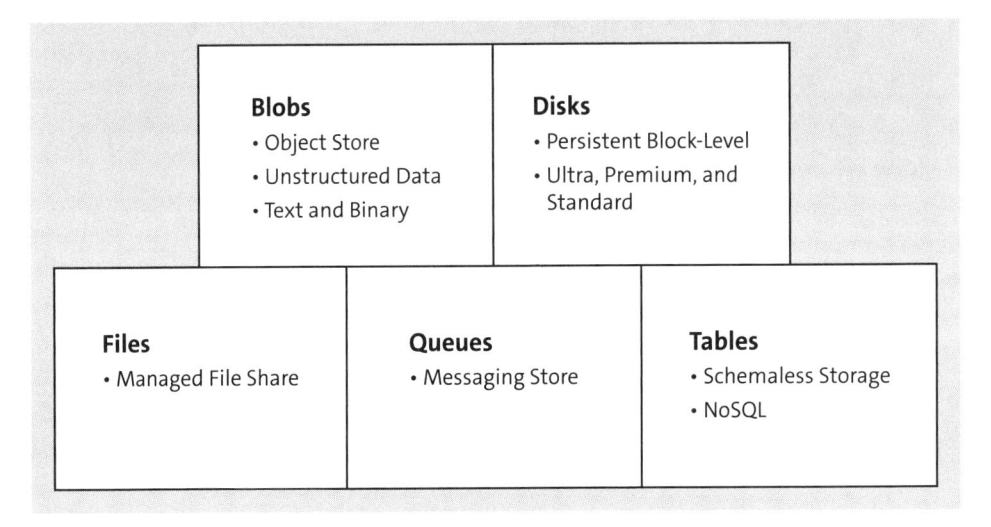

Blobs
- Object Store
- Unstructured Data
- Text and Binary

Disks
- Persistent Block-Level
- Ultra, Premium, and Standard

Files
- Managed File Share

Queues
- Messaging Store

Tables
- Schemaless Storage
- NoSQL

Figure 3.9 Storage Types Offered by Microsoft Azure

Microsoft Azure managed disks are mainly used in conjunction with a VM and are recommended for SAP data for both application and database servers; though virtualized, these are like on-premise physical disks.

Managed disks are resilient, are integrated with availability set and availability zone, and offer encryption. For different use cases and customer scenarios, Microsoft Azure provides the following four types of managed disks, which are a combination of hard disk drive (HDD) and solid-state drive (SDD):

- Standard HDD
- Standard SSD
- Premium
- Ultra

Table 3.2 compares some of the important features of the preceding managed disk types.

3.4 Infrastructure Foundation Pillars

Feature	Standard HDD	Standard SSD	Premium	Ultra
Disk type	HDD	SSD	SSD	SSD
Use case	Noncritical	Development/test apps	Production apps (SAP)	IO-intensive database (SAP HANA)
Cost	$	$$	$$$	$$$$
Performance	★	★★	★★★	★★★★
Dynamic performance adjustment	No	No	No	Yes
Snapshot	Yes	Yes	Yes	No
Microsoft Azure Backup	Yes	Yes	Yes	No
Microsoft Azure site recovery	Yes	Yes	Yes	No

Table 3.2 Microsoft Azure Managed Disks Features Comparison

Microsoft Azure storage accounts provide access to other data objects such as blobs, files, queues, tables, and unmanaged disks. It has a unique namespace that lets you access it over http or https as well. Microsoft Azure blob storage also provides access tiers, such as hot, cool, and archive, with different cost and retention structures. It helps you optimize costs by changing tiers of less frequently accessed data.

Disk Size and Name

Because there are so many disk type and sizes available, the disks are named to identify the disk type and size, usually starting with a letter denoting the type followed by a number denoting the size:

- Standard HDD starts with S; for example, S30 denotes 1 TiB, and S40 denotes 2 TiB.
- Standard SDD starts with E; for example, E30 denotes 1 TiB.
- Premium disk starts with P; for example, P30 denotes 1 TiB.
- Ultra disks aren't yet denoted by a letter, however, they come in the same size categories.

Constraints and Considerations

Microsoft Azure disks have some limitations by design, such as the performance of SSD is better than that of HDD, and others based on maturity of the offering (e.g., restrictions on ultra disk). A few of the important ones are highlighted here:

- Performance (IOPS and throughput) depends on the size; that is, the higher the disk, the better it performs.
- Adding multiple disks to a VM increases throughput, but the combined throughput can't exceed the maximum specified by the VM.
- Premium disks aren't compatible with all VM SKUs either, so when choosing a database server for SAP, you'll have to check compatibility.
- Premium disks smaller than 1 TB support bursting, meaning it can temporarily provide higher IOPS and throughput up to a ceiling.
- Ultra disk is relatively newer so there are more restrictions in terms of VM support, regions, and availability zones.
- Ultra disk can only be used as a data disk; premium disk is recommended for an operating system (OS).
- Managed disks support reservations similar to reserved VMs.
- Disk latency improves as you move from standard to premium and ultra.

Disk Cost Model

Different disk types have their own pricing models. For example, standard HDD and standard SSD are charged by size, number of disks, number of transactions, and number of outbound data transfers. Premium disks aren't charged for transactions, whereas ultra disks are billed based on provisioned size, IOPS, and throughput.

3.4.3 Network

We've already discussed connectivity to Microsoft Azure earlier in this chapter, so here we'll talk more about the Microsoft Azure network setup, isolation, and interconnectivity between different virtual networks.

Virtual Network and Subnet

A virtual network (VNET) in Microsoft Azure is an isolation boundary where internal services can communicate among each other, and external traffic is denied by default. A Microsoft Azure VNET is similar to an on-premise local area network (LAN) in terms of communication among the resources. VNET can be further sliced into smaller networks (called *subnets*) to allow greater control, separate application types, and restrict certain traffic flow.

Figure 3.10 shows an example of the VNET (SAPVNET) and subnet relationship (AzureBastionSubnet, sapsubnet) from Microsoft Azure portal.

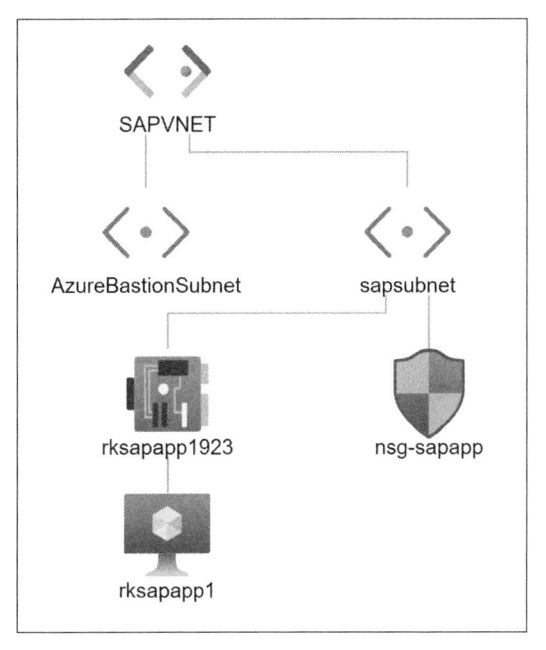

Figure 3.10 VNET and Subnet Representation from Microsoft Azure Portal

Address Spaces

Creating a VNET or subnet requires an IP address space in classless inter-domain routing (CIDR) notation, which specifies the IP address and associated routing prefix, as shown in Figure 3.11. Resources within a VNET or subnet get one of the available IPs assigned. You can either calculate the number of IPs available using the CIDR notation calculation or find it in the Microsoft Azure portal (Microsoft Azure reserves five IPs for each subnet).

Basics

Subscription	rk-azure
Resource group	sap-abc
Name	SAP-SBX-VNET
Region	East US

IP addresses

Address space	10.0.0.0/16

Name	IPv4
AzureBastionSubnet	10.10.8.0/27 (26 available)
sapsubnet	10.10.0.0/21 (2042 available)

Figure 3.11 VNET and Subnet Example with CIDR and Available IPs

Peering

By design, VNETs are isolated and don't talk to external networks. To enable communication, you need to connect the network using Microsoft Azure peering. Peering is a two-way connection, meaning if VNET A is peered to VNET B, it doesn't mean the communication will start because VNET B will have to be peered to VNET A as well in the configuration settings. Peering within the same region is called Microsoft Azure VNET peering; across different regions, it's termed global VNET peering.

Non-peering VNETs have their own use cases as well, such as a DR drill or POC systems that don't need to talk to anything else.

> **Note**
>
> A prerequisite to peer Microsoft Azure VNETs or to peer VNET to on-premise is *non-overlapping IP ranges*. In general, systems or networks that talk to each other wouldn't have overlapping IPs.

> **VNET Peering Is Nontransitive**
>
> If VNET A is peered with B, and B is peered with C, that doesn't mean A and C are automatically peered. You'll have to separately peer A and C if communication between those two is required.

Network Scope

Each network belongs to a subscription and a region. It's possible to connect the networks (peering) that are in different regions as well as different subscriptions. It's also possible for resources such as VMs to connect to the Internet if a public IP is enabled.

You can move a VM from one subnet to a different one without redeploying.

Security Groups

Network filtering using source IP and protocol can be achieved in two ways in Microsoft Azure: via a network security group or an application security group.

Network security groups allow and deny security rules based on IP address (source and destination), port, and protocol. So, if you wanted to block file transfer protocol (FTP) port 21 to all the servers, network security group rules would be the way to go.

Application security groups bring the application-centric approach to these rules. For example, if you have several databases that connect to applications on specific ports (e.g., SAP HANA database connecting to applications), you can create an application security group and apply that to the database group, effectively creating network security micro segmentation using higher granularity.

> **Tip**
>
> To reduce the number of rules, you can also use a group of IP prefixes, called *service tags* in Microsoft Azure.

Figure 3.12 shows how application security groups can be used for application-centric policies in an SAP environment. SAP Web Dispatcher can connect to application servers but not to databases, which it shouldn't anyway.

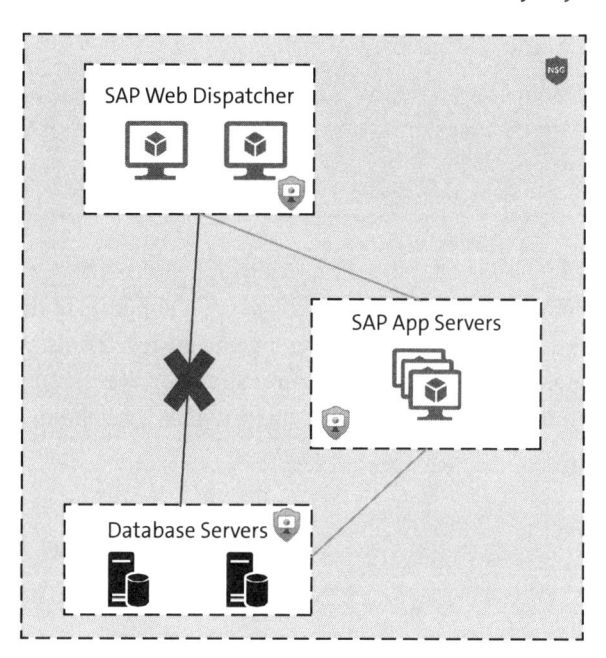

Figure 3.12 Application-Centric Security Rules Using Application Security Groups

3.5 Shared Storage

Use of shared storage has important implications in an SAP environment, including the following most common ones:

- High availability (HA)
- SAP shared directories such as profile and transport
- Interface directory
- SAP HANA scale-out installation (with standby)

3.5.1 Microsoft Azure Shared Storage

While Microsoft Azure provides multiple shared storage services, such as Microsoft Azure files, Microsoft Azure shared disks, and Microsoft Azure NetApp Files, not every service is suitable or optimized for SAP solutions. At the time of publication, Microsoft Azure shared disks and Microsoft Azure NetApp Files meet all the requirements and are supported for SAP use cases such as HA.

3.5.2 Microsoft Azure Shared Disks

Microsoft Azure shared disks allow managed disks to be shared across multiple VMs and supports the small computer system interface persistent reservations (SCSI PR) standard. Shared disks require a cluster manager, such as Windows Server Failover Cluster or Pacemaker, to handle communication and write locking.

For SAP, at the time of publication, Microsoft Azure shared disks supports SAP Central Services clustering on Windows. (Even though shared disks support the Linux OS, HA support for SAP isn't there yet.)

3.5.3 Microsoft Azure NetApp Files

Microsoft Azure NetApp Files is a managed file share service (PaaS) that supports both server message block and Network File System (NFS) technologies and is backed by ONTAP (NetApp's storage OS) technology. It's a Microsoft Azure native service so Microsoft manages the updates and patching behind the scenes and provides the support.

Figure 3.13 shows the Microsoft Azure NetApp Files hierarchy.

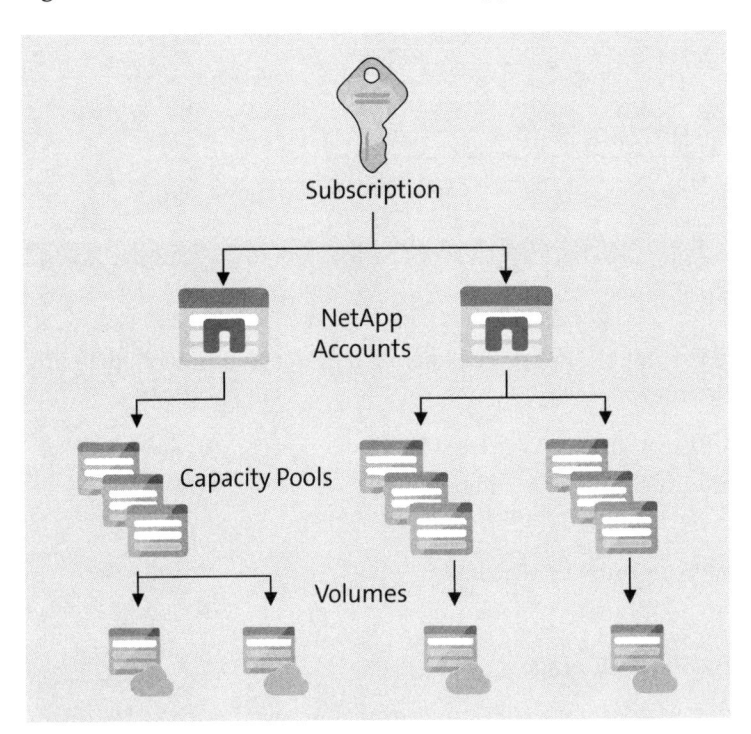

Figure 3.13 Microsoft Azure NetApp Files Storage Hierarchy in Microsoft Azure

The NetApp account resides within a subscription, and this is where a capacity pool is created (minimum 4 TiB, and then increments of 1 TiB). Capacity pools are further subdivided into volumes that can be mounted to different VMs.

Microsoft Azure NetApp Files provides HA out of the box with 99.99% SLA, and within the capacity pool, you can define different service levels based on performance requirements. Microsoft Azure NetApp Files comes in standard, premium, and ultra service levels. Table 3.3 shows the throughput for volume quotas.

Service Level	Throughput (MiB/s per TiB)
Standard	16
Premium	64
Ultra	128

Table 3.3 Microsoft Azure NetApp Files Throughput for Each Service Level

> **Note**
> The throughput is based on volume quota size regardless of capacity pool size.

Cost and other considerations regarding Microsoft Azure NetApp Files are listed here:

- Microsoft Azure NetApp Files cost is higher than that of comparable throughput of Microsoft Azure premium disk, but there is no management overhead, maintenance, or patching hassles.
- You start paying as soon as you provision a capacity pool, and it's pay for what you provision, meaning you'll pay for the whole capacity pool even if you're using only a small portion of it.
- All Microsoft Azure NetApp Files volumes are encrypted at rest, and the key is managed by the service.
- You can increase the performance of a volume by dynamically resizing it.
- All Microsoft Azure NetApp Files volumes are deployed in a delegated subnet, and currently there is no support for network security group in the Microsoft Azure NetApp Files subnet.
- Microsoft Azure NetApp Files supports snapshot, which is great for large volumes.

3.6 Operating System Licenses in Microsoft Azure

Choosing an OS is one of the fundamental decisions for SAP environments mainly because changing the OS requires intense effort and a lot of time. We've already talked about the OSs supported on Microsoft Azure (also listed in this section) for SAP, so this section will talk more about licensing models.

The following OSs for SAP are supported on Microsoft Azure:

- Microsoft Windows
- SUSE Linux Enterprise Server (SLES)
- RedHat Enterprise Linux (RHEL)
- Oracle Linux

Microsoft Azure provides different licensing models for various OS, primarily spanning across pay-as-you-go and bring your own subscription with minor differences across vendors:

- **Pay-as-you-go**
  Use pay-as-you-go when you want to combine the OS license with the VM license in Microsoft Azure and pay together as part of the Microsoft Azure cost. Microsoft partners with OS vendors for the support.

- **Bring your own subscription**
  Use bring your own subscription when you already have a licensing agreement with the OS vendor and want to use that in Microsoft Azure. The OS vendor will be the primary support contact if you're using this licensing model.

> **Note**
>
> Conversion from one licensing model to another may not be supported; in which case, you'll have to migrate SAP systems to new servers or decommission old ones and install new. With this in mind, be careful with the licensing model you choose.

Every vendor has a different name for the offering:

- **RHEL licensing names**
  The pay-as-you-go version is called on-demand support, and bring your own subscription is called cloud access support.

- **SLES licensing names**
  The SUSE on Microsoft Azure support models are called bring your own subscription, basic, standard, and priority. Figure 3.14 shows an example of the available offerings in Microsoft Azure for SLES.

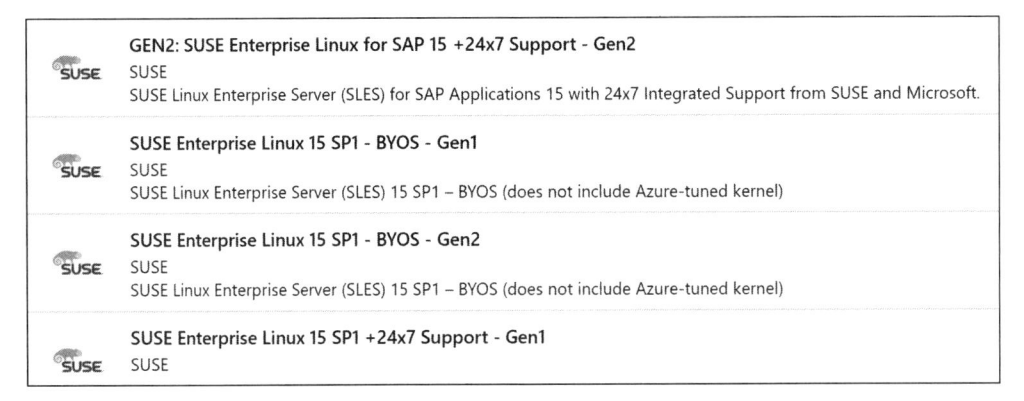

SUSE	**GEN2: SUSE Enterprise Linux for SAP 15 +24x7 Support - Gen2** SUSE SUSE Linux Enterprise Server (SLES) for SAP Applications 15 with 24x7 Integrated Support from SUSE and Microsoft.
SUSE	**SUSE Enterprise Linux 15 SP1 - BYOS - Gen1** SUSE SUSE Linux Enterprise Server (SLES) 15 SP1 – BYOS (does not include Azure-tuned kernel)
SUSE	**SUSE Enterprise Linux 15 SP1 - BYOS - Gen2** SUSE SUSE Linux Enterprise Server (SLES) 15 SP1 – BYOS (does not include Azure-tuned kernel)
SUSE	**SUSE Enterprise Linux 15 SP1 +24x7 Support - Gen1** SUSE

Figure 3.14 OS Licensing Model for SUSE Enterprise Linux in Microsoft Azure

- **Oracle Linux licensing model supported**
  You must have an active Oracle license to use Oracle Linux in Microsoft Azure. More details on Linux support details on Microsoft Azure are available at *https://support.microsoft.com/en-us/help/2941892/support-for-linux-and-open-source-technology-in-azure*.
- **Microsoft Windows licensing model supported**
  For Windows servers, pay-as-you-go and bring your own subscription are offered as well. The Microsoft program name for bring your own licenses is called Azure Hybrid Benefit, wherein if you have active Software Assurance on-premise, you can reuse on-premise Windows licenses in Microsoft Azure.

SAP Flavor for Linux

RHEL and SLES also provide an SAP flavor of the OS (called RHEL for SAP and SLES for SAP), which contains packages such as HA add-ons, and parameters optimized for SAP applications as well as SAP HANA, as recommended by SAP.

SAP License in Microsoft Azure

SAP licenses on Microsoft Azure are bring your own licenses, and support is provided by SAP.

3.7 Platform Maintenance and Notifications

Microsoft Azure updates the platform regularly to enhance security, resiliency, and performance; this includes software and hardware updates as well as decommissions. Microsoft Azure also uses machine learning algorithms to identify disks or nodes that can potentially fail and migrate those to a different infrastructure.

With developments in technology over the years, the maintenance has become less disruptive, and Microsoft uses different techniques depending on the kind of update and impact on hosts:

- **Hot patching**
  Hot patching is applied at the function level and incurs no downtime for customer VMs. This is the preferred mechanism whenever possible.
- **Memory preserving host updates**
  This mechanism preserves the memory in RAM and pauses the VM up to 30 seconds. It's not compatible with all Microsoft Azure VM SKUs, and other methods are used for noncompatible ones.
- **Live migration**
  This involves moving a VM to a different infrastructure while it's still up and running.

While the VM is suspended for a short time, applications that aren't as sensitive can sustain this to adding to the resiliency. Live migration is used to proactively mitigate problems when the machine learning algorithms predict a failure.

- **Self-service notifications**
  SAP systems can be sensitive to even short pauses; therefore, the self-service mechanism is a better way to go. It gives you a maintenance window within which you can schedule the update to minimize business disruption.

3.8 Microsoft Azure Dedicated Host

Whether you're in a regulated business, want greater control over the infrastructure, or think host-level isolation would serve your organization better, Microsoft Azure Dedicated Host can meet your needs.

Figure 3.15 shows the dedicated host structure in Microsoft Azure.

Virtual Machine (Name, Size)
Microsoft Azure VM

Dedicated Host (Name, Host Group, Size)
Physical Server in Microsoft Azure

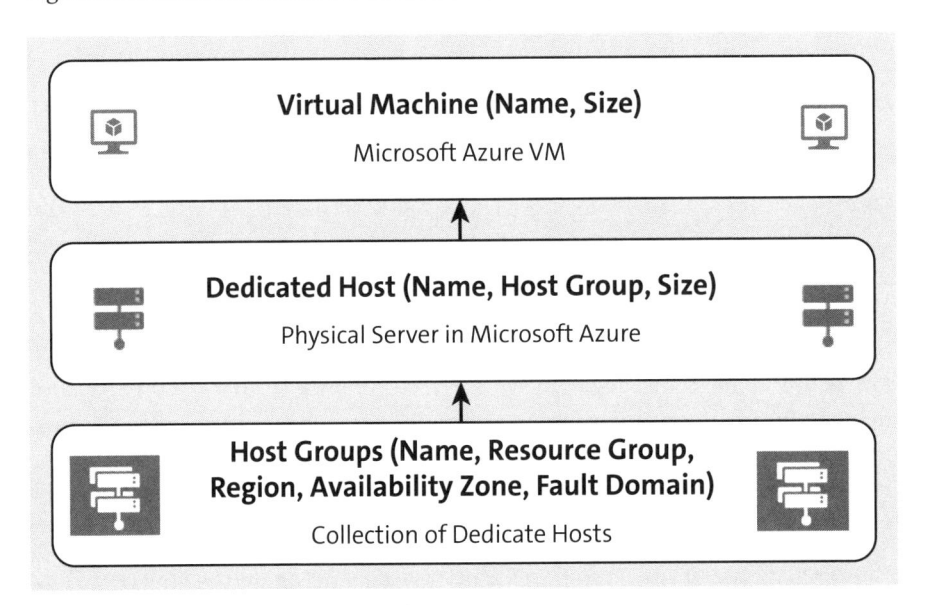

Host Groups (Name, Resource Group, Region, Availability Zone, Fault Domain)
Collection of Dedicate Hosts

Figure 3.15 Microsoft Azure Dedicated Host Structure

3.8.1 Virtual Machine Provisioning and Tracking Capacity

Microsoft Azure Dedicated Host is a dedicated physical server for your organization that you can assign new VMs to via host group, as shown in Figure 3.16. You can either create a new VM or add existing VMs (restrictions apply) to a Microsoft Azure Dedicated Host group.

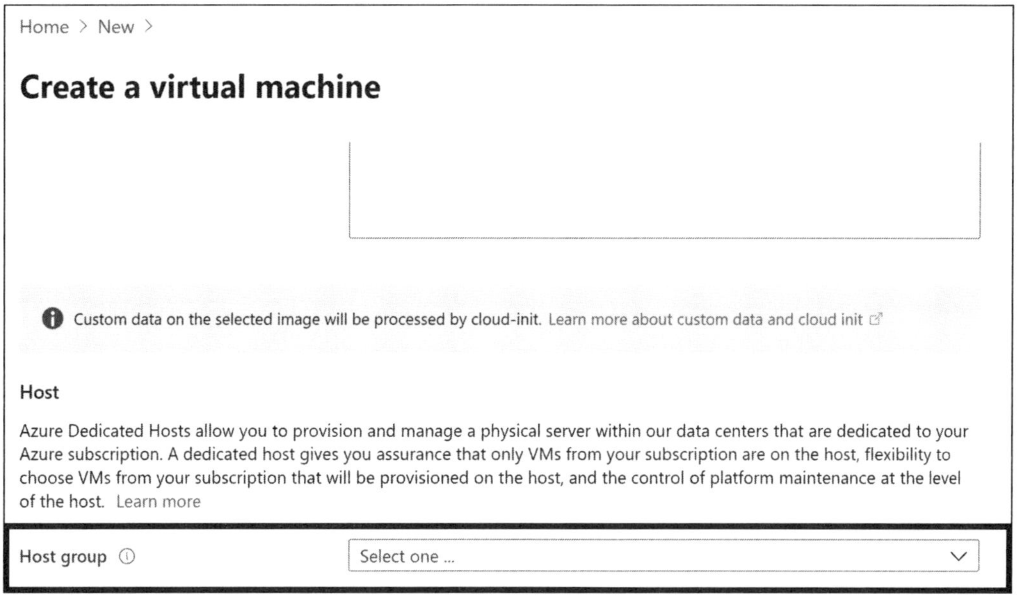

3.8 Microsoft Azure Dedicated Host

Home > New >

Create a virtual machine

ⓘ Custom data on the selected image will be processed by cloud-init. Learn more about custom data and cloud init

Host

Azure Dedicated Hosts allow you to provision and manage a physical server within our data centers that are dedicated to your Azure subscription. A dedicated host gives you assurance that only VMs from your subscription are on the host, flexibility to choose VMs from your subscription that will be provisioned on the host, and the control of platform maintenance at the level of the host. Learn more

Host group ⓘ | Select one ...

Figure 3.16 Assigning a VM to a Microsoft Azure Dedicated Host Host Group

Microsoft Azure Dedicated Host also keeps track of available capacity for VMs, as illustrated in Figure 3.17. You can get support for Microsoft Azure Dedicated Host VMs for SAP by provisioning SAP-certified VMs from SAP Note 1928533.

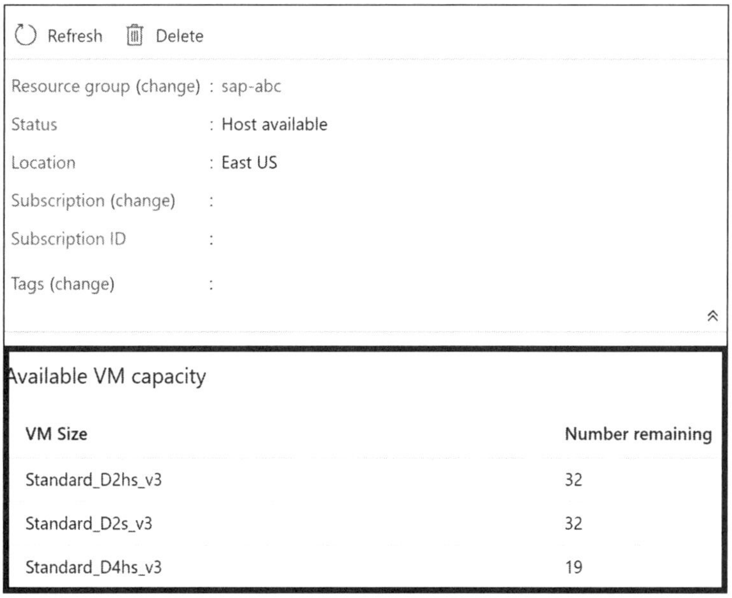

◯ Refresh   🗑 Delete

Resource group (change) : sap-abc
Status : Host available
Location : East US
Subscription (change) :
Subscription ID :
Tags (change) :

Available VM capacity

VM Size	Number remaining
Standard_D2hs_v3	32
Standard_D2s_v3	32
Standard_D4hs_v3	19

Figure 3.17 Microsoft Azure Dedicated Host Showing Available Capacity

3.8.2 Cost

Because the host is dedicated to an organization (not shared), you pay for the whole server regardless of how many VMs are deployed on the host. The host price is dependent on region, VM family, hardware type, and so on.

> **Other Considerations**
>
> Following are a few important considerations for Microsoft Azure Dedicated Host:
>
> - Microsoft Azure Dedicated Host also offers reserved instances, which provides better pricing than pay-as-you-go.
> - You can use the Azure Hybrid Benefit, as applicable for Windows Server licenses, in Microsoft Azure Dedicated Host.
> - Currently, there is a quota limit of 3,000 vCPUs for Microsoft Azure Dedicated Host, per region.

> **Maintenance Control for Microsoft Azure Dedicated Host**
>
> Microsoft Azure Dedicated Host provides better control for patching options than Microsoft Azure VMs because you can schedule the patches at a time of your choice within a 35-day rolling window.

3.9 SAP HANA on Azure (Large Instances)

SAP HANA on Azure (Large Instances) is Microsoft's bare metal offering for SAP HANA databases, which are SAP HANA tailored data center integration-certified. It's different from the Microsoft Azure Dedicated Host offering because SAP HANA on Azure (Large Instances) can't host VM and is only supported for the SAP HANA database.

Figure 3.18 shows the architecture of SAP HANA on Azure (Large Instances), illustrating customer isolation within the infrastructure stamp.

SAP HANA on Azure (Large Instances) (referred to as S series in Microsoft Azure) currently supports up to 24 TB of memory for a single instance and up to 120 TB for an SAP HANA scale-out configuration. Specific configurations and the SAP certification details can be found in the SAP HANA Hardware Directory at *https://www.sap.com/dmc/exp/2014-09-02-hana-hardware/enEN/#/solutions?filters=iaas;ve:24*.

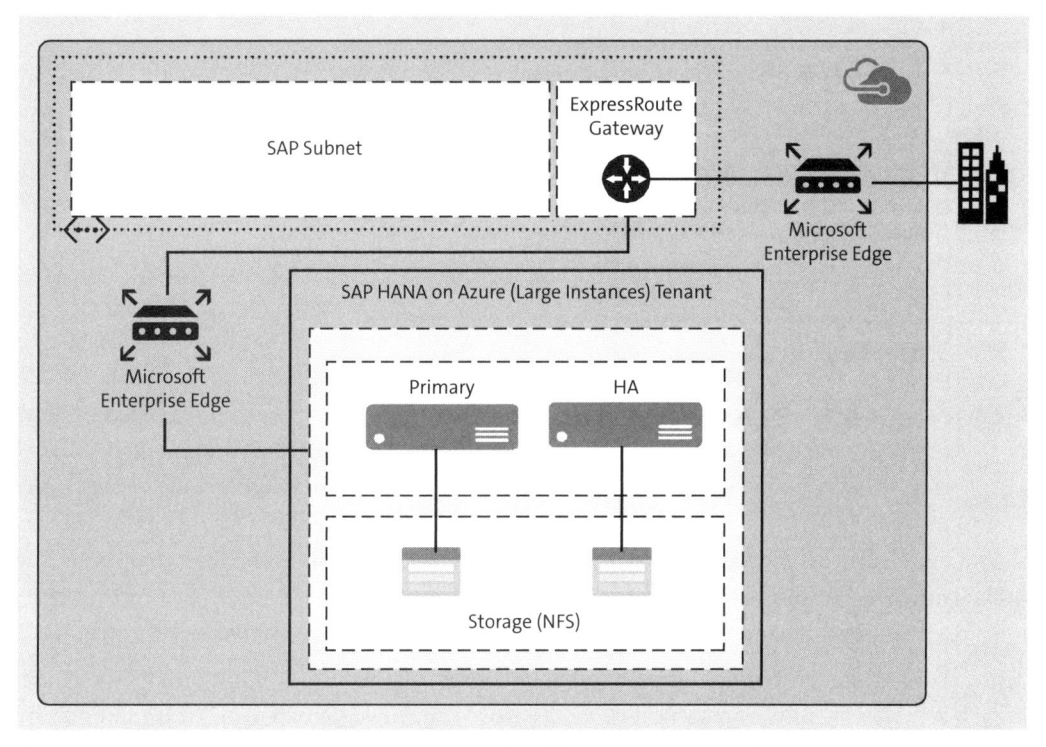

Figure 3.18 SAP HANA on Azure (Large Instances) Architecture in Microsoft Azure

3.9.1 SAP HANA on Azure (Large Instances) Revision 4

Starting July 2019, Revision 4 of SAP HANA on Azure (Large Instances) became available, which puts SAP HANA on Azure (Large Instances) servers in close physical proximity to the Microsoft Azure VM where SAP application servers reside and helps with the latency benchmark between the database and application server, published by SAP. Refer to the Microsoft Azure resource availability matrix to locate the regions that support SAP HANA on Azure (Large Instances).

3.9.2 Deployment Timeline and Communication

Because SAP HANA on Azure (Large Instances) servers are purpose-built for a customer, currently there is no way to provision using Microsoft Azure portal or automation scripts. You have to work with Microsoft to specify the configuration for the deployment, which may take a few weeks, which you should account for during planning.

By design and for security reasons, SAP HANA on Azure (Large Instances) networks are isolated from each other. Therefore, the servers residing in different regions or on-premise can't communicate with each other, except for storage replication. You have to use one of the following mechanisms to enable the communication:

- Reverse proxy mechanism
- IPTables (Internet Protocol tables) rules configuration in the Linux VM
- ExpressRoute Global Reach add-on to the ExpressRoute connection

When considering SAP HANA on Azure (Large Instances), it's important to think about network connectivity architecture and direct communication to SAP HANA on Azure (Large Instances).

3.10 Key Vault

Key Vault is a Microsoft Azure service to store secrets such as passwords, keys, and certificates that are software or hardware security module (HSM) protected. It's a centralized way to manage and control sensitive information in Microsoft Azure that minimizes the chances of getting something accidently leaked; it's also a better way to store secure information, such as password or connection information, than hardcoding in application code. Access to Key Vault is restricted using Active Directory (AD) authentication, and vault management can be done via role-based access control.

For SAP landscape deployment and ongoing management, Key Vault provides a secure way to store and access the several passwords and keys that are used, this method can also be used with DevOps pipelines. It also integrates with Microsoft Azure disk encryption, making it useful when using customer-managed keys. In addition, access to Key Vault can be logged and monitored to provide an audit trail.

3.11 Microsoft Azure Landing Zone

A landing zone can be thought of as infrastructure services that ready the platform to deploy applications. Think of core components that would need to be in place for SAP migration, and that's your landing zone. Each individual service or component is like a building block that fits together to create the landing zone.

Figure 3.19 shows the infrastructure components to consider for building a landing zone in Microsoft Azure before any SAP deployment.

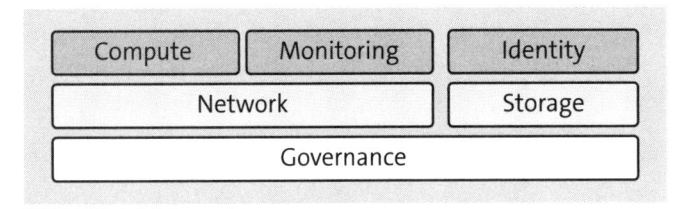

Figure 3.19 Landing Zone Components

All the services we've discussed so far, along with governance structure, play a part in creating the landing zone.

3.12 Summary

Microsoft Azure provides a lot of services, but for SAP deployments, we use only a subset of them for several reasons, such as certification requirements, performance, and architecture. Having said that, a lot of the services that aren't relevant to SAP aren't discussed in this book.

In this chapter, you learned about the services that comprise the core infrastructure needed for SAP deployments. We also talked about different options available, cost and performance aspects, and certifications as they relate to SAP. The next chapter discusses design considerations and architecture pillars; we'll talk about the decisions to be made in the context of SAP for the Microsoft Azure services, including sizing, security, and performance.

Chapter 4
System Design Framework

This chapter provides as a decision-making framework and collection of tools for designing the SAP solution in Microsoft Azure. We'll discuss the design pillars and Microsoft Azure services within those pillars.

Decision-making always involves a lot of issues and trade-offs that must be considered simultaneously. For example, if you're looking for a car, you probably have a fair idea of the features you want, but you also have price in mind because it all goes into the final decision. The same is true for the decisions necessary for designing the SAP solution for Microsoft Azure.

Migrating to the cloud is the first step in the digital transformation, and it serves as a foundation to business agility and integration with other technologies that provide competitive advantage. Figure 4.1 shows the pillars that form the basis of a good solution design, that is, security, performance, resiliency, and operational efficiency; we'll explore each pillar in the following sections.

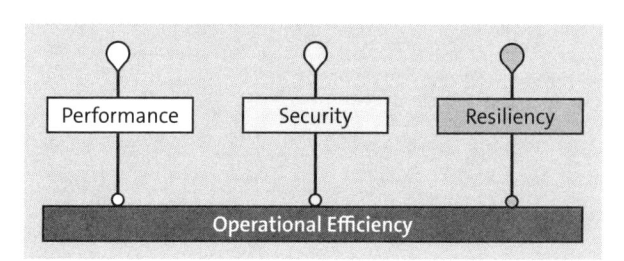

Figure 4.1 Design Excellence Pillars for Cloud Solutions

4.1 Security

Security is in the center of everything we do, and detection is equally as important as prevention in cloud environments. You may be thinking that security is the cloud provider's responsibility, but let's consider that a little bit:

- What level of security are we talking about: physical building, network, application, data?
- Just because security tools and techniques exist, do you implement everything for each scenario?
- Whose responsibility is implementing the recommended practices?

4 System Design Framework

It may seem like *everything* is secure in the cloud by default, but depending on the circle of your control (from cloud infrastructure as a service [IaaS], platform as a service [PaaS], software as a service [SaaS] model, as shown in Figure 4.2), you must secure what you're responsible for. Microsoft Azure provides the tools and allows you to bring your own as well, so security is a shared responsibility.

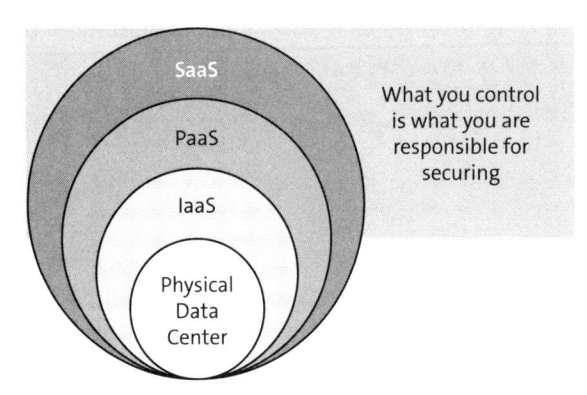

Figure 4.2 Security as a Shared Responsibility

Probably the biggest difference in managing security on-premise versus the cloud is that you don't have to worry about securing everything; you pass some of the responsibilities to Microsoft (in case of Microsoft Azure) who invests significant amounts of time in research and securing Microsoft Azure.

The following sections discuss the key aspects of security highlighted in Figure 4.3.

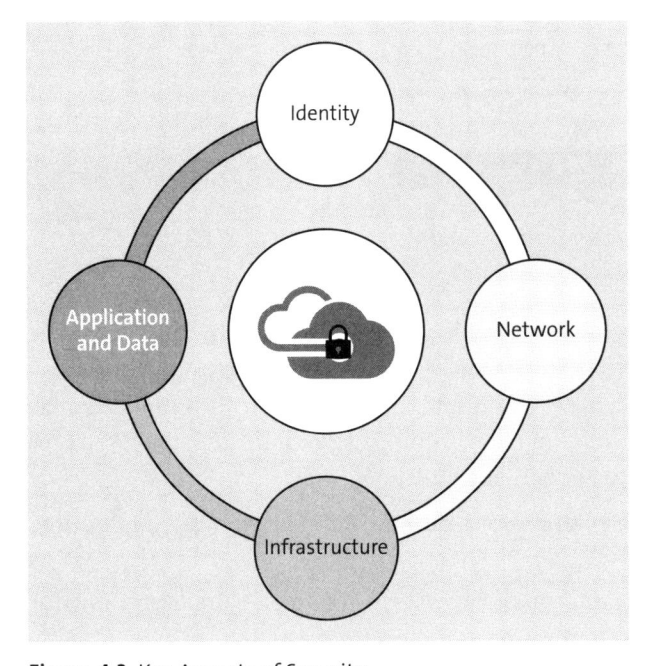

Figure 4.3 Key Aspects of Security

4.1.1 Identity

An important part of keeping your house secure is to give keys only to family members; similarly, identity management is a key part of any cloud security program. Access and authorizations for all Microsoft Azure subscriptions and, thus, services, are governed by Microsoft Azure Active Directory (Microsoft Azure AD); it lets you determine who to grant access to along with the kind of access using the role-based access control model. You can also synchronize your on-premise AD with Microsoft Azure AD to enable organizational single sign-on (SSO).

Custom roles (Figure 4.4) in Microsoft Azure helps you follow the least privilege model. You can also create a team-based model where there is a role for, say, infrastructure, SAP Basis, network teams, and so on, and then assign members to those roles so the Basis team doesn't get access to manage network configurations, for example.

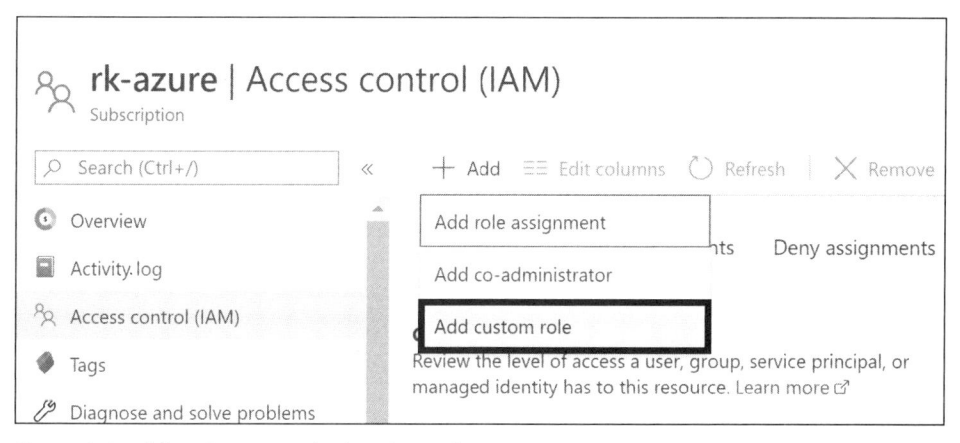

Figure 4.4 Adding Custom Roles in Microsoft Azure

When you're creating resources using automated templates, such as Microsoft Azure Resource Manager or Terraform code, Microsoft Azure provides a way to do it using an app. You register an app in Microsoft Azure AD (see Figure 4.5) and create an identity for the app called a *service principal*. Then you create a client secret (application password in simple terms) with an expiration date.

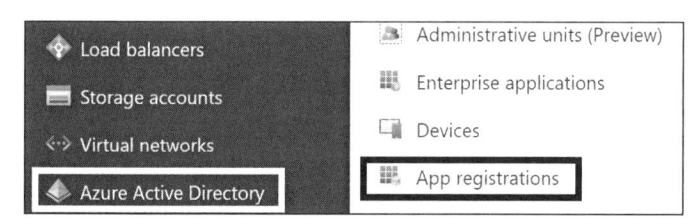

Figure 4.5 App Registrations in Microsoft Azure AD

You add an appropriate role to the app (this ensures that the application has only desired authorizations and creates an audit trail for resources created using the app), and

4   System Design Framework

the automation program makes a call with the credentials, which can be integrated with DevOps processes as well.

SAP systems are mostly on IaaS, so, even after the initial provisioning, you may be managing the virtual machines (VMs) and other infrastructure using automation scripts. When the question of storing keys or passwords arises, the Microsoft Azure Key Vault seems to be a good solution, but you still need to authenticate with Key Vault so it doesn't fix the original problem. The *managed identity* feature addresses that issue by providing Microsoft Azure resources, such as VM, with automatically managed identities in Microsoft Azure AD. Managed identity uses the service principal in the background, and Microsoft Azure internally manages expiration and key rotation, so you don't have to worry about those.

Microsoft Azure provides system-assigned managed identity (which is enabled on the service and tied to the service lifecycle, meaning if the VM gets deleted, the identity will too) and user-managed identity, which acts as a separate resource and can be assigned to the services that support this construct. Figure 4.6 shows an example of user-assigned managed identity for a VM.

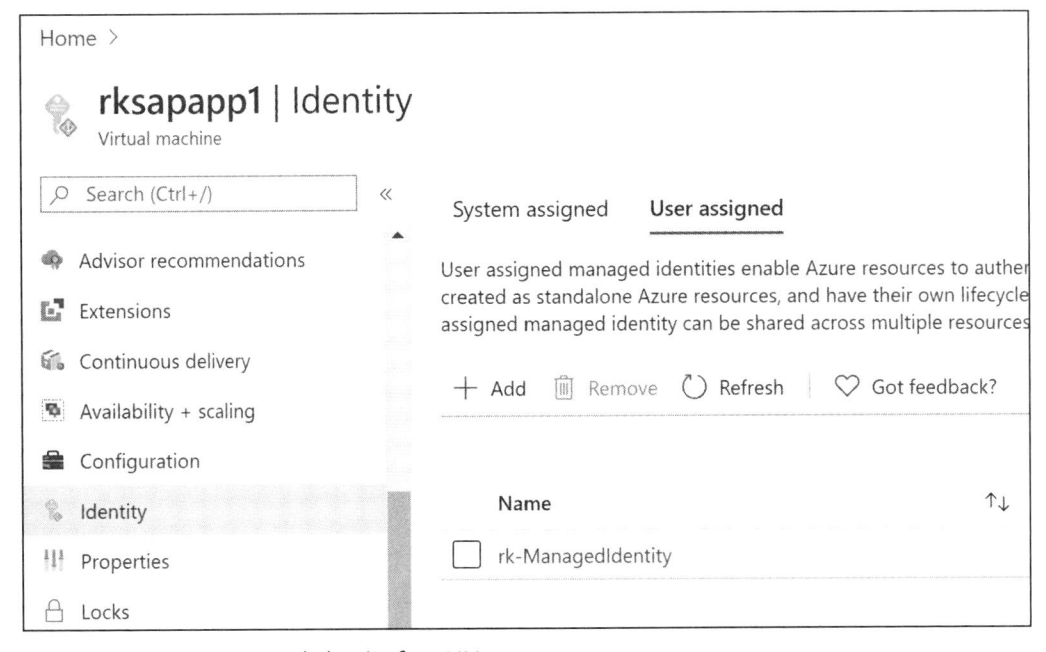

Figure 4.6 Managed Identity for a VM

> **Note**
>
> Not all Microsoft Azure services support managed identity, so always refer to the latest Microsoft Azure documentation as new services get added.

88

SAP supports SSO with AD and Microsoft Azure AD using technologies such as Kerberos and Security Assertion Markup Language (SAML) streamlining the authentication process.

Microsoft Azure AD also provides different kinds of sign-in experiences (besides traditional username/password model) such as *password-less*, *hardware token*, and *multifactor authentication,* and there are built-in security features such as conditional access, risk-based policies, and custom banned passwords.

> **Microsoft Azure AD Features and Licensing**
>
> Not all the features are available with standard Microsoft Azure AD. Depending on the security feature, you may need to subscribe to the premium model, which has cost considerations.

4.1.2 Network Security

Microsoft Azure has a comprehensive network security approach; the underlying idea is to allow only authorized traffic (prevention) and learn quickly if something doesn't look right (detection). Figure 4.7 shows an outside-in perspective for the Microsoft Azure security layered approach that we'll discuss in this section.

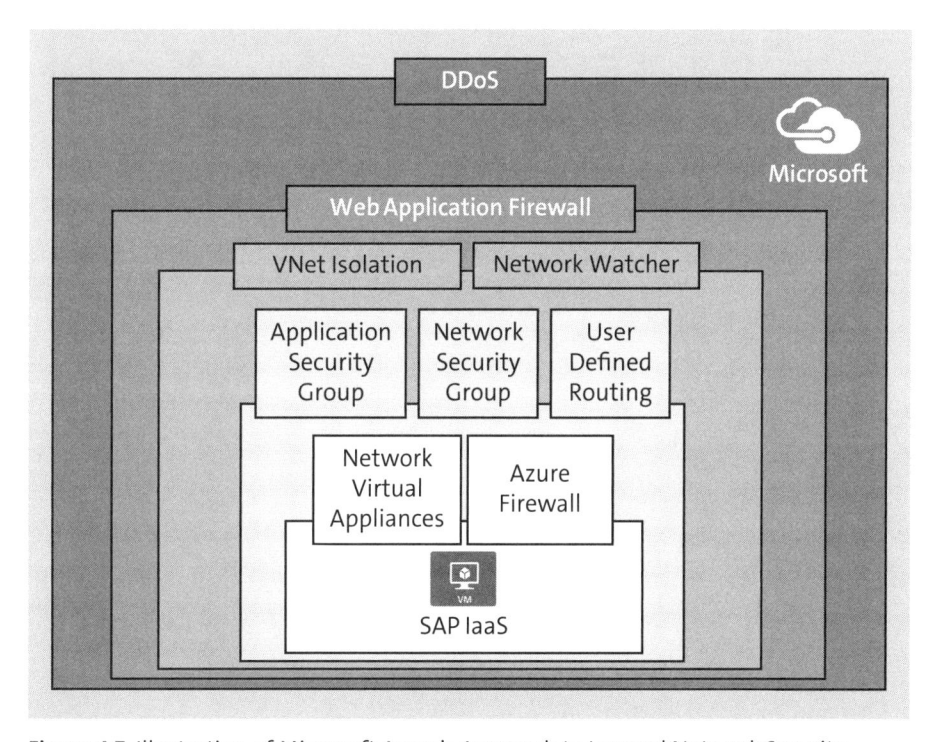

Figure 4.7 Illustration of Microsoft Azure's Approach to Layered Network Security

Microsoft Azure has built-in *distributed denial of service* (DDoS) protection for all services, including public IPs created for a service such as got SAProuter VM. DDoS uses threat detection algorithms to protect against volume-based attacks.

Services such as Microsoft Azure Front Door (global web traffic routing/balancing) and Application Gateway (regional http(s) load balancer) provide Secure Sockets Layer (SSL) termination and web application firewall (WAF).

When it comes to isolating customer networks, *virtual network* (VNet) is the base layer; by design, it blocks all communication unless specifically peered with other networks. From there, you can divide the networks into subnets that use their own private IP range, apply *network security groups* and *application security groups*, and can also define their own routes using *user-defined routes* (UDRs). Microsoft recommends, and provides a tool called *Network Watcher* to monitor and diagnose networks for IaaS use cases such as between a VM and endpoint. You can feed packet capture data from Network Watcher to an intrusion detection system as well to look for malicious activity.

Microsoft Azure provides a cloud native firewall service (*Microsoft Azure Firewall*) and also allows you to bring your own third-party firewall solution (e.g., Palo Alto or Barracuda) in the form of a *network virtual appliance*. You can choose what fits your organization better based on features, licenses, and familiarity.

> **Never Trust; Always Verify!**
>
> We recommend organizations implement *zero trust* based on the principle of "never trust, always verify." The zero trust model assumes that nothing is secure, not even inside the organization boundary; you should assume breach and always verify identity and access requests.

4.1.3 Infrastructure Security

This section focuses on infrastructure components such as VM and operating system (OS) images. VMs run on Microsoft Azure Hypervisor, which is an abstraction hidden from users but controlled and managed by Microsoft.

VM security starts with *access management*:

- Never enable public IP on a VM by default. VMs that require public access can be put in a separate perimeter network with network virtual appliances in front of them. Figure 4.8 shows an example of private IP configuration for a VM (you can find the configuration information from the network interface configuration in the Microsoft Azure portal). For SAP systems, it also needs to be configured as static (rather than dynamic IP).

- Both Windows and Linux VMs can be integrated with Microsoft Azure AD for authentication. This lets you centrally manage access; you can layer the user authentication on Microsoft Azure role-based access control for VM access.
- Enable just-in-time (JIT) access for VMs; JIT locks down open ports using network security group rules in the background. Access is granted for a specified time when requested by a user with correct role-based access control permissions.

IP Version	Type	Private IP address	Public IP address
IPv4	Primary	10.10.0.4 (Static)	-

Figure 4.8 Private IP Configuration Example

> **Tip**
> Configure Microsoft Azure policies to restrict the public IP and minimize the number of uses for a VM across resource groups or subscriptions.

> **Confidential Computing**
> Microsoft Azure also provides confidential computing, which is hardware-based protection while data is in use. These VMs run on specialized hardware and fall under the data center series stock-keeping unit (SKU). Confidential computing VM SKUs aren't certified for SAP use.

Keeping the VMs patched is important not only for security but also for VM *lifecycle management*. You can either use Microsoft Azure Update Management (from Microsoft Azure automation) or integrate this in the DevOps pipeline that you currently use.

When it comes to OS management, security starts right from the time you build the OS image. Security configurations recommended by the OS vendor and SAP should be implemented besides the organizational standard hardening guidelines. Microsoft Azure provides the Image Builder feature, which is based on HashiCorp Packer and lets you bring Windows or Linux images or pick one from the marketplace to create a golden image and patch going forward. Incorporate the anti-malware install during the image build itself to make it consistent and compliant organization wide. Microsoft provides an anti-malware solution in addition to supporting other providers such as Trend Micro, McAfee, Broadcom, and so on.

You can also use the guidance from the Center for Internet Security (CIS) and adopt the controls to quickly establish or benchmark policies. CIS has a benchmark guide specific for securing Microsoft Azure.

4.1.4 Application and Data Security

Application security control refers to securing the application, such as SAP, and data security spans encryption, backups, and databases. SAP provides a way to secure the application, and, to the extent that it reaches the database and OS layer, SAP also recommends specific patches and parameters through SAP Notes. Microsoft Azure as a technology doesn't get too deep into the application layer of SAP, but there are third-party tools available such as Onapsis and ERPScan that can point toward specific application vulnerability. User interface (UI) endpoints such as SAP GUI, SAP Business Client, SAP Web Dispatcher, and SAP Fiori have SAP-specific security mechanisms such as SSL and secure network communications (SNC) support.

Data security in Microsoft Azure can be implemented using encryption and access restriction. As usual, you apply the principle of least privilege when granting access to a storage account and using a shared access signature.

Encryption revolves around data being at rest or in transit. By design, the data at rest is encrypted by Microsoft Azure for both storage accounts (called Microsoft Azure storage encryption) and managed disks (called server-side encryption [SSE]), at the storage layer, using 256-bit Advanced Encryption Standard (AES) encryption.

> **Note**
> Temporary disk storage isn't encrypted by SSE because these aren't managed disks. Temporary disk loses everything with reboot and isn't recommended for customer data.

Because SSE is done at the storage layer, there is no performance impact or additional cost, and you don't have an option to opt out; however, you can bring your own key with customer-managed key feature. Managed disk customer-managed key is integrated with Microsoft Azure Key Vault.

> **Customer-Managed Key and Data Encryption Key**
> Microsoft Azure internally uses data encryption key for encryption and uses customer-managed key to encrypt the data encryption key. In addition, customer-managed key relies on the managed identity feature under the hood.

Managed disks offer another layer of encryption, on top of SSE, called Microsoft Azure Disk Encryption, which can be enabled on the OS and data disks used by VMs. Figure 4.9 shows the difference in scope for SSE versus Microsoft Azure Disk Encryption. Similar to SSE, Microsoft Azure Disk Encryption also allows customer-managed key and is integrated with Microsoft Azure Key Vault.

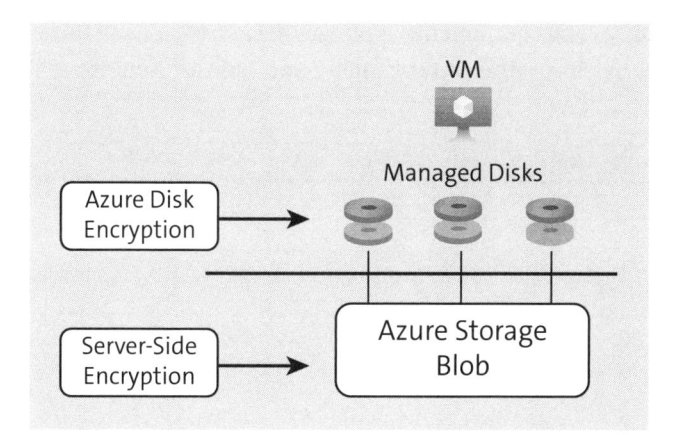

Figure 4.9 Encryption Scope for SSE versus Microsoft Azure Disk Encryption

Microsoft Azure also offers several ways of securing the data while in transit (*encryption in transit*) such as transport layer security (TLS), HTTPS with shared access signature, server message block encryption, Virtual Private Network (VPN) encryption, and so on. We'll discuss more details of these mechanisms in Chapter 10.

> **Enforcing and Monitoring Security Controls**
>
> Good security architecture also focuses on enforcing the controls, so there should be regular auditing to ensure all security controls are in place and are implemented consistently for new resources.
>
> Using *Microsoft Azure Security Center* is a good way to increase visibility of the Microsoft Azure resource security. It allows you to monitor, define policies, and configure security alerts.

Microsoft Azure also provides a collection of cloud-centric recommendations to improve Microsoft Azure security called Microsoft Azure Security Benchmark (find more information here: *https://docs.microsoft.com/en-us/azure/security/benchmarks/introduction*).

4.2 Performance

It's no secret that applications which perform well provide a better user experience; for SAP, it goes beyond that and into background jobs for month end, quarterly earnings report, and response times for interfaces to name a few instances where application performance is crucial.

4   System Design Framework

Designing for performance has several components as shown in Figure 4.10, and these aren't independent of each other but rather intermingled and built on top of each other.

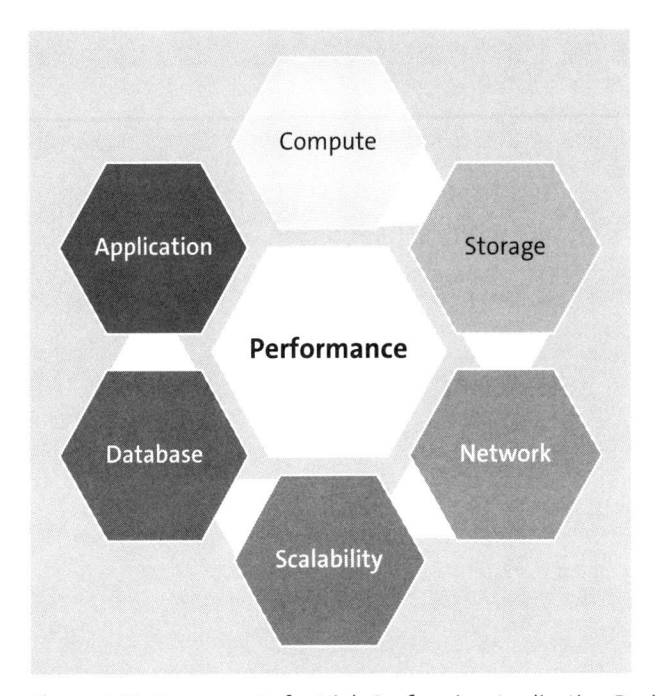

Figure 4.10 Components for High-Performing Application Design

4.2.1 Compute

On the cloud, initial sizing doesn't have to be perfect; getting to a right size is an iterative process. For a migration use case, you may not have SAP Application Performance Standard (SAPS) available, so *reference sizing* is a good way to get a comparable infrastructure. Reference sizing is done by looking at the current infrastructure size on-premise (or on another cloud) and evaluating the usage against an SAP EarlyWatch Alert report. SAP EarlyWatch Alert shows the system utilization stats and historical information to determine where the current system sizing stands with respect to the average and peak loads. We've discussed SAP-certified VMs and associated SAPS from SAP Note 1928533. In this section, we'll talk about the SAP certification benchmarks and the Microsoft Azure compute units (ACUs).

SAPS is based on the Sales and Distribution (SD) benchmark (100 SAPS = 2,000 fully business-processed order line items/hour), and the *hardware benchmarking* is done with almost 100% CPU utilization and < 1 second response time, as shown in Figure 4.11. The certificate can be accessed at *www.sap.com/dmc/benchmark/2020/Cert20017.pdf*.

4.2 Performance

```
Number of SAP SD benchmark users:                    24,400
Average dialog response time:                        0.84 seconds
Throughput:
    Fully processed order line items per hour:       2,701,670
    Dialog steps per hour:                           8,105,000
    SAPS:                                            135,080
Deployment Type:                                     Cloud
Average database request time (dialog/update):       0.018 sec / 0.036 sec
CPU utilization of central server:                   96%
Operating system, central server:                    Windows Server 2016 Datacenter
RDBMS:                                               Microsoft SQL Server 2012
SAP Business Suite software:                         SAP enhancement package 5 for
                                                     SAP ERP 6.0
```

Configuration:

No. of servers	Usage	Hardware	Segmentation / CPU utilization in cloud instances
1	Central Server	2 processors / 64 cores / 128 threads, AMD EPYC 7452 Processor, 2,35 GHz, 64 KB L1 cache and 512 KB L2 cache per core, 128 MB L3 cache per processor, 768 GB main memory	Instance Type: Microsoft Azure Virtual Machine Services D96as_v4 96 vCPUs, 384 GB memory

Figure 4.11 Hardware Benchmarking Certificate for Microsoft Azure VM

SAP also highlights a few other things that you should be aware of when interpreting the cloud benchmarks:

- The cloud has shared resources, so the service-level agreement (SLA) should be defined to mitigate performance impact.
- Wide area network (WAN) connectivity (VPN or ExpressRoute connectivity for Microsoft Azure) and throughput should be considered as well because these can impact end user experience even when the cloud resources are performing well.
- Underlying hardware may change over time in the cloud, so the SLA should be defined for a single computing unit for consistent performance. SAP Note 1501701 talks more about single computing unit while sizing for a few SAP products in SAP.

You may be wondering how you can compare CPU performance across Microsoft Azure VM families. Microsoft Azure provides a comparison in terms of ACUs; ACU for Standard_A1 is 100, and other SKUs represent the speed for the standard benchmark compared to that. Figure 4.12 shows the)ACU for a few SKUs, and the full list can be found at *https://docs.microsoft.com/en-us/azure/virtual-machines/acu*.

> **Tip**
> If you're running into performance issues, but CPU and memory stats look fine, remember that each VM also has a throughput limit, which can be a factor.

4   System Design Framework

SKU Family	ACU \ vCPU	vCPU: Core
A0	50	1:1
A1 - A4	100	1:1
A5 - A7	100	1:1
A1_v2 - A8_v2	100	1:1
A2m_v2 - A8m_v2	100	1:1
A8 - A11	225*	1:1
D1 - D14	160 - 250	1:1
D1_v2 - D15_v2	210 - 250*	1:1

Figure 4.12 Microsoft Azure ACU for VM Families

4.2.2 Storage

With different use cases, such as application files, databases, and global file systems for SAP, there is no one-size-fits-all storage. Microsoft Azure supports both managed disks and unmanaged (storage account), but using managed disks is recommended for SAP.

Microsoft also publishes new guidelines based on experience such as not supporting standard storage for the SAP global transport directory (as of February 2020). Microsoft Azure doesn't provide SLA-based guaranteed capacity, input/output operations per second (IOPS), and throughput for standard disks, so for most uses in SAP systems, premium disk (or ultra, in some cases) is a better fit. SAP Note 2367194 also states the details behind the premium disk recommendation for database servers.

IOPS, throughout, and latency are the main performance indicators for storage, and the following techniques help optimize those:

- **Striping**
  Multiple disks can be striped together to get combined throughput, IOPS, and size (as long as it doesn't exceed the maximum allowed IOPS and throughput for the VM). This is especially important for database servers because the SAP application server's IOPS and throughput requirements are relatively low. Because Microsoft Azure keeps three copies of data, there is no additional redundant array of independent disks (RAID) required, and RAID level 0 is recommended.

> **Note**
> You shouldn't mix disks of different sizes when striping; otherwise, the performance will be restricted to the slower disk.

Figure 4.13 shows the IOPS and throughput of a disk as the size increases. Notice the change from P30 to P50: the disk doubles in size, but the IOPS and throughput don't; so, with bigger disks, it gets to the point of diminishing return.

Premium SSD sizes	P30	P40	P50
Disk size in GiB	1,024	2,048	4,096
Provisioned IOPS per disk	5,000	7,500	7,500
Provisioned Throughput per disk	200 MiB/sec	250 MiB/sec	250 MiB/sec

Figure 4.13 Premium Disk Throughput and IOPS Increase with Size

Premium Storage
Not all VMs support premium storage; keep this in mind when selecting a SKU for SAP.

- Bursting
  Disk bursting is a temporary increase in IOPS and throughput; it's enabled by default for new deployments on premium disks up to P20 (512 GiB). Bursting is useful if there is, for example, an important SAP background job that needs higher throughput during month end.

  Bursting works on a credit system, meaning unused IOPS and throughput accumulate when running under the provisioned limits. When needed, the credit allows 30 minutes burst and maximum allowed rate, as shown in Figure 4.14.

Premium SSD sizes	P1	P2	P3	P4	P6
Max burst IOPS per disk	3,500	3,500	3,500	3,500	3,500
Max burst throughput per disk	170 MiB/sec	170 MiB/sec	170 MiB/sec	170 MiB/sec	170 MiB/sec

Figure 4.14 Premium Disk Bursting Limits

4   System Design Framework

- Caching

  The cache is specialized storage that has faster read/write capabilities than disk, so disk caching improves performance of the VM. Because cache storage is limited, it's important to enable caching for the right workload demands, such as SAP databases.

  By default, the Microsoft Azure OS disk has read/write caching enabled, and the recommendation is to enable read-only caching for read-intensive disks.

> **Disk Size for Caching**
>
> Disks larger than or equal to 4 TiB don't support caching. Supported options for caching are read-only, read/write, and none.

- Write accelerator

  This feature of Microsoft Azure premium managed disk improves write latency. It's suited for use with database log file writes and is available for M series SKUs. Write accelerator disk supports none and read-only caching and currently doesn't support snapshots.

> **Tip**
>
> Ensure that the log disk for SAP HANA databases on M series has write accelerator enabled.

> **Disk Benchmarking**
>
> You can use tools such as Iometer and fio (flexible I/O) to benchmark premium disk to determine the application performance level.

4.2.3   Network

ExpressRoute and VPN speed comes to mind immediately when we think of network performance, but there are other configuration items as well that may help. With the growth of Microsoft Azure, the number of data centers in the same region has grown as well. Combining that with the fact that not every VM SKU is available in all data centers means provisioning SAP systems may result in the application server and database being in different data centers, impacting performance due to higher latency. *Proximity placement groups* address that problem by provisioning the VMs inside a proximity placement group in the same data center.

Figure 4.15 shows scenarios for SAP system with and without (worst case) proximity placement groups in place. You can use either SAP executable NIPING tool or report

/SSA/CAT -> ABAPMeter to check latency between SAP servers with and without proximity placement groups to get an idea of latency.

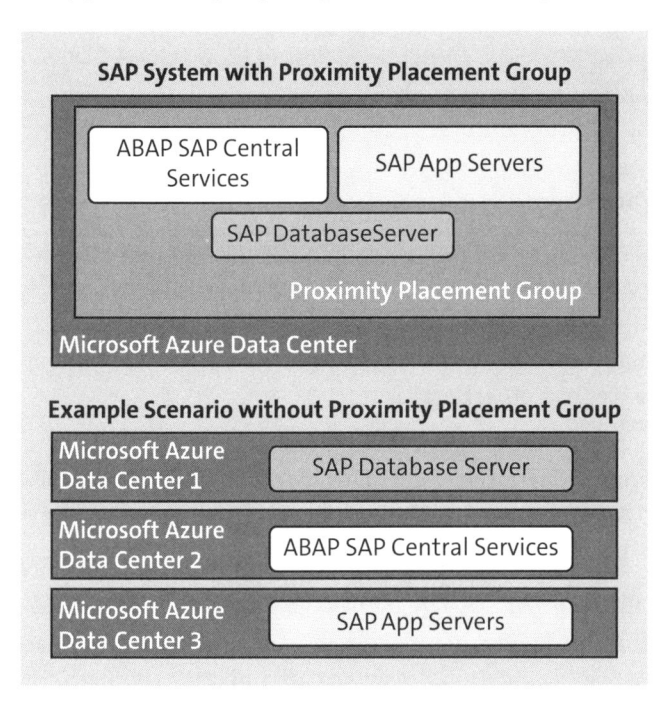

Figure 4.15 SAP System with and without Proximity Placement Groups

> **Note**
> Because not all VM types are available in all data centers, the recommendation is to create the largest VM (usually the database server) first, and then anchor application servers to the database.

Another recommended mechanism to boost performance is to enable **Accelerated networking** for all supported VMs. It enables single-root input/output virtualization (SR-IOV), which takes Microsoft Azure's software-defined networking off the CPU into the network interface controller (NIC), resulting in lower latency and CPU utilization. It can be enabled on a VM either during the provisioning or afterward and then can be viewed from networking configuration, as shown in Figure 4.16.

Figure 4.16 Accelerated Networking Option in Networking Section

4   System Design Framework

> **Note**
> Accelerated networking improves the throughput only up to Microsoft Azure's max allocated throughput for that VM. This also applies regardless of how many NICs are provisioned for that VM.

4.2.4 Database and Application

SAP provides recommendations about how to optimize performance using parameters and configurations for both databases and applications. It may be as simple as zero memory management or a little more involved such as updating SAP HANA to the next patch level. Your choice of database is a factor too: SAP HANA, which is an in-memory database, has better performance than other databases.

Note that though many of the recommendations remain the same regardless of where the SAP system is located (public cloud, private cloud, or on-premise), SAP publishes recommendations, as needed, specific to Microsoft Azure as well. Here are a few examples (SAP support access is required to view SAP Notes):

- SAP Note 2731110: Support of Network Virtual Appliances (NVA) for SAP on Microsoft Azure
- SAP Note 2791572: Performance Degradation Because of Missing VDSO Support for HyperV in Microsoft Azure
- SAP Note 2787703: Poor Performance While Loading Data into Microsoft Azure SQL Datawarehouse Database - SAP Data Services 4.2
- SAP Note 2931465: Reduce Network Latency (RTT) Using Proximity Placement Groups on Microsoft Azure
- SAP Note 2814271: SAP HANA Backup Fails on Microsoft Azure with Checksum Error

From a design point of view, follow the Microsoft Azure infrastructure, SAP database, and application recommendations; if you run into performance issues, look for SAP Knowledge Base Articles (KBAs) for specific Microsoft Azure-related findings.

4.2.5 Scalability

Designing or optimizing SAP system performance isn't a one-time activity; it's also how you manage ongoing demands and spikes during special events and as technologies evolve. The ability to scale up (or down) plays an important role not only in performance management but also in cost management. Microsoft Azure offers VMs with up to 12 TB memory for SAP HANA databases, as well as a variety of other SKUs for application. With the ease of moving from one server to another, you don't have to size the system for several years or for peak load. More systems can be added based on demand or schedule. The same goes for adapting new technologies; it's easier and cheaper to replace older VMs for new ones in Microsoft Azure than on-premise.

4.3 Resiliency

We define resiliency as the ability to do the following:

- Resist or avoid system failure.
- Recover from failure within an intended, designed time frame with acceptable data loss.

This section discusses the services and tools Microsoft Azure provides to achieve resiliency in the context of application architecture.

4.3.1 Platform Resiliency

We've talked about how Microsoft Azure performs different kinds of updates without downtime, such as hot patching, memory preserving updates, and live migration in Chapter 3, Section 3.7. All of these methods contribute to Microsoft Azure providing financial-backed SLAs. Even for a single VM with premium (or ultra) storage, Microsoft Azure's current SLA is 99.9%, which may be sufficient for SAP nonproduction (development/test) and sandbox applications.

> **SLA and Microsoft Azure Credit**
>
> The financial-backed SLA for Microsoft Azure is reflected as a Microsoft Azure service credit that Microsoft provides for not meeting the uptime or connectivity commitment (service level) on a monthly period. It doesn't account for the loss of business revenue you may incur as a result of Microsoft Azure service downtime, so you may want to think about how to mitigate business risk when Microsoft Azure services aren't available. Part of that risk mitigation is to design for business continuity and disaster recovery (BCDR).

> **SLA versus Service Level Objective**
>
> If your organization doesn't have any formal SLA for the service availability, you can think in terms of the service level objective (SLO) that you want to meet and compare Microsoft Azure service resiliency against that.

Because we're getting into an SLA discussion, Table 4.1 shows the downtime information in minutes/hours again (originally provided in Chapter 1).

4 System Design Framework

SLA	Potential Monthly Downtime	Potential Yearly Downtime
99.99%	4.32 mins	52.55 mins
99.95%	21.6 mins	4.38 hrs
99.9%	43.2 mins	8.76 hrs

Table 4.1 SLA Percentages with Corresponding Downtime in Minutes/Hours

Even with the best of the measures, unexpected events happen causing service downtime. As a guiding principle to resiliency, *redundancy* of service is recommended, especially for production workload. Microsoft Azure provides the following constructs to increase availability (with higher SLAs) when redundant components are deployed.

4.3.2 Availability Set

An availability set is a configuration for VMs to provide redundancy with SLAs of 99.95% for availability of at least one instance. For an SAP use case, this means that if you have a high availability (HA) configuration, say, ABAP SAP Central Services/ERS setup with two VMs in an availability set, at least one of the VMs will be available at least 99.95% of the time.

Microsoft Azure assigns update and fault domains to VMs in an availability set to further mitigate multiple VM outages because of a failure or platform updates. VMs in an update domain will be restarted together when Microsoft Azure rolls out an update that requires a reboot; only one update domain is restarted at a time. Fault domains share the power source and physical network switch. Figure 4.17 shows an example of VM distribution between fault and update domains. In this example, if VMs in UD0 are rebooted after a platform update, you still have other VMs running the instance, making use of redundancy.

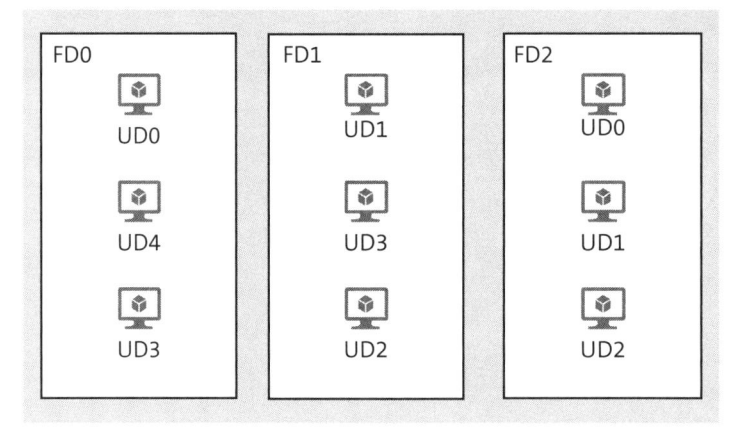

```
FD0           FD1           FD2
 UD0           UD1           UD0
 UD4           UD3           UD1
 UD3           UD2           UD2
```

Figure 4.17 Illustration of Update and Fault Domains

By default, Microsoft Azure separates VMs into three fault domains and five update domains (configurable up to 20), and you can set an availability set only during VM creation. Figure 4.18 shows fault and update domain configuration while creating an availability set.

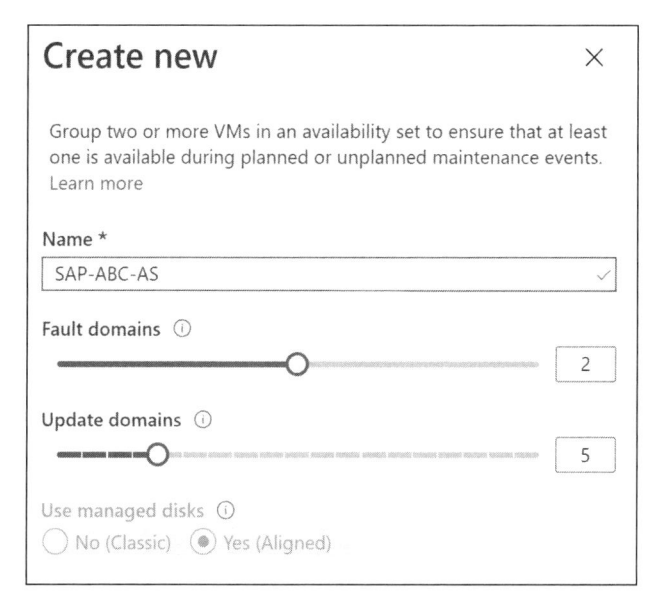

Figure 4.18 Fault and Update Domain Configuration Options

> **Disks in an Availability Set**
> When you use managed disks, Microsoft Azure ensures that these are isolated as well to avoid a single point of failure. This highlights another advantage of using managed disks.

4.3.3 Availability Zone

Expanding the circle of resiliency are availability zones, which are different physical locations within a region; a single availability zone may have more than one data center, each with its own power, networking, and cooling capabilities. Availability zones are split into update and fault domains (similar to availability sets), providing the SLA of 99.99% for VMs split across availability zones. You can think of availability zones as resilience from data center failure if lightning were to strike a data center and take the main and backup power out.

Services that follow the availability zone model are divided into two categories: one that is pinned to a zone (*zonal services*, such as VM, managed disk, IP address, and so on, and others that are replicated across zones (*zone-redundant services*), such as zone-redundant storage.

4   System Design Framework

For SAP setup, think of single point of failures such as central services, database, and application servers, each split into availability zones (there are three zones in a region that support availability zones), as shown in Figure 4.19.

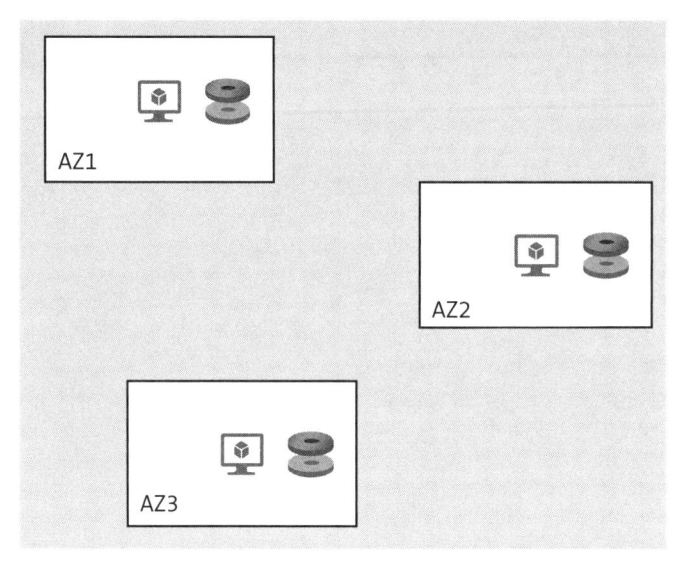

Figure 4.19 Availability Zone VM Setup Example

> **Note**
>
> Availability zones are independent in their logical mapping to physical locations, so AZ1 in one subscription may not be the same location for AZ1 in a different subscription.

> **Availability Set and Availability Zone**
>
> **Q: We have 10 application servers divided across availability zones, how can we put them in availability set within a zone?**
>
> A: Availability sets within an availability zone isn't supported, but you can use proximity placement groups to achieve this. Create an availability set that references proximity placement groups, and then deploy the application server VM referencing availability sets and proximity placement groups.
>
> **Q: Choosing availability sets and availability zones provides higher SLAs for VMs, but how does it ensure application availability?**
>
> A: Microsoft Azure resiliency and higher SLA is only for the infrastructure; it relies on application replication and features to ensure continued access. For SAP, we'll talk about how OS clustering, ABAP SAP Central Services/ERS replication, and database replication are combined for HA.

4.3.4 Region Resiliency

When we expand the scope of protection for something such as an earthquake or other big natural disaster, the importance of planning for disaster recovery (DR) comes into play. Microsoft Azure pairs each region with another in a geography, called *regional pairs* (e.g., East US and West US), to manage serial updates and prioritize recovery. Some services such as storage, recovery vault, and so on also use regional pairs to replicate data.

You can either pick regional pairs (e.g., if you're planning to use storage reapplication) or any other region of your choice as a secondary DR region.

If we were to map the resiliency layers in Microsoft Azure, it would look something like Figure 4.20.

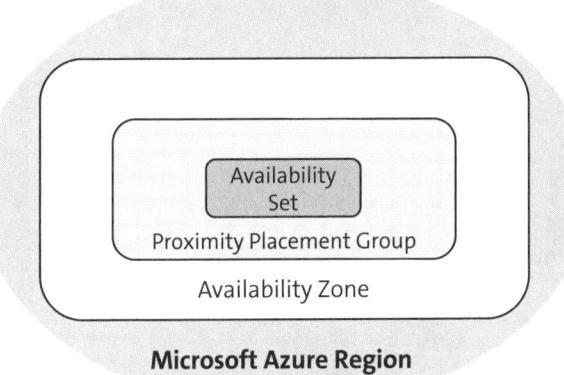

Figure 4.20 Microsoft Azure Resiliency Layers

Regional Pairs

By default, there is no data replication between pairs for all services; you have to enable/configure replication to make use of a regional pair as DR.

Not all services may be available in regional pairs (e.g., M series VM SKU); in which case, you can pick a nonpaired region based on service availability. Note that in case of nonpaired regions, you may not be able to use replication technologies that use pairing for replication.

Following are a few tools from Microsoft Azure for regional resiliency for VMs that can be used in the SAP environment.

4.3.5 Microsoft Azure Site Recovery

Microsoft Azure Site Recovery replicates Microsoft Azure VMs to a secondary region, which doesn't necessarily need to be Microsoft Azure paired regions. Microsoft Azure

Site Recovery also provides failover and failback capabilities, which are helpful not only in real disasters but also during DR tests and drills. You can also think of Microsoft Azure Site Recovery as DR as a dervice (DRaaS) on Microsoft Azure.

Figure 4.21 illustrates how Microsoft Azure Site Recovery can be used to protect VMs by replicating them to a secondary region.

- Source region (West US 2)
- Selected target region (East US 2)
- Available target regions

Figure 4.21 VM Replication Example Using Microsoft Azure Site Recovery

> **Microsoft Azure Site Recovery Use Cases**
>
> Microsoft Azure Site Recovery is more versatile than just replicating VMs on Microsoft Azure. Other use cases include replication from on-premise or other cloud providers, Microsoft Azure stack VMs, and physical servers.

Microsoft Azure Site Recovery replicates the primary region VM with settings to the secondary region of your choice, but it doesn't bring the VM up on the other side by default. That also means you're not paying for compute services on the DR site, just the storage and transfer bandwidth costs. You can also create a replication group to maintain multi-VM replication consistency. Under the hood, Microsoft Azure takes disk snapshots and creates recovery points, which is helpful when you perform failover because you have the option to choose specific recovery points (currently up to 72 hours). When you're ready to perform failover, you can use a recovery plan for orchestration, which lets you define things such as dependencies, VM groups, custom actions, and so on.

4.3.6 Microsoft Azure Backup Service

Microsoft Azure Backup is a native service that lets you back up Microsoft Azure VM, SQL Server, and SAP HANA into the Microsoft Azure Recovery Services vault. It also does automatic storage management and lets you define the frequency, retention, and so on.

Microsoft Azure Backup takes snapshots in the background, which can be application-consistent (captures memory and pending I/O operations), file system–consistent (all file systems captured at the same time), or crash-consistent (if the VM crashes or shuts down during backup, it captures the disk available at the time). You can see the status either in the recovery vault or by going to the backup blade (Microsoft Azure portal) of the VM, as shown in Figure 4.22.

Restore points (30)

This list is filtered for last 30 days of restore points. To recover from restore point older than 30 days, click here.

CRASH CONSISTENT	APPLICATION CONSISTENT	FILE-SYSTEM CONSISTENT
6	0	24

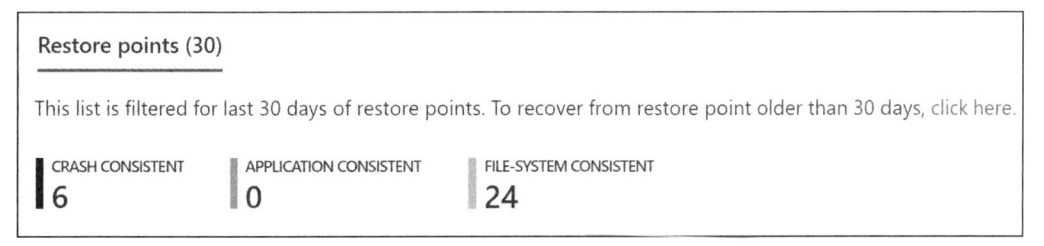

Figure 4.22 Microsoft Azure VM Backup History

Depending on the use cases, it can either replace your current backup solution or work alongside any third-party solution you bring to Microsoft Azure. Currently, Microsoft Azure Backup supports full and incremental backup for a VM.

> **Microsoft Azure Backup Cross-Region Restore and Soft Delete**
>
> Microsoft Azure provides the cross-region restore feature that allows more control by enabling you to restore the backup in Microsoft Azure paired regions acting as a DR solution.
>
> Soft delete is a feature (at no additional cost) that retains backup data for an additional 14 days, which helps with accidental or malicious deletions.

4.3.7 Microsoft Azure Storage Resiliency

Microsoft Azure keeps multiple copies of all storage and provides options to replicate the storage across availability zones and regions. Cost, availability, performance, and resiliency are the factors to consider when deciding which type of storage to use. Following are the storage redundancy and durability options provided by Microsoft Azure:

- **Locally redundant storage**
  Locally redundant storage replicates the data within the same data center synchronously and keeps three copies. It provides high performance and lower cost but doesn't protect the data if a disaster were to disrupt the whole data center. Managed disks currently support only locally redundant storage to ensure high performance.

- **Zone-redundant storage**
  Zone-redundant storage replicates the data, synchronously, across availability zones within the same region to provide resiliency for an outage of a data center.

- **Geo-redundant storage**
  Geo-redundant storage protects against regional failure by copying data to the Microsoft Azure paired region. It uses locally redundant storage in the primary region and asynchronously replicates to the secondary region, where it's copied using LRS again, making a total of six copies of data.

- **Geo-zone-redundant storage**
  Geo-zone-redundant storage combines zone-redundant storage and geo-redundant storage, replicating within the zone in the primary region synchronously and asynchronously to the secondary region.

- **Read-access geo-redundant storage and read-access geo-zone-redundant storage**
  These options add read access to the secondary region of geo-redundant storage and geo-zone-redundant storage storage types.

Locally redundant storage has a durability of 99.999999999% (11 nines), geo-redundant storage has 12 nines, and geo-redundant storage has 16 nines over a year.

> **Microsoft Managed Failover**
>
> In an unlikely event of a zone or region failure, Microsoft will initiate a failover after which you'll have write access to the storage. However, if you have read-enabled storage, you'll have continued read access from the secondary region.
>
> In addition, because replication to a secondary region is asynchronous, there is a chance of data loss, so factor that into your DR plan.

4.3.8 Microsoft Azure Load Balancer

Microsoft Azure Load Balancer is a Microsoft Azure native transport layer (layer 4 of Open Systems Interconnection [OSI] model) load balancer that facilitates traffic flow to the backend pool based on health probes. Public load balancer balances Internet traffic to VMs, whereas the internal load balancer is inside a VNet and can act as the frontend to VMs, as shown in Figure 4.23.

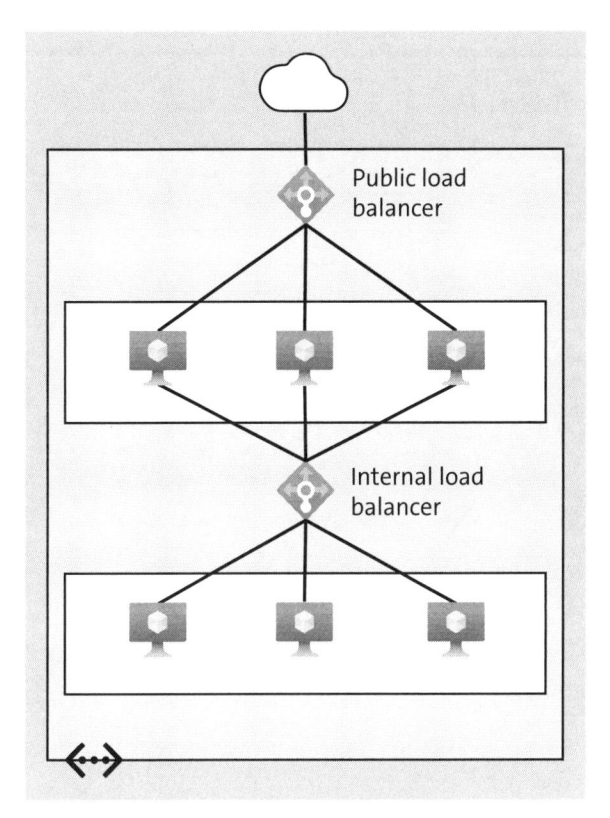

Figure 4.23 Microsoft Azure Load Balancer

The basic tier load balancer, which is offered at no charge, is open to the Internet by default and there's no specified SLA, whereas the standard load balancer comes with 99.99% SLA and is part of a VNet offering more security. Standard load balancer supports availability zone use cases and is also zone redundant, which means it will survive a zone failure.

> **Backend VM Configuration for Microsoft Azure Load Balancer**
> VMs behind a load balancer can be standalone, in an availability set, or in an availability zone.

4.4 Operational Efficiency

Operational efficiency is a design pillar because operations shouldn't be an afterthought; they should be part of the design considerations right from the beginning. Figure 4.24 shows the elements to be considered when designing for a solution with operations in mind.

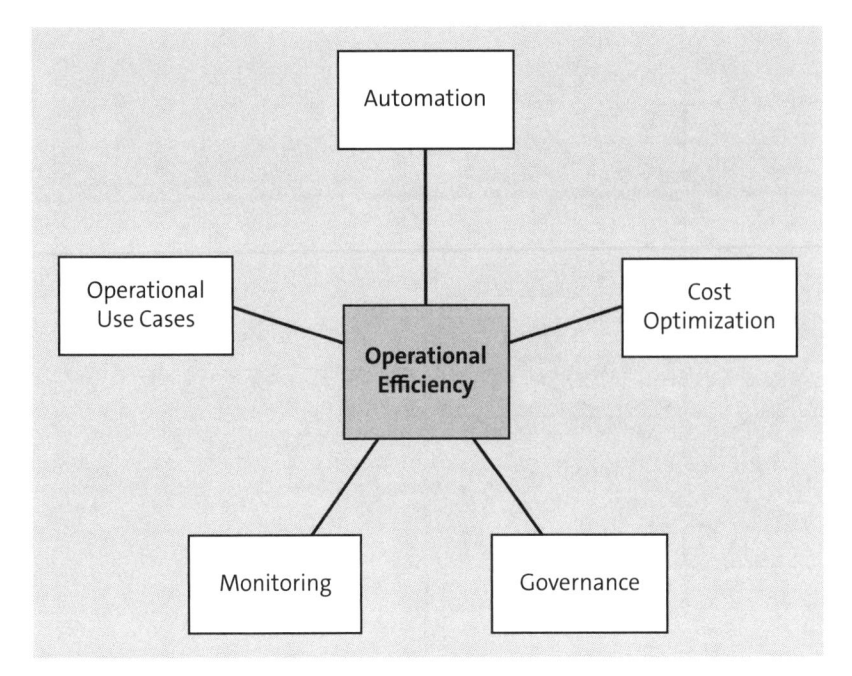

Figure 4.24 Elements of Operational Efficiency

4.4.1 Operational Use Cases

Consider the tasks that you perform for SAP operations and think about how you'd do it if you picked something during design; then find out whether a different element of design would make it more optimized.

Here are few examples:

- **SAP system copy**
  If you have a large database and do monthly system copies, you may want to explore snapshots and which storage provides snapshot capabilities. Depending on the frequency and ease of use, you can compare Microsoft Azure premium disk versus the Microsoft Azure NetApp Files snapshot process for SAP HANA, and adopt one with the better fit. If you use SAP Landscape Management, then you also have to evaluate how the Microsoft Azure LaMa connector integrates and influences your system copy process and timelines.

- **OS patching**
  Consider your organization's patching cycle and whether it makes sense to adopt immutable architecture, wherein you create a new VM and decommission old ones instead of patching. This also requires automation consideration and may be easier to do for SAP application servers than for SAP Central Services or database VMs.

This may also uncover how different OSs (e.g., SUSE Linux Enterprise Server [SLES], Red Hat Enterprise Linux [RHEL], or Windows) manage rollback and help you decide which OS to proceed with.

- **DR drill and organization-specific requirements**
  How often you perform DR drills and organizational requirements may impact the choice of how may copies of the database you have to have in the secondary region. For example, if you do a DR drill every six months, and there is a requirement to have DR available while you're doing the drill, then you'd have to configure another database server for the drill.
- **Operational SLA**
  SLAs may determine whether you need HA configuration or not, which is an important part of the landscape design.
- **Business-critical jobs**
  Do you have business-critical jobs that run monthly with a dedicated application server just for those? Instead of having an application server running all the time, you may want to use automation to build one and then destroy it after the jobs are done.

4.4.2 Monitoring

When moving to cloud services, it's always a good idea to explore native monitoring tools such as Microsoft Azure Monitor, but it may not have all the extensions and application programing interfaces (APIs) for SAP monitoring.

If you're using SAP Solution Manager, it can be migrated to Microsoft Azure as well, and your choice of infrastructure monitoring tool influences design elements. You should also consider business process monitoring and how it fits in with the target Microsoft Azure architecture.

4.4.3 Governance

Design decisions that have been optimized for operations can be governed using Microsoft Azure tools. Here are few examples:

- After you've decided on the primary and secondary Microsoft Azure regions, you can implement a policy that lets you create resources in only those regions.
- You can use Microsoft Azure tags to manage monitoring alerts, identify sap landscape information, and track compliance requirements.
- Microsoft Azure blueprints can be used to comply with build standards and patterns.

4.4.4 Cost Optimization

Operational cost is an important metric for everyone, and it certainly affects design decisions. Examples of design decisions to optimize cost include the following:

- Right size a VM rather than overprovision for growth. It's easy to scale up and down in the cloud, so paying for capacity that you'd use in two to three years doesn't make much sense.
- Use Microsoft Azure Site Recovery for application servers DR so you're not paying for compute services.
- Stack multiple application servers or databases on a single VM to optimize cost.
- Shut down (deallocate) nonproduction VMs during nonbusiness hours.

These are just a few examples, and you'll discover more scenarios where design decisions must consider the cost aspect.

4.4.5 Automation

All other elements discussed previously have automation components as well right from the deployment of infrastructure, monitoring, and cost optimization, all the way to SAP operational use cases. Automation enables a lot of efficiencies in the "operational efficiency" context.

Whether it's standardization of deployments, repetition of certain tasks, or gaining efficiency in time, automation has it all. Having said that, automation has a wide application, and creating templates to automation everything isn't just a day's job. Therefore, it's important to get started early.

> **Automation for Ongoing Evolution**
>
> Microsoft Azure provides new features that often present opportunities to optimize the environment further; automation framework should be flexible to evolve with Microsoft Azure and adapt to new use cases, such as moving from availability sets to availability zones or incorporating proximity placement groups.

> **Trade-Offs**
>
> During any system design, you'll make a lot of decisions involving trade-offs usually revolving around cost, performance, and complexity. So, it's always a good idea to think whether a solution meets the goals you've set rather than looking at different solutions to arrive at a goal. A good example is availability SLAs: placing VMs in an availability set or availability zone provides a higher SLA, but it also increases cost and complexity. If your organizational SLA is met with a single VM, there isn't much value in comparing availability set and availability zone architectures.

4.5 Summary

There is no single design that works best for everyone because everyone's goals and success criteria are different. Having said that, knowing all the tools and options gives you a way to consider multiple scenarios and choose the best one for your situation.

In this chapter, we discussed the concepts and relevant tools and how they fit together as design elements for a system that's secure, performs well, and remains resilient. In the next chapter, we'll discuss governance and compliance aspects of Microsoft Azure and how these topics relate to SAP solution deployment.

Chapter 5
Governance and Compliance

Governance is the key to the long-term success of the cloud strategy. Whether it's controlling cost, following security guidelines, or ensuring compliance, it all comes together to form the basis of successful deployments.

Governance of an organization refers to policies, practices, and procedures followed by a company based on a framework to mitigate risk and ensure compliance. Compliance in itself can be thought as a subset of governance where organizations demonstrate conformation to specific laws and regulations such as General Data Protection Regulation (GDPR) or data residency.

It often boils down to the aspects of process, people, and technology throughout the cloud lifecycle, as highlighted in Figure 5.1.

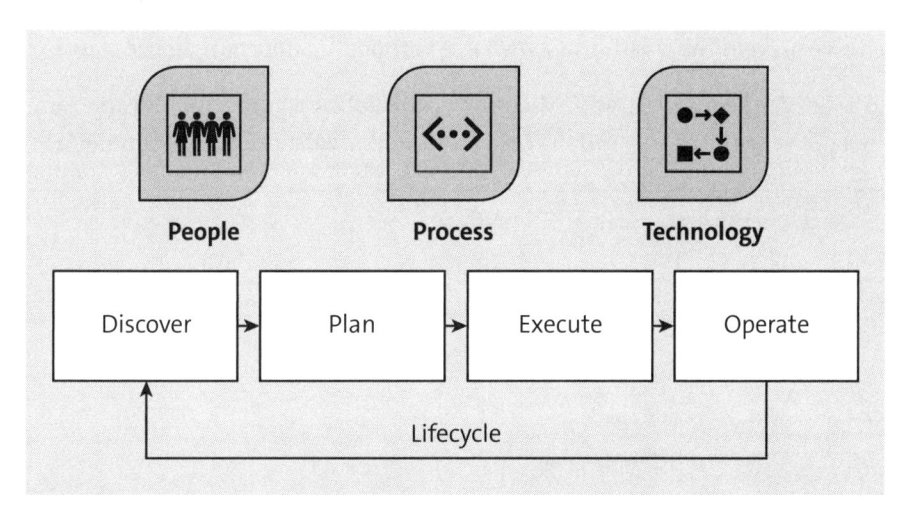

Figure 5.1 People, Process, and Technology across the Cloud Lifecycle

Throughout this chapter, we'll discuss aspects of how Microsoft Azure provides governance across people, process, and technology aspects. You'll also understand how cloud lifecycle scenarios such as the following can be handled:

- Automation makes it easier to create and consume Microsoft Azure services quickly and efficiently, so is it possible that a mistake could wipe it all?

- After we spin up hundreds of servers, how do we know which server does what? Or whether the operating system (OS) and configurations are consistent across the board?
- How do we control, report, and forecast cost for a project?
- How do we ensure only authorized people are creating new services?
- How do we ensure the infrastructure follows regulatory compliance?
- How do we track and audit Microsoft Azure builds?

5.1 Policies

Microsoft Azure policies enforce rules on resources by evaluating those for noncompliance. These policies can be assigned to management groups (explained in the next section), subscriptions, or resource groups.

Think about the following scenarios:

- How do we prevent virtual machine (VM) creation with a public IP or VMs with only E series stock-keeping units (SKUs)?
- How do we prevent resource creation outside of selected regions as a part of the data residency requirement?
- How do we prevent the creation of a resource without organization-defined tags?

All these issues can be managed with Microsoft Azure Policy. Figure 5.2 shows an example of a policy that ensures only certain VM SKUs are allowed in resource group **sap-abc**.

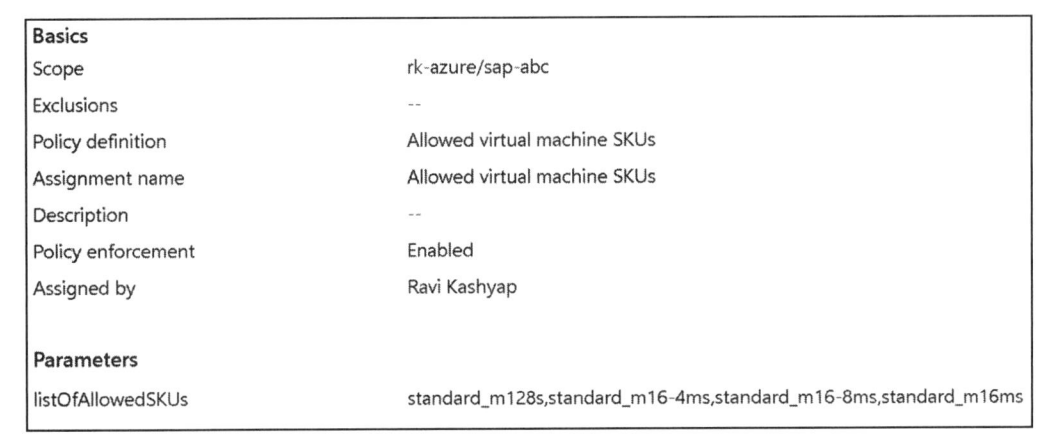

Basics	
Scope	rk-azure/sap-abc
Exclusions	--
Policy definition	Allowed virtual machine SKUs
Assignment name	Allowed virtual machine SKUs
Description	--
Policy enforcement	Enabled
Assigned by	Ravi Kashyap
Parameters	
listOfAllowedSKUs	standard_m128s,standard_m16-4ms,standard_m16-8ms,standard_m16ms

Figure 5.2 Example of Microsoft Azure Policy: Allowed VM SKUs

Policies can monitor compliance for audit and remediate as well (for resources created before the policy was implemented, as shown in Figure 5.3). For example, if all the disks are supposed to be encrypted, Microsoft Azure Policy can audit and alert or initiate a remediate task for existing resources if it finds an unencrypted disk.

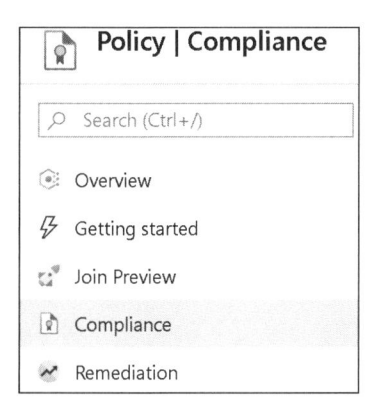

Figure 5.3 Microsoft Azure Policy Compliance and Remediation Option

Microsoft Azure Initiative

The Microsoft Azure initiative is a way to combine policies for a specific goal. For example, if you wanted to combine all policies for a particular regulatory compliance such as GDPR, all policies related to the compliance can be grouped in the form of an initiative.

5.2 Management Groups

Often organizations have more than one subscription, and sometimes dozens or even hundreds. Creating and managing policies across all of them can be tedious and error prone. That's where management groups come into play to help manage policies and compliance across multiple subscriptions. All subscriptions within the management group inherit the restrictions applied to the group.

Figure 5.4 shows an example of the hierarchy of management groups and subscriptions; there can be multiple management groups with up to six levels of depth.

Let's say an organization has a data residency requirement. Management groups can be used to enforce the policy that the subscription owners can't create resources outside of selected regions.

5 Governance and Compliance

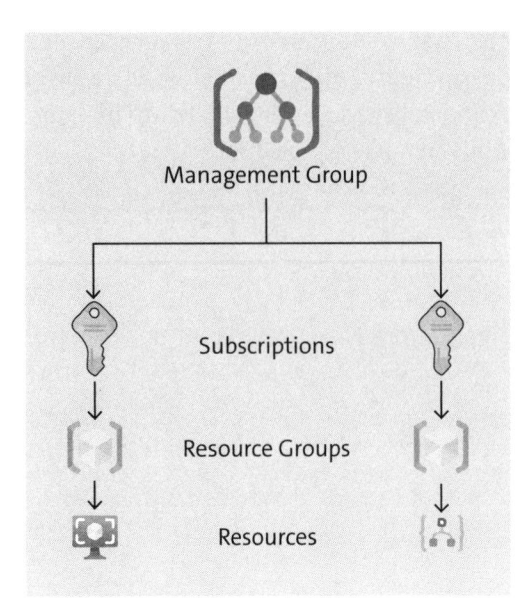

Figure 5.4 Management Group and Subscription Hierarchy in Microsoft Azure

5.3 Resource Groups

A resource group belongs to a subscription and is the logical grouping of resources with the same lifecycle; that is, they're created, updated, and deleted together. Figure 5.5 shows an example of a resource group hierarchy containing other Microsoft Azure resources.

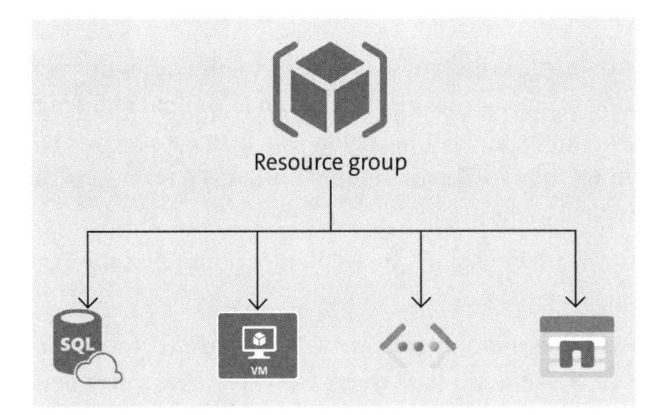

Figure 5.5 Resource Group Containing Microsoft Azure Resources

Following are a few properties of resource groups (full list is available at *https://docs.microsoft.com*):

- A resource group can itself be assigned to only one region, but the resources within the group can span different regions.
- A resource can belong to only one resource group.
- Resource groups can be used as administrative and access boundaries.

The last item in the preceding list is particularly important as we'll discuss in the next sections.

In the context of SAP, because SAP Central Services, database, and application server together make a SID, all Microsoft Azure resources within a SID can be in a resource group.

5.4 Role-Based Access Control

Role-based access control is the authorization mechanism for Microsoft Azure, which ensures that we're doing exactly what we're allowed, by the administrator, to do.

5.4.1 How to Use Role-Based Access Control

Here are few examples of role-based access control in use:

- Allow only administrators to create VMs, and allow only the network team to create virtual networks (VNets) and subnets.
- Allow the database team to have access to the database layer only and not the OS.
- Allow the SAP infrastructure team to manage everything in the SAP subscription.

It's like providing data center access only to folks who need to maintain equipment even though there may be other teams in the same building.

Microsoft Azure out of the box roles include the following:

- **Reader**
  Provides read (view) access to existing Microsoft Azure resources.
- **Contributor**
  Provides access to create and maintain all resources (restriction: this role doesn't allow you to grant access to others).
- **Owner**
  Provides complete access to all resources, including granting access to others.
- **User access administrator**
  Provides user access management capabilities.

These roles are considered primary roles, and there are several more resource-specific roles as well, such as VM contributor. *Custom roles* can be created, and it's a good idea to follow the least privilege model; that is, assess what's the least access a team or person needs to get the job done and create a custom role for that.

5.4.2 Role-Based Access Control Scope

The scope of role-based access control is the boundary for the access or resources that the access is applicable for. Scope can be any of the following:

- Management group
- Subscription
- Resource group
- Individual resources

In a hierarchy, the child inherits the access of the parent. Figure 5.6 illustrates the role-based access control scope and inheritance concept.

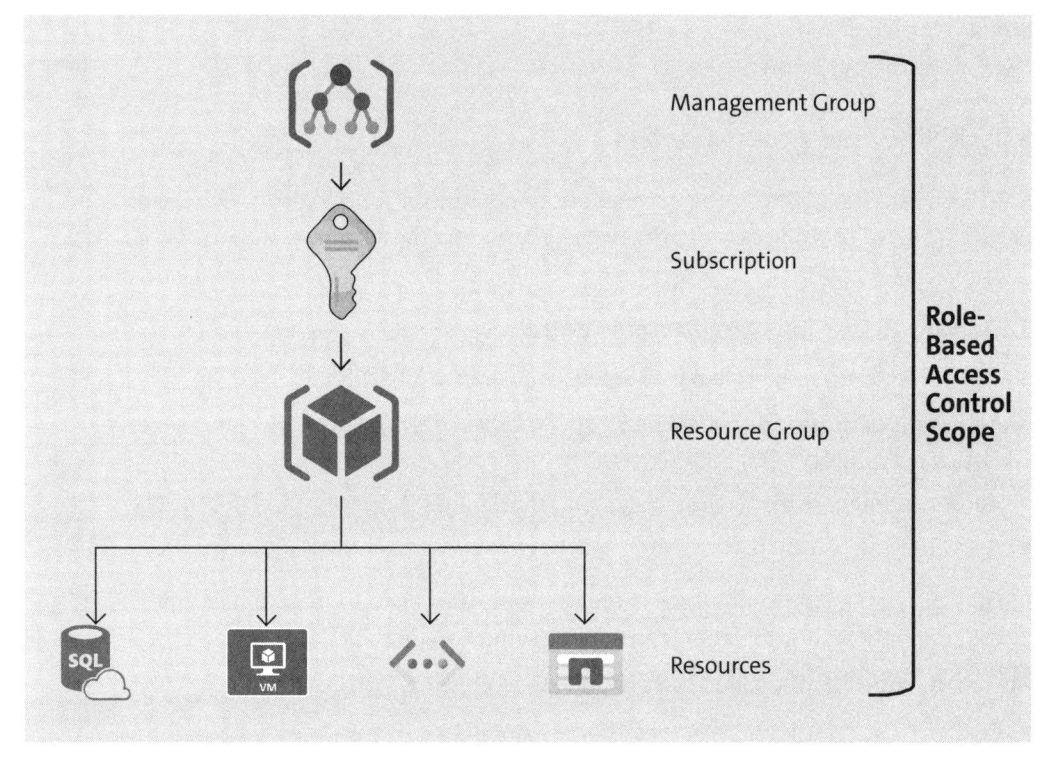

Figure 5.6 Role-Based Access Control Scope and Inheritance Hierarchy

5.4.3 Role-Based Access Control versus Policy

If you're thinking role-based access control sounds similar to policies and whether both are required, they're actually not similar and both are required. Here are the major differences:

- Role-based access control focuses on user actions such as create or delete access, whereas policy focuses on resource properties such as resource type, region, VM SKU, and extensions.
- Microsoft Azure policy's default is to allow, which means to deny something, we must explicitly say so.

- Originally, role-based access control was allow-only, but now it supports deny as well. Deny takes precedence over a role that has allow for the same resource.

> **Note**
>
> The control plane for role-based access control is Microsoft Azure level resources. Access inside of a VM or application and who/how can it be controlled, depends on the VM/application user roles.

5.5 Naming Conventions

When you're dealing with a lot of resources, and each resource has a unique name, naming conventions are instrumental in effective management. There will be hundreds of VMs associated with different SAP installations and probably in different regions too. Establishing a naming pattern is important for several reasons:

- Makes it easier to identify and manage resources not only during the deployment but also during operational activities such as patching
- Ensures there are no conflicting names
- May show the hierarchy or relationship such as region or production versus nonproduction

Most of the organizations have naming conventions regardless of whether the systems are on-premise or in a private cloud. Microsoft Azure provides includes more resources to name, so expanding on the current naming convention is a good idea.

Here's an illustration for a naming convention:

- Divide the name into segments.
- Each segment can be two to three characters and may show the hierarchy or identifier.
- Use a shortened version of resource names such as VM for Virtual Machine and VNet for Virtual Network.
- Be familiar with naming restrictions (e.g., special characters) and character limits (e.g., disks can have up to 80 characters).

Example for SAP VMs derived from segments shown in Table 5.1.

Segment	seg1	seg2	seg3	seg4	seg5	seg6
meaning	region	landscape	Resource type	SID	application	number
name1	ea2	prd	vm	abc	hana	01
name2	ea1	dev	vm	def	ascs	10

Table 5.1 Example of Naming Convention Divided into Segments

In these instances, the names of VMs are as follows:

- ea2-prd-vm-abc-hana-01
  This is a production SAP HANA VM located in US East 2 with SID = ABC.
- ea1-dev-vm-def-ascs-10
  This is a development VM located in US East; SAP Central Services is installed with instance #10 and SID = DEF.

> **Warning!**
> Ensure that Microsoft Azure naming conventions are compatible with your company's naming requirements and SAP restrictions such as 13 character length for SAPLOCAL-HOST.

5.6 Resource Locks

Mistakes happen and we've all been there when some important file got deleted accidently and had to be restored (assuming we had a backup), but what if someone deletes the whole production system by mistake? That's probably the number one situation in the avoid list rather than the fix list.

Unlike role-based access control, resource locks are applicable for all users regardless of assigned roles, so even though role-based access control can defend against unauthorized deletes, it can't prevent accidental ones.

Locks can be applied to either an individual resource or resource groups. For SAP systems, we like to lock the whole resource group so nobody can delete even the storage that seems like it doesn't belong to the system when it's actually the interface directory shared across the landscape.

Microsoft Azure provides two levels of locks:

- **CanNotDelete** (or simply Delete on Microsoft Azure Portal)
  The resource can be modified by authorized users (via role-based access control) but can't be deleted.
- **ReadOnly**
  The resource can only be read, but neither modified nor deleted, even by authorized users.

Figure 5.7 and Figure 5.8 show an example of how to set a Delete (NoDelete) lock on a resource group (**sap-abc**) in this example.

Figure 5.9 shows the error message when trying to delete the locked resource group.

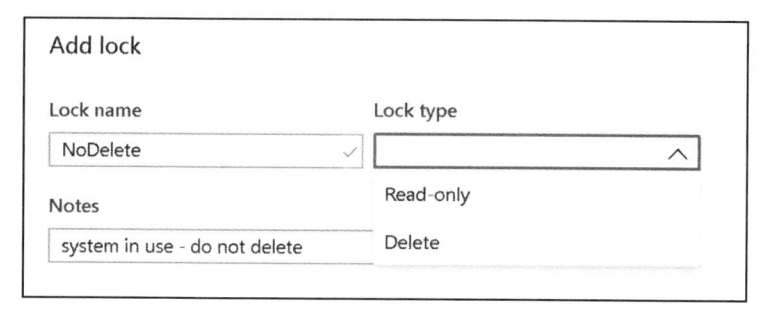

Figure 5.7 Lock Configuration from Microsoft Azure Portal

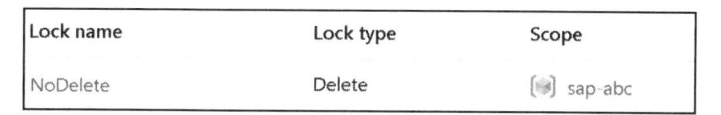

Figure 5.8 Example of Delete Lock on Resource Group sap-abc

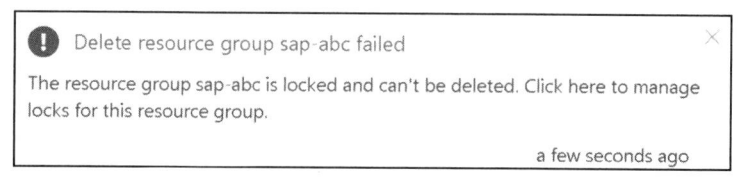

Figure 5.9 Error Message Trying to Delete the Locked Resource Group

5.7 Tagging

Microsoft Azure tags provide a mechanism to logically organize resources with a name and value pair; tags can be applied to a subscription, resource group, or a resource directly.

Here are a few scenarios that tags address:

- How do we create a report showing that all production systems are configured consistently?
- How do we apply automation to several systems based on definitions?
- How do we set up cost management for each business unit or SAP environment?

Figure 5.10 shows an example of tags that are applied to the **sap-abc** resource group.

> **Use of Policy for Tagging Compliance**
>
> A good way to enforce tagging compliance is to use Microsoft Azure Policy. In addition, resources created before the policy was enforced can have tags added using a policy remediation task.

5   Governance and Compliance

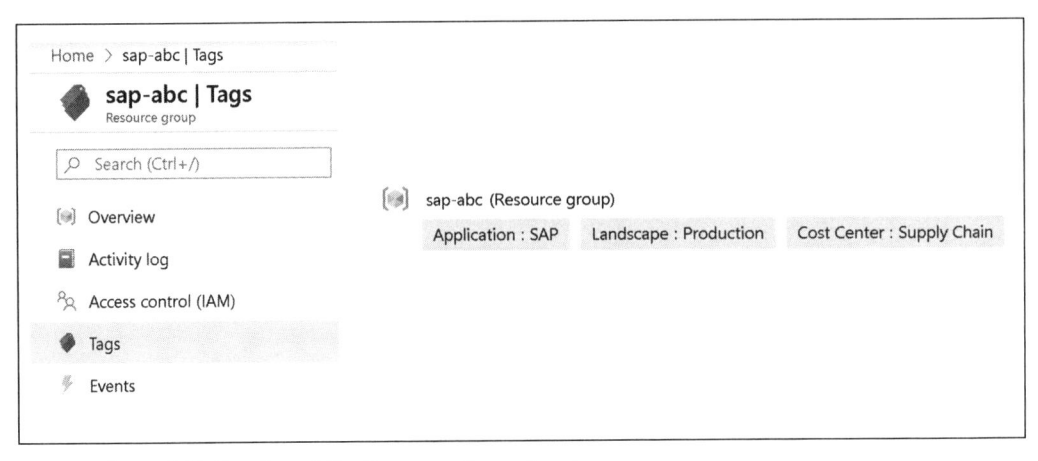

Figure 5.10 Tagging at the Resource Group Level

5.8 Microsoft Azure Blueprint

Microsoft Azure Blueprint packages different resources together as definitions that can be applied to environments. Microsoft Azure also provides built-in examples.

Figure 5.11 shows a graphical representation of how it works.

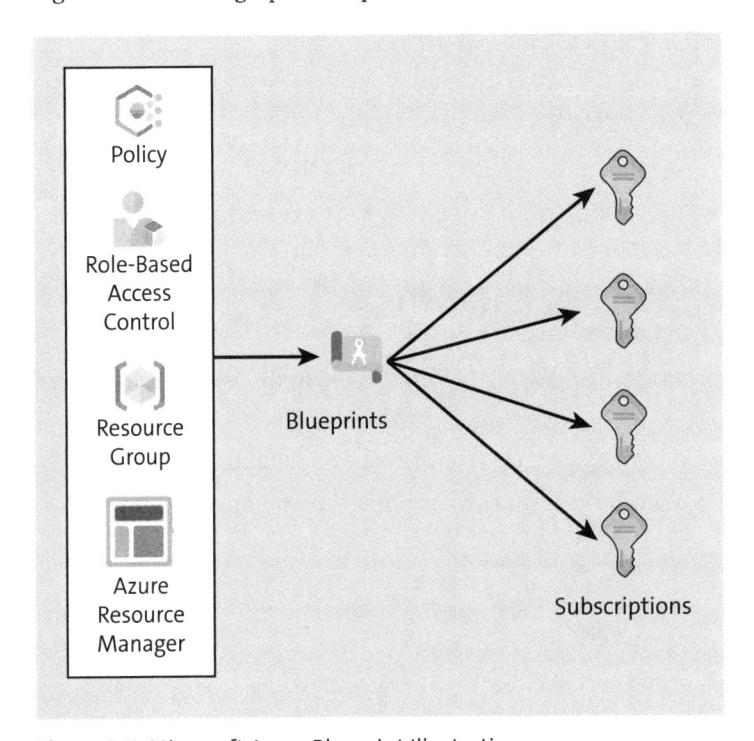

Figure 5.11 Microsoft Azure Blueprint Illustration

Here are few ways to use Microsoft Azure Blueprint:

- **Orchestrate a consistent environment**
  In a large SAP environment, you may be creating hundreds of VMs with other supporting resources. The first issue to arise is how to ensure that everything will be built consistently, and the answer almost always is "automation."

  Blueprints act as orchestrators in the sense that they contain all the automation definitions and can trigger the deployment in multiple subscriptions from a central place. They can also be version controlled to bring more flexibility to the process.

- **Microsoft Azure landing zone**
  Creating a Microsoft Azure landing zone is a great use case for blueprints. It accelerates the deployment with all the governance in place and processes with fewer errors.

> **Microsoft Azure Blueprint versus Microsoft Azure Resource Manager Template**
>
> Because blueprints contain SAP Microsoft Azure Resource Manager (ARM) templates, blueprints can be thought of as a superset of individual components, such as ARM, policy, and so on.
>
> Blueprints sustain the relationship between Microsoft Azure resources that are deployed, which leads to better tracking and auditing.

5.9 Regulatory and Audit Compliance

As we've discussed, organizations want to ensure compliance with their processes and policies to reduce risk; in addition, there are certain compliance requirements set by laws and regulations such as the Sarbanes-Oxley Act (SOX) and GDPR, as well as country-specific regulations.

Compliance with regulatory mandates is crucial because a violation can result in legal action. This section highlights tools provided by Microsoft Azure that are geared toward regulations and ways to audit cloud activities. There are two parts to the compliance:

- Is the cloud compliant?
- Is the organization using the cloud compliant with the applicable regulations?

Microsoft caters to the first part by providing more than 90 compliance certifications, which include country- and industry-specific regulations. The full list is available at the Microsoft Azure compliance site: *https://azure.microsoft.com/en-us/overview/trusted-cloud/compliance/*.

Microsoft Azure provides several tools to ensure organizations can track and audit company- or industry-specific regulations; the following sections discuss these tools in detail.

5.9.1 Regulatory Compliance

Microsoft Azure Security Center lets you monitor subscriptions for regulatory compliance risks. It generates reports (can also filter by regulations), highlights risk, and enables you to remediate. Figure 5.12 shows the **Regulatory compliance** section in Microsoft Azure Security Center.

Figure 5.12 Microsoft Azure Security Center: Policy and Compliance Offering

5.9.2 Microsoft Azure Logs

Microsoft Azure provides several mechanisms for logging, security alerting, and auditing, which can also be forwarded to Microsoft Azure Monitor for central analysis and insights.

Logs can help in scenarios such as following:

- How do we know when and how a VM or service was deleted that broke a business process. We'll be looking at activity logs for this answer.
- A server didn't come up after maintenance, and we need to find out what's happening. Resource logs will be of help here.
- Something happened in Microsoft Azure, and it raised an alert. This will be logged as a Microsoft Azure Security Center alert.

Figure 5.13 shows an example of a log that captures the deleting of a resource.

Figure 5.14 shows how to configure diagnostic setting and forward logs to the target system.

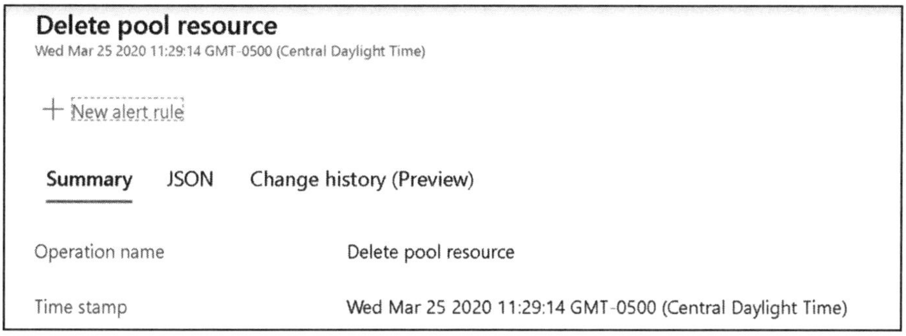

Figure 5.13 Example of Microsoft Azure Activity Log

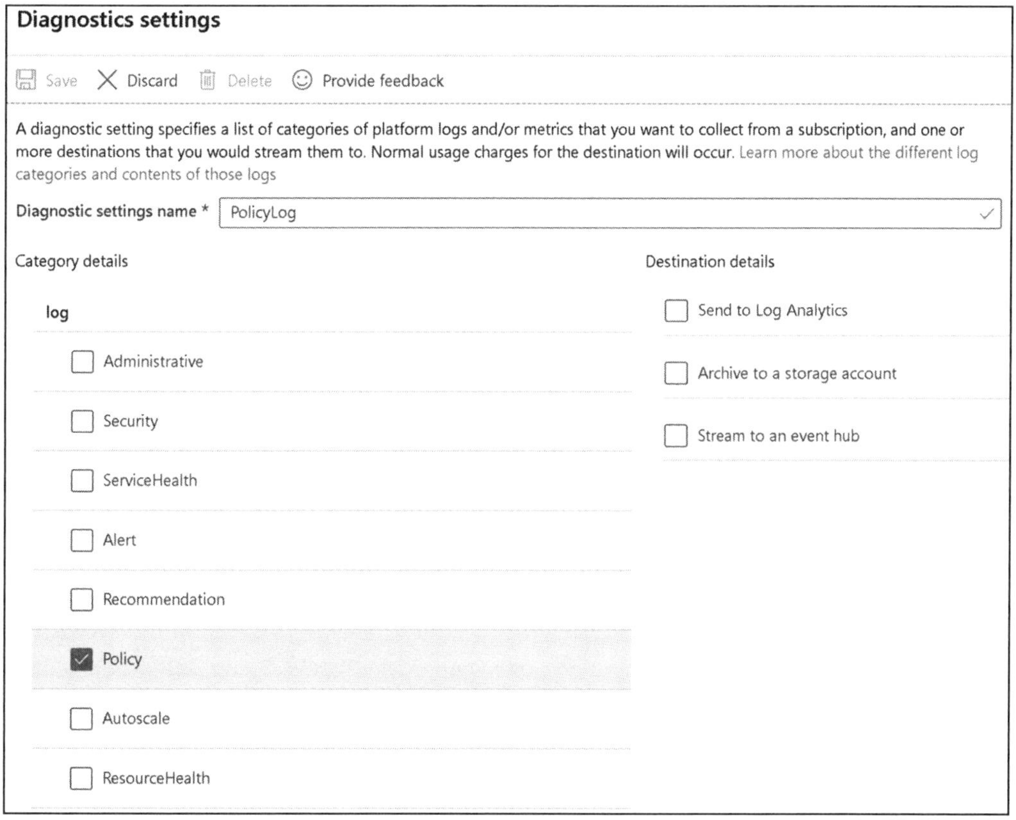

Figure 5.14 Example of Diagnostic Setting and Target Configuration

5.9.3 Reporting

Microsoft Azure provides many services for collecting and analyzing telemetry from Microsoft Azure resources and applications, which generate reports that can be used for troubleshooting as well as auditing. Following are some of the commonly used methods for monitoring and reporting:

5   Governance and Compliance

- **Microsoft Azure Monitor**
  Collects the diagnostics and other monitoring data at a centralized location that gives you a view of all the resources.
- **Microsoft Azure Service Health**
  Provides a personalized dashboard showing the availability incidents and maintenance for the services that an organization is using. You can also configure alerts and tie them to ticketing tools, such as Service Now.
- **Microsoft Azure Advisor**
  Looks at the current resource configuration and shows optimization options based on Microsoft Azure deployment recommended practices in areas such as high availability, security, performance, cost, and so on.

Figure 5.15 shows an example of **Service Health** and root cause analysis availability (**Analysis** column) in Microsoft Azure.

Figure 5.15 Microsoft Azure Service Health Illustration

> **Tip**
> When looking for cost optimization opportunities, for example, for an SAP environment, Microsoft Azure Advisor is the place to look for underutilized VMs.

5.10   Summary

With the ease of use and automation in the public cloud, it's easy for things to get out of hand, so having good governance framework is crucial. For successful cloud implementations, governance should be incorporated right from the beginning and shouldn't be an afterthought; research also suggest that organizations with good governance have higher profits in the long run.

In the next chapter we'll build on what we've learned so far and dive into infrastructure architecture for SAP on Microsoft Azure.

Chapter 6
Infrastructure Architecture Guidance

Infrastructure as a service (IaaS) architecture can be more involved because you have to look at each component and ensure that it's optimized for SAP. Unlike platform as a service (PaaS), where most of the implementation details are abstracted, IaaS architecture exposes what's under the hood.

Now that you're familiar with Microsoft Azure concepts and its IaaS offerings and design considerations, we'll discuss how to marry SAP and Microsoft Azure, also known as the SAP on Microsoft Azure architecture.

We'll make architectural decisions based on the following guidance:

- **Keep it simple**
  Wherever possible, choose simpler architecture over a complex setup if it achieves the same goal.

- **Base it on business requirements**
  Given enough time, money, and skill, most things are possible; in lack of that, prioritize based on business requirements such as whether you need high availability (HA) and what kind of disaster recovery (DR) solution you're looking for.

- **Data-driven decision to improve architecture**
  In the cloud, experimentation is easier, so you can collect data from different choices to improve architecture over time because architectural improvements are an ongoing effort.

6.1 Microsoft Azure Regions

A Microsoft Azure region is a set of data centers with a low latency network that reside within a geography, ensuring a data residency boundary. For example, regions within the United States store the data at rest in the United States.

Architecture questions to consider include the following:

- What Microsoft Azure region should I choose for my SAP deployment?
- What is the DR or secondary region? Can I pick one, or is it always Microsoft Azure paired regions?

Choosing a region has several considerations such as data residency requirement, availability of SAP supported services, locations of users, and cost. For a global company based out of the United States, there may be users all over the world, and even within the United States, the users may be scattered around. So, you may want to pick a US region that has all SAP services such as M Series Virtual Machine (VM) or SAP HANA on Azure (Large Instances). From there, you can narrow it down based on cost.

Microsoft Azure divides its services into foundational, mainstream, and specialized categories with SAP services under specialized because of the type of hardware requirements.

> **Tip**
> If your corporate headquarters have a lot of users, you can also pick the closest region provided it supports all the services you're looking for.

As far as choice of a secondary region goes, Microsoft Azure doesn't mandate the paired region, and, in some cases, specific services such as SAP HANA on Azure (Large Instances) may not be available in both regions. However, note that geo replication services such as geo-redundant storage (GRS), Microsoft Azure Backup cross-region restore, and so on replicate to paired regions. Microsoft Azure Site Recovery works with any pair within a geography.

6.2 Subscription Design

There are several ways to go about subscription, so you should start with business need and priorities. Here are a few common ways to decide about subscription creation:

- Production versus nonproduction systems across applications
- Workload category (SAP versus non-SAP)
- Business unit
- Geography
- Any combination of the preceding, such as workload and geography

Architecture questions to consider include the following:

- How many subscriptions do I need for my SAP landscape?
- Do I need different subscriptions for each region?

In the spirit of keeping it simple, given a choice, we prefer one subscription for all SAP systems. Subscriptions aren't bound to a region, so even for resources spanned across multiple regions, the same subscription would work; therefore, you don't need a regional subscription strategy.

> **Subscription Limits and Quotas**
>
> Keep in mind that there are limits on resources in subscriptions; some of the default quotas can be increased to the maximum limit be contacting Microsoft Azure support. A few examples include 25,000 VMs per region or 2,500 availability sets per region. There are limits per VM stock-keeping units (SKUs) as well; refer to the Microsoft Azure documentation for limits on all services.
>
> Usually, the limits are high enough to not exceed for the SAP landscape, but in the rare instance you expect to exceed, you can have a separate subscription for production and nonproduction systems.

6.3 Connectivity and Network Design

After you've procured the subscription, next is to determine how you'll connect and the network configuration inside it.

Architecture questions to consider include the following:

- How do I connect to Microsoft Azure resources?
- What kind of topology does the Microsoft Azure network need?
- How do multiple virtual networks (VNets) communicate in Microsoft Azure?
- What IP ranges do Microsoft Azure networks have?
- Is there a cost associated with data transfer between multiple networks?
- Does SAP HANA need a different network for client versus storage communication?
- Should there be separate networks for application connectivity and operational activities, such as backups?

6.3.1 Connectivity to Microsoft Azure

ExpressRoute is the preferred way to connect to Microsoft Azure because it supports higher bandwidth and is a private connection. ExpressRoute can take weeks to set up, so during the initial stages, setting a site-to-site Virtual Private Network (VPN) can get you going.

ExpressRoute connects on-premise systems' resources to the Microsoft Azure subscription via the gateway that's deployed in a VNet with its own dedicated subnet.

6.3.2 Network Design

The VNet, similar to on-premise networks, is the foundational component of a network inside a subscription. Each VNet is bound to a region and a subscription, and VNets can be divided into smaller parts called subnets.

The factors to consider when determining the number of VNets are security model, available IP ranges (classless inter-domain routing [CIDR]), and cost. Because VNets are isolated by design, when you have multiple networks, you need to connect them using the peering process. VNet peering enables the communication and makes the network space bigger, but it comes at a cost; Microsoft Azure charges for inbound and outbound data transfer between peered VNets.

> **VNet Peering Isn't Transitive**
> If VNet A is peered with VNet B, and B is peered with C, then A isn't peered with C. If you need communication between A and C, then those VNets should be peered separately.

With cost optimization in mind, minimizing the number of VNets should be the target; however, because each VNet also requires a contiguous IP address range in CIDR format, depending on whether you have the range available, the number of VNets will change. Microsoft recommends using the IP range for private networks as recommended by the Internet Assigned Numbers Authority (IANA):

- 10.0.0.0–10.255.255.255 (10/8 prefix)
- 172.16.0.0–172.31.255.255 (172.16/12 prefix)
- 192.168.0.0–192.168.255.255 (192.168/16 prefix)

In addition, in Microsoft Azure, you can't use the following ranges because they are reserved by the platform:

- 224.0.0.0/4 (Multicast)
- 255.255.255.255/32 (Broadcast)
- 127.0.0.0/8 (Loopback)
- 169.254.0.0/16 (Link-local)
- 168.63.129.16/32 (internal domain name service [DNS])

When you move SAP systems to Microsoft Azure, there are other supporting systems such as DNS, network virtual appliance, identity management systems, domain services, bastion hosts, and so on that may not be exclusively used by SAP systems, or security teams might want more control over those. It may make sense to put those systems in a separate VNet—we'll call it hub network—that peers with SAP network (or spoke VNets). If you already have a hub network in another subscription, that can be used by peering to the SAP subscription as well. Figure 6.1 illustrates this hub and spoke approach.

Following a *micro segmentation* strategy, you can divide the SAP VNet into application and database subnets. By default, all the subnets (inside a VNet) can communicate with each other using automatically created system routes. If you need to restrict traffic flow in a certain way, you can create custom routes called user-defined routes. You can put further restrictions on subnets, and workload-specific VMs (e.g., databases) using network security groups and application security groups. At the subnet level, network security groups define the access policies for the subnet.

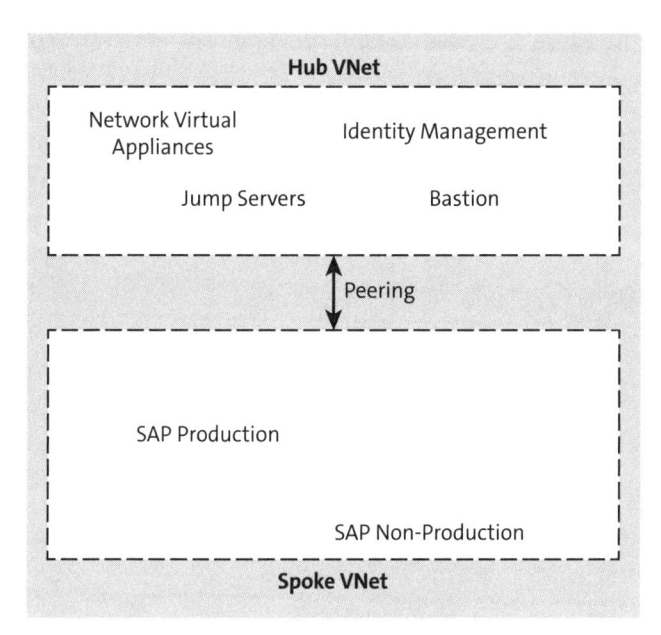

Figure 6.1 Hub and Spoke Network Representation

6.3.3 Subnet Sizes for Gateway, Bastion, and Microsoft Azure NetApp Files

Depending on the setup and growth considerations, there are a minimum number of IPs that Microsoft Azure recommends for certain subnets, such as gateway, bastion, Microsoft Azure NetApp Files, and so on (because Microsoft Azure reserves five IPs for each subnet, the number of available IPs need to be considered, not the total as represented by CIDR notation).

The following IPs are reserved by Microsoft Azure:

- x.x.x.0: Network address.
- x.x.x.1: Default gateway.
- x.x.x.2, x.x.x.3: To map the Microsoft Azure DNS IPs to the VNet space.
- x.x.x.255: Network broadcast address.

At the time of publishing, following are the recommendations from Microsoft:

- GatewaySubnet: /27 or larger
- AzureBastionSubnet: /27 or larger
- Microsoft Azure NetApp Files Subnet: /28 or higher

> **Network Security Groups and Subnets**
> At the time of publishing, gateway and Microsoft Azure NetApp Files subnets don't allow network security groups. Bastion subnets allow network security groups but don't support user-defined routes.

6   Infrastructure Architecture Guidance

Figure 6.2 shows the architecture we've discussed so far for regions, connectivity, and networks (VNet, subnet, network security groups).

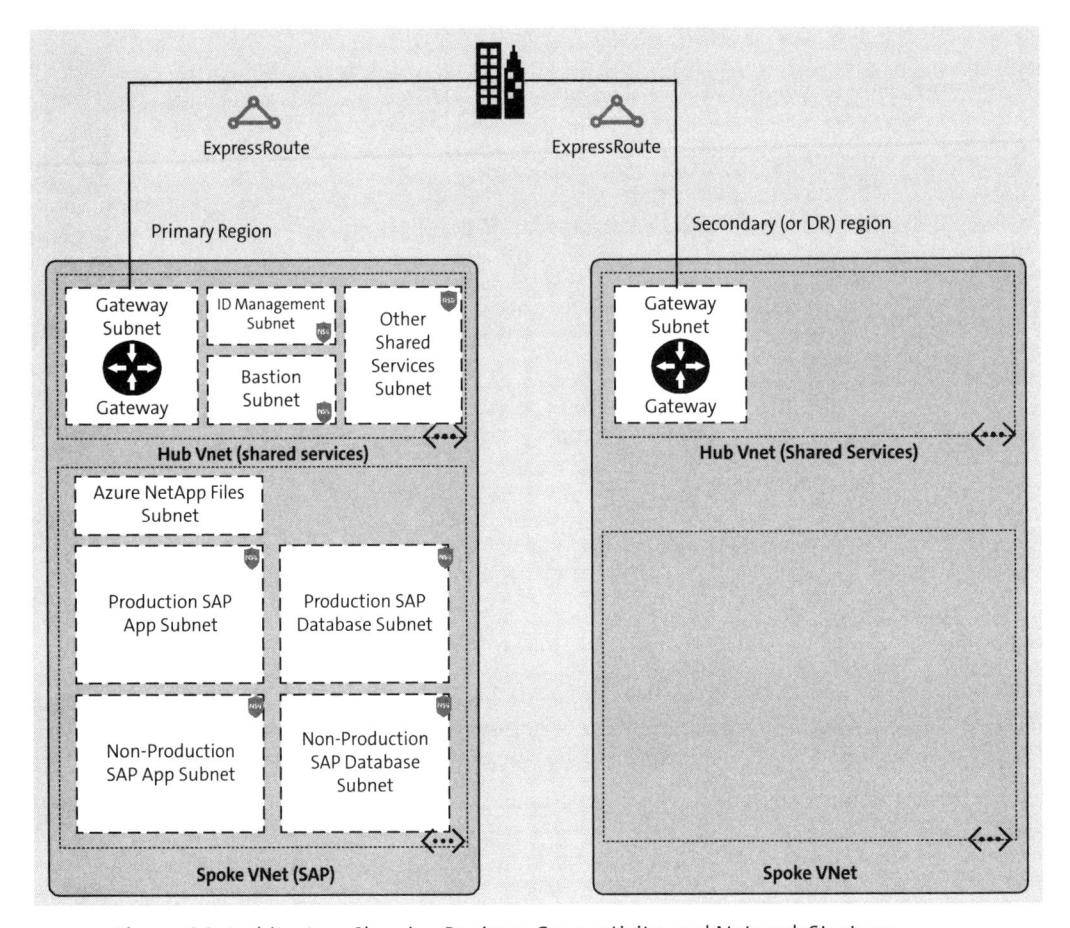

Figure 6.2 Architecture Showing Regions, Connectivity, and Network Strategy

6.3.4 SAP HANA Network Zones

SAP HANA components use different logical network zones for communication, that is, client, internal, and storage zone, which can be implemented using subnets in Microsoft Azure. Each zone may have different configurations for performance and security:

- **Client zone**
  This zone includes SAP application servers, browser-based sources, and other data sources (e.g., a business intelligence solution).
- **Internal zone**
  This zone spans communication between hosts for SAP HANA system replication and among nodes for scale-out configuration.
- **Storage zone**
  This zone is important for data write processes in persistent storage, especially when it's accessed over a network.

6.3 Connectivity and Network Design

The network setups for the different zones are illustrated in Figure 6.3.

Figure 6.3 SAP HANA Network Zones

6.3.5 Database App Connectivity and Management Network

For database servers, traffic segregation is recommended in which you can have a subnet for application connectivity and another for operational activities and management such as backup traffic. You can also apply different security policies to these using network security groups. This can be achieved by creating multiple vNICs for each VM, as shown in Figure 6.4.

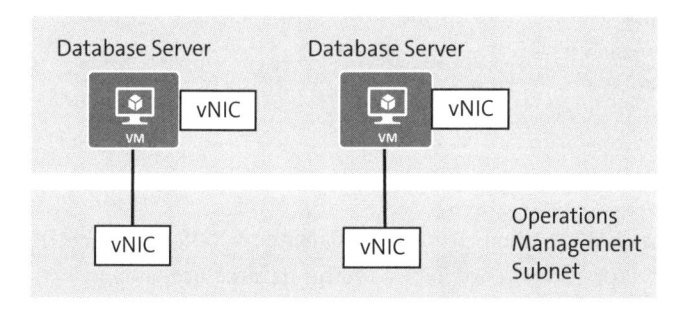

Figure 6.4 Multiple Network and vNIC Setup for Database Servers

6.3.6 Perimeter Network

The perimeter network, also called the demilitarized zone (DMZ), enables a secure connection using techniques such as packet sniffing, intrusion detection, policy enforcement, and so on between Microsoft Azure and the Internet.

In the SAP context, systems such as SAP Web Dispatcher (when external facing) and SAPRouter that have connections to and from the Internet should be protected. In

6   Infrastructure Architecture Guidance

addition, you can also use it for security between Microsoft Azure and on-premise systems.

Figure 6.5 shows the setup using network virtual appliance (or the Microsoft Azure firewall); it provides a secure network boundary by inspecting all Internet traffic. Network virtual appliance can be a single point of failure as well, so consider putting two network virtual appliances in an AS for a better SLA.

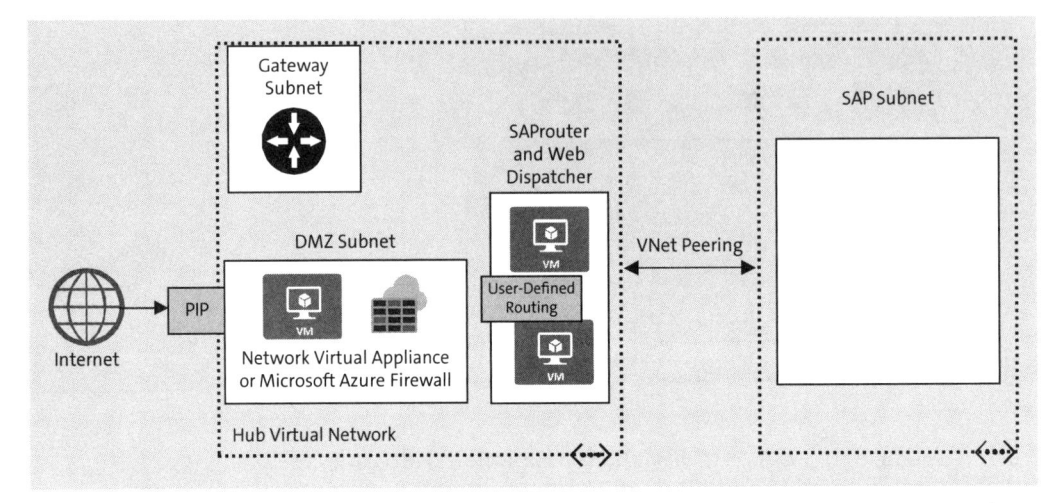

Figure 6.5 Perimeter Network (DMZ) Setup for SAPRouter and Externally Facing SAP Web Dispatcher

> **Note**
> Microsoft Azure doesn't support the setup with network virtual appliance between SAP application and database servers.

6.4   Compute

We've discussed how to choose SAP-certified VMs from SAP Note 1928533 and the certified SAP HANA Hardware Directory, so here we'll explore the architecture details.

Architecture questions to consider include the following:

- Can we choose any size for the compute process, or do we have to pick from a defined list?
- Does Microsoft Azure offer both Intel and AMD processor VMs for SAP?
- Can all the VMs listed be used for application and database processes, or are there restrictions?
- How do we enable accelerated networking?

- What extensions do we need to install for VMs?
- Does Microsoft Azure support Intel Optane for SAP HANA?
- How does provisioning of SAP HANA on Azure (Large Instances) work?
- How do we find out which SKUs support SAP HANA scale-up versus scale-out?
- Can we install multiple application servers or databases on the same VM?

Because all the servers for SAP need to be certified, Microsoft Azure doesn't provide an option to create one by providing CPU/RAM; instead, you need to pick one from the certified list. However, Microsoft Azure provides compute options in several different ranges (combination of CPU/RAM and processor type, e.g., Intel and AMD) to meet the sizing requirement. There are certain VM SKUs, such as the DV2 series, that don't support premium storage and can't be used for databases. If you're moving from a different hardware platform and aren't sure how it compares to Intel or AMD processors, pick a server closest to the current configuration and then optimize it based on the load. Reference sizing is an iterative process.

For VMs where accelerated networking is supported, we recommend enabling it when provisioning the system. It's an option both from automated deployment and from the Microsoft Azure portal (in the **Networking** section), as shown in Figure 6.6.

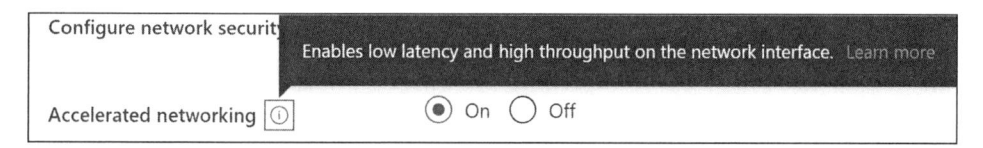

Figure 6.6 Accelerated Networking Option during VM Deployment

Microsoft Azure VMs support extensions, which are applications to support activities such as monitoring, configurations, and automation on VM. These extensions reside outside of VMs, so no direct connection is required. Common extensions include Microsoft Azure Enhanced Monitoring for SAP (required for SAP support), Microsoft Azure Diagnostics, Microsoft Azure Custom Script, Microsoft Azure Monitor, and Microsoft Azure Site Recovery. When you perform certain activities from the Microsoft Azure portal, such as configuring Microsoft Azure Site Recovery, extensions may be provisioned in background by the process, but you can install those using automation scripts ahead of time. Figure 6.7 shows what it looks like in the Microsoft Azure portal after the extensions are installed. Third-party extensions, such as Chef, Puppet, and anti-virus, are also available.

When it comes to the SAP HANA database, besides VMs (which go up to 12 TB of memory at the time of publication), Microsoft Azure's bare-metal offering can be used for larger databases. Currently, it doesn't integrate with the Microsoft Azure portal or automation scripts for provisioning, so you'll have to work with Microsoft (this may take a couple of weeks because those are purpose built).

6 Infrastructure Architecture Guidance

```
rksapapp1 | Extensions
Virtual machine

Search (Ctrl+/)          « + Add

Security                   Search to filter items...
Advisor recommendations    Name                 ↑↓  Type
Extensions                 LinuxDiagnostic
Continuous delivery        MonitorX64Linux          Microsoft.AzureCAT.AzureEnhancedMonitoring.MonitorX64Linux
```

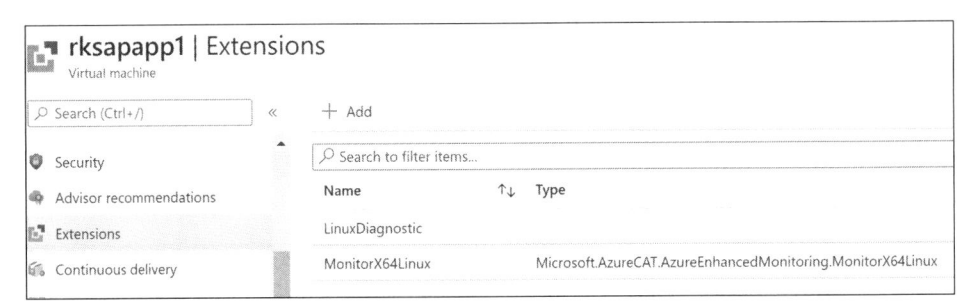

Figure 6.7 Microsoft Azure VM Extensions

SAP HANA Hardware Directory (*www.sap.com/dmc/exp/2014-09-02-hana-hardware/enEN/iaas.html#categories=Microsoft%20Azure*) is the single point of truth to find SAP certification details in terms of size, configuration (scale out, scale up), and application (Online Transactional Processing [OLTP], Online Analytical Processing [OLAP]). Figure 6.8 shows an example of instance M416s_v2 certification.

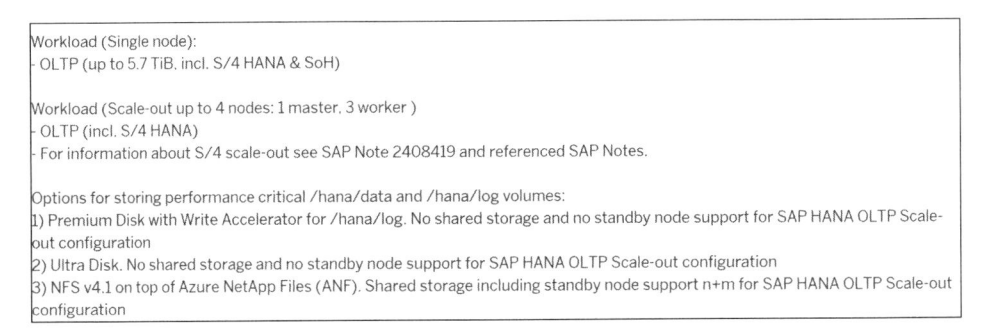

```
Workload (Single node):
- OLTP (up to 5.7 TiB, incl. S/4 HANA & SoH)

Workload (Scale-out up to 4 nodes: 1 master, 3 worker )
- OLTP (incl. S/4 HANA)
- For information about S/4 scale-out see SAP Note 2408419 and referenced SAP Notes.

Options for storing performance critical /hana/data and /hana/log volumes:
1) Premium Disk with Write Accelerator for /hana/log. No shared storage and no standby node support for SAP HANA OLTP Scale-out configuration
2) Ultra Disk. No shared storage and no standby node support for SAP HANA OLTP Scale-out configuration
3) NFS v4.1 on top of Azure NetApp Files (ANF). Shared storage including standby node support n+m for SAP HANA OLTP Scale-out configuration
```

Figure 6.8 Microsoft Azure on SAP HANA Certification Details for M416s_v2

Multiple Instances on the Same VM

Having multiple instances on the same host can have cost and management optimization motivations, but you have to ensure that they're not competing for the same resources and that SAP sizing and parameter (memory cap) recommendations are followed. Keep VM throughput in mind, and size the storage for multiple instances as well. Note that multiple instances can't share the same disk.

Running multiple instances on the same server is supported for databases (SQL Server on Windows, SA HANA [multiple components on one system – MCOS], IBM DB2, and Oracle) as well as applications, as long as you follow SAP recommendations and restrictions. The setup looks like that shown in Figure 6.9.

HA Support for Multiple Instances

HA is supported for SAP Central Services (called multi-SID HA), but it isn't supported for databases when multiple instances are present on the same host.

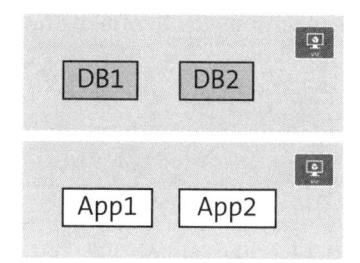

Figure 6.9 Multiple Instances on the Same Server (VM)

6.5 Storage

Choosing storage is a use case-based exercise because several types are available in Microsoft Azure and not all disks are fit for every use case. Architecture questions to consider include the following:

- What storage solution should be used for Microsoft Azure Diagnostics?
- What storage type fits SAP applications and databases?
- What are recommended practices for disk layout?
- What are the available options for shared storage for SAP?
- What disk encryption options are available?
- What is the SAP use case for the write accelerator?

Microsoft Azure Diagnostics agent collects monitoring data from the guest OS and keeps it in a storage account. During deployment, a standard storage account can be used for this, which also enables console login from the Microsoft Azure portal. For SAP storage, a managed disk is recommended, and because standard disks don't guarantee performance, premium managed disks are a better fit for both applications (SAP Central Services, application servers) and databases.

Because disks have input/output operations per second (IOPS) restrictions, striping should be done to maximize the IOPS and throughout (with RAID 0) and for databases on M series VMs. Enabling the write accelerator (feature of premium disk to optimize write latency) on the database log directory improves write I/O latency.

File system naming conventions follow SAP guidelines with the following considerations for sizing and striping:

- Disk IOPS and throughput
- Number of disks supported by the VM type
- Total VM throughput
- Type of storage being used (premium, ultra, etc.)

SAP HANA tailored data center integration includes recommendations from SAP for storage.

There are different ways of implementing shared storage solutions for the following SAP use cases:

- SAP shared file systems such as interface and transport directory
- HA using a shared file system (*/sapmnt*)
- SAP HANA scale-out configuration with standby

In Microsoft Azure, shared storage for SAP can be implemented in the following ways (at the time of publication):

- Enabling Network File System (NFS) on a Linux VM
- Microsoft Azure shared disk (windows)
- Scale-out file system (windows)
- Microsoft Azure NetApp Files for server message block as well as NFS

> **HA for Shared Storage**
>
> HA for shared storage is highly recommended because it's a single point of failure; however, if your use case doesn't require a strict SLA, then you can use a single server as well.

As we've discussed, all disks are encrypted at the storage layer, and you can also use Microsoft Azure Disk Encryption at the disk level. Microsoft Azure Disk Encryption supports both a platform-managed (managed by Microsoft Azure) or customer-managed (bring your own key) model. There may be certain restrictions for VM size or OS, and the details for this are found in the Microsoft Azure documentation.

> **Database and Disk Encryption**
>
> Usually, databases have their own encryption mechanism too, which is recommended for SAP systems. In those instances, for example, when SAP HANA encryption is turned on, don't turn disk encryption on for those database disks.

6.6 Summary

This chapter discussed the building blocks of SAP architecture on Microsoft Azure starting with choosing regions and subscription design. Next, we walked through components such as compute, network, and storage. If you're looking get started in Microsoft Azure with a demo, proof of concept, or non-production SAP system, these are the architecture decisions you'll be making.

The next chapter takes this a step further and introduces resiliency into the architecture in terms of high availability and disaster recovery.

Chapter 7
Resiliency

Reliability of services is always on top of the list for any cloud provider, and it's always a shared responsibility. Microsoft Azure ensures the service availability and performance at the fabric layer, and you have to include resiliency in the application architecture.

Resiliency has several layers and almost always starts with business requirements. Discussing high availability and disaster recovery (HA/DR) without business context doesn't result in an optimal design because every decision has trade-offs and costs associated with it.

Architecture questions to consider include the following:

- Our organization has no formal service-level agreement (SLA), do we need HA?
- How do we achieve HA for shared storage?
- How do we choose among availability set, availability zone, and proximity placement groups?
- What does HA/DR architecture look like in Microsoft Azure?
- Is there a Microsoft Azure native tool for DR, or will we have to use SAP and third-party tools?

7.1 High Availability

A Microsoft Azure single virtual machine (VM) (with premium storage) has the SLA of 99.9%. Understanding the potential downtime (43.2 minutes per month) is a good starting point for the HA discussion.

Does 99.9% infrastructure availability meet your organization's SLA (or service-level objective [SLO])? If yes, then you can simplify the architecture and operations by deploying the SAP environment without HA. If a single VM SLA doesn't meet your organization's requirements, then you need HA configuration. The objective of HA for SAP is to protect the system from single point of failure components, which are shown in Figure 7.1 for SAP NetWeaver and the ABAP platform.

7 Resiliency

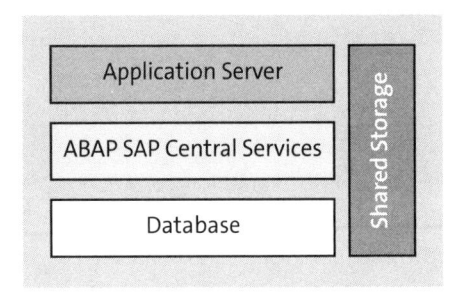

Figure 7.1 Single Point of Failure Components for SAP NetWeaver and ABAP Platform

Shared storage HA is achieved by clustering multiple systems and replicating the data. For Linux systems, the Network File System (NFS) server cluster (in the availability set) with data replicated using Distributed Replicated Block Device (DRBD) can be used, as shown in Figure 7.2. It also achieves HA with two VMs configured in an availability set or availability zone.

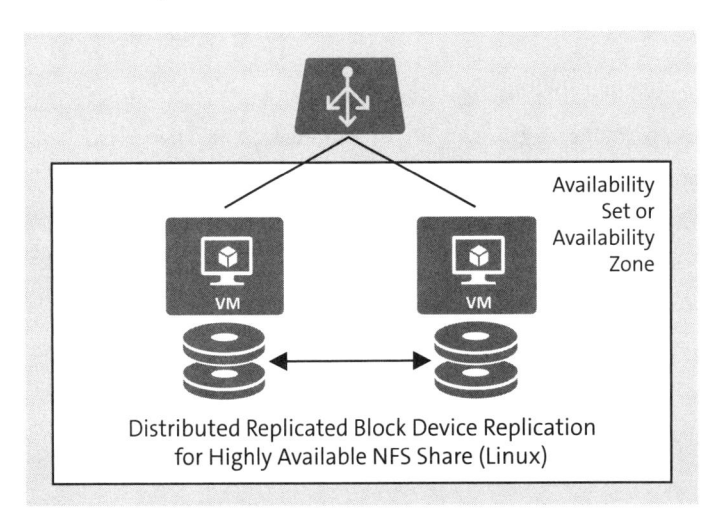

Figure 7.2 Highly Available NFS Cluster Setup

Pacemaker for NFS HA

For the HA setup of NFS, DRBD manages the disk replication while Pacemaker manages the cluster failover. We'll discuss more about Pacemaker in Section 7.1.6.

GlusterFS

Red Hat Enterprise Linux (RHEL) also supports GlusterFS cluster as HA shared storage in Microsoft Azure.

For the Windows operating system (OS), HA shared storage can be achieved by Scale-Out File Server (SOFS) using Storage Spaces Direct (S2D), as shown in Figure 7.3. S2D synchronizes data on disks to provide the combined disk as a storage pool.

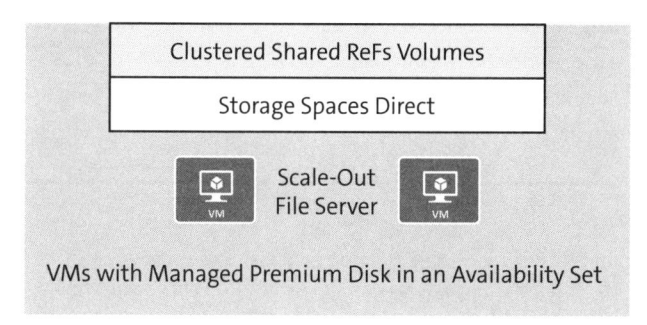

Figure 7.3 Scale-Out File Share with Storage Space Direct Setup

7.1.1 Shared Storage Using Platform as a Service

Platform as a service (PaaS) solutions such as Microsoft Azure NetApp Files simplify the setup because Microsoft Azure NetApp Files supports both server message block and NFS protocols and comes with a 99.99% SLA without the effort of managing the underlying infrastructure. At the time of publication, SAP HANA scale-out with standby configuration is only certified with Microsoft Azure NetApp Files.

> **Third-Party Solutions for Clustered Shared Disk**
>
> Besides S2D (starting in Windows 2016) or DRBD for HA shared disk, you can also use third-party solutions such as SIOS to achieve a clustered shared disk. For Windows OSs, SAP supports SAP Central Services clustering using file share for SAP NetWeaver ≥ 7.40 with SAP Kernel ≥ 7.49. If you're on an earlier version, SIOS DataKeeper is a good option to create a clustered shared disk for SAP Central Services HA, and SIOS also supports later version as well as Linux.

7.1.2 SAP Application Server

SAP application server HA is achieved by redundancy, that is, deploying multiple application servers, all active, in a landscape to mitigate the single point of failure. Load balancing for ABAP systems is done using message server, which is a part of SAP Central Services. For Java-based systems or web services, load balancing can be done either by using SAP Web Dispatcher or a hardware load balancer such as F5 or A10 (acting as reverse proxy).

7.1.3 SAP Central Services and Database

SAP Central Services and database HA is achieved by configuring more than one server in a cluster configuration so that when any of those fail, the service can be failed over to the secondary server. This configuration is in active-passive mode where the service on only one server is active at a time. A virtual IP (VIP) is used by the application servers to connect to the active central service and database; in Microsoft Azure, VIP is configured using the internal load balancer.

> **Microsoft Azure Load Balancer**
>
> The Microsoft Azure internal load balancer isn't performing any load balancing for SAP Central Services and database because only one is active at a time; it's primarily used for VIP and port forwarding for this use case. For SAP environments, standard load balancer is recommended because basic load balancer doesn't come with an SLA and isn't zone resilient.

SAP Central Services (for SAP NetWeaver and ABAP platform) consists of the message server and enqueue server. The message server acts as a communication channel and performs load balancing for application servers; it doesn't contain any persistent data so restart of the service doesn't lose any SAP transactional or crucial data. The enqueue server, on the other hand, contains the lock information for user and system transactions (background jobs, data loads, etc.), and losing this information will cause data inconsistency so it must be protected. That's where the enqueue replication server (ERS) comes into play, as it replicates the lock table to a secondary server that can serve as the primary in case of failover.

> **Standalone Enqueue Server 2**
>
> Starting with SAP NetWeaver ABAP 7.51, SAP introduced a new mechanism for enqueue server failover, which improves scalability. In the earlier version, SAP Central Services followed ERS for failover, meaning the services started on the same server (VM) that was running ERS. If the ERS server fails for some reason before the original SAP Central Services is recovered, it would cause downtime for the application. With the new Enqueue Server 2, you can have more than two servers in the cluster, and the failover can happen on a different server with enqueue replication happening over the TCP layer. SAP Central Services doesn't have to follow the ERS server in the new mechanism.

Figure 7.4 shows the VM configuration in an availability set (with internal load balancer) for SAP Central Services and database that enables infrastructure HA at the infrastructure layer. SAP application servers are HA by redundancy.

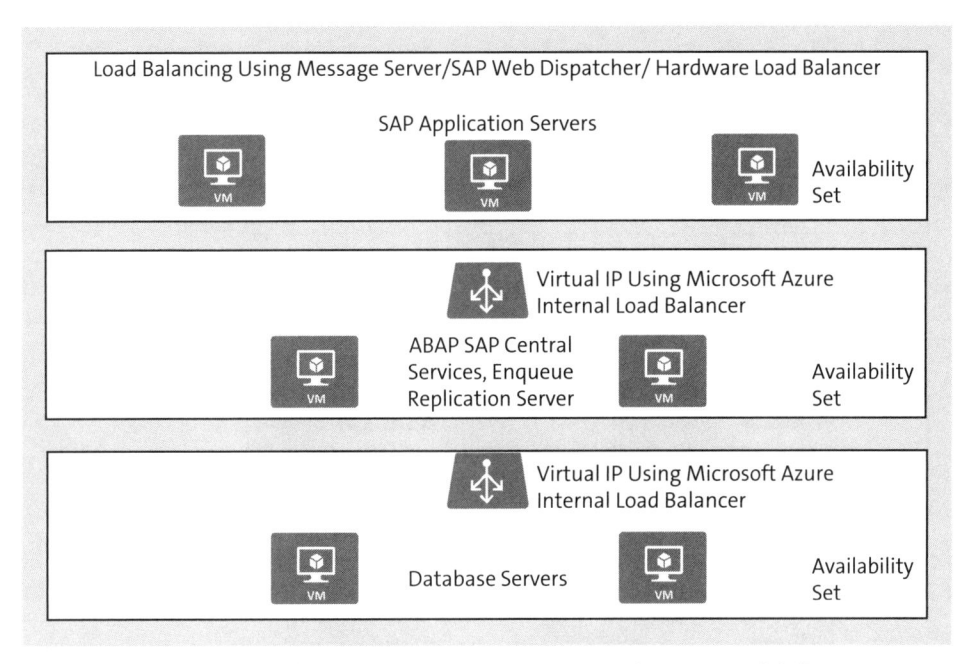

Figure 7.4 SAP NetWeaver/ABAP Platform HA Using Microsoft Azure Availability Sets

Availability sets in Microsoft Azure has a 99.95% SLA (21.6 mins of potential downtime per month). Another way to get a higher SLA (99.99%) is to use an availability zone construct. Couple of things to keep in mind before you decide on using an availability zone:

- Not all Microsoft Azure regions support availability zones (at the time of publication).
- Microsoft doesn't publish or guarantee the distance between data centers located in an availability zone.
- Related to the previous point, not all availability zones are equal; check latency using NIPING to ensure it meets SAP requirements.
- Availability zone mapping is tied to a subscription, meaning AZ1 may be different for another subscription.
- Availability zones aren't meant to be a DR solution; they are a better fit for SAP HA.

Figure 7.5 shows the HA setup using availability zones with a 99.99% SLA (4.32 minutes of potential downtime per month).

With the growth of Microsoft Azure and the introduction of availability zones, which can be a combination of multiple data centers, latency between VMs could suffer and affect SAP performance. To combat that scenario, Microsoft Azure introduced proximity placement groups, which ensure that all the VMs in a proximity placement group are placed in the same data center.

7 Resiliency

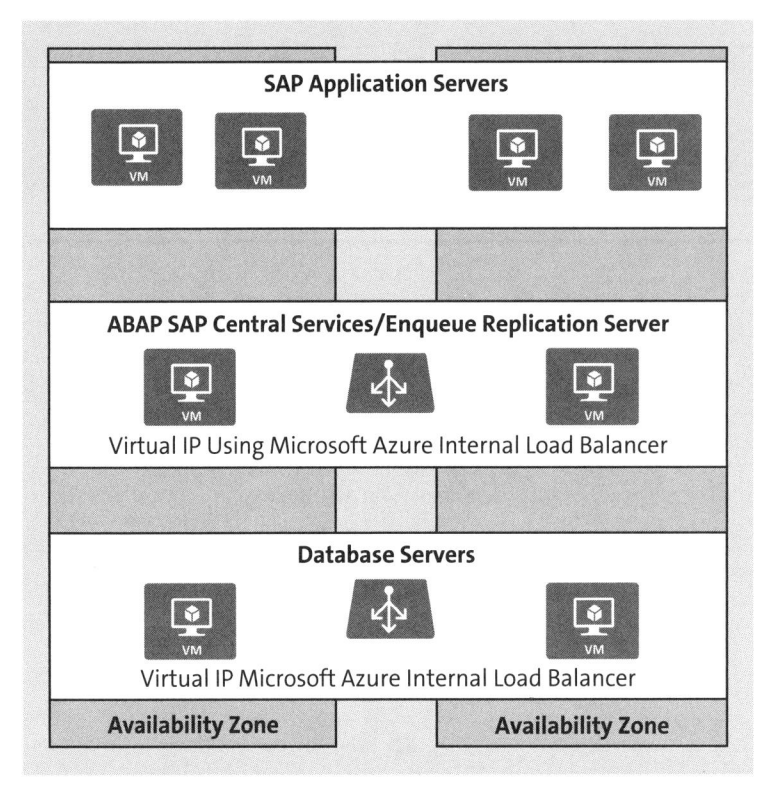

Figure 7.5 SAP NetWeaver/ABAP Platform HA Using Microsoft Azure Availability Zones

Proximity placement groups can contain multiple availability sets, so for a nonzone deployment, create a proximity placement group for all the servers in an SAP <SID> that contains availability sets for application, SAP Central Services, and database. Because not all the VM types may be available in all data centers, create the database VM first, and anchor all other VMs to that (the database is the anchor because usually that's the VM with largest size). Figure 7.6 shows the setup that combines the availability set and the proximity placement group.

With the cross-zone (availability zone) setup, SAP Central Services and database servers are part of different fault and update domains just by being in different zones. However, with multiple application servers in the same zone, there is no guarantee of individual servers to be in different fault or update domains. Consider the scenario in Figure 7.7 in which groups of application servers in each zone aren't guaranteed to be in different update and fault domains. The solution seems as simple as putting those in an availability set, except that Microsoft Azure doesn't support availability set and availability zone configuration together.

7.1 High Availability

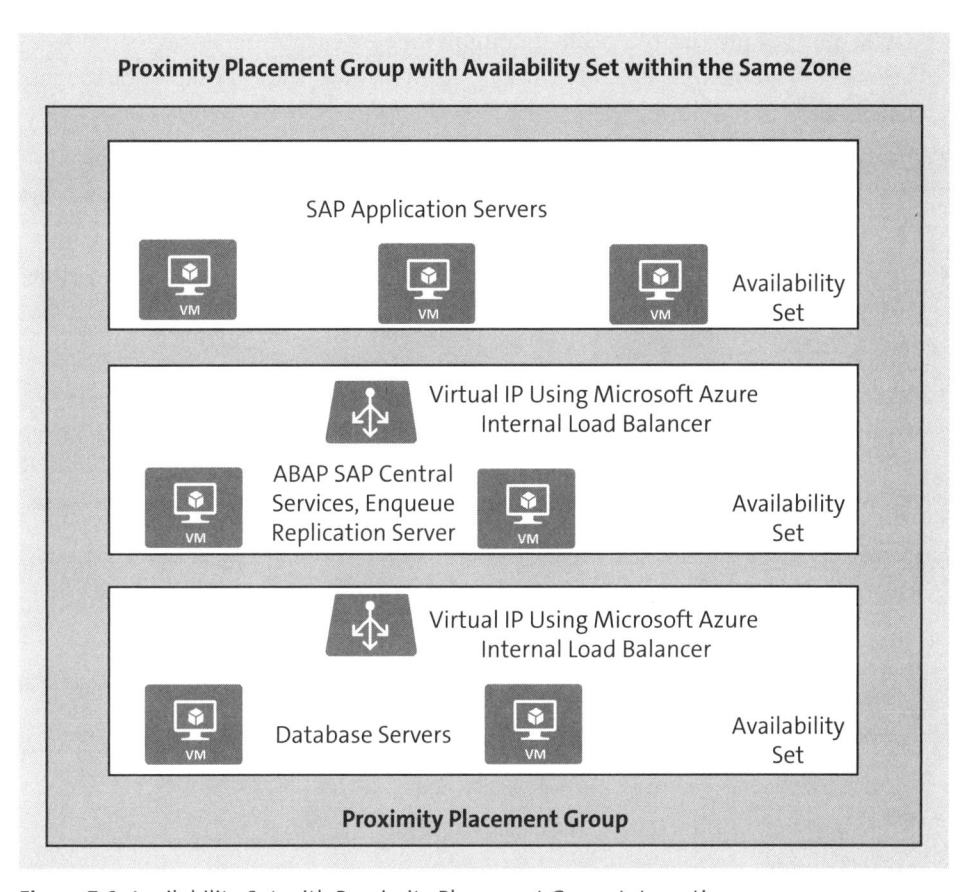

Figure 7.6 Availability Set with Proximity Placement Group Integration

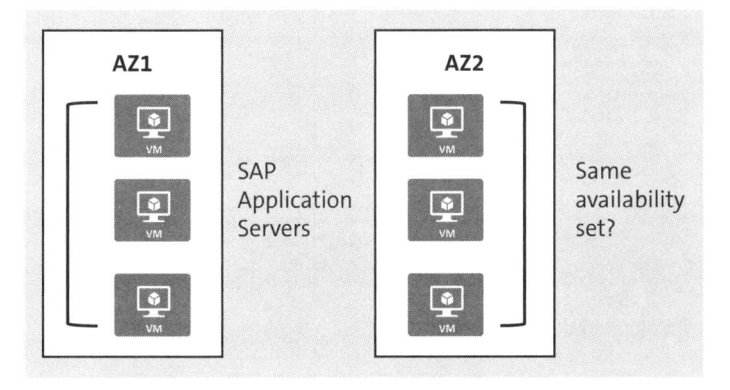

Figure 7.7 SAP Application Server Groups in Different Zones

Proximity placement groups come to the rescue here because proximity placement groups can hold availability sets. Here's how to create the setup highlighted in Figure 7.8:

- Create multiple proximity placement groups (one for each zone; this is logical separation because creation of the proximity placement group doesn't allow you to specify zones).
- Create the anchor VM (i.e., database) and reference the availability zone and proximity placement group together. During the VM creation configuration, you can specify both.
- Create availability sets within the proximity placement group (one for each zone; this is logical separation because creation of the availability set doesn't allow you to specify zones).
- When you create application server VMs, you can reference the proximity placement group and availability set together. Because the proximity placement group is tied to the zone when deploying the anchor VM, the application servers within that proximity placement group go to the same zone and also follow the availability set model for update and fault domains.
- You can also move existing VMs into a proximity placement group, although it requires downtime.

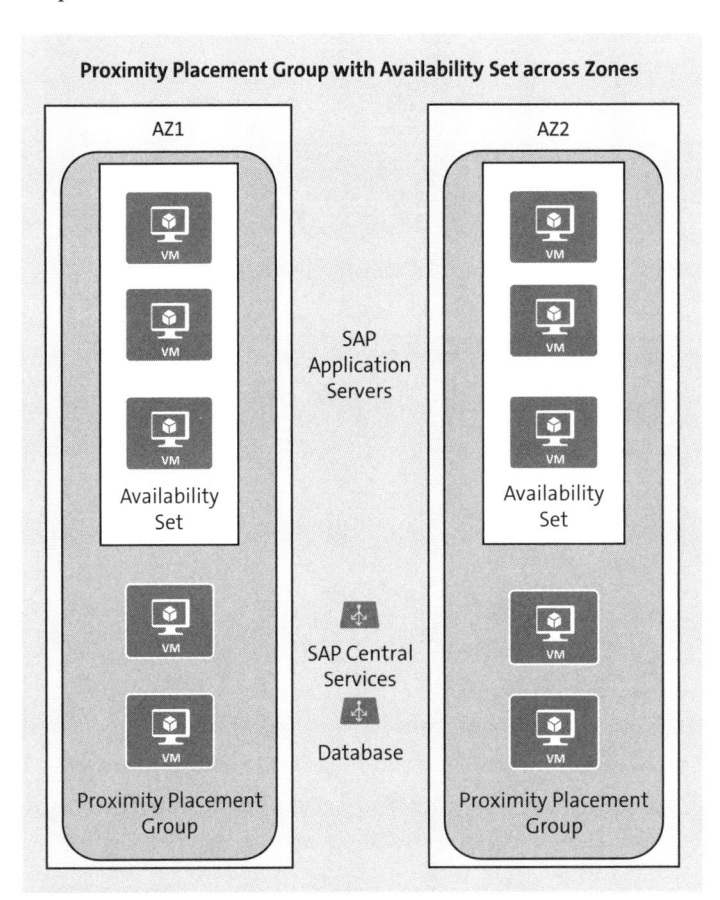

Figure 7.8 SAP Application Server Groups in Different Zones with Availability Sets

> **Proximity Placement Group and SAP HANA on Azure (Large Instances)**
>
> If you're using SAP HANA on Azure (Large Instances) instead of VM for SAP HANA database, revision 4 stamps are deployed with the proximity placement group. You can use the same proximity placement group name for application services and SAP Central Services VMs to be in the same data centers as SAP HANA on Azure (Large Instances) server.

Because recommended managed disks are used for the SAP VMs, those are part of availability set and availability zone resiliency as well. We've talked about shared storage HA, which adds on to the application VM setup (in availability set or availability zone). Figure 7.9 and Figure 7.10 show how VM HA for applications works in combination with shared disk HA and Microsoft Azure NetApp Files, respectively.

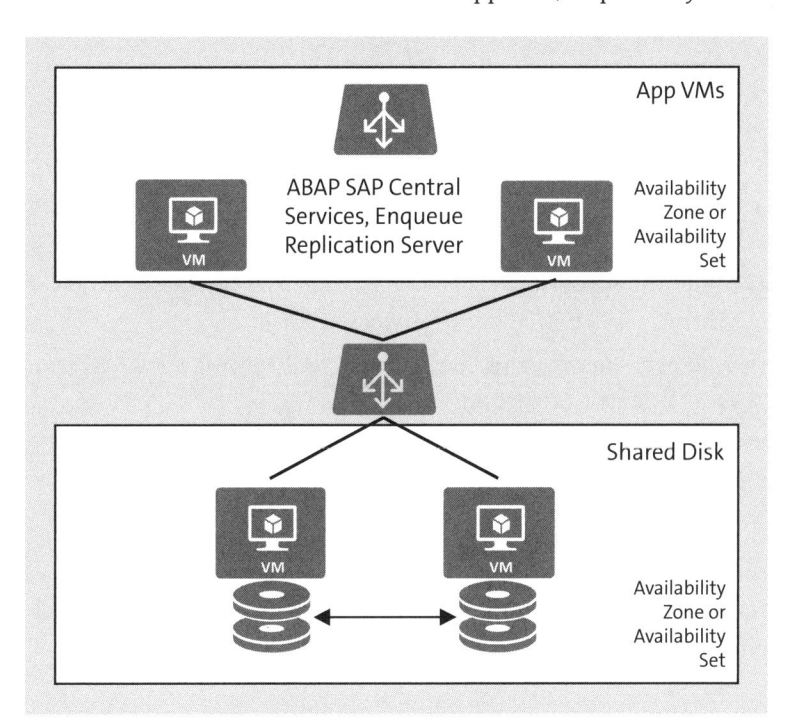

Figure 7.9 HA Setup of VM with HA Shared Disk

> **Application versus Infrastructure HA**
>
> Microsoft Azure infrastructure level resiliency as discussed previously isn't application aware; therefore, an application- or OS-level clustering and failover mechanism is required for SAP HA.

Now that you understand the Microsoft Azure infrastructure resiliency options, we'll discuss how clustering solutions complement this setup to achieve application-level HA.

7 Resiliency

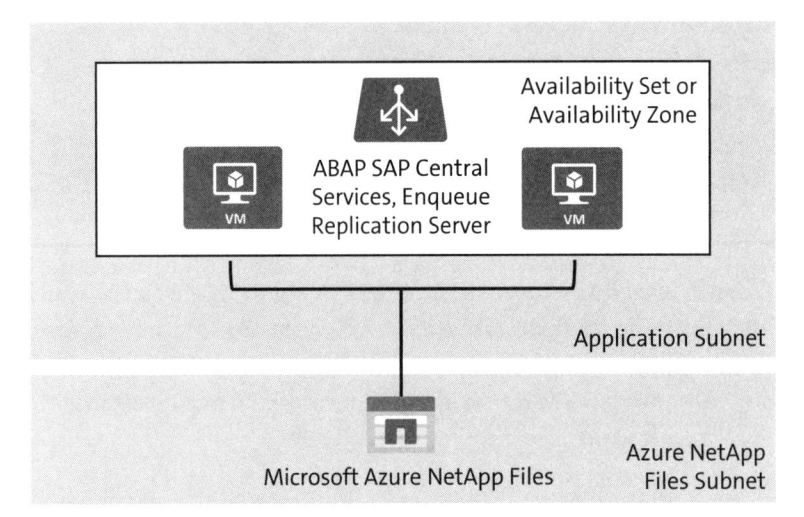

Figure 7.10 HA Setup of VM with Microsoft Azure NetApp Files

At the time of publication, Microsoft supports the following HA solutions for SAP:

- Windows Server failover cluster for SAP Central Services and database services on Windows VMs
  - Windows Server failover cluster with clustered shared disks for SAP NetWeaver < 7.40 with SAP kernel < 7.49 (SAP Central Services)
  - Windows Server failover cluster using file share for SAP NetWeaver ≥ 7.40 with SAP kernel ≥ 7.49 (SAP Central Services)
- Pacemaker cluster for SUSE Linux Enterprise Server (SLES) and RHEL (for both SAP Central Services and database VMs)

Before we get into platform-specific details, it's worth highlighting that the virtual hostname (and associated VIP) is used for SAP installation in HA configuration. In Microsoft Azure, VIP is created using Microsoft Azure Load Balancer, and in the load balancing rule configuration, you enable the **Floating IP**, as shown in Figure 7.11:

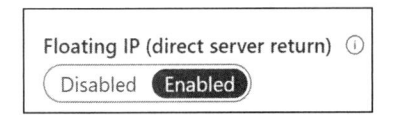

Figure 7.11 Enabling Floating IP in the Load Balancing Configuration

7.1.4 SAP Central Services on Windows Operating System

Because the SAP Central Services cluster (including ERS) is a two-node cluster, the node with file share majority can be used to determine the quorum. In this configuration, each node and the file share (witness) gets the vote to determine the majority for the cluster to function. The Microsoft Azure blob storage account (also called the cloud witness) or a HA file share can be used as the file share witness because this shouldn't be the single point of failure for the cluster.

Figure 7.12 shows an architecture for SAP Central Services HA configuration on the Windows OS using SOFS and cloud witness.

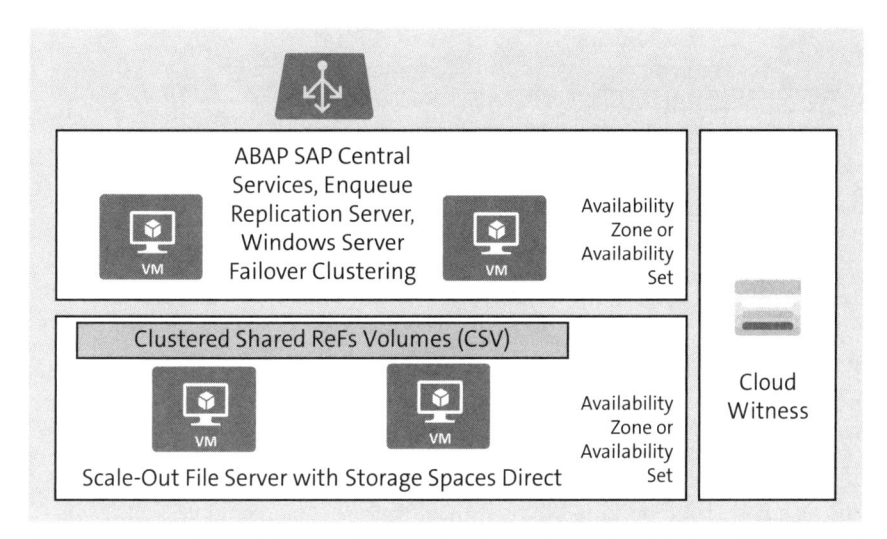

Figure 7.12 SAP Central Services/ERS HA Configuration Using SOFS on Windows OS

Following are a few recommendations for SOFS setup:

- Load balancer isn't required for the disk share.
- Microsoft recommends the Resilient File System (ReFS) format per SAP Note 1869038 - SAP Support for ReFs File System.
- Premium managed disks are recommended.
- Mirroring resiliency is recommended for performance.
- Microsoft recommends three cluster nodes for SOFS with three-way mirroring for better scalability and resiliency.

  The SOFS setup doesn't need to be dedicated to a single system; instead, it can be shared across multiple SAP <SID> servers, optimizing the cost and effort of managing multiple clusters. You can also simplify the architecture using the Microsoft Azure NetApp Files server message block share instead of SOFS, as shown in Figure 7.13.
- Server message block 3.0 (or later) is required, which is supported by Microsoft Azure NetApp Files.
- Create Active Directory (AD) connections before creating the server message block volume.
- Server message block share being HA isn't a problem because Microsoft Azure NetApp Files comes with a 99.99% SLA.

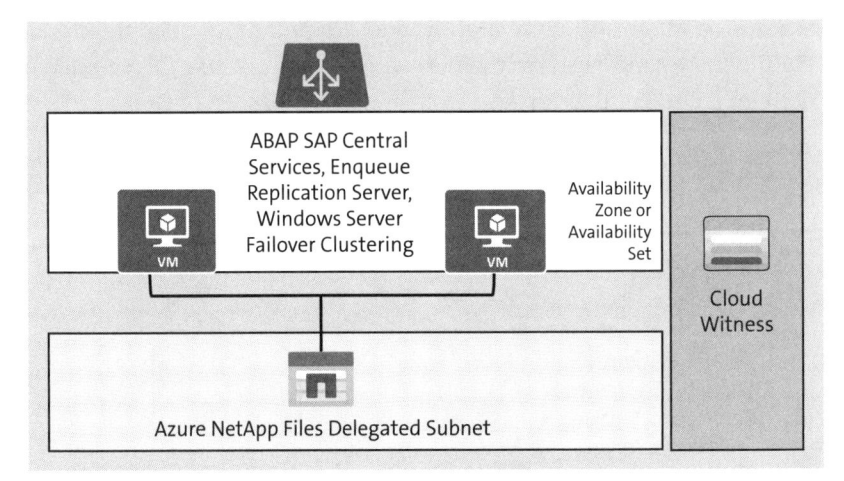

Figure 7.13 SAP Central Services HA for Windows Using Microsoft Azure NetApp Files Server Message Block

> **File Share HA Setup**
>
> File share setup for HA is applicable for SAP NetWeaver ≥ 7.40 with SAP kernel ≥ 7.49 and Windows ≥ 2016. Third-party solutions such as SIOS are required for versions lower than these, and the SIOS solution, in particular, also supports higher versions of SAP.

> **Microsoft Azure Shared Disk**
>
> Microsoft Azure also supports shared disk for the SAP Central Services cluster on the Windows server; however, there are certain restrictions such as mandatory use of proximity placement group (restricting this to be used in availability zone setups), storage fault domain unenforced when using availability sets, and no support for Linux/SAP cluster making (this isn't as versatile as Microsoft Azure NetApp Files). As it evolves and more features get added, shared disk would be a good candidate for SAP use cases.

7.1.5 SQL Server Database on Windows Operating System

HA for SQL Server on Microsoft Azure can be achieved either using a SQL Server failover cluster based on SOFS or SQL Server AlwaysOn. The latter is preferred (and supported on Microsoft Azure) because it uses separate storage that provides better resiliency. Similar to SAP Central Services, there are two VMs in an availability set or availability zone with a witness and database replication keeping the data in sync. For failover, the clustering software (Windows Server failover cluster) promotes the secondary node to primary, and because the cluster connection is routed through the internal load balancer, SAP connects to the new database server without any explicit configuration change. The setup in Microsoft Azure is shown in Figure 7.14.

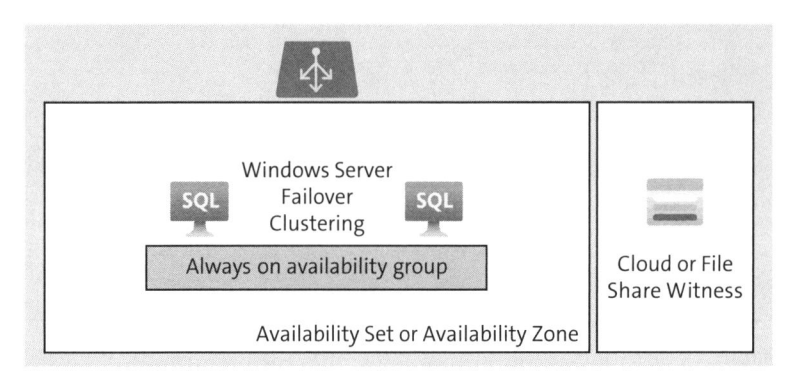

Figure 7.14 SQL Server AlwaysOn with HA

The load balancer IP address has the listener for the SQL Server availability group, and the data replication is in synchronous mode.

> **SQL Server on Linux**
>
> SAP doesn't support SQL Server on Linux even though it's available in a Linux flavor for other applications.

7.1.6 High Availability on the Linux Operating System

Both SLES and RHEL provide an HA extension add-on, which comes by default with the SAP flavor of the OS (SLES for SAP and RHEL for SAP). VIP (i.e., floating) and fencing are the important considerations for the HA implementation in Microsoft Azure.

Under the hood, both SLES and RHEL use the open-source Pacemaker solution to manage HA. Pacemaker is a cluster resource manager that runs on nodes (servers) to maintain consistency and minimize downtime; it uses Corosync as the communication framework. Figure 7.15 shows how Pacemaker and Corosync work with Microsoft Azure servers and shared storage to make HA work.

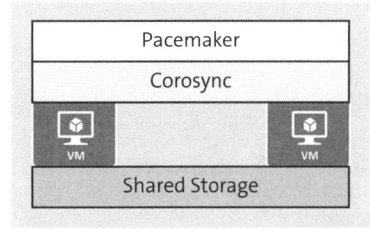

Figure 7.15 Pacemaker Integration with Microsoft Azure Servers

> **Fencing**
>
> Fencing ensures that the cluster state is consistent; when it can't find the status of resources (services) in a node, it ensures that the node doesn't run any important service

7   Resiliency

by killing the node (node level fencing). The Pacemaker node-level fencing implementation mechanism is STONITH (shoot the other node in the head).

In Microsoft Azure, STONITH fencing can either be implemented using a storage-based death device or Microsoft Azure fence agent allowing STONITH to fence the cluster.

Storage-based death implementation in Microsoft Azure requires a VM that acts as an Internet Small Computer Systems Interface (iSCSI) target server. For better quorum management, three devices (servers) are recommended; these can be put in an availability set or availability zone (one server in each zone). Similar to SOFS, the storage-based death device setup can be shared among multiple HA clusters in an SAP environment. The Microsoft Azure fencing agent works on Python-based software development kit (SDK) and doesn't require VM deployment. For the Microsoft Azure fencing agent, STONITH uses a service principal to authorize against Microsoft Azure. Figure 7.16 and Figure 7.17 show the setup with storage-based death and the Microsoft Azure agent, respectively.

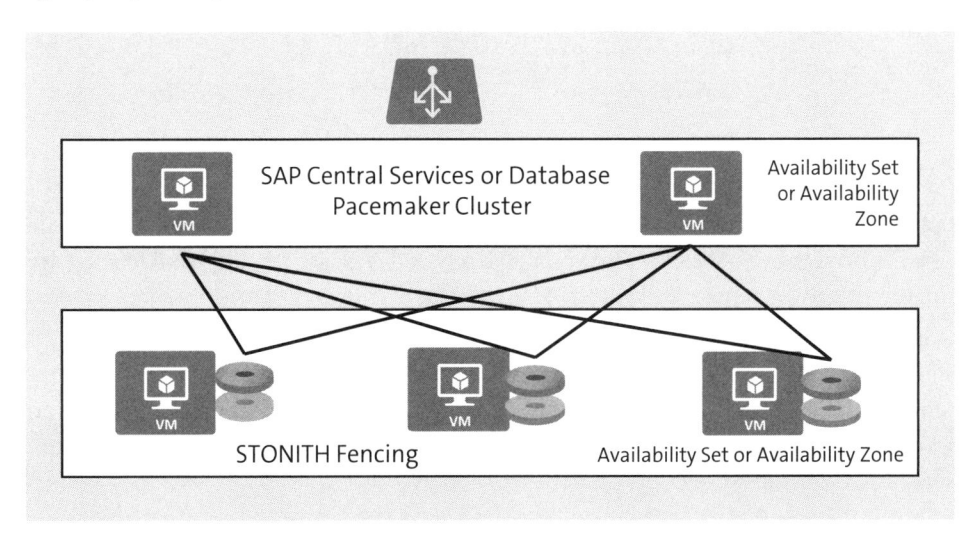

Figure 7.16 Pacemaker Cluster Using Storage-Based Death Devices

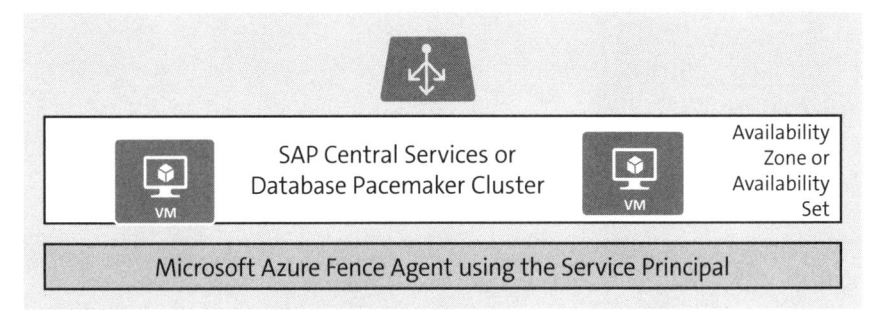

Figure 7.17 Fencing Using Microsoft Azure Agent

7.1 High Availability

> **SLES versus RHEL Fencing Agent Support**
>
> SLES supports both storage-based death and the Microsoft Azure fence agent, whereas RHEL supports only the Microsoft Azure fence agent in a cloud environment.

SAP Central Services on Linux

Now that you have all the building blocks, there are a few different ways to make these combinations as follows:

- Cluster for SAP Central Services/ERS
  - Pacemaker
- Shared disk (*/sapmnt*)
  - NFS cluster
  - Microsoft Azure NetApp Files
- Fencing
  - Storage-based death device (SBD)
  - Microsoft Azure fence agent (RHEL supports only this mechanism)

Figure 7.18 shows a setup for SLES with the NFS cluster and SBD devices (RHEL doesn't support storage-based death).

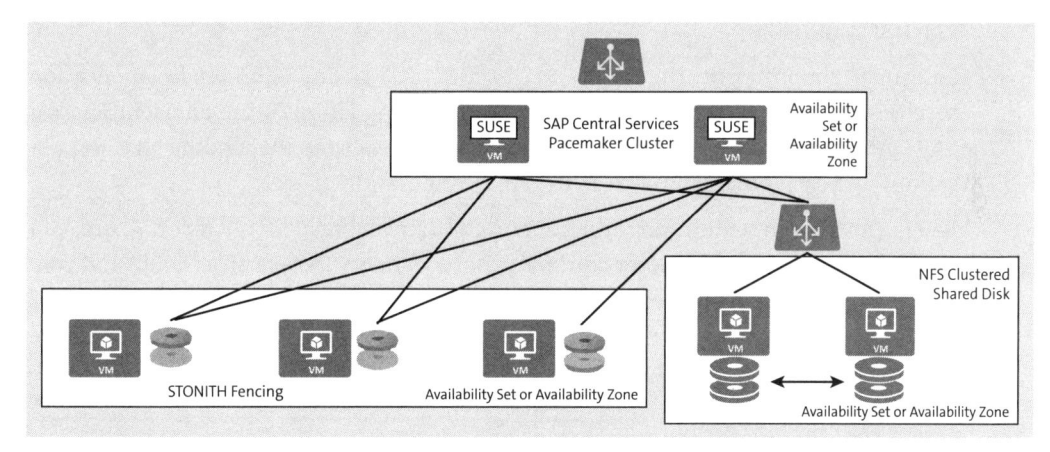

Figure 7.18 SAP Central Services HA Setup Using NFS Cluster, Pacemaker, and Storage-Based Death Devices

Figure 7.19 shows a different setup with Microsoft Azure NetApp Files and Microsoft Azure fence agent for RHEL (SLES supports this as well).

7   Resiliency

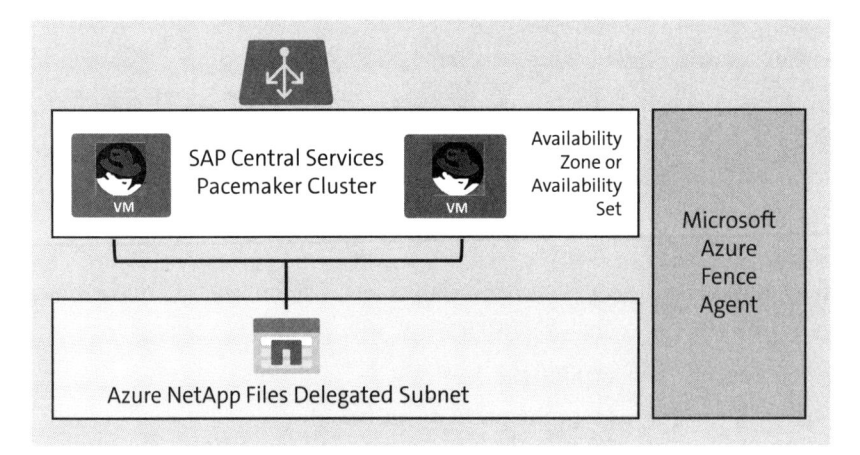

Figure 7.19 RHEL HA Setup for SAP Central Services Using Microsoft Azure NetApp Files and Microsoft Azure Fence Agent

> **Integrated SAP Web Dispatcher and Gateway**
>
> SAP Web Dispatcher and gateway configuration can be integrated with SAP Central Services. You can optionally use that to protect those with HA configuration of SAP Central Services.

SAP HANA Database

SAP HANA supports only the Linux OS so even if you're using Windows for application services and SAP Central Services, you'll end up using Linux in the environment for SAP HANA. The deployment models are scale up and scale out (depending on the application), and each differ a little bit in the HA configuration.

SAP HANA system replication is the supported HA mechanism in Microsoft Azure; you install SAP HANA on two servers (primary and secondary in case of scale up) and configure SAP HANA system replication in synchronous mode. Cluster management is done by Pacemaker, and fencing is handled by either storage-based death or by the Microsoft Azure fence agent, as shown in Figure 7.20.

> **SAP HANA Network Zones**
>
> Figure 7.20 doesn't explicitly show different network zones for SAP HANA for ease of understanding; however, it's still applicable. We'll highlight this in the scale-out HA configuration.

For SAP HANA scale out, you can either do a setup similar to scale up, meaning there would be corresponding secondary to each primary (n + n) with SAP HANA system replication or host an auto failover recovery scenario (n + m where m < n) with a standby host. When any of the active nodes fail, SAP HANA triggers failover to the standby node. SAP HANA manages this mechanism, and no external cluster software is required. This setup also requires NFS shared storage; on Microsoft Azure, it's certified with only Microsoft Azure NetApp Files (NFS v 4.1), at the time of publication.

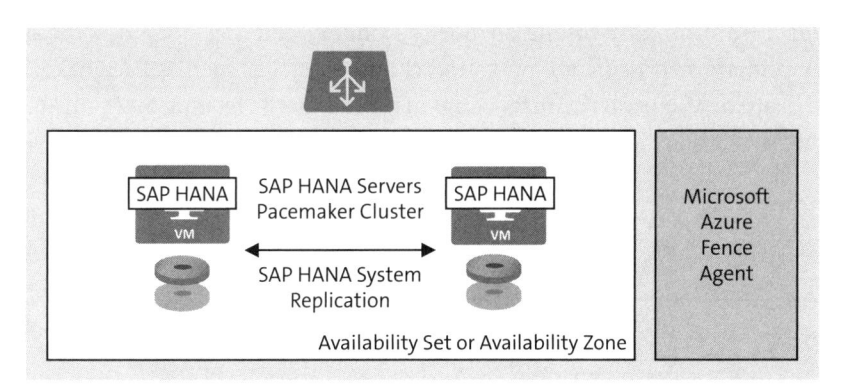

Figure 7.20 SAP HANA HA Using Pacemaker, SAP HANA System Replication, and Microsoft Azure Fence Agent

Figure 7.21 shows the scale-out scenario with Microsoft Azure NetApp Files and also highlights different network zones for SAP HANA communication.

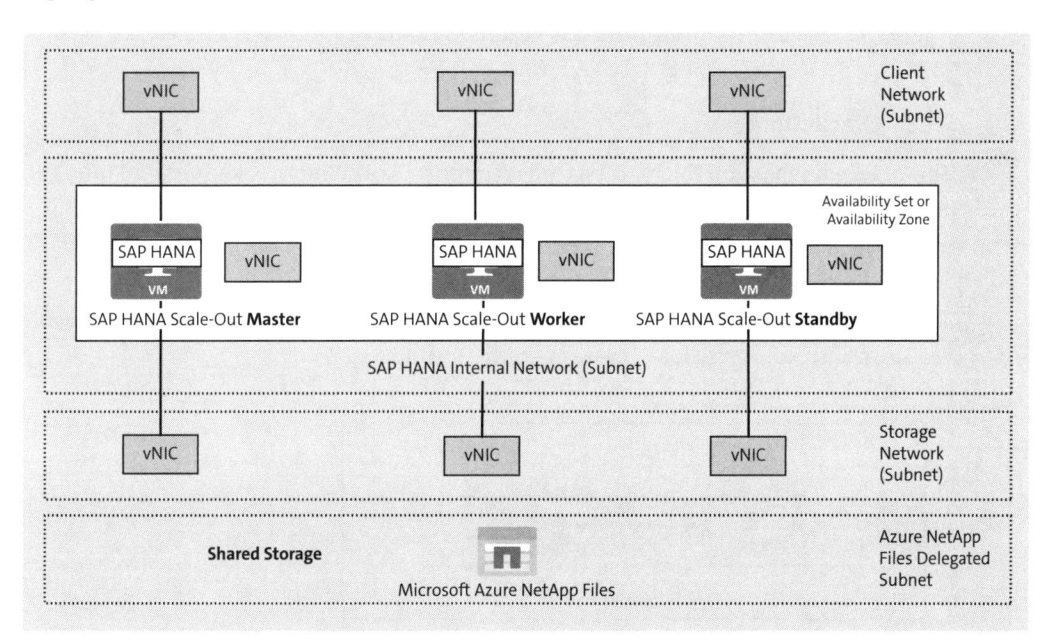

Figure 7.21 SAP HANA Scale-Out Setup with Standby Using Microsoft Azure NetApp Files

> **HA on SAP HANA on Azure (Large Instances)**
>
> Microsoft supports both HA configurations, described previously for VM, on SAP HANA on Azure (Large Instances) as well.

7.1.7 IBM DB2

DB2 in Microsoft Azure is supported on Windows, RHEL, and SLES; however, HA configuration isn't supported on Windows at the time of publication. DB2 HA/DR features replicate the data from primary to one or more secondary databases. Standby takes over when the primary fails using an integrated cluster manager such as Pacemaker. Storage-based death or Microsoft Azure fence agent is used for the fencing mechanism. This setup is highlighted in Figure 7.22.

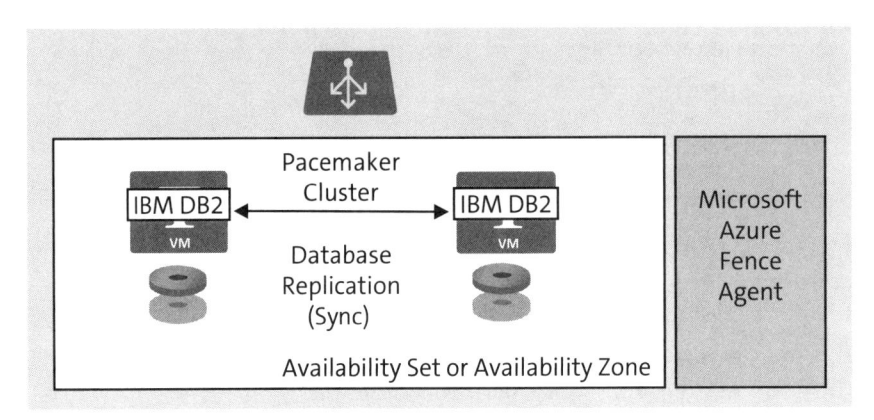

Figure 7.22 IBM DB2 HA Using Database Replication and the Pacemaker Cluster

7.1.8 Oracle Database

The Oracle database on Microsoft Azure is supported on Windows and Oracle Linux OS. The HA solution is achieved using the mechanism called Data Guard (DG), which has a similar setup for both Windows and Linux OS. It uses Oracle VMs in an availability set and an observer that triggers the failover using the fast start failover mechanism, as shown in Figure 7.23. Automated failover is managed by the observer and doesn't require Microsoft Azure load balancer configuration.

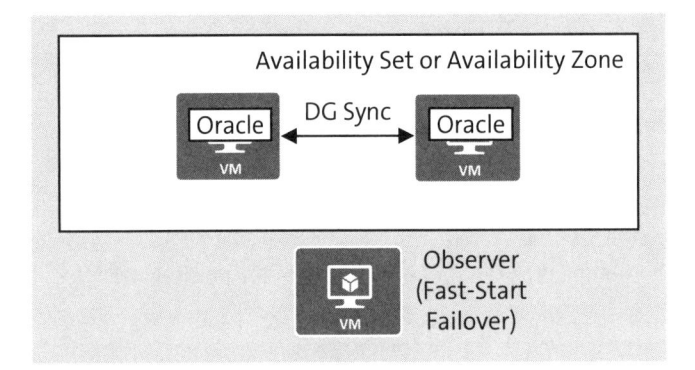

Figure 7.23 HA Using Oracle Data Guard

7.1.9 SAP Adaptive Server Enterprise Database

Microsoft Azure supports SAP ASE on Windows, SLES, and RHEL, and the HA setup is similar. SAP ASE provides an always-on feature for HA/DR, which uses an embedded replication server to replicate (in synchronous mode for HA) data between primary and companion (secondary) servers. It supports a fault manager (on a different host) for failover management.

In Microsoft Azure, at the time of publication, the fault manager (without floating or VIP) is the only supported configuration, so there is no need for the load balancer. This setup is illustrated in Figure 7.24.

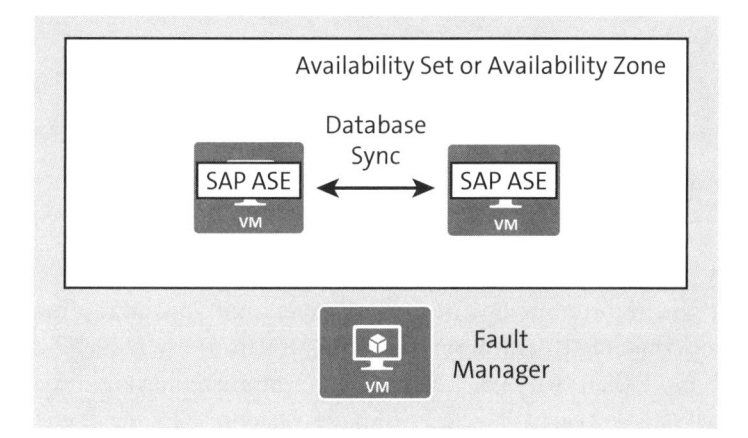

Figure 7.24 SAP ASE HA Setup

HA for Observer or Fault Manager

Both Oracle and SAP ASE use a third server for failover, so the observer and fault manager server should be configured to be HA too. The preceding illustrations don't explicitly show that.

7.1.10 SAP BusinessObjects Business Intelligence

Besides SAP NetWeaver and ABAP platform, SAP BusinessObjects is another commonly used SAP application. The main components include the following:

- Web Tier
- Central Management Server (CMS)
- File repository server, which is a shared file system
- Database, such as SQL Server

The HA setup for SAP BusinessObects BI is illustrated in Figure 7.25.

7   Resiliency

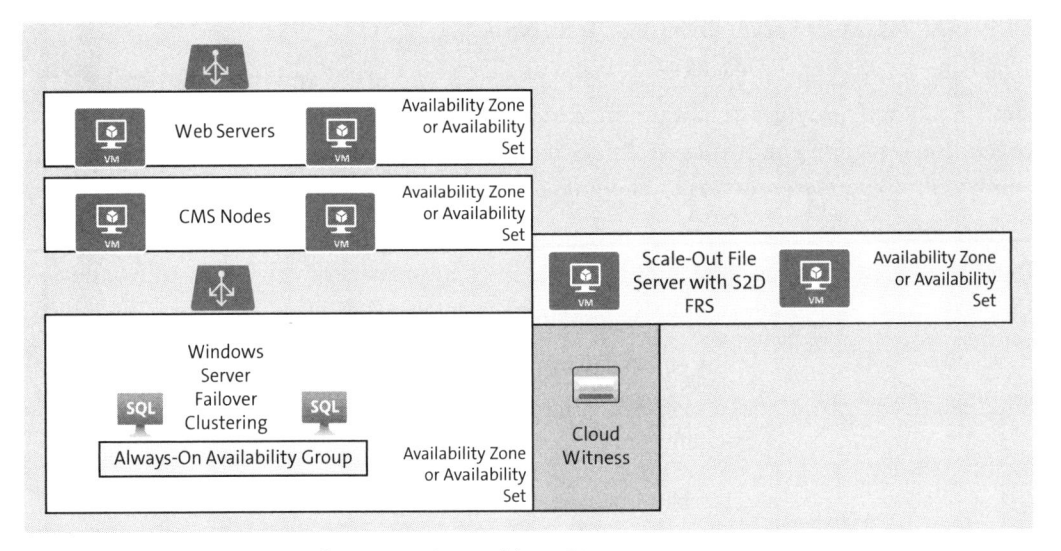

Figure 7.25 HA Setup for SAP BusinessObjects BI

7.1.11 Standalone Enqueue Server 2

Enqueue Server 2 was originally introduced with SAP NetWeaver ABAP 7.51 and became the default installation option for SAP Central Services from ABAP platform 1809. It's a more scalable way with more than two-node support. We recommend having three nodes for better resiliency, but you can still have a two-node cluster setup for Enqueue Server 2. Figure 7.26 illustrates the architecture of the three-node SAP Central Services/ERS cluster setup.

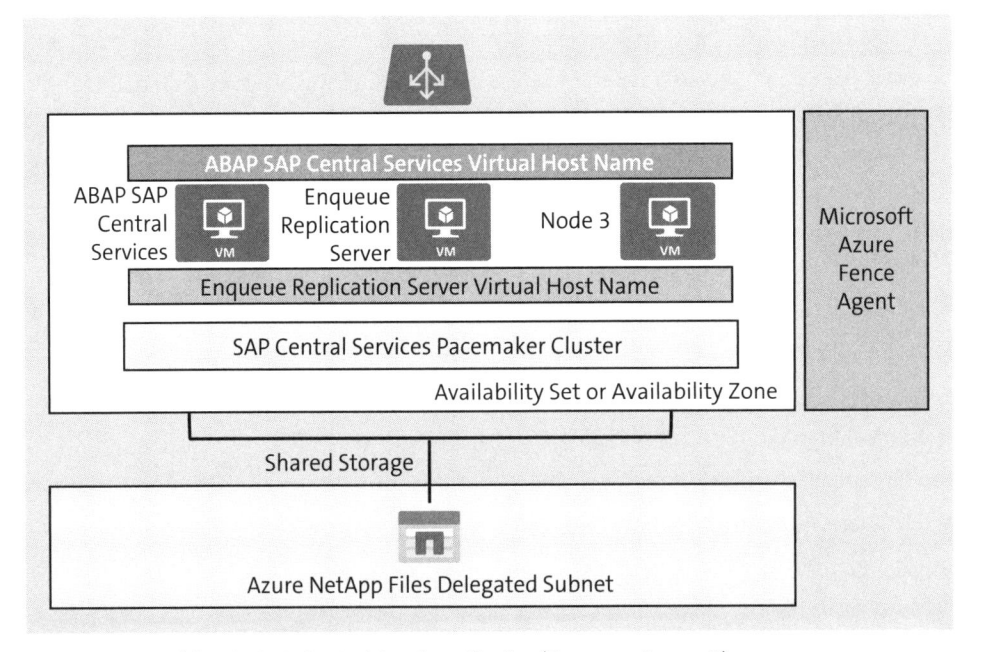

Figure 7.26 Multinode SAP Central Services Cluster (Enqueue Server 2)

> **If SAP Central Services Doesn't Use ERS, Do We Still Need a Cluster Manager?**
>
> In a cloud environment, if the SAP Central Services server fails, it gets rebooted and comes back a lot quicker than on-premise; the locks sync back, and there is no data loss. That begs the question of whether the cluster manager such as Pacemaker is still required or adds any value. The crashed VM may become available quickly, but there is no SLA available with it; therefore, even though it may be faster most of the times, it takes what it takes and may not produce desirable results in the long run. Hence, SAP recommends Enqueue Server 2 setup to be managed by HA software.

7.1.12 Multi-SAP System ID for SAP Central Services

Multi-SID (SAP system ID) HA can be described as an HA configuration where multiple SID central services reside on the same host cluster and connect to their respective application servers. The motivation behind this is to reduce the number of hosts either for cost optimization or the operational efficiency associated with management of fewer VMs. Multi-SID HA is supported with Windows, RHEL, and SLES OSs. Multiple VIPs for application installation are configured through the internal load balancer because it supports multiple frontend IPs.

Following are some considerations and restrictions with multi-SID HA:

- The clustered VMs must be sized for the extra load associated with multiple SIDs.
- Each SID can failover independently depending on the type of issue the services run into.
- If you're using storage-based death fencing, the same storage-based death cluster can be shared with multiple SAP Central Services clusters.
- Even though this configuration brings less management of VMs, it can be complex from the configuration and application maintenance point of view.
- For Linux (RHEL and SLES), the maximum number of SIDs supported is five.
- For Windows, the maximum number of SIDs supported is equal to the maximum number of private frontend IPs associated with the Microsoft Azure internal load balancer, and at the time of publication, the setup isn't supported in an availability zone configuration.
- The mix of standalone enqueue server and Enqueue Server 2 isn't supported at the time of publication.
- The setup shouldn't include any application server of any of the associated (or other) SIDs.

Figure 7.27 illustrates the architecture of the setup.

7 Resiliency

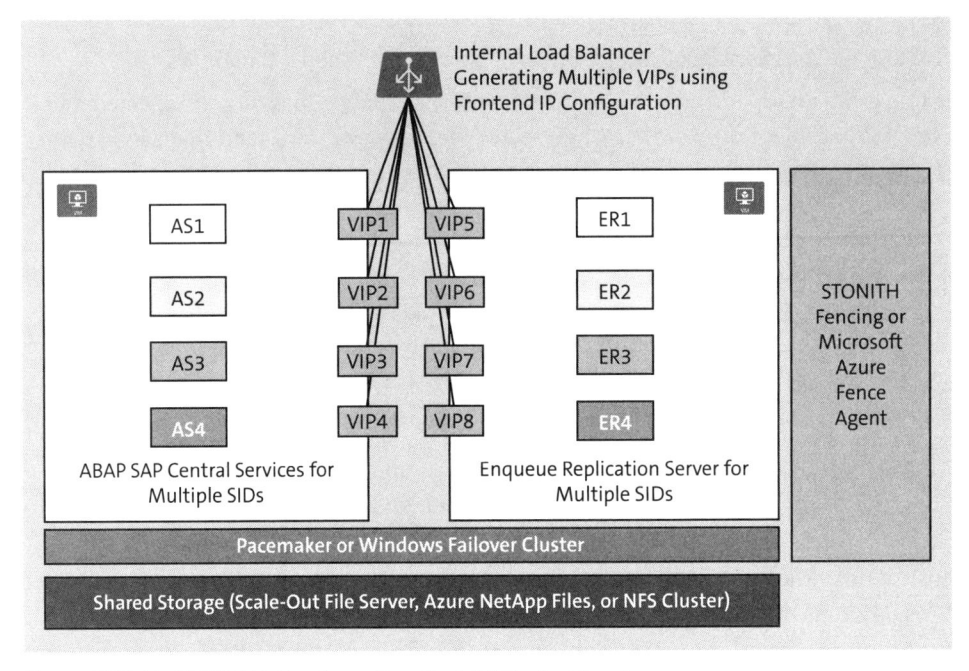

Figure 7.27 Multi-SID HA Configuration for SAP Central Services

Database Multi-SID HA
Multi-SID HA for database instances isn't supported at the time of publication.

HA Server Sizing
The sizing for the HA system should be the same as the primary because during the failover, the HA system takes over and function as the primary.

7.2 Disaster Recovery

Expanding the scope of resiliency, HA configuration ensures the system availability in case of localized failure such as power failure, hardware issue, and so on or in case of availability zone configuration or resiliency from a data center failure.

Now consider a wider failure radius, that is, something that affects a data center such as lightning or flooding, or something that affects the whole region, such as a hurricane. How can we design systems to survive that kind of failure? When we think of bigger failures, natural disasters often come to mind, but it could be a lot less dramatic, such as long power failures or communication disruptions. Disaster recovery (DR) planning is the key to surviving these kinds of catastrophes. DR plans always start with the business, and you need to understand which business processes need that kind of resiliency. Given the time and cost constraints, not everything qualifies for DR protection. Work with the business to understand which areas are prioritized, and then tie these areas to the SAP systems used for them. Categorizing systems in different tiers (e.g., tier 1, 2, 3) based on business-critical processes (business impact analysis) is a common exercise that should be used in DR planning as well.

7.2.1 Recovery Time Objective and Recovery Point Object

The next step in the process is determining how much data the business can afford to lose and the time it can sustain while the SAP systems are in recovery. These metrics are known as recovery point objective (RPO) and recovery time objective (RTO), as illustrated in Figure 7.28.

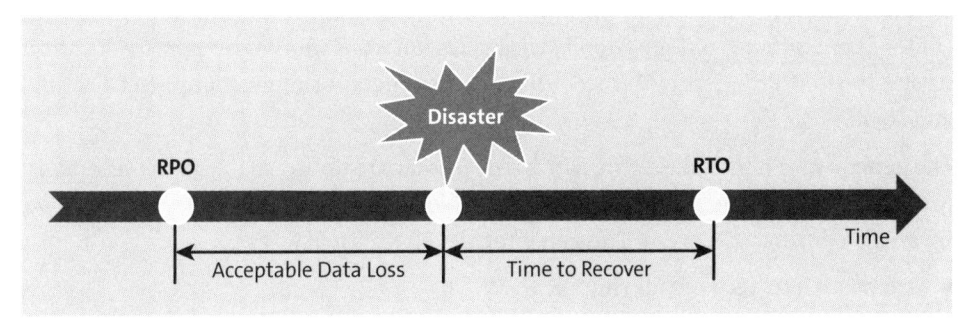

Figure 7.28 RPO and RTO

When we think of HA configuration options, the first thing that comes to mind is the availability SLA. You must consider how much availability is required so the systems can be designed accordingly by using features such as availability set versus availability zone, NFS server versus Microsoft Azure NetApp Files, and so on. Similarly, all DR conversations start with knowing RPO and RTO.

7.2.2 Microsoft Azure Paired Regions

Microsoft Azure's approach to resiliency follow the same principles when designing for DR. Microsoft Azure geographies usually have two or more regions to meet data residency and compliance restrictions, and within a geography, it pairs a region with another to form a regional pair; where possible, regional pairs are 300 miles apart. For example, the East US is paired with West US, and East Asia is paired with Southeast Asia. Besides the physical separation, the regional pair concept has some other advantages such as georedundant storage replicates to paired regions (which is also used by Microsoft Azure

Backup cross region restore [CRR]), planned Microsoft Azure platform updates are rolled out sequentially, and one region recovery is prioritized in an event of a widespread calamity.

Given the advantages of following the regional pair model, it's a good idea to pick the paired region to deploy the SAP DR systems; however, given that SAP SKUs are considered specialized, there is a chance that some infrastructure such as M series VMs and SAP HANA on Azure (Large Instances) aren't available in the paired region. In those scenarios, you may have to pick a different region in the same geography. Choosing a nonpaired region still lets you use other tools such as Microsoft Azure Site Recovery.

7.2.3 Disaster Recovery for SAP

From the architecture point of view, the DR scope should consider not only the SAP and ancillary systems but also the communication and network infrastructure. This includes ExpressRoute configuration to the DR region from another on-premise location or site-to-site VPN, preprovisioned VNets and subnets for replication, VNet peering, and so on.

The general idea is to make all the data in the primary region available in the secondary (or DR) region, so either the systems are available in the DR region, or they can be stood up quickly during a DR event. This can be achieved multiple ways:

- Offsite backup/recovery during DR
- Near real-time replication from the primary to secondary region to bring the system up quickly during DR

Usually recovery from backup can take longer, and the data loss may not be acceptable; that is, backup/restore as a DR mechanism has higher RTO and RPO. This mechanism may rely on geo-redundant storage (using Microsoft Azure backup or third-party backup integration), which can be restrictive when regional pairs don't have the same services chosen for the SAP landscape deployment.

The replication mechanism is more reliable and has better RPO/RTO; thus, it's better suited for DR of critical SAP systems. We'll discuss the details of this mechanism for the following SAP architectural components (for SAP NetWeaver and ABAP platform):

- SAP Central Services
- Application servers
- Database
- Shared storage

> **Backup versus Replication**
>
> Choice between backup and replication mechanisms isn't an all or nothing proposition. You can create a hybrid strategy with backup/restore for tier 2 and 3 systems and replication for tier 1 systems.
>
> There are trade-offs of time, effort, and cost for RTO/RPO. While it's not uncommon to achieve 15 minutes RPO and 2 hours RTO with replication, backup/restore can take hours and can have significantly higher data loss.

> **HA Configuration at the DR Site**
>
> Usually, we assume that there is no HA for the DR systems and, to that extent, the architecture discussed here doesn't show the HA configuration at the DR site. However, if your organization requires it, after the failover, you can use automation scripts to create additional servers and configuration. HA configuration at the DR site would be similar to what we've discussed in the previous section.

7.2.4 Disaster Recovery of SAP Components

Database DR using the replication mechanism is similar to HA, but it's done asynchronously so the primary system isn't affected. Each database has its own technology (as discussed in Section 7.1) and mechanism for replication, but the overall concept and configurations are similar. These replication mechanisms commonly have an RPO ≤ 15 minutes:

- SAP HANA: SAP HANA system replication
- SQL Server AlwaysOn
- Oracle: Data Guard
- DB2: HA/DR replication
- SAP ASE: Database replication

Figure 7.29 shows a setup with database HA in the primary region and DR in the secondary region.

> **Failover to DR**
>
> Unlike HA, DR failover isn't automatic because disaster must be declared by the organization based on the severity of the issue and time to recover. After the decision to proceed with the DR system is made, you can use automation to bring the systems up quickly at the DR site.

7   Resiliency

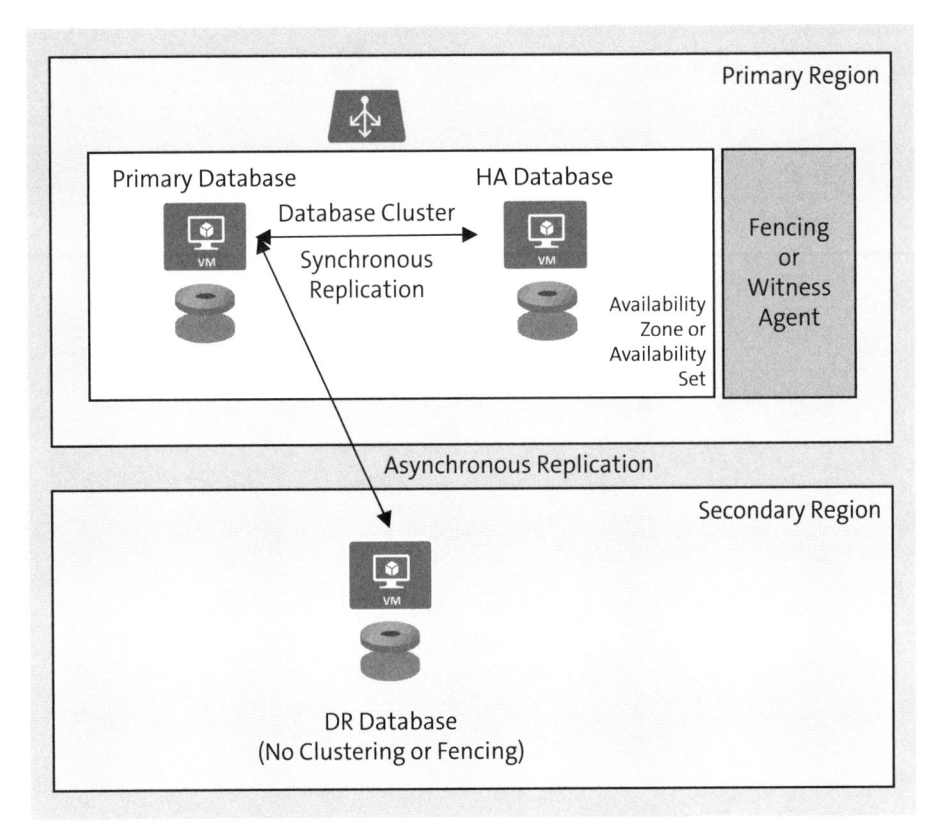

Figure 7.29 Database DR Setup Using the Replication Mechanism

7.2.5 Application Disaster Recover

Protection of SAP Central Services and application servers can be achieved using a Microsoft Azure native service called Microsoft Azure Site Recovery, which replicates VMs across regions (doesn't have to be Microsoft Azure paired regions) or availability zones at the block level. Microsoft Azure Site Recovery uses the Microsoft Azure automation account under the hood and stores data and snapshots in the Microsoft Azure Recovery Services vault. It provides features such as disk exclusion, multi-VM consistency, and failover orchestration.

Figure 7.30 shows a typical Microsoft Azure Site Recovery setup. Because the VMs aren't up and running while replication is in progress, you're not incurring cost for those, however, you still pay for storage, data transfer, and site recovery license fee (per instance). Given that compute cost is probably the biggest factor in the cost model, Microsoft Azure Site Recovery is significantly cheaper than any other solution that has VM up at the DR site. Microsoft Azure Site Recovery is availability set-, availability zone-, and proximity placement group-aware, meaning Microsoft Azure supports those in conjunction with Microsoft Azure Site Recovery.

Figure 7.30 Microsoft Azure Site Recovery as DR Setup

> **Microsoft Azure Site Recovery to Different Zone within the Same Region**
> Microsoft Azure also provides zone-to-zone Microsoft Azure Site Recovery, but because there is no guarantee of distance between data centers within a region, zone-to-zone Microsoft Azure Site Recovery isn't a robust DR solution.

Microsoft Azure Site Recovery provides crash-consistency (disk snapshot, every 5 mins) and application consistency (disk + memory snapshot, every hour). The first run may take a little longer because it does all the preparation work and full replication, and, from there, it's delta. If you're using Microsoft Azure portal to configure Microsoft Azure Site Recovery, you can do it either by going to a recovery vault or directly from the VM by selecting the DR blade. Figure 7.31 shows some of the steps that are performed as a part of replication enablement, and Figure 7.32 shows the infrastructure view from the Microsoft Azure portal.

7　Resiliency

Name	Status
Prerequisites check for enabling protection	✓ Successful
Installing Mobility Service and preparing target	⟳ In progress
Enable replication	
Starting initial replication	
Updating the provider states	

Figure 7.31 Microsoft Azure Site Recovery Internal Steps to Enable Replication

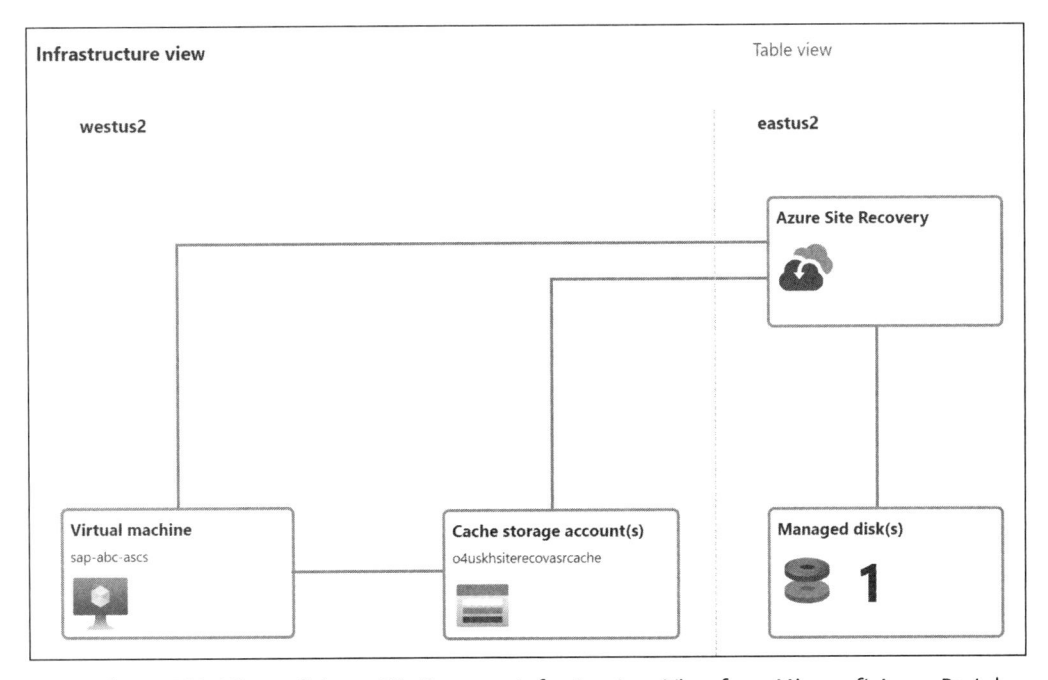

Figure 7.32 Microsoft Azure Site Recovery Infrastructure View from Microsoft Azure Portal

Once configured, you can also see the health status from the portal, as shown in Figure 7.33.

Essentials

Health and status
- Replication Health: ✓ Healthy
- Status: Protected
- RPO: 31 secs

Failover readiness
- Last successful Test Failover:
- Configuration issues: ✓ No issues
- Agent version: ✓ 9.34.5648.1
- Agent status: ✓ Healthy

Figure 7.33 Microsoft Azure Site Recovery Health Status

Other items of note are as follows:

- **Recovery time objective and recovery point objective**
  Site recovery RTO for VM failover is 2 hours, but there is no defined RPO because it depends on several factors such as distance between regions, replication health, chosen recovery point, and so on. However, both time to recover and data loss, in practice, are generally on the order of minutes, not hours.

- **Encryption and security**
  Microsoft Azure Site Recovery supports encryption in transit as well as in rest; it's certified for ISO 27001:2013, 27018, HIPAA, and DPA.

> **Microsoft Azure Site Recovery Support Matrix**
> You can find all the supported configurations and restrictions for Microsoft Azure Site Recovery in Microsoft Azure documentation at *https://docs.microsoft.com/en-us/azure/site-recovery/azure-to-azure-support-matrix*.

> **Microsoft Azure Policy to Enable Microsoft Azure Site Recovery**
> At the time of publication, the Microsoft Azure policy to automatically enable DR using Microsoft Azure Site Recovery configuration isn't supported.

7.2.6 Shared Storage in the Secondary Region

Following are the recommended methods for shared storage DR:

- Shared storage using S2D (for Windows) is supported by Microsoft Azure Site Recovery.

- NFS clusters using DRBD aren't supported by Microsoft Azure Site Recovery at the time of publication. Use tools such as rsync to copy the files from the primary to secondary region. This would require the NFS VM to be present in the secondary region.

- The Microsoft Azure NetApp Files CRR feature for Microsoft Azure, which uses NetApp SnapMirror technology to replicate Microsoft Azure NetApp Files volumes to another region, is used for DR. You can also use other mechanisms such as rsync when not using Microsoft Azure NetApp Files CRR.

- Cloud witness doesn't contain any data, so the recommendation is to create a new one in the target location (if HA after failover is in the plan).

Figure 7.34 shows a reference architecture (simplified to highlight the concepts) for the DR setup for SAP NetWeaver and ABAP platform.

7   Resiliency

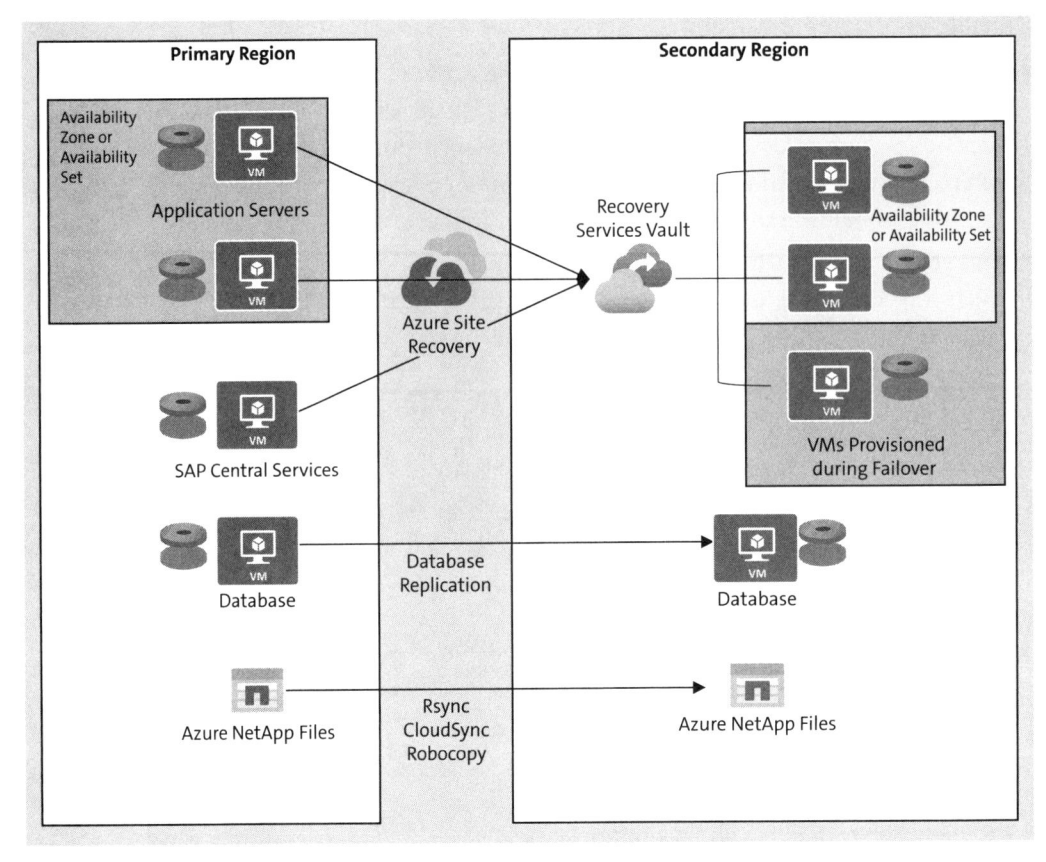

Figure 7.34 SAP Components DR Setup Illustration

> **Non-SAP NetWeaver or ABAP Platform SAP Systems**
> Other SAP systems, such as SAP BusinessObjects, use a similar approach for DR configuration.

7.2.7   Test and Drills

Part of business continuity is to prepare for disaster. But even after everything has been configured, there are unknowns in terms of organization process, documentation, coordination among teams, sequence of events, and so on. DR testing is the perfect way to understand the unknowns and test the knowns.

It's not uncommon for an organization to perform a DR test yearly or even every six months. Doing a DR test also allows you to learn and make continuous improvements not only to processes but also to configurations by identifying gaps and optimizations and thus reducing RTO and RPO.

For a complete DR test, each component needs to go through failover, be brought up, and be isolated so it doesn't impact the production run. Microsoft Azure Site Recovery provides recover plans that not only help with orchestration but also allow pre- and post-scripts, further streamlining the failover using automation. It also provides an option to perform a test failover. For systems not covered by Microsoft Azure Site Recovery, such as database and Microsoft Azure NetApp Files systems, you can either perform the steps individually or integrate them into pre- or post-scripts of the Microsoft Azure Site Recovery plan. Remember to clean up after the test and put the database replication back in place.

> **Cost-Optimized DR Setup**
>
> If you have production and nonproduction system in different regions, you can also dual purpose some of the nonproduction database servers for DR. Because the database doesn't need the same capacity during replication, it could run on another server hosting a nonproduction database. This approach reduces the compute process cost if you're replicating many large databases. In a DR event, that nonproduction system needs to shut down to run the production database, so plan accordingly.

7.3 Reference Architecture

So far, we've discussed all the building blocks for SAP on Microsoft Azure architecture. Putting it all together to get a holistic view helps with planning so you're not missing something obvious that causes rework later.

Making decisions about each area requires collaboration among several teams such as network, security, infrastructure, SAP, and so on, and one decision affects the other; for example, the number of SAP systems with HA/DR directly relates to the number of IPs required. Thinking about it holistically also saves you from going back and forth with evolving requirements. Following are some example of the areas that you need to think about (not a comprehensive list) and plan for:

- Storage
- Performance
- Connectivity
- Computation
- Subscription
- Security
- Network
- Resiliency

7   Resiliency

- Cost
- Backup
- Microsoft Azure services
- Identity and governance
- Operating system

Figure 7.35 shows a reference architecture for SAP on Microsoft Azure that combines all the building blocks.

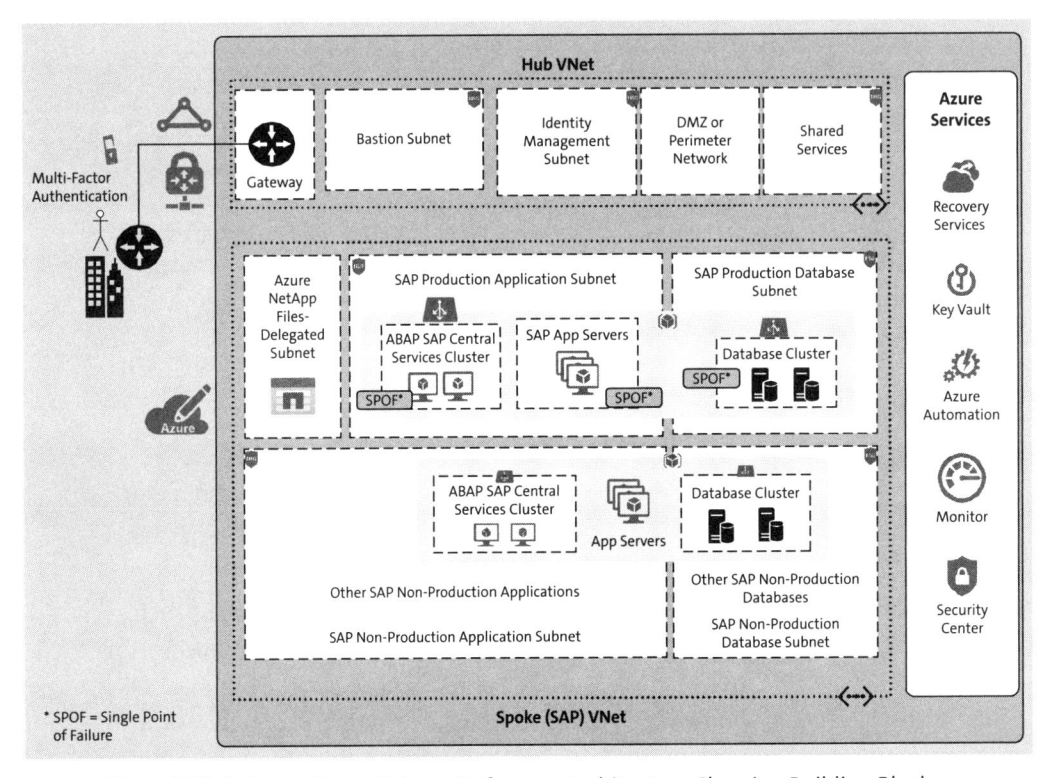

Figure 7.35 SAP on Microsoft Azure Reference Architecture Showing Building Blocks

If your production and nonproduction systems are in different regions, you can use database servers as dual purpose with replication and nonproduction active databases in a cost-optimized setup, as shown in Figure 7.36.

> **Tip**
> The right architecture for you is what aligns with your use case, not necessarily using everything that Microsoft Azure offers. Use the reference architectures as a starting point, and customize for your environment.

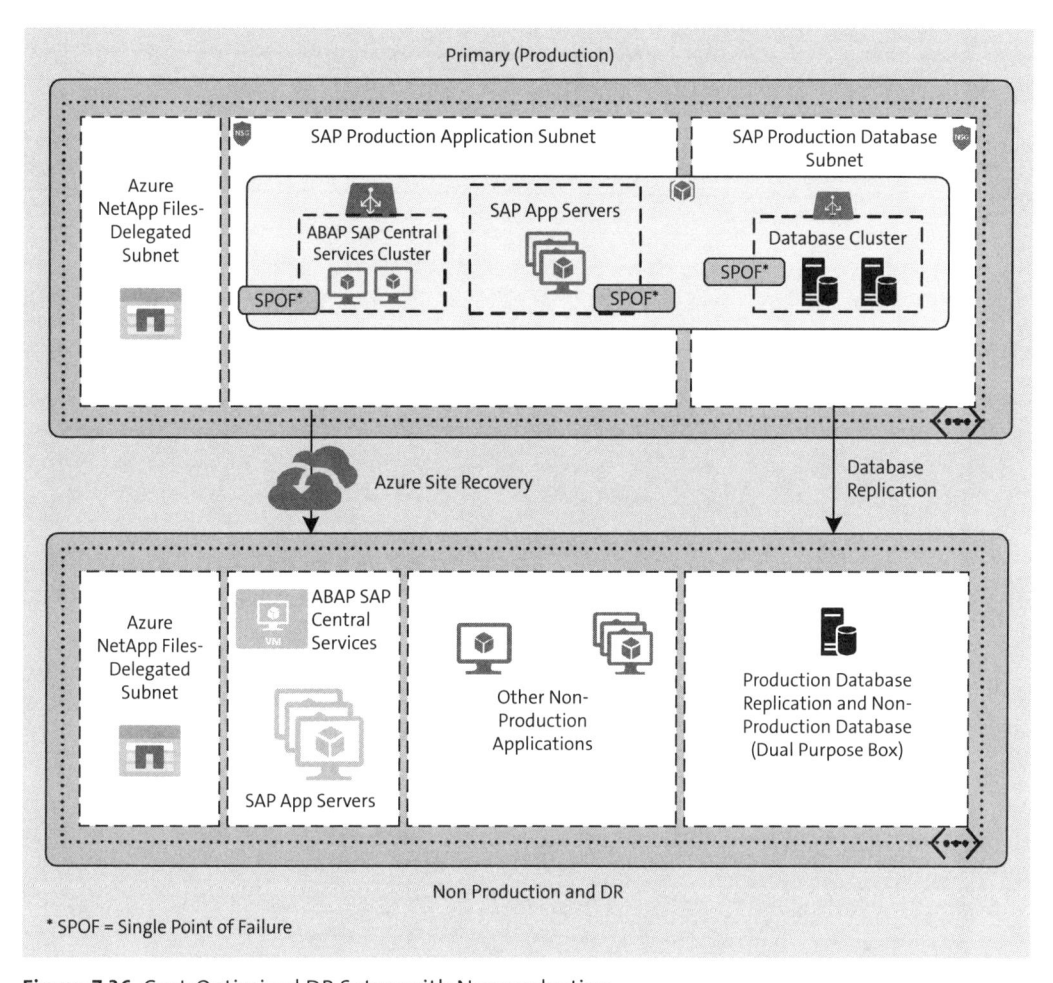

Figure 7.36 Cost-Optimized DR Setup with Nonproduction

7.4 Summary

The role of technology is to provide options, and you, as decision maker, translate business requirements into your technology architecture. Resiliency is a large part of the reliability discussion that you have control over; this chapter discussed the options for HA and DR for infrastructure (Microsoft Azure IaaS) as well as application. Remember, there is no application resiliency without infrastructure resiliency, but just having a resilient infrastructure doesn't make the application that way.

In the next chapter, we'll discuss business continuity in terms of the backup and restore architecture. We'll also cover Microsoft Azure tools for backups and snapshots.

Chapter 8
Backup Architecture and Mechanisms

From a business continuity point of view, backing up SAP data plays an important role. The ability to failover to a secondary region in case of a regional failover is critical for business; however, this shouldn't replace backup planning. A good business continuity plan should have established disaster recovery (DR) as well as backup processes.

Regular backups for operating systems (OSs), databases, and applications is a crucial component of managing infrastructure not only to restore in an event of failure or human error but also for other use cases such as DR and system copy.

The backup design approach should consider the following key items:

- What components need to be backed up versus what can be created new in an event of a failure
- Use cases of the backup and restore mechanism
- Length of time you can afford to have the system down in an event of failure or data corruption
- Amount of data can you afford to lose
- The budget available or financial considerations for the solution to consider along with all of the preceding items

This chapter will discuss these approaches in the context of the SAP environment and tools available in Microsoft Azure.

8.1 Backup and Restore Overview

Backup and restore go hand in hand, and the backup strategy is part of the overall success criteria. The restore approach should be tested as a part of the project to ensure that it adheres to the metrices set during requirements gathering, such as time to restore, retention, and so on.

Figure 8.1 highlights the elements of a backup/restore design.

8 Backup Architecture and Mechanisms

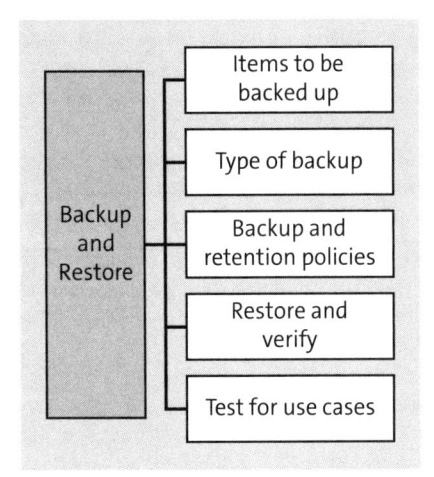

Figure 8.1 Backup and Restore Design Approach

For SAP NetWeaver and the ABAP stack, the components to back up are virtual machines (VMs), databases, and shared storage, as illustrated in Figure 8.2. Backup frequency and retention is organization dependent and sometimes governed by law such as for medical data retention.

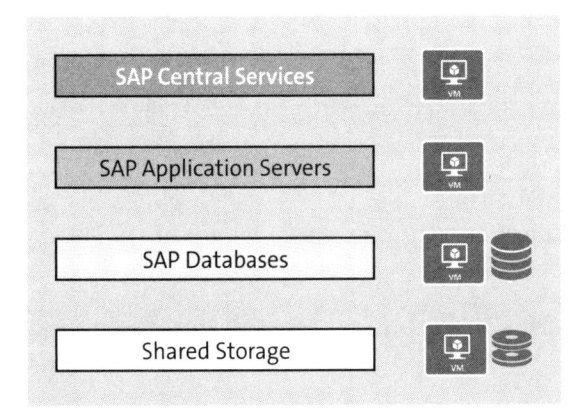

Figure 8.2 Components to Back Up for the SAP Landscape

Following are the most common use cases for backup/restore:

- Restore to the original system in case of failure or data corruption
- System copy/clone/restore
- DR by storing backups off-site

There are several mechanisms available for these use cases in Microsoft Azure, such as Microsoft Azure Backup for VMs, Microsoft Azure Backup for SQL Server and SAP HANA, and snapshots.

8.2 Backup Classifications

There are several types of backups and classifications. Following are some of the most common:

- **Online and offline**
  These are based on the system status while the backup is in progress. Online is used with the system running, whereas offline is used when the system is taken down for backup. Most of the SAP system backups are online with offline initiated in exceptional cases.

- **Full, incremental, and differential**
  Full backup copies all data, while differential and incremental backups use the full backup as a base and build on top of it. Incremental backups contain data that has changed *since* the *previous backup*, and differential backups contain all the data *since the last full backup*. The concept of full, incremental, and differential backups is illustrated in Figure 8.3.

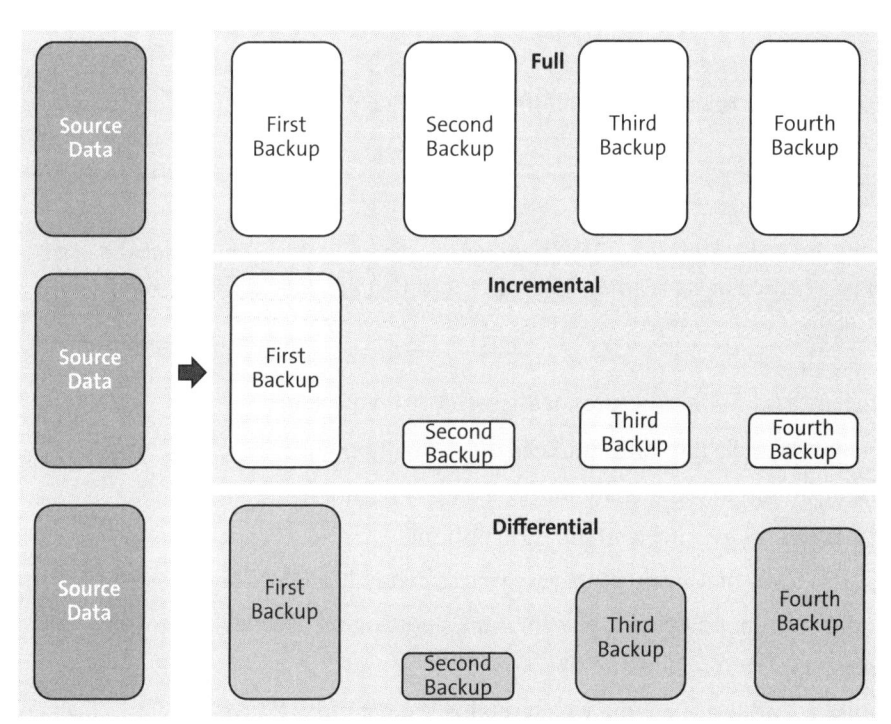

Figure 8.3 Full, Incremental, and Differential Backups

Note

When choosing among backup strategies, the first thing you need to find out is whether it's supported on Microsoft Azure. From there, the trade-offs are time taken for backup and restore, storage used, cost for the solution, and ease of recovery.

8   Backup Architecture and Mechanisms

8.3 Microsoft Azure Backup and Recovery Vault

Microsoft Azure Backup is a built-in service that can protect VMs, file shares, SQL Server, and SAP HANA databases, as illustrated in Figure 8.4. It stores the data in recovery vaults, which are used for backup as well as site recovery. The recovery services vault manages storage in the background and can use local and geo redundancy.

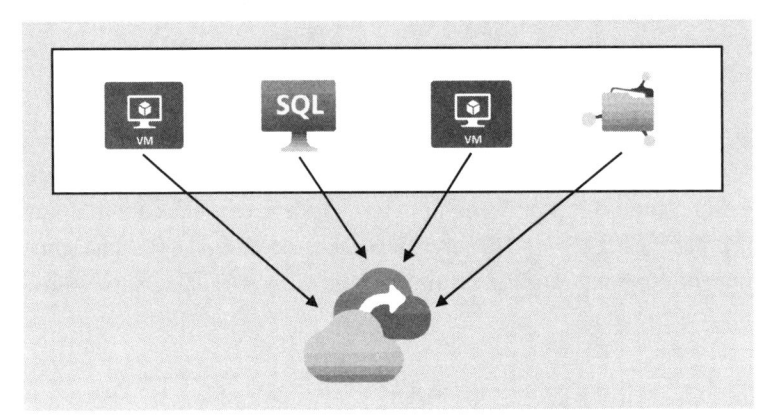

Figure 8.4 Microsoft Azure Backup for Different Components

> **Note**
>
> Microsoft Azure Backup also offers on-premise resource backup, which could be used either as a backup or DR solution for applications that you may choose to remain on-premise.

Following are a few salient features of Microsoft Azure Backup:

- Provides high scalability without need of any maintenance
- Manages storage automatically, and you pay for what you use
- Manages retention using configuration options
- Supports locally redundant storage as well as geo-redundant storage
- Provides built-in monitoring, alerting, and reporting capabilities
- Supports application-consistent backup
- Provides a soft delete option, which retains the data for 14 days even after backup deletion (accidental or malicious)

8.4 Virtual Machine Backup

SAP Central Services and application servers don't have constantly changing data like a database does and can be protected by Microsoft Azure VM backup. The backup process

8.4 Virtual Machine Backup

internally takes a snapshot of the VM and moves it to the vault with no performance impact on the server or application.

You can configure backup from the Microsoft Azure portal by going to the backup blade, as shown in Figure 8.5. If you don't already have a recovery vault and policy, it allows you to create a new one.

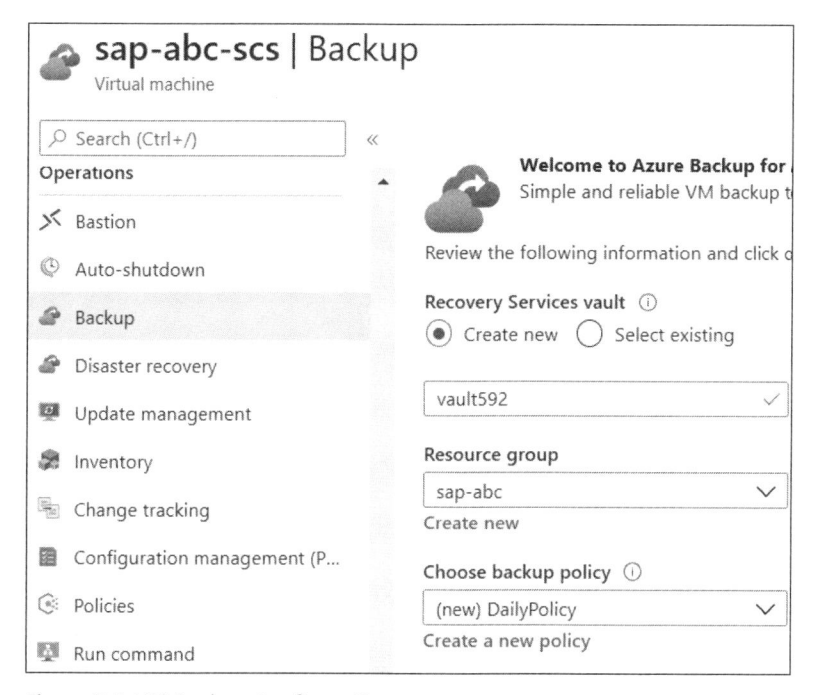

Figure 8.5 VM Backup Configuration

Backup policy triggers the backup, and it's optimized using parallel disk backup. In addition, for each disk, only the delta (data changed since the last backup) is transferred to the vault. Figure 8.6 shows the flow of steps for a VM backup.

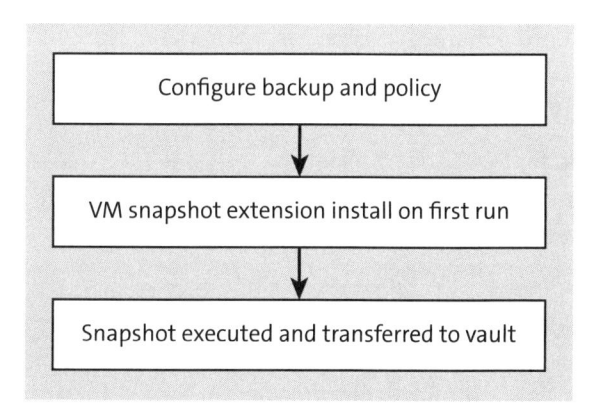

Figure 8.6 Microsoft Azure VM Backup Flow

> **Note**
> The snapshot transfer to the recovery vault may not be immediate depending on the load. For backups scheduled daily, the total backup time will be less than 24 hours.

8.5 Database Backup

For databases, the rate of change is high, so VM backup isn't an ideal solution. There are several ways to back up a database, and this chapter discusses the following mechanisms:

- Microsoft Azure Backup for SQL Server and SAP HANA
- Disk-based database backup
- Storage snapshot
- Third-party tools

8.5.1 Microsoft Azure Backup for SQL Server and SAP HANA

Support for SQL Server and SAP HANA backups is integrated into the Microsoft Azure Backup service.

SQL Server

Microsoft Azure Backup provides stream-based solution for SQL Server databases on the Windows OS that supports full, differential, and log backup using SQL native application programming interfaces (APIs). Log backups can be done with a frequency of 15 minutes, making this a low data loss use case.

Figure 8.7 illustrates the backup architecture; the solution uses a backup extension that gets installed for the VM as a part of configuration. It also uses your Windows account to connect to the database, and the account requires SQL sysadmin permission. The coordinator works with the SQL plug-in to start streaming the backup data directly to the recovery vault.

Microsoft Azure portal configuration for SQL Server backup has the same interface as the VM (see Figure 8.8), and after you select **SQL Server in Azure VM**, it discovers databases and highlights the configuration steps.

> **Restrictions**
> You should be familiar with the restrictions of Microsoft Azure Backup for SQL Server, such as supported regions, OSs, database size, number of files, and so on, which may limit your SAP landscape from using this solution.

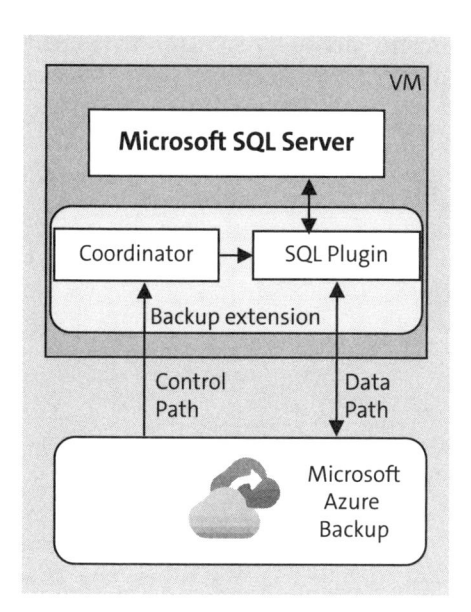

Figure 8.7 Architecture for Microsoft Azure Backup for SQL Server

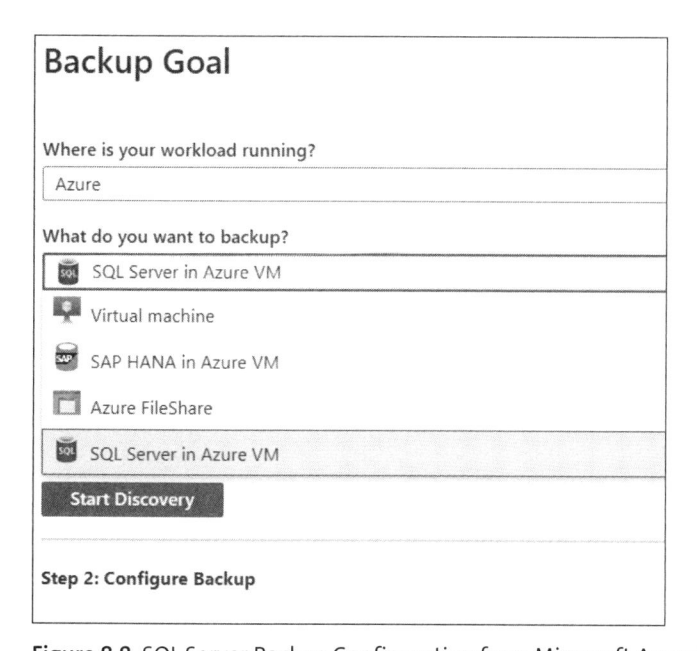

Figure 8.8 SQL Server Backup Configuration from Microsoft Azure Portal

SAP HANA

SAP HANA integration with Microsoft Azure Backup uses SAP-certified interface BACKINT, which uses SAP HANA native APIs to stream the data into the recovery vault. It supports full, differential, and log backups; daily database backup combined with 15-minute log backups enable recovery with minimal data loss.

8 Backup Architecture and Mechanisms

Figure 8.9 shows the architecture for Microsoft Azure Backup for SAP HANA. As a part of configuration, OS and database users are created to enable the backups.

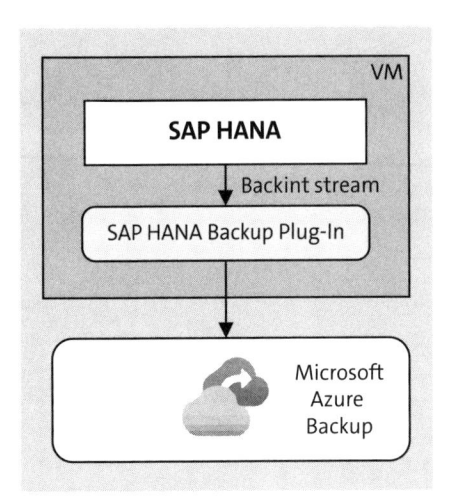

Figure 8.9 Microsoft Azure Backup for SAP HANA Architecture

The SAP HANA Backup plug-in maintains the schedule and communicates with the SAP HANA backup engine through BACKINT APIs. Full and differential backups ae initiated by the plug-in, while log backups are managed by the SAP HANA backup engine. The portal experience is consistent with Microsoft Azure Backup, as shown in Figure 8.10.

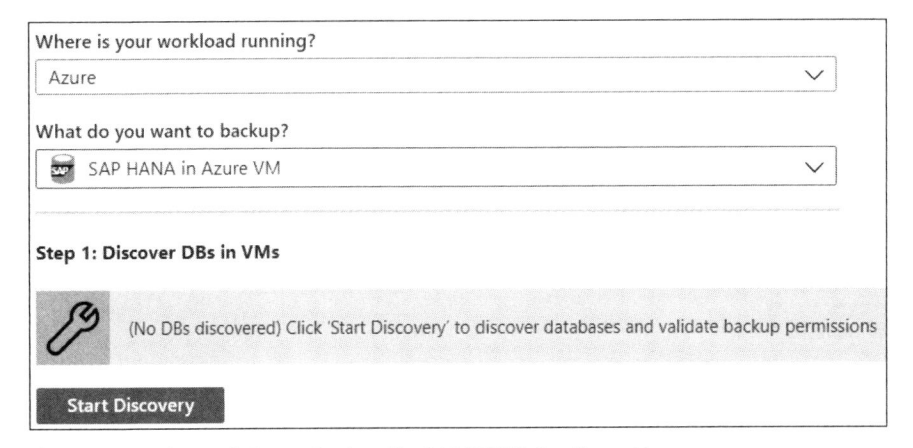

Figure 8.10 Microsoft Azure Backup for SAP HANA Configuration

Limitations

At the time of publication, Microsoft Azure Backup for SAP HANA is available only on VMs excluding SAP HANA on Azure (Large Instances). In addition, SAP HANA scale-up and dynamic tiering scenarios aren't supported. Be sure to review OS and database size support requirements.

> **Backup Management**
>
> Managing Microsoft Azure Backup for VMs and databases provides monitoring capabilities grouped with common management experience.

8.5.2 Virtual Machine Backup with and without Database File Systems

When you're backing up the database, it just ensures the recoverability of the database itself not necessarily the VM that the database resides on, so a separate VM backup is required. Because backup cost is based on the amount of storage, backing up the whole server, including database file systems, isn't only redundant (and possibly unrecoverable because database file systems won't be consistent) but also costs more. That's where the *selective disk backup* feature is useful as it lets you exclude database-related file systems when backing up the server using Microsoft Azure Backup.

On the other hand, if you're using SAP HANA with Microsoft Azure premium disk, you can use pre- and postscripts (SAP HANA commands) to put the database in a consistent state and execute an application-consistent VM backup. Database consistency management is the key when working with database servers.

> **Write Accelerator Disks**
>
> If you're using write accelerator-enabled disks for SAP HANA logs, the snapshot doesn't guarantee the consistency for logs. Recovery using logs from Microsoft Azure Backup will be required.

8.5.3 Disk-Based Database Backup

All the databases, including in-memory ones such as SAP HANA, support backup on a file system either via graphical user interface (GUI) tools or the command line. You can either use local storage or shared storage, such as Microsoft Azure NetApp Files for SAP HANA backup; from there, copy or move to a long-term storage based on your retention policy, as illustrated in Figure 8.11.

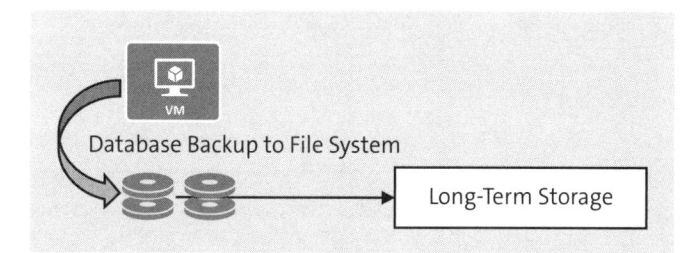

Figure 8.11 Database Backup to File System (Disk)

8   Backup Architecture and Mechanisms

This method is simple, convenient, and doesn't require any expensive licensed products or specialized skillset. However, it has its own challenges, and you'll have to figure out how to do the following either using custom scripts or manually:

- Retention management
- Restore process
- Other administrative tasks

This is better suited for some use cases than others, such as system refresh—an ad hoc backup to disk after certain data events can be a winner!

> **Cost Optimization**
> When using blob storage to store backups for longer duration, use cool and archival access tiers.

8.5.4 Storage Snapshot

With smaller databases, the backup times are manageable so there is no performance impact, and full backups can be done more frequently. For backup and restore of large databases, storage snapshot can be a valuable tool.

Microsoft Azure premium disk and Microsoft Azure NetApp Files support storage-level snapshots. To ensure application-consistent snapshots, the database has to support it as well because disk snapshots aren't application aware. It involves database-specific preparation, and SAP HANA provides native SQL commands to do that. Figure 8.12 shows the steps to perform an SAP HANA snapshot combining SQL native commands and storage technology. Snapshot with Microsoft Azure NetApp Files as SAP HANA storage follows a similar pattern and also supports compression and deduplication.

Prepare
- Create internal database snapshot
- Freeze XFS file system

Snapshot
- Create data snapshot using Microsoft Azure tools/storage commands

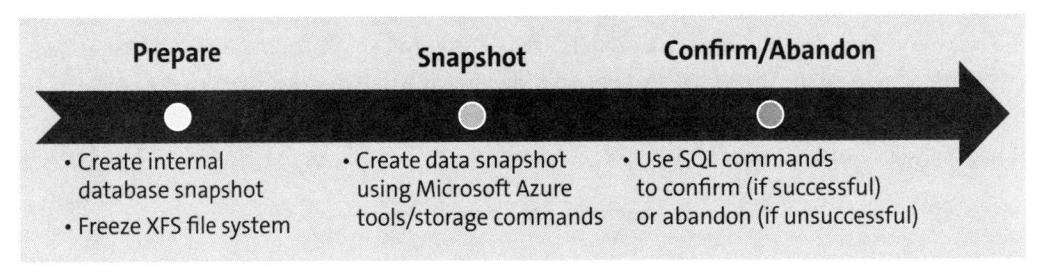

Confirm/Abandon
- Use SQL commands to confirm (if successful) or abandon (if unsuccessful)

Figure 8.12 SAP HANA Storage Snapshot

> **Tip**
> Snapshot doesn't provide an integrity check at the block level, so SAP doesn't recommend snapshots as the only backup mechanism. Rather, it should be combined with

184

other backup mechanisms. For example, you can do snapshots more frequently, say daily, combined with a weekly file level backup.

Snapshot Compatibility
Microsoft Azure follows SAP guidelines for SAP HANA snapshot compatibility. For example, multitenant snapshot isn't supported until SAP HANA 2.0 SPS 4, which is applicable for Microsoft Azure as well.

8.6 Shared Disk Backup

SAP environments use shared disks for high availability, interface files, profile directory, and so on, and the backup of those are crucial for full system recovery. Depending on the configuration, you may have to employ different backup and retention mechanisms. If you're using a Network File System (NFS) server, backup of the VM is required versus if you're using Microsoft Azure NetApp Files, snapshots are an option as well.

Another method is to copy the data to a replicated geo-redundant storage or zone-redundant storage using tools such as AzCopy or rsync.

Tip
Don't assume that if you're using a platform as a service (PaaS) solution such as Microsoft Azure NetApp Files, the backups are automatically taken care of by Microsoft Azure. You're responsible to ensure that the data is being backed up and configured to be sent to a potentially different location.

8.7 Third-Party Tools

If none of the other backup methods meet your requirements, or your organization has an enterprise-level backup solution that you want to use for SAP as well, third-party solutions such as Commvault would be a good fit. For SAP databases, third-party tools use the BACKINT interface and are also compatible with snapshot management.

The advantage of third-party tools also includes flexibility, such as the Commvault integration with SAP Landscape Management and the same software for multiple database types (SQL Server, SAP HANA, DB2, Oracle) and VMs, additional features such as incremental backup support, and the same experience as on-premise. Deduplication and compression features are other considerations as well, which aren't supported by Microsoft Azure Backup for SAP HANA at the time of publication. These solutions also have built-in retention management.

8 Backup Architecture and Mechanisms

Figure 8.13 shows the use cases supported by Commvault for the SAP landscape on Microsoft Azure.

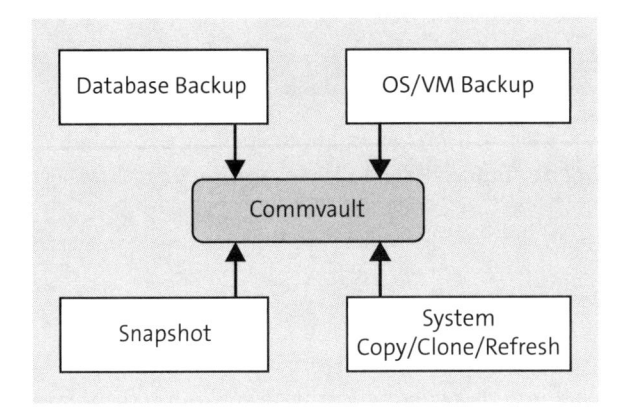

Figure 8.13 Commvault Integration with Microsoft Azure Use Cases

8.8 Backup and Retention Policy

When you configure the backup for the first time, there are prerequisites and configurations; after those are completed, the backup can be kicked off at a regular interval without much intervention. However, backup is a regular activity, and managing the frequency and retention can be more involved than anticipated if you're not using a tool that has built-in options to do that.

For Microsoft Azure Backup, frequency and retention management is built-in to the policy, as shown in Figure 8.14. After you create a new policy, you can also assign the same one to subsequent VMs and databases. There are a couple of items to keep in mind, such as the following:

- Supported backup frequency is once a day, at the time of publication.
- Backup can be done at the same region where resources are located.
- You can't move data between different vaults and vaults across different subscriptions.
- Policy doesn't account for daylight savings time, so unless you've configured UTC, ensure either the schedule is adjusted or the hour difference doesn't have any impact on the operations.
- Encryption in transit and at rest is supported.
- Using more than one backup solution, such as Microsoft Azure Backup and third-party tools, at the same time for the same resource isn't recommended.
- If you make any change in retention in an existing policy, it will affect not only the new backup retentions but also the existing recovery points.

Backup policy

Policy name *
ABC-VM-Backup-Policy

Backup schedule

Frequency *	Time *	Timezone *
Daily	3:00 AM	(UTC) Coordinated Universal Time

Instant Restore

Retain instant recovery snapshot(s) for

2 Day(s)

Retention range

☑ Retention of daily backup point.

At	For	
3:00 AM	7	Day(s)

☑ Retention of weekly backup point.

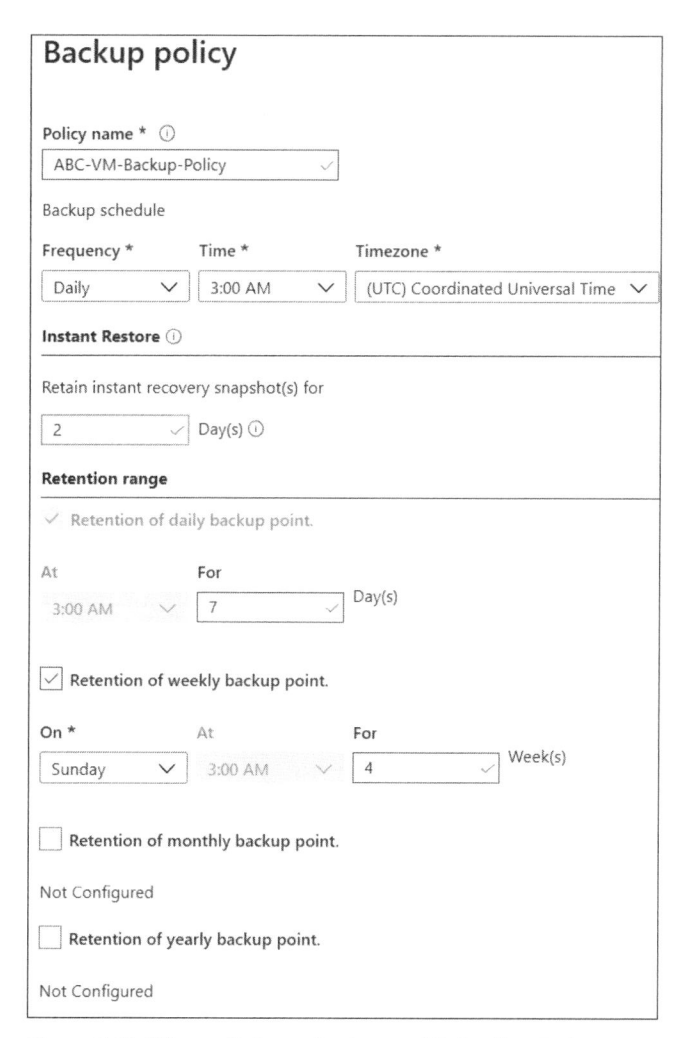

On *	At	For	
Sunday	3:00 AM	4	Week(s)

☐ Retention of monthly backup point.
Not Configured

☐ Retention of yearly backup point.
Not Configured

Figure 8.14 Microsoft Azure Backup and Retention Policy

8.9 Restore and Recovery

Depending on the scenario, such as failure, error, or other use case, the level of restore and recovery is different. You may need just the VM, database, a few files, or everything. You also need to know your organization's tolerance for data loss to make recovery decisions. If there is a logical error, then you need an older recovery point than when the error occurred.

8.9.1 Virtual Machine Restore

Depending on whether a VM has encrypted disks, Microsoft Azure Backup has several restore options as shown in Figure 8.15 (encrypted disk doesn't support file-level restore).

8 Backup Architecture and Mechanisms

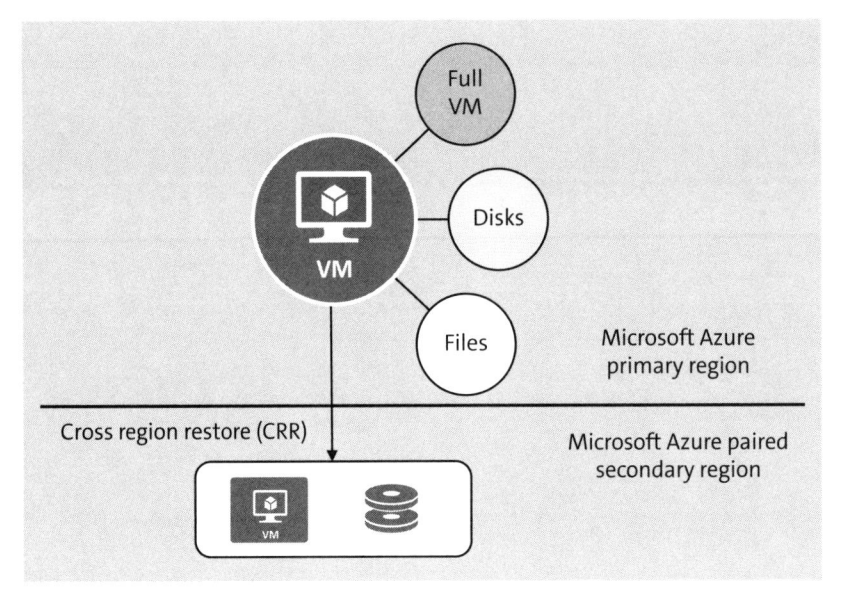

Figure 8.15 Microsoft Azure VM Restore Options

Restore can either be in the same region on the original or alternate VM if failure occurred because of corruption, logical error, and so on, or it can be to a Microsoft Azure paired region (if enabled) for disaster events or drills. The cross-region restore feature uses geo-redundant storage under the hood managed by Microsoft Azure Backup. From Microsoft Azure portal, the restore options can be invoked from the backup blade of a VM (or from a recovery vault), as shown in Figure 8.16.

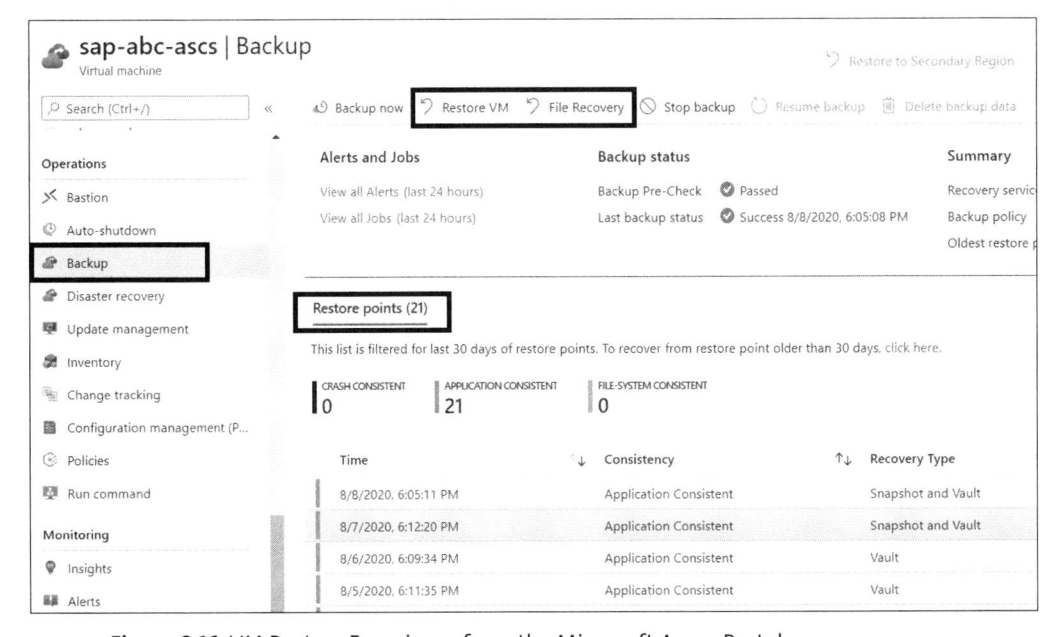

Figure 8.16 VM Restore Experience from the Microsoft Azure Portal

8.9 Restore and Recovery

> **Instant Restore**
>
> Microsoft Azure Backup has the option—called instant restore—to retain the VM snapshot locally up to five days, which significantly reduces the restore time. Instant restore has an impact on storage cost, but the feature can't be disabled; if you don't anticipate using this feature, set it to one day to minimize cost.

8.9.2 SQL Server and SAP HANA

Database restores are more involved because you can do point-in-time recovery using logs. For SQL Server as well as SAP HANA, log backups can be done as frequently as 15 minutes. Microsoft Azure Backup understands point-in-time recovery and presents you with an option to do so, as highlighted in Figure 8.17. Similar to the VM restore, there are options to either override the existing database or restore at an alternate location.

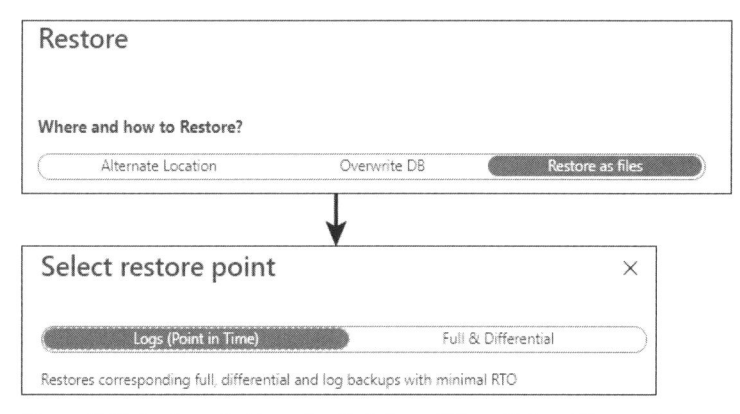

Figure 8.17 Restore Options for Database When Using Microsoft Azure Backup

Another useful option is **Restore as files**, which comes in handy when you're trying to restore the database in a different subscription or region, such as a system copy if your nonproduction systems are in a separate subscription.

> **Cross-Region Replication**
>
> Microsoft Azure Backup also supports cross-region restore for both SQL Server and SAP HANA backups.

8.9.3 Testing for all Use Cases

Whether you're using the same tool across the board for backups or a combination of different tools based on use case, you should test and document the backup, restore, and recovery processes for all the use cases identified in scope.

8   Backup Architecture and Mechanisms

There may be database-specific steps that you'll need to perform; for example, if you restore as files for the SAP HANA database, you'll need to recreate the backup catalog (using SAP HANA executable `hdbbackupdiag`), which should be documented and operationalized.

> **Third-Party Tools**
> When using third-party tools, refer to the product-specific restore/recovery procedures.

8.10 Management and Reporting

Microsoft Azure Backup provides management functions such as triggering ad hoc backups, alerting, and reporting. You can do a lot of activities from the resource itself (e.g., the VM), but the recovery vault shows a centralized view of all the items configured for that vault and is easier to navigate.

Figure 8.18 highlights some of the common tasks. Alerting is integrated with Microsoft Azure Monitor and provides same experience for alert configuration and action items through action groups.

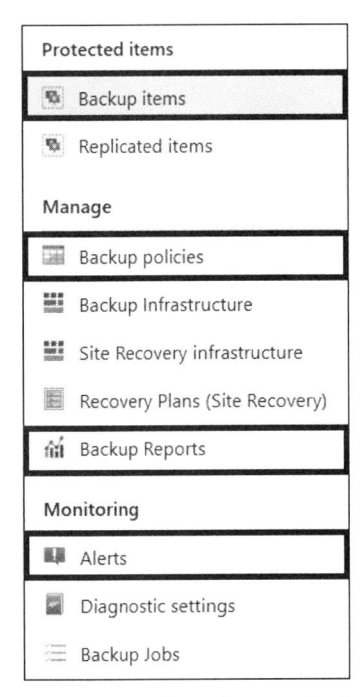

Protected items
- Backup items
- Replicated items

Manage
- Backup policies
- Backup Infrastructure
- Site Recovery infrastructure
- Recovery Plans (Site Recovery)
- Backup Reports

Monitoring
- Alerts
- Diagnostic settings
- Backup Jobs

Figure 8.18 Microsoft Azure Backup Management Options

8.11 Summary

Backups aren't fruitful unless you can restore them, so it's important to do a test periodically and improve the process as you go. This chapter discussed backup and restore options for all SAP components and use cases. Choice of tool depends on several factors, and it should align with your organization strategy. Use native Microsoft Azure tools when possible, and supplement with others as appropriate.

In the next chapter, we'll talk about how automation can be used to deploy and manage infrastructure in Microsoft Azure and integration with SAP installation and maintenance.

Chapter 9
Automation

The top three things you need to do for consistent on-time SAP deployments and streamlined operations are automate, automate, and automate. Gone are the days when SAP provisioning used to take weeks and databases went down because it took too long to increase the disk space. Automation is the new currency to buy (save) time in the cloud world.

Automation comes in various forms, and the cloud became the breeding ground for infrastructure-related automation. In the SAP on Microsoft Azure deployment context, when we talk about automation, it's about how to use scripts, tools, and technology to orchestrate and execute tasks in the background. Here are a few examples:

- Microsoft Azure Resource Manager (ARM) templates, Terraform, or Ansible scripts to create and configure virtual machines (VMs), storage, networks, and so on
- Microsoft Azure automation accounts to run custom scripts based on monitoring triggers
- SAP Cloud Appliance Library to deploy a solution in your Microsoft Azure subscription
- SAP Landscape Management to perform system copy tasks

Before getting into the how, you should understand the why, that is, what's the motivation behind using automation. Figure 9.1 shows the benefits. Keep in mind that it's not an all or nothing proposition; while it takes time to build automation capabilities, you don't have to wait for it to be perfect. Start small and integrate into the build process.

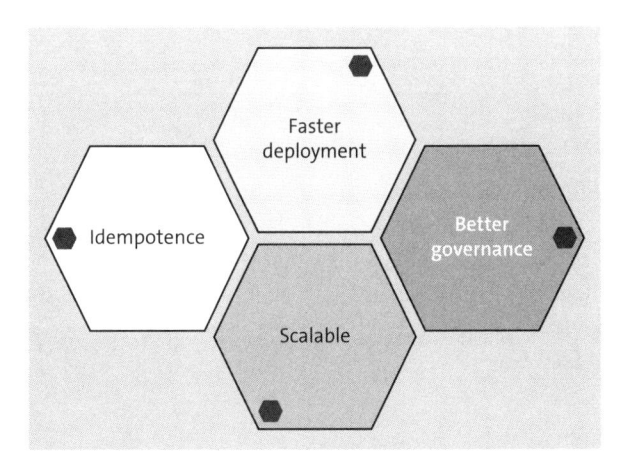

Figure 9.1 Advantages of Using Automation

9   Automation

When thinking about automation, consider the whole scope, including what can't be automated or can only be semi-automated and how to integrate that into the workflow. Figure 9.2 shows the areas that the automation scope will cover.

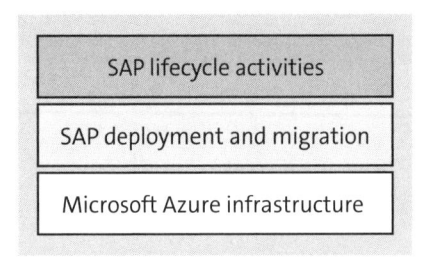

Figure 9.2 Overview of Automation Scope

9.1 Infrastructure as Code

Infrastructure as code (IaC) is the concept that fuels the automation journey: it's a mechanism to deploy and manage the IT infrastructure as code rather than traditional manual processes. Cloud provides an application programming interface (API) for services making IaC implementation possible. Figure 9.3 helps visualize this better by showing how code can turn into infrastructure components.

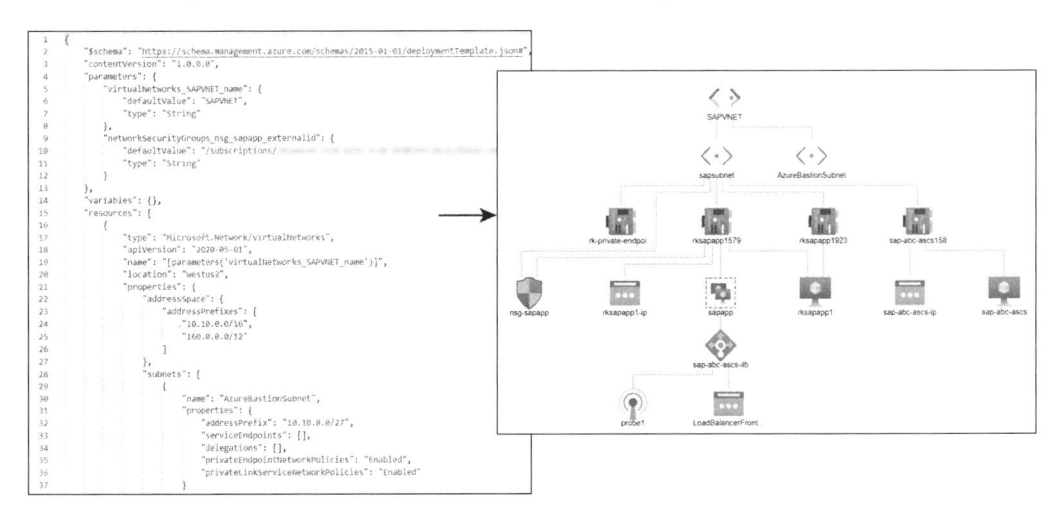

Figure 9.3 Infrastructure Creation from Code

Idempotence is an important part of IaC, which means regardless of how many times the script is run, the status in the beginning and the end state will have the same configuration. Figure 9.4 illustrates the workflow to create Microsoft Azure resources using code (automation scripts or templates).

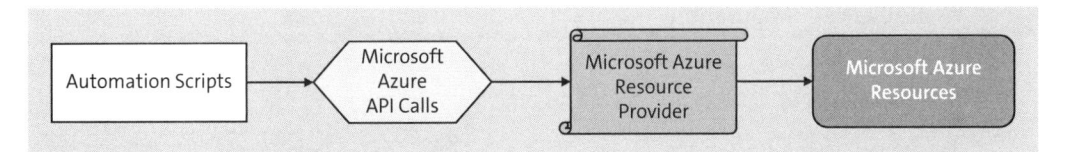

Figure 9.4 IaC Workflow to Create Resources

> **Microsoft Azure Resource Provider**
> In Microsoft Azure, the resource lifecycle is managed by a resource provider, so when code is triggered to, say, provision a VM, it makes a request to resource provider Microsoft.Compute, which deploys the machine. resource providers are registered at the subscription level and can be managed from the resource provider blade in the subscription. If you have contributor or owner access to the subscription, the resource providers are registered on the first request, and everyone can use it from there on. If you just have access to a resource group, and a resource provider isn't registered, you may not be able to provision the resource provided by the resource provider.

9.2 Automation Use Cases

From the automation scope, you should drill down to the use cases that you'll be automating and how they will incrementally add to one another. For example, not every VM you create will have SAP HANA installed, but every SAP HANA installation requires a VM; therefore, the SAP HANA install is an incremental automation that tacks on to the VM. This also highlights the importance of modularity. Modular templates are like Legos in that they can be independently created, adjusted, and added together to achieve the final output.

> **Note**
> At the time of publication, SAP HANA on Azure (Large Instances) has limited automation options, and you can't use either code or the Microsoft Azure portal to provision those options.

9.2.1 Infrastructure Deployment

The infrastructure groups a lot of items together, and, depending on the scenario, you may not need all the components. Some of the common elements are as follows:

- Compute (VM), storage, network
- Load balancer
- Network File System (NFS)

9   Automation

- Resilience configuration
- Microsoft Azure Site Recovery
- Governance

The automation goes beyond initial deployment into configuration as well, such as managing load balancing configuration to disaster recovery (DR) testing, all of which can be performed using API calls.

9.2.2   Application Deployment

Application deployment includes database and SAP application components. Installation using scripts is also called *unattended install* or *silent install*. The underlying idea is to use a configuration file to provide user inputs with the install binaries. Most of the databases, including Microsoft SQL Server and SAP HANA, support silent installations. SAP software provisioning manager (SWPM) supports unattended mode as well.

Now the question is how you get the configuration file, and the answer may seem circular—you get the configuration file from your first manual install. During the very first time when you go through all the options and it lets you review the inputs, the configuration file is generated that is used by the installer:

- *.cfg* for SAP HANA
- *.ini* for SQL Server
- *.params* for SAP

After you have the configuration file, you can either complete the installation or cancel and trigger it using scripts by supplying the file. The recommendation is to complete the manual installation to ensure that all the prerequisites are met. If you run into an issue, it can be sorted out and the fix implemented going forward. Figure 9.5 shows the overall workflow for an unattended install.

Manual first install → Harvest config file → Automated installs ↻ Repeat

Figure 9.5 Workflow for Unattended Installs

For databases, you can often deploy the latest or target release right from the beginning; for example, SAP HANA 2.0 SP 05 can be installed directly instead of installing SP 02 and upgrading the database. This isn't true for SAP application versions; to get to the latest version, you need to use the Software Update Manager (SUM) tool after the initial installation. Alternatively, SAP supports up-to-date installation using a stack XML file, which can be performed in an automated fashion after you get the configuration file using the Maintenance Planner option.

> **New Install versus Migration**
>
> When doing a migration for SAP, you bring your own database content, which is a consideration for automating the overall process. In that scenario, you'll have to split the migration process into smaller parts and try to automate individually and integrate with manual process where needed. For example, if it's a homogenous migration with database replication, there are more automation opportunities for cutover than if it's a heterogenous migration using parallel export/import. Some steps are always manual such as requesting an SAP license from the SAP Marketplace with the VM hardware ID.

9.2.3 Infrastructure and Application Lifecycle

After everything is up and running on Microsoft Azure, lifecycle management tasks become the norm. Some of the common tasks are as follows:

- Operating system (OS) patching
- SAP kernel update
- SAP and OS parameter tuning
- Snoozing SAP when not in use (nonproduction)
- SAP system copy

Automation for each use case should be considered, and, if you're in the immutable architecture camp, where you don't patch a server but rather create a new one and decommission old ones, you need to consider the impact on application components as well. In Chapter 12, we discuss how to achieve operational tasks using the immutable architecture.

9.3 Automation Tools

Because automation has a broad definition, the tools range from the command-line interface (CLI) to enterprise software such as Terraform. Each tool has its pros and cons, and some are a better fit for particular use cases.

9.3.1 Microsoft Azure Cloud Shell

Microsoft Azure Cloud Shell is a CLI to manage Microsoft Azure resources. It goes through an authentication process and lets you customize the subscription you want to use. You can either access it using a browser by going to *http://shell.azure.com* or from Microsoft Azure portal; Microsoft Azure Cloud Shell allows you to use both bash and PowerShell (not at the same time).

Microsoft Azure CLI is a simple yet powerful tool, as shown in Figure 9.6, in which a few lines of declarative code can create a VM in minutes. As you may have noticed, there are a lot of other parameters that VMs can have, such as region and VM stock-keeping unit, which weren't provided, and Microsoft Azure used default values for those. Of course, you can still provide those options from the command line.

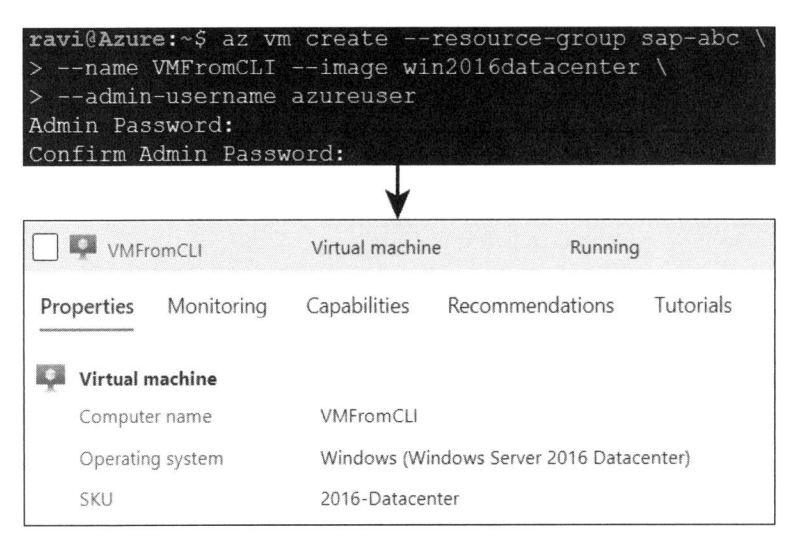

```
ravi@Azure:~$ az vm create --resource-group sap-abc \
> --name VMFromCLI --image win2016datacenter \
> --admin-username azureuser
Admin Password:
Confirm Admin Password:
```

| VMFromCLI | Virtual machine | Running |

Properties Monitoring Capabilities Recommendations Tutorials

Virtual machine
Computer name   VMFromCLI
Operating system   Windows (Windows Server 2016 Datacenter)
SKU   2016-Datacenter

Figure 9.6 Microsoft Azure CLI Commands to Create a VM

CLI commands are useful to quickly deploy and terminate resources, but not all commands are idempotent, so you may end up with duplicate resources when a script is executed multiple times. To mitigate that, you can add a code to check for existing resources before provisioning.

> **Tip**
> Microsoft Azure Cloud Shell can also be deployed in a virtual network (VNet) so you can connect via Secure Shell (SSH) to a VM with only a private IP or perform other tasks restricted within a VNet.

9.3.2 Microsoft Azure Resource Manager Template

ARM templates are the way to implement IaC in Microsoft Azure; the template is a JavaScript Object Notation (JSON) file that defines the infrastructure components. You trigger the whole deployment once, and it manages the orchestration and does parallel execution when creating nondependent resources. Other salient features include the following:

- You need to use the *declarative approach* to specify the final desired state, and ARM handles the details behind the scenes to provision the resources (unlike the *imperative approach* where you have to provide step-by-step instructions).

- ARM has out-of-the-box validation before the resources are created, and all the provisioning can be tracked from Microsoft Azure deployment history.
- You can use Microsoft Azure policy and blueprints with ARM templates.

Listing 9.1 is an example of an ARM template to create a storage account.

```
"resources": [
  {
    "type": "Microsoft.Storage/storageAccounts",
    "name": "[variables('storageAccountName')]",
    "location": "[parameters('location')]",
    "sku": {
      "name": "[parameters('storageAccountType')]"
    },
    "kind": "StorageV2",
    "properties": {}
  }
]
```

Listing 9.1 ARM Code Example for New Storage Account

A low code approach to creating resources in Microsoft Azure is to download the template from the Microsoft Azure portal for already-provisioned resources, as shown in Figure 9.7, and then use that as a base to create similar resources by making necessary changes.

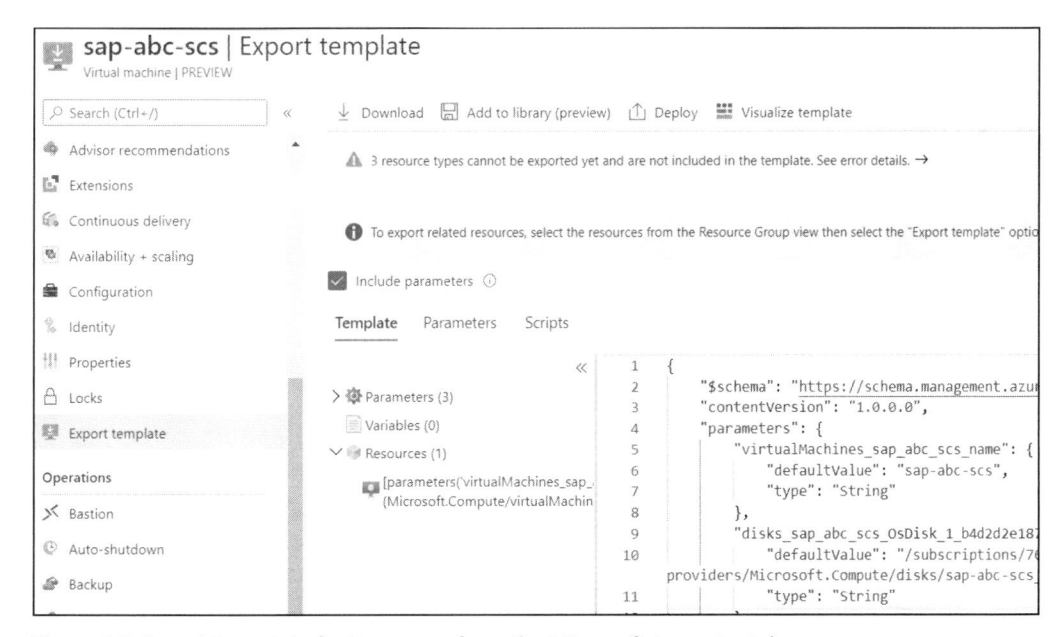

Figure 9.7 Export Template for Resources from the Microsoft Azure Portal

9 Automation

> **ARM API**
>
> ARM is the provisioning engine in Microsoft Azure that is exposed as an API that the template uses to create and manage resources.

9.3.3 Terraform

While ARM templates can be used only with Microsoft Azure, Terraform is a cloud-agnostic tool with a lot of similar features such as being declarative and has orchestration capabilities. It uses YAML (which cyclically stands for YAML Ain't Markup Language) format for the code as opposed to JSON used by ARM templates. Under the hood, it uses azurearm as the provider, which understands the API interaction with Microsoft Azure. It also provides error handling as well as validation.

Listing 9.2 is an example of a Terraform template to create a resource group and storage account.

```
provider "azurerm" {
}
resource "azurerm_resource_group" "RGTest" {
  name     = "SAP-Production"
  location = "East US"
}
resource "azurerm_storage_account" "StorageTest" {
  name                     = "${var.storageAccountName}"
  resource_group_name      = "${azurerm_resource_group.testrg.name}"
  location                 = "${var.region}"
  account_tier             = "${var.tier}"
  account_replication_type = "${var.replicationType}"
}
```

Listing 9.2 Terraform Code Example to Create a New Resource Group and Storage Account

Terraform connects to Microsoft Azure using the service principal, which should have correct access to provision and manage resources. It stores all the resource details in a flat file called a state file and uses that to determine new deployments and changes when a template is executed.

> **Template versus Script**
>
> CLI or PowerShell scripts are most useful for doing smaller tasks, whereas templates such as ARM or Terraform takes the overall deployment, versioning, and repeatability to an elevated level.

9.3.4 Orchestration versus Configuration Management

Tools such as Terraform, ARM, and CLI do a good job of provisioning, managing, and deleting the infrastructure, but when you need to do something within the infrastructure, such as installing software in a VM, that spans into configuration management, and there are other tools (e.g., Ansible, Chef, Puppet) that are better at configuration management. Figure 9.8 shows an example of tools for each area.

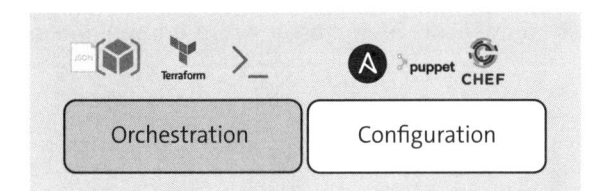

Figure 9.8 Tools for Orchestration versus Configuration Management

In the SAP deployment context, provisioning of infrastructure components such as compute, network, and storage can be done using orchestration tools, whereas OS configuration and database and application install require configuration management tools. There may be overlap in cross-functionalities of the tools, but, in general, it's a good idea to pick a tool from each area for the best experience.

Microsoft Azure Automation

Microsoft Azure's cloud-based automation can be used to process, configure, and update management for both Windows- and Linux-based systems within Microsoft Azure's framework for role-based access control, governance, Key Vault, and so on.

It executes runbooks to achieve those tasks and supports multiple languages such as PowerShell and Python. Figure 9.9 shows the types of runbooks that can be created in automation accounts. Several Microsoft Azure services, such as Microsoft Azure Site Recovery, use automation accounts in the background.

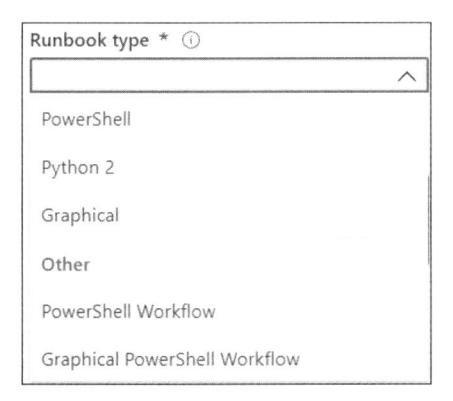

Figure 9.9 Microsoft Azure Runbook Types

9 Automation

Golden Operating System Images

Most organizations don't just pick a marketplace image to deploy their SAP solutions; instead, they customize the image with the organization compliance and security standards. Add SAP and Microsoft Azure recommendations to it, and the process becomes complex to say the least. Microsoft Azure Image Builder, built on HashiCorp Packer, lets you customize an image and store it in the Microsoft Azure shared image gallery. You can patch images as well as connect to existing configuration management servers such as Chef or Puppet. Figure 9.10 shows components of Microsoft Azure Image Builder, which is represented by a template.

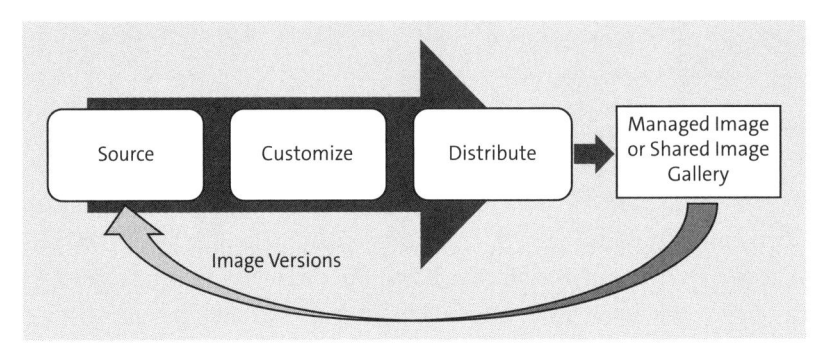

Figure 9.10 Components of Microsoft Azure Image Builder

9.3.5 SAP Landscape Management

A common limitation of third-party and open-source tools is application awareness. In the context of SAP, none of the IaC tools effectively perform lifecycle management steps of the application. SAP Landscape Management addresses that gap: it's an orchestration and automation solution by SAP for centralized management of SAP systems.

Figure 9.11 highlights some of the automation capabilities, and notably there is a Microsoft Azure connector that helps manage Microsoft Azure resources (refer to SAP Note 2343511 for more details about the connector's requirements and prerequisites).

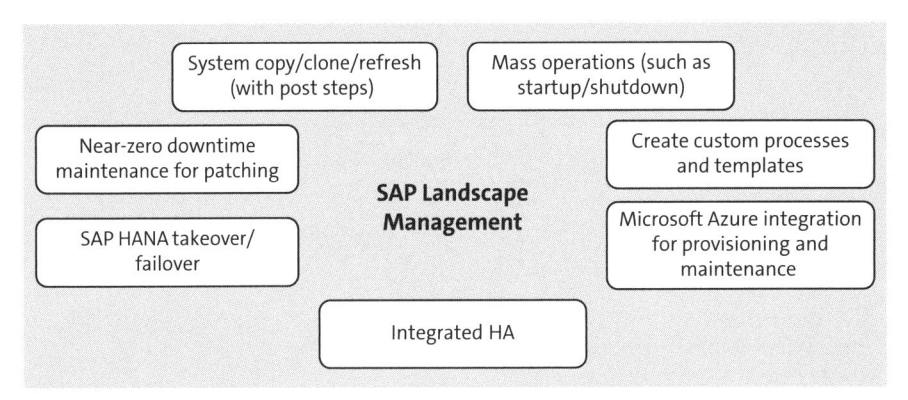

Figure 9.11 SAP Landscape Management Automation Capabilities

With the Microsoft Azure connector and the ability to use custom scripts, SAP Landscape Management may fit well with your overall automation approach.

9.4 DevOps Integration

IaC brought infrastructure management and DevOps together, combining the flexibility of resource management with the agility of continuous integration and continuous delivery (CI/CD).

All the IaC tools integrate with DevOps tools such as Microsoft Azure DevOps, and the pipeline can have not only all the tasks but also a combination of languages and tools. For example, you can have a Terraform template for orchestration, Ansible for configuration management, and CLI commands for something else. Figure 9.12 shows an example of how all the automation can be a part of the pipeline and work together.

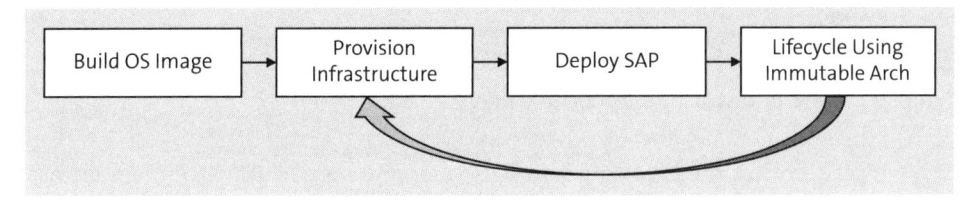

Figure 9.12 Activities Using DevOps Pipelines

9.5 Quickstart Templates

Quickstart templates act as automation accelerators, and if you're just starting or understand IaC but would like to use something as a base, these would be a good fit. There are several templates available online, most notably on GitHub. Following are some SAP-focused GitHub repositories:

- *https://github.com/Azure/sap-hana*
- *https://github.com/SUSE/azure-resource-manager-sap-solution-templates*
- *https://github.com/redhat-sap*

SUSE also provides templates for the SAP solution (just the infrastructure) in Microsoft Azure marketplace, as shown in Figure 9.13.

> **Tip**
> Templates are a good way to deploy environments quickly, but you'll have to use the tool that the template is using. For example, if it's using a Terraform and Ansible combination, you'll have to learn that even if you're more familiar with ARM templates. Keep that in mind when choosing a template, and when using different sources, ensure that you don't end up mixing too much code that you don't understand.

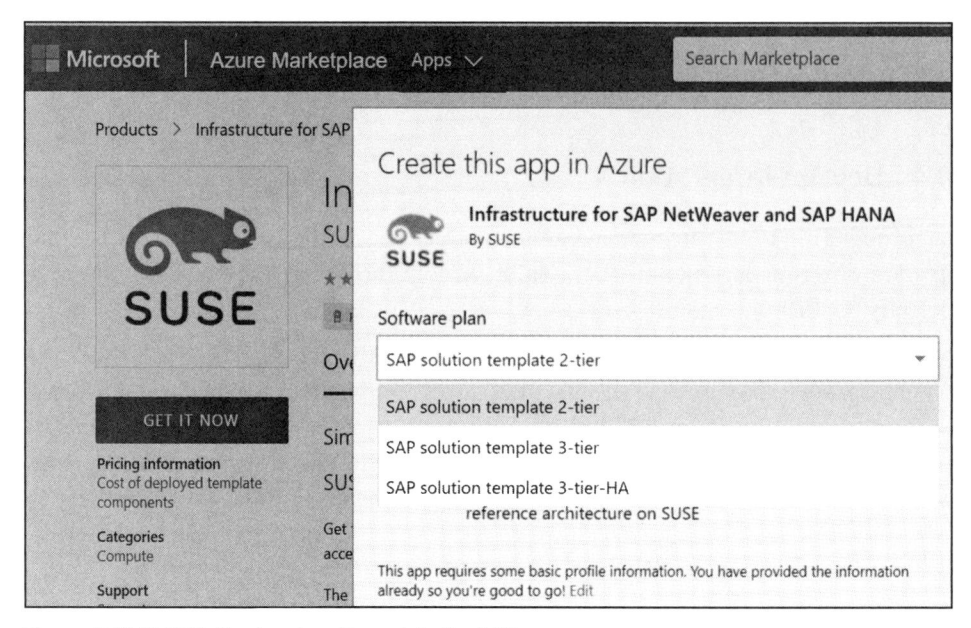

Figure 9.13 SUSE Infrastructure Template for SAP

The template creates the following infrastructures and installs SUSE Linux Enterprise Server (SLES) for SAP flavor:

- VMs
- VNet and subnet
- Storage according to VM sizes
- Availability set (AS) and internal load balancer if the HA option is selected

You can also clone the GitHub repositories and customize them for your environment. A lot of templates focus on SAP HANA, so you'll have to create your own for other databases.

9.6 Disadvantages of Using Automation

You've now learned why automation is important and the benefits of using it, but can there be disadvantages; that is, what could go wrong? Here are some things that you should be careful about when using automation:

- **Mistake propagation**
  Automation can propagate mistakes as fast it can fix something. Be careful when trying to do something in mass; perform pretesting and version control the code.
- **Accidental deletion**
  When you're working with hundreds of servers and make changes frequently, there is a chance that a typo or simple mistake can delete the infrastructure as well. Be

sure to use delete lock on the entire production environment to prevent accidental deletion.

- **Correct access**
  Ensure that the right people have access (principle of least privilege) to create and manage infrastructure. Someone who doesn't understand IaC well can damage things across the board.

- **Cost**
  With the ease of creating servers, costs can get out of hand. Be sure to use Microsoft Azure policies and integrate the approval process in your DevOps pipelines to minimize spinning up unnecessary items.

- **Learning the infrastructure**
  If you have a small landscape, the cost of learning and implementing IaC may be high compared to the yearly infrastructure cost. Weigh the cost versus benefit factors for using automation for smaller landscapes.

- **Code management**
  It can be difficult to manage code if it grows large, especially when multiple teams are collaborating.

9.7 Automation Recommend Practices

Just like autonomous cars have several levels of autonomy, ranging from parking assist to full driving, IaC can be used from basic automation such as just the infrastructure to sophisticated use cases such as application install and lifecycle management. Therefore, define the milestones in terms of use cases and work toward those rather than boiling the ocean right from the start.

Following are some of the recommendations for automation:

- **Use modular approach**
  Instead of grouping everything together, create smaller modules for infrastructure, database, and application. Besides being simpler to execute and troubleshoot, it also promotes reuse; for example, if SAP HANA is your choice of database, having a module for SAP HANA that can be called in all the deployments makes maintenance and software version management easier.

- **Use open-source tools**
  Open source promotes the power of community, and you wouldn't have to create everything yourself. A good example of this is using the open-source Prometheus tool to monitor SUSE HA cluster.

- **Integrate security into code**
  Don't think of security as a separate exercise; integrate security controls in the code and use Microsoft Azure features such as managed identities and Key Vault.

- **Use immutable architecture when possible**
  DevOps pipelines make using immutable architecture easier and consistent in the long run.

- **Reuse code**
  Jump-start your automation using templates available at GitHub and combine different types of scripts using DevOps pipelines. For example, if you have something working well using CLI commands, you may want to integrate that instead of rewriting using Ansible.

- **Look at the bigger picture**
  Don't think of automation as a provisioning tool; rather, consider it as a part of the infrastructure management strategy.

9.8 Summary

Automation can save you time, money, and a lot of headache that comes with mistakes made trying to do things manually. This chapter discussed the concept of IaC and tools to achieve that in Microsoft Azure. It also addressed application-level automation and lifecycle management using DevOps.

In the next chapter, we'll discuss encryption and how to apply it at different levels such as network, storage, database, and application.

Chapter 10
Encryption

Encryption helps keep the data secure, but it doesn't replace other security practices such as role-based access control, network security, or identity management. It should be part of a larger security practice and consider data in rest as well as in transit.

Security is a shared responsibility in the cloud—Microsoft Azure provides the technology and tools while you're responsible to implement those for your landscape. Encryption should be a part of the larger security story to keep the data secure and spans infrastructure, data, and backups. In this chapter we'll discuss key areas of encryption (as shown in Figure 10.1): encryption at rest, in transit, and encryption key management in the context of SAP landscapes.

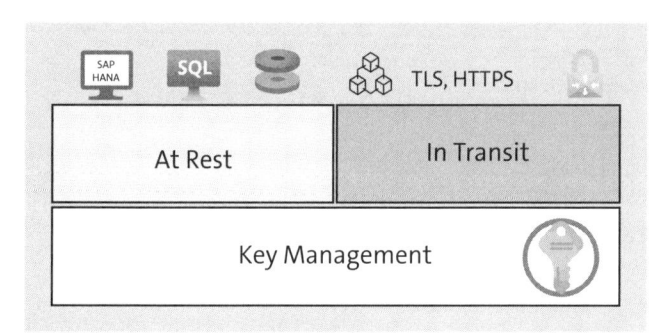

Figure 10.1 Key Areas of Encryption

Encryption can be implemented either at the client side, when it's performed outside of Microsoft Azure, or at the server side within Microsoft Azure fabric. With client-side encryption, Microsoft Azure doesn't have access to the keys, and you have sole control, while server-side encryption model allows both platform-managed keys (PMKs) and customer-managed keys (CMKs). For client-side encryption, you can use tools such as Microsoft Azure storage client library for .NET NuGet or Java.

10.1 Encryption at Rest

Encryption at rest protects persistent data and is applicable to compute, manage disks, storage accounts, snapshots, and backups. Microsoft Azure provides encryption at rest

10 Encryption

for services across infrastructure as a service (IaaS), platform as a service (PaaS), and software as a service (SaaS) solutions. The use case for encryption at rest is to protect the access of data if an attacker gets hold of the physical hardware, such as the hard drive, and attempts to retrieve the data stored there. It may also be a regulatory compliance requirement such as Health Insurance Portability and Accountability Act (HIPPA) or Payment Card Industry (PCI).

Microsoft Azure's implementation for encryption at rest is illustrated in Figure 10.2; more than one key is used.

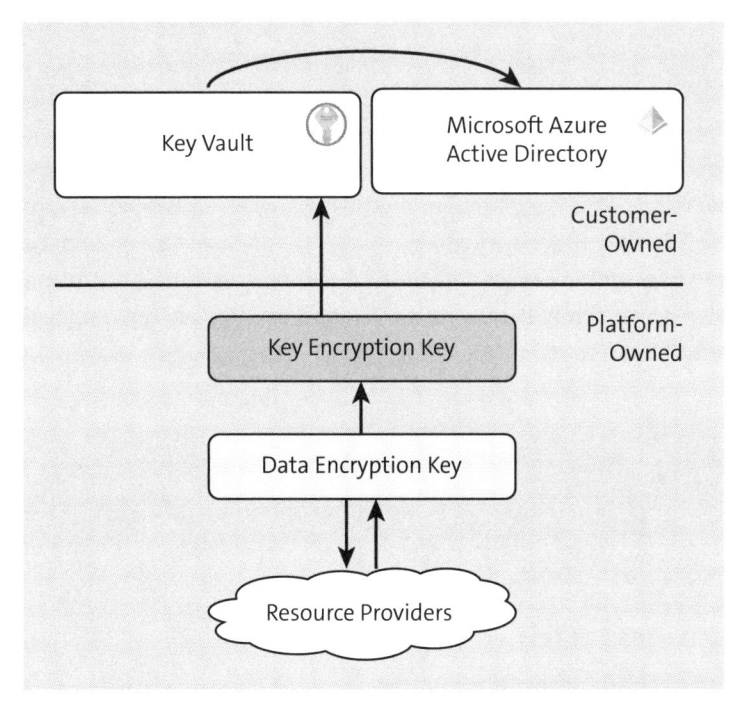

Figure 10.2 Microsoft Azure Encryption at Rest Implementation

Data encryption key (DEK) is a symmetric 256-bit advanced encryption standard (AES) key that encrypts a block or partition, which also means a single resource may have multiple DEKs, and when it's replaced or rotated, only the data encrypted by that key is re-encrypted. The second layer on top of the DEK is the key encryption key (KEK), which encrypts DEK; both keys are stored separately, and a service with access to KEK can decrypt DEK, making it a single access point.

To access and manage the keys, you need a solution that not only acts as a gatekeeper using the right permission from Microsoft Azure Active Directory (AD) but also provides a common management experience across services and allows you to bring your own keys (customer-managed keys). The Microsoft Azure Key Vault fits right in for this use case.

10.1.1 Storage Service Encryption

Microsoft Azure storage uses 256-bit AES to encrypt anything that goes in and automatically decrypts on retrieval. It's automatic and enabled for all storage accounts and all tiers, such as standard, premium, hot, cool, and so on.

10.1.2 Microsoft Azure Disk Encryption

Managed disks can be encrypted using Microsoft Azure Disk Encryption (ADE), which uses BitLocker for Windows and dm-crypt for Linux. If you guessed that keys are stored in the Key Vault, you're right!

This also integrates with Microsoft Azure Backup, which uses KEK to back up and restore encrypted virtual machines (VMs). Figure 10.3 shows an illustration of ADE in the Microsoft Azure portal, which can be viewed from the disks blade of a VM.

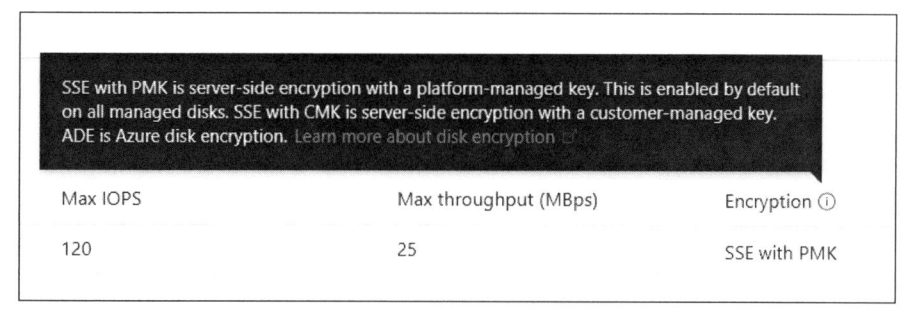

Figure 10.3 Microsoft Azure Disk Encryption

> **Custom Linux Images**
>
> ADE isn't supported for custom Linux images, meaning you have to use the Microsoft Azure image as the starting point if you're planning on using ADE; however, you can rely on server-side encryption (SSE) if that satisfies the organization's encryption policies.

10.1.3 Database Encryption

Most of the databases provide their own mechanisms for encrypting the database content such as data and log encryption for SAP HANA, transparent data encryption (TDE) for SQL Server, and so on. Encrypting the database using database methods may be beneficial depending on the key management preferences and keeping the database and platform encryption separate. It may also provide additional features always encrypted, such as SQL Server.

Considerations using database mechanisms include backup and restore procedures in terms of how database encryption will work together with encrypted VMs and enabling database encryption along with disk encryption, which would be double encryption and isn't recommended.

10.1.4 Backup Encryption

Because Microsoft Azure Backup uses storage in the background, everything is encrypted using SSE. By default, recovery vault uses PMKs, but you can also bring your own for when backing up, for example, VMs, and the model is called customer-managed keys (CMK). So, in that sense, there are two levels of encryption: at the storage layer and at the recovery vault layer.

CMK gives you more control over the keys, but it also can be a single point of failure (SPOF); if you lose the key, Microsoft Azure won't be able to decrypt anything that was encrypted using that key. Microsoft Azure Backup also supports ADE when using managed disks in VMs. It's also important to understand the restore process when encrypting the backups—an encrypted VM can only be restored by restoring the disks and creating a VM. Replace existing and restore VM operations aren't supported, at the time of publication.

10.1.5 Microsoft Azure NetApp Files

Microsoft Azure NetApp Files volumes are encrypted using the Federal Information Processing Standard Publication (FIPS) 140-2 standard, and keys are managed by the service. Because the encryption keys are at the volume level, if you delete a volume, the key used for encrypting the volume is deleted too.

CMKs using a dedicated hardware security module (HSM) are being rolled out and aren't available in all regions at the time of publication.

10.1.6 Third-Party Software

You can also use third-party software, such as Vormetric, for encryption if you're not looking to use Microsoft Azure and/or database-specific tools. There is a cost-benefit trade-off when using third-party tools plus additional hardware that may need to be provisioned. These tools may also have additional regulatory compliance and are a good way to maintain consistency if your organization has a hybrid or multicloud model.

> **Data Scrambling versus Encryption**
>
> Data scrambling is different from encryption. While encryption focuses on securing the data from unauthorized access, scrambling focuses on anonymizing the data by masking. Data scrambling is often used when doing system copy from production to non-production environments.

10.2 Encryption in Transit

Encryption in transit protects from interception of data transfer between on-premise and Microsoft Azure, between Microsoft Azure services, or over the Internet. Data is encrypted before transmission and decrypted upon arrival. Microsoft Azure offers several mechanisms for in-transit encryption:

- **ExpressRoute encryption**

  ExpressRoute supports *MACsec*, which encrypts the data at the media access control (MAC) or layer 2, and *IP Security* (IPSec), which works at layer 3.

  MACsec is supported only for ExpressRoute direct, and it can be used to encrypt the physical link between your network devices and Microsoft's network devices. It's based on the CMK paradigm and uses the Key Vault to store the keys. MACsec has to be enabled because it's not active by default.

  IPSec can be used for end-to-end connection encryption between Microsoft Azure virtual network (VNet) and on-premise. Microsoft Azure also supports IPSec and MACsec to be used together (for ExpressRoute direct). If you're using the Microsoft Azure Virtual Private Network (VPN) gateway, the throughput will follow the specifications based on the stock-keeping unit (SKU).

- **VPN**

  Point-to-site VPN uses the secure socket tunneling protocol (SSTP) to create a tunnel and site-to-site uses the IPSec/Internet Key Exchange (IKE) tunnel for encryption. Because point-to-site allows individual client machines to connect to the Microsoft Azure VNET, you can use your own public key infrastructure (PKI) root certificate authority that can be generated using PowerShell.

- **Between Microsoft Azure data centers**

  When the data moves between different data centers, and if it goes outside boundaries beyond Microsoft's control, MACsec encryption is used, which encrypts and decrypts the data on the device. This is applied by default for all traffic within and across Microsoft Azure regions.

- **Microsoft Azure storage**

  All the interaction with storage using the portal happens over HTTPS; API calls and shared access signature (SAS) can enforce HTTPS as well.

  If you're using client-side encryption, the data going to storage is secure, in transit, as well.

- **Virtual machines**

  Microsoft Azure allows encryption for data in and out of a VM in different ways depending on the OS. For the Windows OS, remote desktop sessions are encrypted using transport layer security (TLS). For Linux VMs, Secure Shell (SSH) uses an encrypted connection, and the recommendation is to use a public-key pair (which is asymmetric) for logon instead of passwords.

10   Encryption

- **Microsoft Azure Backup**
  Backups are transferred to the recovery vault over HTTPS and remain within the Microsoft Azure network.

- **Microsoft Azure NetApp files**
  When using Network File System (NFS) 4.1, traffic between Microsoft Azure NetApp Files and NFS clients (e.g., VM) can be encrypted using Kerberos with the AES-256 standard. NFS 3.0 and SMB 3.0 don't provide an encryption option; however, the traffic is internal to Microsoft Azure data center networks.

- **Microsoft Azure Site Recovery**
  For replication between Microsoft Azure regions, Microsoft Azure Site Recovery supports encryption in transit as well as at rest. In addition, TLS 1.2 is enforced by default.

> **Encryption and Authorized Access**
> It's important to understand that encryption prevents unauthorized access to data. Authorized users can still access data by either using the key or other authentication means (e.g., where there is automatic decryption when using correct access); therefore, encryption and authorization (role-based access control) work together to ensure that only the right folks have access.

10.3   Key Management

Managing the encryption key is the key to securing data from unauthorized access! Cloud-native tools such as Microsoft Azure Key Vault not only provide a way to manage keys but also support HSM, where the key never leaves the HSM boundary.

As we've discussed, there are multiple paradigms for keys such as PMKs, where Microsoft Azure creates and manages the key, and CMKs where you bring your own key to Microsoft Azure by generating it using on-premise HSM.

Depending on whether your organization has a centralized key management policy, and/or you require the keys to be generated using your own hardware, you choose either PMKs or CMKs. You can also enable logging in the Microsoft Azure Key Vault to monitor key access activities.

10.4   Summary

Encryption goes hand in hand with authentication and authorization in securing an environment. This chapter discussed the aspects of encryption in rest, in transit, and key management to give you a bigger picture of how to incorporate encryption in larger security practice. In the next chapter, we'll discuss process and technical mechanisms for migrating your existing SAP landscape (whether on-premise or in the private cloud) to Azure.

Chapter 11
Migrating SAP to Microsoft Azure

Migration seems like a simple term but there is a lot to unbox, especially for SAP landscapes. A large part of migration projects consists of planning, testing, and optimizing, so there are no surprises during the final cutover.

Migrating SAP systems is a big undertaking and can take months (or sometimes years) to plan and execute. Whether it's the journey to SAP S/4HANA or a good old lift-and-shift, there are a lot of decisions to be made and several iterations to be done to get it right. One of the common challenges is learning a new platform such as Microsoft Azure while doing SAP migration—that's why we split architecture and migration into different chapters so by the time you're reading about migration, you have a fair understanding of Microsoft Azure and how SAP architecture on Microsoft Azure works. This chapter focuses on planning, optimizing, and learning about methods and processes related to migration.

11.1 Planning and Readiness

When you're moving to a new house, you inventory everything in the current house to decide what to take and how to move; similarly, when moving SAP and connected systems, you should know what is in scope. Without such an exercise, migration may break business processes or system workflows, if something is missed. Here are important pieces of information to gather:

- List of SAP and non-SAP systems that connect with SAP such as printer servers, tax solutions, application lifecycle management tools, and so on
- List of all the interfaces, internal and external, and how they connect, for example, with IP address, host name, load balancing, and so on
- Systems that are tightly coupled and need to move together
- Dependency map to determine the sequence of migration

The next step in the planning process is to rationalize the application landscape, working with the business, and determine the path forward to what applications can be retired, rehosted, rearchitected, or replaced. This can be an iterative process; the final result should be something like that shown in Figure 11.1.

11   Migrating SAP to Microsoft Azure

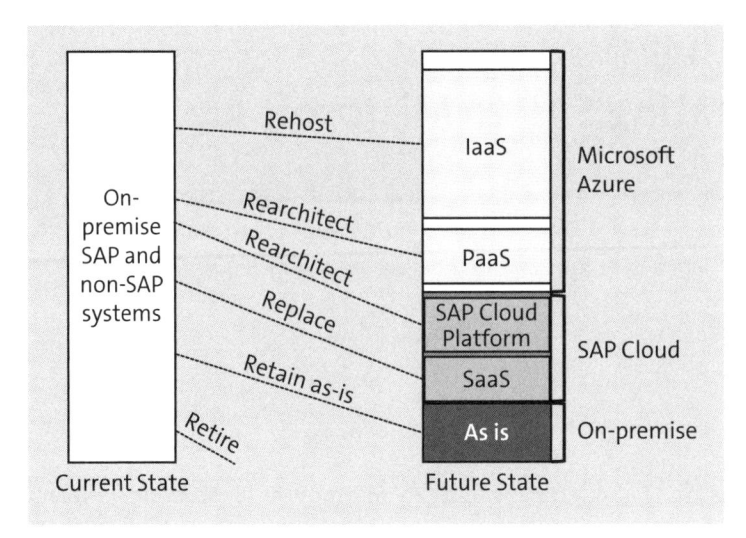

Figure 11.1 Systems Rationalization as Migration Planning

11.1.1   Readiness Evaluation

After you know what needs to be migrated, you need to evaluate, for each system, what preparation work has to be done before the migration. For some SAP systems (to be rehosted), it may be as simple as getting to a new kernel level, or it may be as involved as upgrading to a newer version before a supported configuration can run on Microsoft Azure (refer to SAP Note 1928533 for minimum application release and kernel requirements).

Systems that will be replaced by software as a service (SaaS) (e.g., moving from SAP ERP Human Capital Management [SAP ERP HCM] to SAP SuccessFactors) solution need even more due diligence to figure out what business processes are being used, how it aligns with the cloud solution, and the steps to move to the new model. Similar analysis for refactoring is needed to move to the platform as a service (PaaS) solution either in Microsoft Azure or SAP Cloud Platform. When retiring a system, you need to ensure that all the functionalities are either included in some other system or that it's not being used anymore because of a change in business.

Following the cloud adoption framework, readiness not only includes technical aspects but also organizational and employee skills (people), as shown in Figure 11.2. The following questions allow you to explore the details:

- Is our organization ready to adopt the cloud operating model?
- Do we have all the skills and resources needed for the migration?
- When can we get system downtime for the migration while ensuring availability during big events?
- What other upcoming projects can potentially conflict with migration?

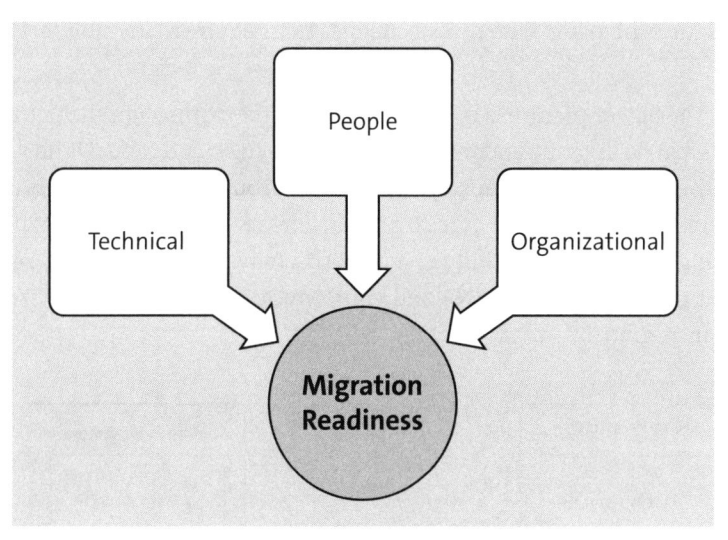

Figure 11.2 Migration Readiness Aspects

11.1.2 Archiving and Cleanup

The size of the database is an important factor in migration timelines, downtime, and complexity. Start data archiving early in the project by working with the business to set retention. A slim database also means lower cost for the Microsoft Azure infrastructure. While business data retention is often governed by laws and can take years, retention of technical data, such as SAP Basis-related tables (refer to SAP Note 2388483) and logs, is usually more flexible.

Along with database tables, file system cleanup is important too. Older transports, upgrade files, interface files, and system logs can occupy a large amount of space over time and incur additional storage costs in Microsoft Azure if not cleaned up regularly.

11.2 Migration Paths and Methodologies

In the beginning of 2020, SAP announced the extension of mainstream maintenance of SAP Business Suite (AnyDB and SAP HANA) from 2025 to the end of 2027 (refer to SAP Note 2881788). It still means that you should plan to move SAP S/4HANA, but you have a little more time to plan and transition.

Depending on your readiness and timelines (marching toward an exit event from the data center or contract termination from the private cloud), moving to Microsoft Azure can be a window to migrate to SAP HANA as well. As shown in Figure 11.3, there are several ways of combining Microsoft Azure migration with the upgrade to SAP Business Suite on SAP HANA or SAP S/4HANA. Lift-and-shift (rehost) is the most straightforward and least complex method compared to SAP S/4HANA conversion, which is more complex and involves functional and data model changes that require regression testing and remediation.

One way of looking at the bigger picture is to get to Microsoft Azure through the path of least resistance and then do upgrade and migrations because the cloud model is flexible and scalable. On the other hand, because you're going through a lot of planning and testing cycles, you might as well go to at least SAP Business Suite on SAP HANA, if not SAP S/4HANA. Going to SAP Business Suite on SAP HANA may make sense if you're already thinking about going to SAP S/4HANA and your AnyDB license may be expiring, or you're due for an upgrade.

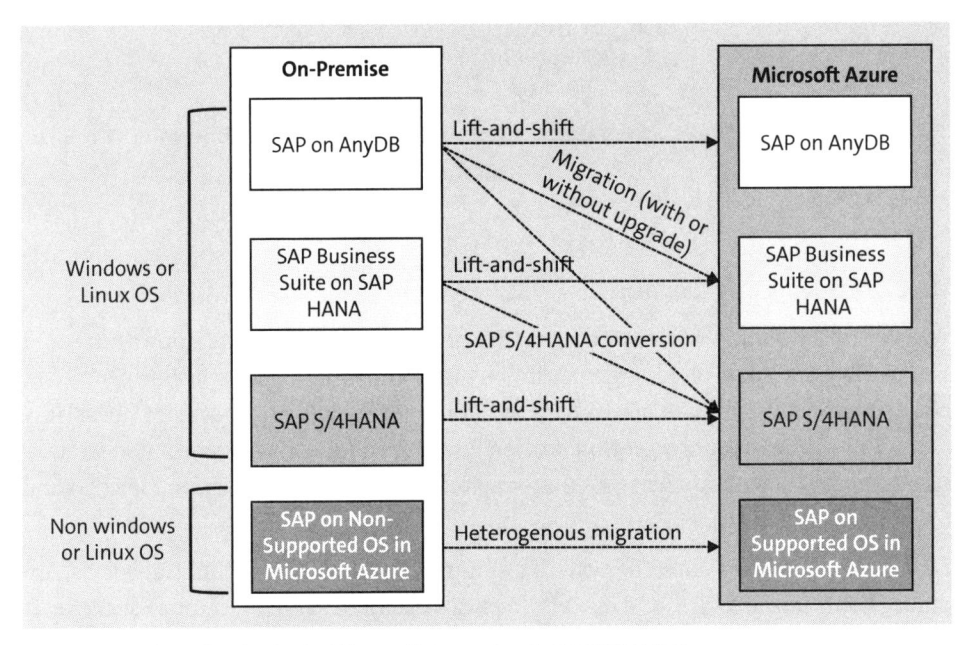

Figure 11.3 Migration Paths to Microsoft Azure (and SAP S/4HANA)

Regardless of the path you choose, it's important to understand that the support model for the database isn't the only thing that SAP is changing; in addition, operating systems (OSs) will be restricted too. SAP Note 2620910 says that new SAP products will support only widely used OSs. Table 11.1 show the list of OSs that are being discontinued starting with SAP S/4HANA 1809 and SAP BW/4HANA 2.0.

SAP S/4HANA up to 1709 SAP BW/4HANA up to 1.0	SAP S/4HANA 1809 and Higher SAP BW/4HANA 2.0 and Higher
Windows Server 64-Bit	Windows Server 64-Bit
Linux on x86_64	Linux on x86_64
AIX	AIX

Table 11.1 OS Support for New SAP Products

SAP S/4HANA up to 1709 SAP BW/4HANA up to 1.0	SAP S/4HANA 1809 and Higher SAP BW/4HANA 2.0 and Higher
Linux on Power Little Endian	Linux on Power Little Endian
Linux on Power Big Endian	- Support discontinued -
HP-UX on IA64	- Support discontinued -
Solaris on SPARC and Solaris on x86	- Support discontinued -
IBM i	- Support discontinued -
IBM z/OS	- Support discontinued -
Linux on IBM Z	- Support discontinued -

Table 11.1 OS Support for New SAP Products (Cont.)

The decision to move forward should include all these technical considerations as well as an organizational road map for SAP.

11.2.1 Database Migration Methodologies

Broadly, SAP data migration (also called system copy in some instances) falls under one of the following three scenarios:

- **Change of hardware, keeping OS and database the same**
  This is considered a homogenous migration (also called lift-and-shift) and usually is done either when the current hardware is old or you're moving to a different location such as to a different cloud provider.

- **Change of OS and/or database**
  This is considered a heterogenous migration and is useful when you're looking to move to a modern in-memory database such as SAP HANA, use more open-source platforms such as the Linux OS, or move to a cloud provider that's better optimized for a different OS/database combination than you currently have. SAP also calls this OS/database migration.

- **Combine SAP upgrade, move to SAP HANA, or transform to SAP S/4HANA with OS/database migration**
  When you're going through a migration, for example, to a cloud such as Microsoft Azure, sometimes it's prudent to combine the upgrade and transformation to achieve multiple goals in the same downtime.

There are several ways to do each of these methods with trade-offs such as downtime, effort, cost, and complexity.

11.2.2 Homogeneous Migration

Keeping the database and OS the same means faster migration and less regression testing. You can also use newer patches or versions at the target system such as Windows 2012 at source to 2016 at target; similarly, a higher patch can be used for the database as long as it's backward compatible.

Backup/Restore

This is the simplest mechanism for system copy and isn't much different from a regular system refresh as you do have the latest production data available for testing or creating a new sandbox system for a project.

Figure 11.4 shows the backup/restore method to migrate the SAP system to Microsoft Azure. Data transfer can be done either via the network (need connectivity and faster speed for transfer) or using Microsoft Azure Data Box (a cloud solution that allows you to send large amounts of data to Microsoft Azure using a physical storage device); this may be the only option in scenarios where you can't establish connectivity from the source to Microsoft Azure, such as a private data center (or cloud) that doesn't allow external connectivity.

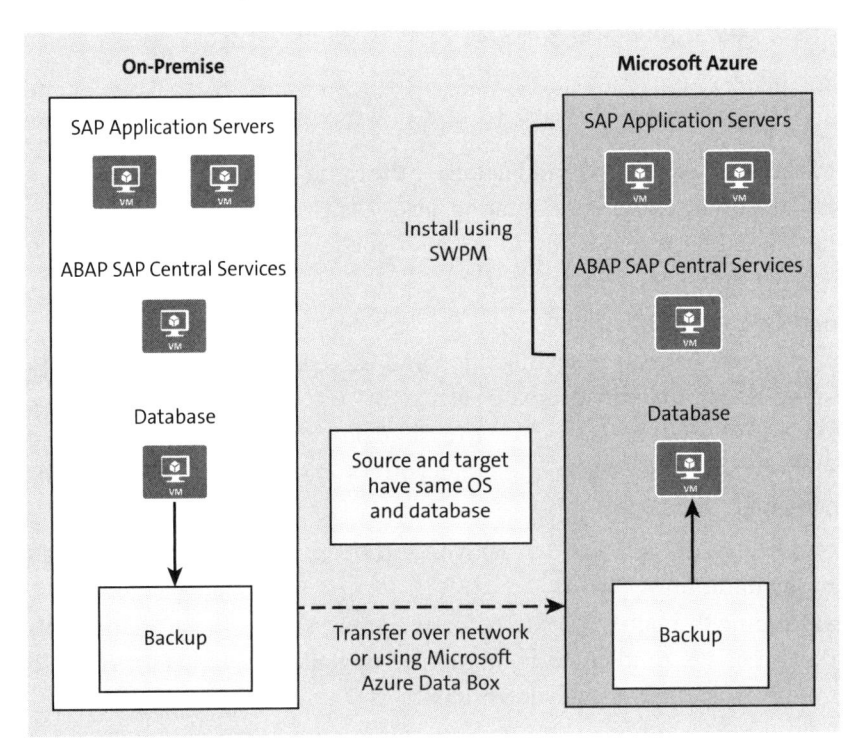

Figure 11.4 Migration Using Backup/Restore

You can use different kinds of backups, such as full offline backup, full online backup with logs, or full online backup, in the beginning, and then use either incremental or differential to catch up. The longer you can keep the source database up, the shorter the migration window will be.

This method may be simple, but it has a bigger downtime window even with the optimizations (e.g., full backup ahead of time and incremental from there). Other options discussed in the following are better suited unless those aren't possible because of technical or cost restrictions.

Database Replication

We've discussed the database replication mechanism as a part of the high availability (HA) and disaster recovery (DR) solution; the idea here is to treat Microsoft Azure as a remote data center and establish replication database-specific methods such as Data Guard for Oracle, AlwaysOn for SQL Server, and SAP HANA system replication in asynchronous mode.

This doesn't require the source system to be down, so the downtime window is at a minimum. At the time of cutover, you do a final sync and shut down the source database before bringing the target up. This setup is illustrated in Figure 11.5. Domain name service (DNS) changes can route users to the new system, so they don't have to change any configuration on their side.

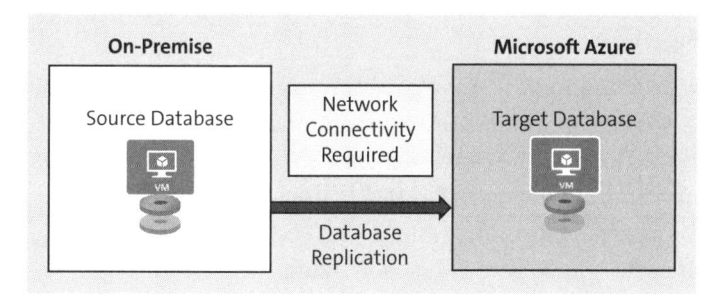

Figure 11.5 Migration Using Database Replication

This is the most downtime efficient method of migration, but it requires more planning, network connectivity between source and target, and additional open ports for replication. In addition, the database version and patch don't need to match; that is, the target can have a higher version as long as it's backward compatible (it's important to check for backward compatibility ahead of time from the database vendor or SAP documentation).

Microsoft Azure Site Recovery

Microsoft Azure Site Recovery as a technology isn't restricted to Microsoft Azure but can be used to replicate virtual machines (VMs) on Hyper-V, VMWare, and physical servers from on-premises to Microsoft Azure. As long as you meet the prerequisites (needs configuration and may need patching for on-premises servers), you can set up the replication and failover to Microsoft Azure for migration. The source OS needs to be among those supported in Microsoft Azure.

Because Microsoft Azure Site Recovery doesn't guarantee database consistency when it's running due to rate of change, as a last step, you'll need to shut down the database and let the application-consistent snapshots synchronize. At the time of publication, Microsoft supports only SQL Server replication for Microsoft Azure Site Recovery.

> **Microsoft Azure Site Recovery: Failover and Target Optimization**
>
> VMs are created during failover, similar to the DR use case, because the new VMs are exact replicas; disk sizes, files, and configurations are copied as is; and there is no opportunity for optimization. So, Microsoft Azure Site Recovery serves as a quick way to migrate, but there are trade-offs with cost as well as configuration optimizations.

> **Microsoft Azure Site Recovery and SAP Support**
>
> Because Microsoft Azure Site Recovery is a Microsoft Azure tool, SAP doesn't specifically support it as a migration method. However, it's supported by Microsoft.

11.2.3 Heterogenous Migration

At times, moving to a new database and/or OS is a good way to get to the latest or open-source technologies and also keep up with the SAP support model for the OS and database; examples include restrictions on the Oracle database to be only on Oracle Linux (or Windows) in Microsoft Azure, moving to SAP HANA to use in-memory capabilities, or SAP deprecating OSs for newer application versions. This section discusses heterogenous migration methods as the way to get to Microsoft Azure.

> **Note**
>
> Since the launch of SAP HANA, other databases have rolled out their own in-memory technologies too, but SAP's direction of not remaining database agnostic and supporting only SAP HANA going forward makes the case for migrating to only SAP HANA for in-memory technologies.

Export/Import

When you're moving to a platform where the target OS, database, or both are different from the source, database-specific mechanisms (e.g., backup/restore) don't work; the data needs to be converted (exported) into a database-independent format that can be imported at the target. Therefore, it's called the export/import mechanism. SAP provides tools to do this in software provisioning manager (SWPM). Use SAP Note 82478 as a starting point for planning the OS/database migration. The main steps of this process include the following:

- Source system preparation
- Source database export, using SWPM, into database-independent files
- Transfer of files to the target host
- Target system installation using source data
- Target system postprocessing steps

> **Parallel Export/Import**
>
> SWPM provides the parallel export/import capability to import the files as they get generated. SWPM internally calls the programs needed, such as R3LOAD, R3LDCTL, R3SZCHK, and so on.

If there's no direct connectivity available from the source to the target, then the files need to be transferred using Microsoft Azure Data Box or something similar. However, the preferred method is to do it over the network to ensure that connectivity either exists or can be temporarily established. Transfer of files can be done using several techniques:

- Use the Migration Monitor tool to perform a file transfer protocol (FTP) copy (in binary mode).
- Copy the export directory using tools such as rsync, AzCopy, and so on.
- Share the export directory over the network as server message block or Network File System (NFS) file share.

> **SAP Migration Check Service**
>
> SAP offers a migration check service for OS/database migrations, which is mandatory for production systems. It includes remote services for analysis (sizing, configuration, prerequisites for migration) and verification (performance analysis and configuration validation of target) of migration.

The heterogenous migration method using the export/import method is illustrated in Figure 11.6.

> **Classical Migration**
>
> Over time, SAP developed methods to combine upgrade with migration in the Software Update Manager (SUM) tool with Data Migration Option (DMO).
>
> The popularity of SUM with DMO (we'll discuss it next) rendered the export/import method as the classical way, hence the term "classical migration" was born.

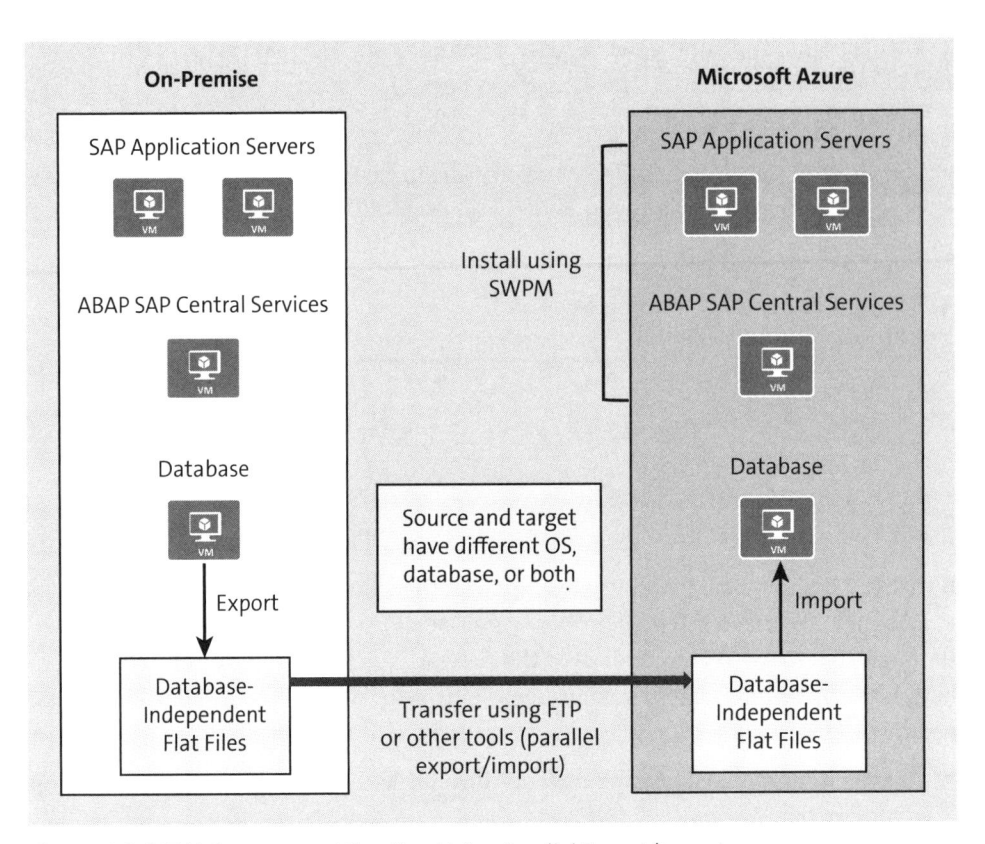

Figure 11.6 SAP Heterogenous Migration Using Parallel Export/Import

Combining Migration and Update

SAP introduced DMO in the SUM tool to simplify upgrade and migration into a one-step process for SAP NetWeaver ABAP-based systems. It started as a way to migrate to the SAP HANA database, but now SAP supports other target databases as well. Besides the reduced number of steps and less downtime (than for upgrade and migration individually), the DMO process also benefits from an easier reset functionality because the source and target databases are consistent during the process. DMO with the system move option is used to move to a different host and, for this use case in particular, move to Microsoft Azure.

> **Target Databases**
>
> At the time of publication, SAP HANA and SAP Adaptive Server Enterprise (SAP ASE) options are available in the tool while other databases are available on request. Table 11.2 shows the source (left) and target database (top) combinations for SUM SP 08; refer to SAP Note 2882441 for more details on other databases and restrictions. Because DMO is meant as a migration tool, source and target databases must be different.

11.2 Migration Paths and Methodologies

Database	SAP HANA	SAP ASE	Microsoft SQL	DB6	SAP MaxDB
Oracle	X	X	X	X	X
SAP MaxDB	X	X	X	X	
Microsoft SQL	X	X		X	X
IBM Db2 for z/OS (DB2)	X	X			
IBM Db2 for i (DB4)	X				
IBM Db2 for Linux, Unix, and Windows (DB6)	X	X	X		X
SAP HANA					
SAP ASE	X		X	X	X

Table 11.2 Source to Target Database Combination as of SUM 2.0 SP 08

DMO with SUM migration (and upgrade) has higher complexity than classical migration, and several preparation steps may be necessary, such as Unicode conversion, dual-stack split (because it supports only ABAP), and so on. Figure 11.7 shows the schematic of this process.

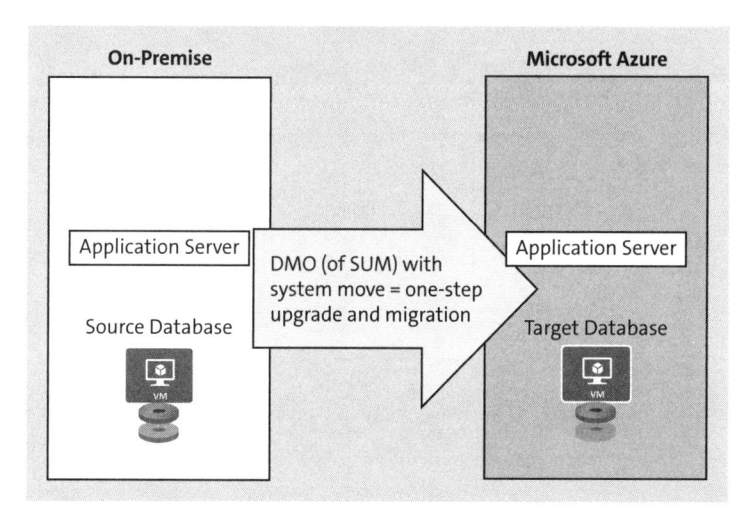

Figure 11.7 Combined Upgrade and Migration: DMO with System Move

Parallel Mode
DMO with system move supports parallel mode as well, similar to parallel export/import of classical migration.

11   Migrating SAP to Microsoft Azure

> **Near-Zero Downtime for Migration and SAP S/4HANA Conversion**
>
> SAP provides near-zero downtime (nZDT) option for migration as well as SAP S/4HANA conversion, but it's a tool offering (at the time of publication) rather than a consulting offering from SAP. It's a solution provided by SAP as part of a minimized downtime service (MDS). Refer to SAP Note 693168 - Minimized Downtime Service (MDS) for more information.

11.2.4 Application Server and SAP Central Services Migration

Database move is the biggest part of any SAP migration; it's often easier to install SAP Central Services and application servers in the target host instead of migrating from the source. Files such as interfaces, logs, and transports can be copied using scripts from the source to the target, as shown in Figure 11.8. This method also ensures that you don't carry any clutter from an older system to Microsoft Azure and provides flexibility to optimize the system in the cloud.

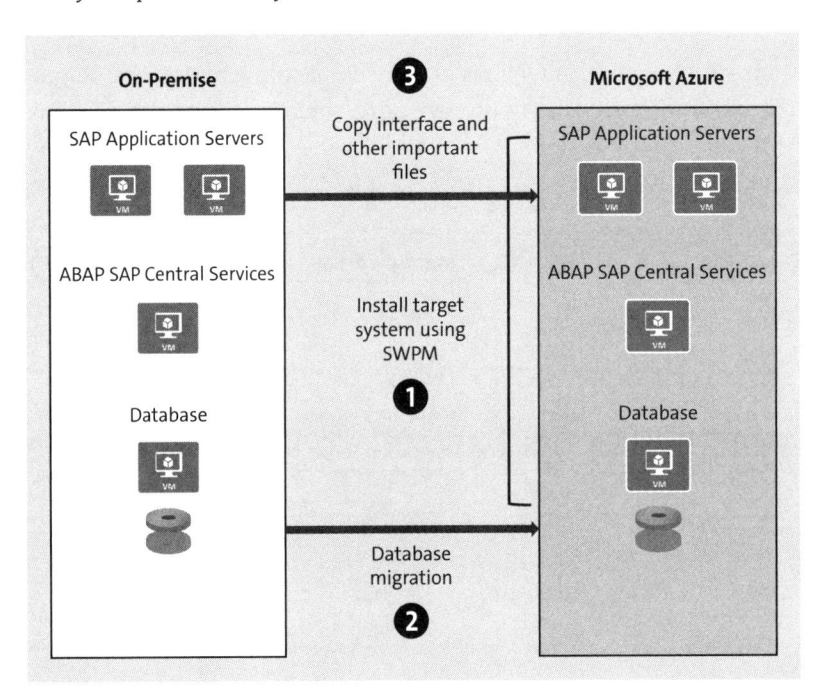

Figure 11.8 SAP Central Services and Application Servers during Migration

> **Microsoft Azure Site Recovery**
>
> We've discussed using Microsoft Azure Site Recovery for application server migration earlier, it's a valid use case but doesn't have wider applicability due to the inflexibility of the Microsoft Azure Site Recovery method in terms of target configuration.

11.2.5 Third-Party Solutions for Migration

SAP supports migration using only SAP tools and techniques. There may be third-party solutions available, by database or other vendors, but the support for those are available only from those vendors. SAP's support during the migration when not using SAP tools is available only as a consulting service. Refer to SAP Note 1767253 – SAP's Recommended Approach to System Copy and SAP Note 82478 - SAP System OS/DB Migration for more details. Microsoft Azure Site Recovery comes under third-party solution space for SAP and the support comes from Microsoft.

11.2.6 Migration Options Trade-Offs

Each migration method has its own use case, pros, and cons. Largely it's a trade-off among complexity, downtime, flexibility, and cost. Table 11.3 summarizes some of these aspects.

	Migration Use Case	Downtime	Complexity	Flexibility
Backup/Restore	Homogenous	High	Low	Low
Database Replication	Homogenous	Low	Medium	Low
Export/Import	Heterogenous	High	Medium	Medium
DMO	Heterogenous	Low	High	High
nZDT	Heterogenous	Lowest	High	High

Table 11.3 Comparing Various Migration Methods

The way to read the table is in the use case context. For example, the database replication mechanism may have lower downtime than DMO, but DMO is also doing an upgrade along with migration. Homogenous migration has lower flexibility in terms of OS and database at the target, but if you're already using, say, Linux with the SAP HANA database, then you don't necessarily care about the flexibility because both are currently supported and are in the support road map for new application versions going forward.

> **Choosing a Migration Strategy**
>
> The best migration strategy is the one that fits your use case and aligns with your organization's objectives. If the objective is to move to Microsoft Azure faster through the path of least resistance, DMO may not be the best path. Similarly, if you've already decided to move to SAP S/4HANA, and the current system is an older version (not supported on Microsoft Azure), then upgrade with transformation may be a good option.
>
> Recognize the motivations for moving to Microsoft Azure and balance that against the trade-offs to choose the right strategy.

11.3 Large Databases and Migration Optimizations

Migrations aren't one-round processes because downtime and resource optimizations need tuning and testing. You usually take SAP recommendations, test the approach with optimizations available for Microsoft Azure, and then finalize the steps for the final migration. Figure 11.9 illustrates the stages to optimize the migration process.

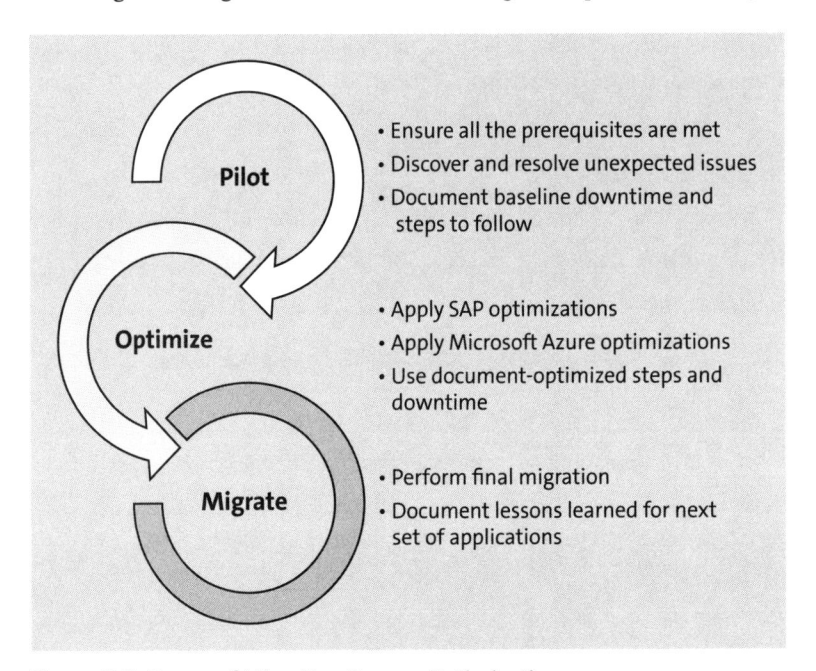

Pilot
- Ensure all the prerequisites are met
- Discover and resolve unexpected issues
- Document baseline downtime and steps to follow

Optimize
- Apply SAP optimizations
- Apply Microsoft Azure optimizations
- Use document-optimized steps and downtime

Migrate
- Perform final migration
- Document lessons learned for next set of applications

Figure 11.9 Stages of Migration Process Optimization

11.3.1 Large Database Challenges

If your organization had SAP for a while, there is a good chance that the database size is multiple terabytes (TB), and the migration of such databases isn't without its challenges.

Higher Downtime

Even with the optimizations, large databases incur higher downtime. They also usually have a higher growth rate, so even if initial tests meet your downtime, by the time you get to the production system, the database size has increased, adding to the technical downtime. If you're using the database replication mechanism, efficiently transferring more transaction logs requires higher network bandwidth as well.

> **Technical versus Business Downtime**
>
> The downtime being referred to here is called *technical downtime* because it accounts for only the downtime during the migration process. There are several pre- and

> post-activities, such as locking users, adapting OS-level scripts, performing testing, and so on, that requires business users get off the system, constituting *business downtime*. Optimizing those activities would decrease the total business downtime, but it's not in the scope of this book.

Expertise

A certified OS/database migration consultant would be familiar with the intricacies of migration steps, but, in general, there is a lot more analysis that goes into the optimizations for larger databases. For example, table splitting is an optimization recommendation, but the largest tables don't always have the longest runtime, so you can't identify the candidates for splitting by just looking at the largest table list. You have to look at the stats from an iteration of export and import and do another run to see the impact on runtime.

Time and Effort to Optimize

Besides table splitting, as mentioned previously, increasing the number of R3LOAD processes helps up to a certain level and then has the opposite effect after that, and identifying the optimal number of processes requires testing. Likewise, there are several optimizations, and a single run won't be able to identify the best configuration. You'll have to do multiple iterations for testing different optimization techniques to get the best result (i.e., lowest downtime). Analyzing dependencies, looking at migration run statistics, and testing several optimization configurations is time and effort intensive. Larger databases lead to higher downtimes and complexity, hence archiving and cleanup should always be a consideration to reduce the database size before any migration project.

11.3.2 Downtime Optimization Techniques

This section explores configurations and practices to optimize the technical downtime for migration. In general, these methods decrease the export and/or import timings and, in some cases, avoid known issues, such as by using the latest patch of tools.

We've discussed migration optimization as being an iterative process, and every time you do an optimization, you need to analyze the time to ensure that you're moving in the right direction with downtime optimization. As you do multiple iterations and capture the downtime, you can compare the runtime of packages using the time analyzer report to see where the improvements were and what else can be optimized. You can use *migtime.sar* for ABAP and *jmigtime.jar* for Java packages. Figure 11.10 shows an example output of time analyzer where you can see the package name and time.

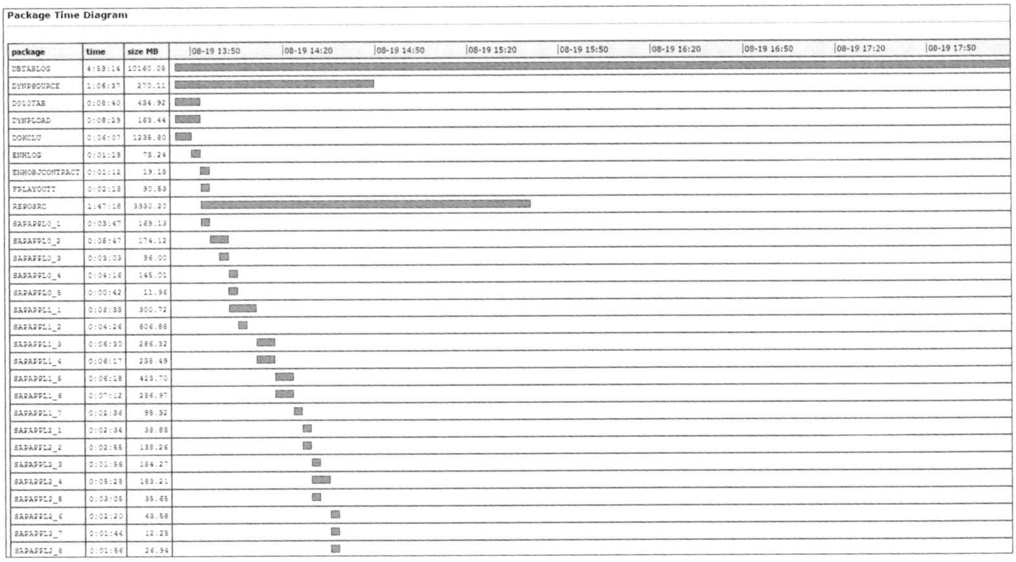

Figure 11.10 Sample Time Analyzer Report

Network Throughput

Whether you're doing backup/restore, database replication, or export/import, restrictions in network bandwidth can hamper the transfer speed, increasing the downtime. Microsoft recommends ExpressRoute for SAP migrations instead of transferring the files over a Virtual Private Network (VPN) connection. If you're running into throughput issues with your originally provisioned ExpressRoute speed, you may want to increase it until the migration project concludes. It's also faster to use multiple threads for copying files than a single process.

Database Parameter Tuning

Each database has its own recommendation for parameters optimized for migration (or system copy)—refer to SAP Notes for database-specific recommendations. This applies to both source and target databases, and the recommended parameters/values may be different for source versus target.

SAP Tools and Kernel

SAP recommends using the latest tools and kernel patch for the migration. After you've done the test migrations and finalized the version and patch level, it's a good idea to stick to it through the migration, unless you run into an issue that's fixed in a patch released afterwards.

Export Directory

SAP supports using NFS disks for export/import, however, for performance reasons, using a local directory is recommended. The same goes for sharing the export directory from the source system to the target system—the latency and throughput at the target may be so high that it would be faster to use FTP or rsync to copy.

Unsorted Export

Exports using unsorted unload are faster and, at some point, SAP changed the default option from sorted to unsorted (with certain hard-coded exclusions). This applies for all databases except when SAP MaxDB is either source or target, in which case, sorted export is required. Refer to SAP Note 54268 for more details.

> **Import for Unsorted Exports**
>
> Importing unsorted data with a clustered index may be slower. During the test runs, identify the impact of time savings during export versus loss during import.

Package and Table Splitting

Certain packages and tables may take longer depending on the data to be exported; splitting the packages and tables (using package and table splitter) is a good way to improve performance. This is especially important for large databases.

Figure 11.11 shows an example of how splitting tables and packages provide shorter downtimes by making export/import faster. SAP doesn't provide a general recommendation on which tables/packages need to be split, so you need to look at the migration logs to determine that. This highlights the iterative nature of migration and challenge that comes with large databases.

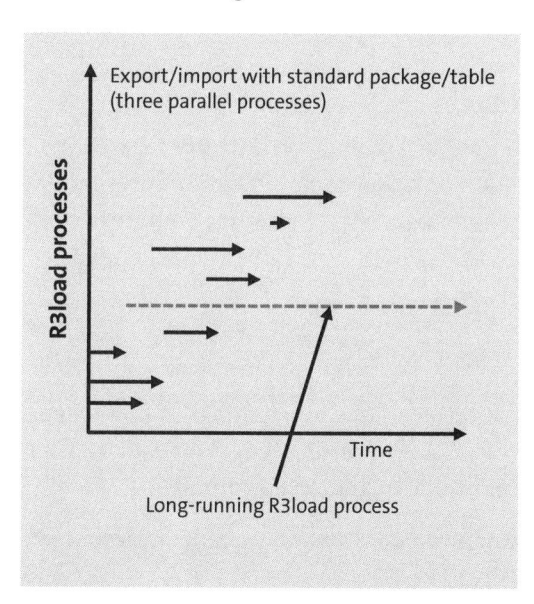

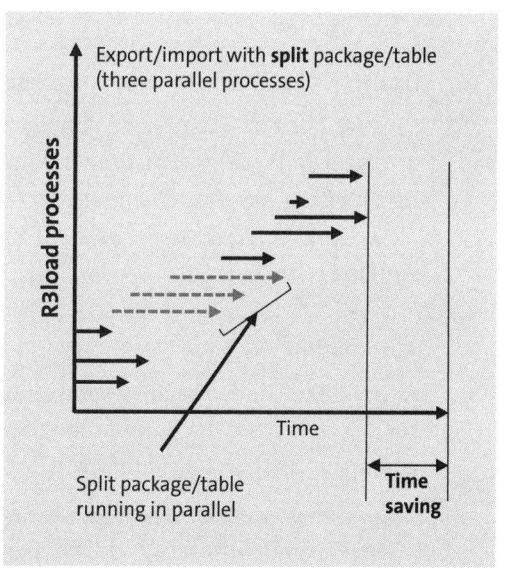

Figure 11.11 Comparison of Export/Import Process without and with Package/Table Splitting and Time Saving

11 Migrating SAP to Microsoft Azure

R3load Process and Dedicated Servers

The rule of thumb for the number of R3load processes is three, but you need to perform some testing to find out the optimal number because too many processes may be counterproductive. You can also use dedicated servers for R3load processes (it can either be application servers or temporary VMs).

Downtime Optimized Data Migration Option

DMO (of SUM) to SAP HANA provides a downtime optimized option, which lets you migrate select large application tables during uptime. The changes made during the uptime migration are part of delta record and replay. Figure 11.12 illustrates this concept and how it differs from standard DMO.

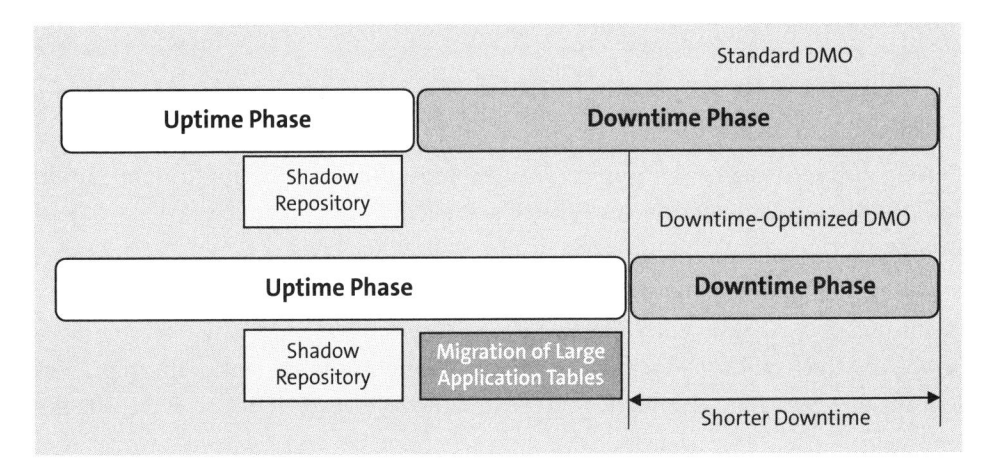

Figure 11.12 Reducing Downtime Using Downtime Optimized DMO

Upsizing Virtual Machines in Microsoft Azure

Because Microsoft Azure lets you resize a VM quickly, and you only pay for what you use, using a bigger VM just for the migration duration comes in handy. A bigger VM helps with a number of import processes and bandwidth; after the import is completed, you can resize to the original-sized VM. In addition, be sure that accelerated networking is on.

Automation

Although not directly a downtime optimization technique, automating any of the steps, such as infrastructure automation in Microsoft Azure, writing scripts for data transfer, and updating source system kernel, reduces overall migration downtime.

> **Near-Zero Downtime Migration Consulting Service**
>
> If you've tried all the optimizations documented by SAP (and Microsoft Azure), and the downtime still doesn't meet the business expectations, you can use SAP's consulting

service portfolio that provides nZDT migration. Refer to SAP Note 693168 for more information.

Downtime and Complexity

SAP migrations have multiple moving pieces, and optimization for downtime adds more. In general, downtime and complexity are inversely proportional, as illustrated in Figure 11.13. Keep that in mind and strike a balance during the project.

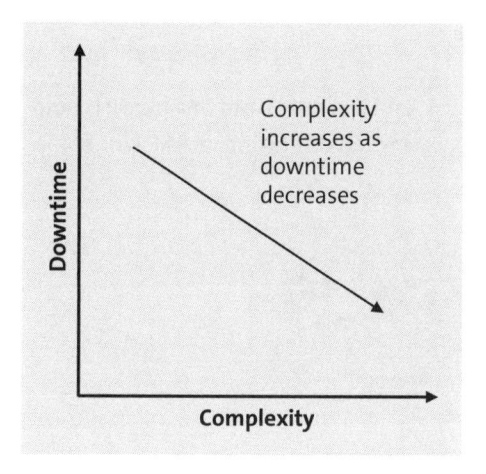

Figure 11.13 Inverse Relationship between Downtime and Complexity

11.4 SAP Landscape Migration Phases

So far, we've talked about how to migrate an SAP system to Microsoft Azure, but there's not just one system to migrate—there are many—and you've got to migrate other systems from the landscape as well, such as development (Dev), quality (DA), sandbox (SBX), and so on, besides production (PRD).

Table 11.4 shows an example of what your SAP landscape may look like, and migrating everything to Microsoft Azure requires a lot of planning, testing, and coordination. You may have more landscapes such as validation, parallel development and QA for projects, and so on.

Application	SBX	Dev	QA	PRD	HA	DR
SAP S/4HANA	X	X	X	X	X	X
SAP Business Warehouse (SAP BW)	X	X	X	X	X	X
SAP Supplier Relationship Management (SAP SRM)	X	X	X	X	X	X

Table 11.4 Typical SAP Landscape Example

11 Migrating SAP to Microsoft Azure

Application	SBX	Dev	QA	PRD	HA	DR
SAP Customer Relationship Management (SAP CRM)	X	X	X	X	X	X
SAP Supply Chain Management (SAP SCM)	X	X	X	X	X	X
SAP Process Integration (SAP PI)	X	X	X	X	X	X
SAP Governance, Risk, and Compliance (SAP GRC)		X	X	X		
SAP Solution Manager		X	X	X		

Table 11.4 Typical SAP Landscape Example (Cont.)

SAP migration projects go through several phases, and learning from one phase is helpful to the next. Figure 11.14 shows the typical phases when migrating an SAP landscape.

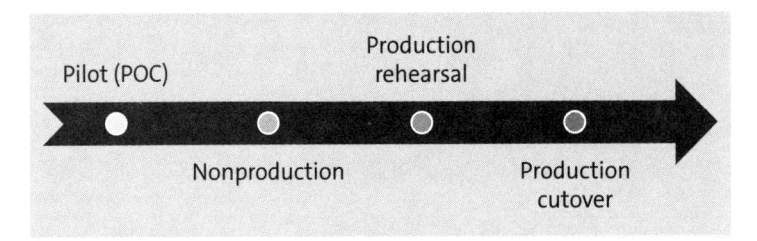

Figure 11.14 Phases for the SAP Migration Project

11.4.1 Pilot

This can also be thought of as proof of concept (POC) because you're migrating the first set of systems to Microsoft Azure. The objective of this phase is to validate the target architecture and then test and document all the migration steps, including pre- and post-configurations.

Depending on the scope of testing, for example, performance testing, you usually do the pilot with a copy of production to get a realistic idea with the database size. If sandbox systems are recent copies, you can use that for the pilot. On the target side, that is, Microsoft Azure, test all the features that you'll be using for production migration such as availability set/availability zone, proximity placement group, accelerated networking, and so on. If the landscape design has HA/DR, then that gets tested in this phase as well, so you understand the configurations and what to automate and how to automate. You validate the OS hardening and patches, encryption, and performance aspects, and it's a good stage to test automation scripts and enhance with detailed steps.

The end result of the pilot comprises the following:

- Target architecture validation
- Initial performance testing results for comparison
- Migration approach validation

11.4 SAP Landscape Migration Phases

- Automation steps validation
- Documentation and learning

These form the basis for all the upcoming phases. In addition, you can leave the migrated system as is or stripped down (get rid of HA/DR configuration), which would be the sandbox system in Microsoft Azure. You can always refresh it later to get the latest data.

11.4.2 Nonproduction

Nonproduction is a broad term that can include multiple landscapes such as development, QA, validation, and so on. There are multiple permutations to migrate all nonproduction systems, and the following are common ways of going about it:

- Migrate development systems *first* because those are small in size and potentially are connected to fewer interfaces.
- Migrate development systems *last* if there's another project in progress that has developers working on and frequently needing to move transports to production. Transport route modification and considerations for testing are still required.

At this stage, you also need to consider how often and which systems you refresh from production to consider a slightly modified plan to move to Microsoft Azure using system refresh rather than migrating. Usually DEV and PRD has their own data, and other systems are refreshed from production, so use that instead of migrating everything. Figure 11.15 shows an example of this method. Because at this stage, production isn't migrated, you can use the SBX as source data (that was migrated during the pilot). This achieves another goal of validating the system refresh process in Microsoft Azure!

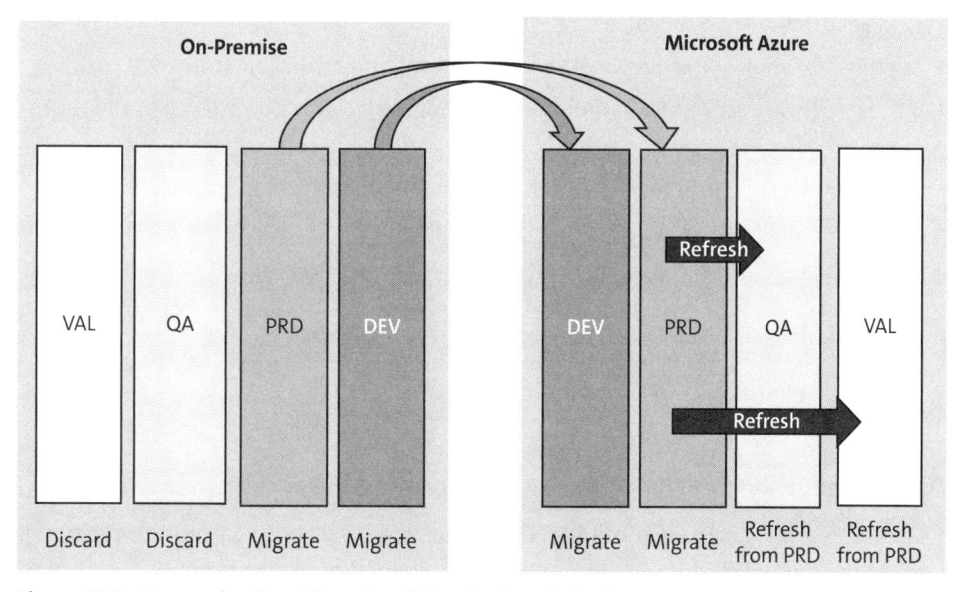

Figure 11.15 Nonproduction Migration Using System Refresh

233

> **Parity with Production System**
>
> At least one of the nonproduction system's setups should be similar to production, such as HA configuration. This helps with testing any update/patching and with replicating problems that you may have in production.

The nonproduction migration phase should meet the following objectives:

- Incorporate learning from the pilot and document new findings.
- Document the usage pattern for source nonproduction so you can save money, in Microsoft Azure, by shutting down systems when not in use (not applicable for reserved instances).
- Understand how Microsoft Azure does platform maintenance, configure notifications, and ensure the architecture is resilient.
- Test and document the system refresh procedure.
- Test regular maintenance and patching using automation.
- Optimize the original design based on learning from this phase.

11.4.3 Production Rehearsal

Production migration rehearsal works along the lines of a wedding rehearsal: you follow each and every step as you would during the cutover. It can be done a week or even a month ahead of the actual cutover; however, if you have a fast-growing database, it's better to do it closer to the cutover so the size change doesn't bring in unexpected elements.

This phase should accomplish the following:

- All the migration steps documented, and timing captured against those steps
- All the software and tools, same versions, and patch that's going to be used for production
- VM images, OS parameters, SAP and database parameters finalized
- All the required Microsoft Azure services configured and tested
- End-to-end downtime window captured, not just technical downtime but business downtime
- Rollback plan prepared and practiced just in case the cutover is unsuccessful (a good migration plan always includes rollback steps)

11.4.4 Production Cutover

This is the D-day, and you should follow the execution playbook from the rehearsal; don't make any last-minute changes to technology, architecture, or steps. In some sense, migration is like a theater play in that you practice a lot but still have to perform live on the final day. Things can go wrong, and you should expect issues; being prepared for a problem that never happens is better than getting caught by surprise.

After the migration, remember to resize the VMs to original if they were upsized before doing the performance testing. Ensure backups, HA, and DR setups are looking good. All the operational activities should be performed in Microsoft Azure now; source systems should be kept down and decommissioned at the earliest.

11.4.5 Large Landscape Migration

Moving all the DEV (or QA, PRD) systems sounds possible if you have a couple of systems to migrate, but what if your SAP landscape is large with 10–20 products? This is where eating an elephant strategy is helpful—you do it one bite at a time.

You group your systems into smaller waves and migrate one group at a time. There are several ways you can group the systems:

- Tightly coupled systems go as a group
- Based on importance of the systems to business (low risk to high risk)
- Based on business unit
- Based on geography
- Some combination of the preceding

Figure 11.16 shows an example of grouping systems and migrating them in different waves.

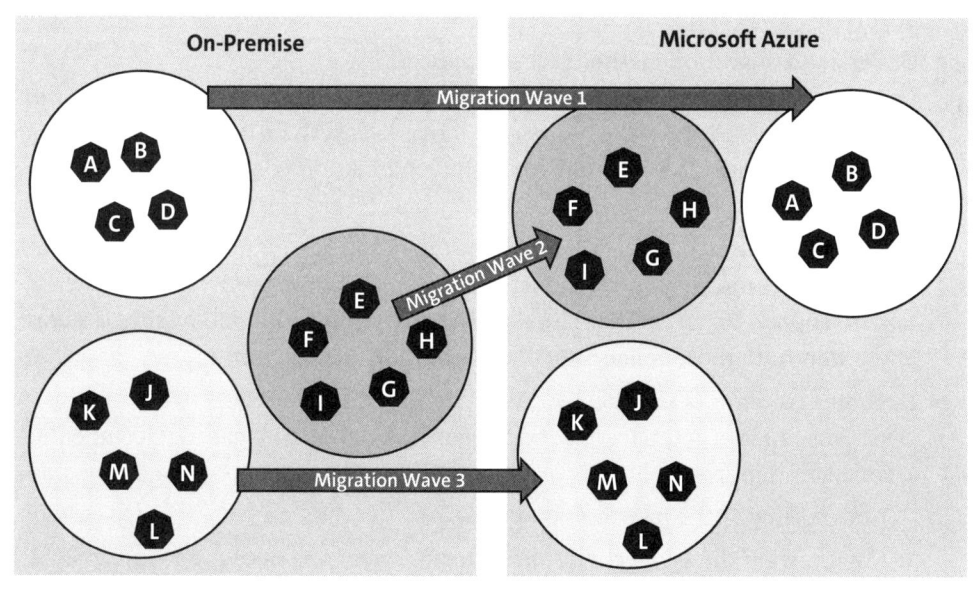

Figure 11.16 System Grouping and Migration in Waves

11.5 Lessons Learned

During your migration journey, there will be roadblocks, unknowns, and learning from overcoming issues. Some situations will be unique to your organization, whereas others are encountered by many folks. This section highlights some of the common lessons learned so you don't have to go through these yourself (like standing on the shoulder of giants):

- **Choose the right Microsoft Azure regions**
  Not all Microsoft Azure regions are created equal. Choosing the right region is important not only from a latency point of view but also for available services. Ensure that the region of your choice has all the services, especially SAP optimized ones such as M Series, SAP HANA on Azure (Large Instances), and so on as applicable.

- **Implement a cloud first strategy**
  As soon as the decision to move to Microsoft Azure is made, consider implementing all new systems directly in Microsoft Azure. That saves you from having to migrate those systems later and also provides an opportunity to understand how cloud and on-premise systems work together.

- **Integrate security at every step**
  Don't think about security as something to be implemented when systems are live; it should be a part of the architecture and implementation process at each and every step of the way.

  You may run into situations where having too many restrictions makes troubleshooting complicated, such as HA cluster configurations, so consider a balanced approach. It also gives you the opportunity to further refine your security policy during the project phase.

- **Understand migration methods for all applications**
  Different systems may have their own requirements for migration. The migration approach should focus on the best way to move each system. It could be a combination of homogenous, heterogenous, new implementation, consolidation of systems, and so on.

  In addition, ensure that you understand the migration process of third-party systems such as tax solutions, print solutions, and so on. SAP doesn't provide recommendations or support for any of the bolt-on and ancillary system migration, so it's important to work with those vendors for documentation and support.

- **Document interfaces and their connectivity mechanism**
  Over time, a lot of interfaces get added without necessarily getting documented. This creates multiple problems:
  - Not knowing all the interfaces that exist
  - Not knowing the connectivity mechanism, such as remote function call (RFC), web services, and so on

- Not knowing the connection parameters such as whether it uses IP address, host name, or DNS alias

Never assume you have the complete list unless you've verified it from the system and business—imagine missing something critical that becomes a single point of failure during the cutover triggering rollback. You may find more of these during testing rounds, but you don't want to go into cutover not knowing them all. During the discovery process, you may also come across connectivity mechanisms that aren't optimized, such as using hard-coded IP addresses, not using load balancing, and so on. Migration is a good juncture to correct those.

- **Anticipate problems**
  SAP migrations tend to follow Murphy's law (anything that can go wrong will go wrong). So even through you may have practiced and documented everything, expect issues and be ready to troubleshoot.

  In addition, it's a good idea to think about some of the common failure scenarios, such as the following and document recovery or workaround:
  - What if a VM goes down during the migration where export or import is running? How would you recover?
  - What if there is a network problem or bottleneck on the day of cutover impacting the transfer rate?
  - What happens if the backup solution isn't working as expected? What other options exist to take a backup before releasing the system to users?
  - What is your plan if you encounter storage issues, database log directory space issues, and so on?

- **Test availability zone configurations**
  When choosing availability zone configuration, perform latency tests to ensure that it meets the SAP standards. Because, usually, there are three zones, you should test different combinations to see which ones gives the best performance (there may be slight differences because Microsoft doesn't guarantee the distance between data centers in the same region).

  In addition, not all services are zone aware, so it's important to test the whole configuration. For example, at the time of publication, Microsoft Azure NetApp Files isn't zone aware, so for HA configuration with availability zone, it may introduce additional latency.

- **Understand Microsoft Azure configurations that you use**
  Because Microsoft Azure brings a lot of new configurations, it may be overwhelming initially. Take your time to go through all the configurations you're using to ensure you understand what's happening behind the scenes. Read about service restrictions and the support matrix as well.

  For example, if you're configuring HA, explore the internal load balancer and how it manages virtual IP. Similarly, if you have just in time access enabled, to use it optimally, you need to understand that it restricts access using network security groups.

- **Keep up with Microsoft Azure service evolution**
  Microsoft Azure keeps evolving constantly with new service/VM introduction and enhancements to current ones. So, if there was a use case during the design phase that you didn't find a good solution for (e.g., backup) and ended up going with a workaround, check back to see whether new features were released for that use case.
  In general, also look for optimization opportunities with new service offerings.

- **Optimize data transfer**
  Bandwidth is one factor that affects the data transfer rate (from on-premise to Microsoft Azure for migration); besides that, parallelization by using multiple transfer streams, testing transfer rate with multiple smaller files versus larger single file separation, and so on are some of the ways to optimize.
  Perform a thorough testing with different approaches to identify the best way forward.

- **Have a rollback plan**
  It's worth repeating—always have a rollback plan. There are many variables during a cutover spanning from technical to business reasons that may require a rollback or need to postpone the cutover to a later date.
  Rollback planning is often underestimated but is a crucial step for a successful project.

11.6 Summary

Given the time and effort it takes to migrate the SAP landscape to Microsoft Azure, it's like training for a marathon. You have a plan and you practice and optimize your time, but there are a lot of factors on the final day that can still affect you. This chapter explained the mechanisms and optimizations that you should include in the planning. We discussed both SAP and Microsoft Azure aspects of migration and lessons learned. Remember to always have a rollback plan!

In the next chapter, we'll talk about what happens after the migration, that is, the operational aspects of SAP on Microsoft Azure, including monitoring, cost management, and optimizations.

Chapter 12
Operations

Because the end goal of migrating systems to the cloud is running them efficiently, the architecture calls for operational aspects, and the feedback loop from operational learning makes the design better.

When thinking about moving to cloud, migration is often the biggest focus, but don't let that get in the way of thinking about how everything will work after the migration. Operational aspects should be in mind right from the beginning and that's why it's one of the elements of architectural guidance.

This chapter talks about the SAP operational processes, common use cases, monitoring, and cost management capabilities.

12.1 Cloud Operating Model

Consider the following scenarios:

- When your SAP systems are in the cloud, do you operate the same way as you have on-premise?
- What about the speed and flexibility? How can you make the best use of it?
- Is moving to the cloud only a technical change or organizational as well?

Operating in the cloud requires different skills, team structures, and, most important of all, a different mind-set:

- **Skillset**
  DevOps, infrastructure as code (IaC), and platform as a service (PaaS) are some of the new things that are more prominent in the cloud environment. Utilizing these are key to operating the cloud estate better.

- **Team structure**
  The line among hardware, operating systems (OSs), network configuration, and application services management is blurred with automation cross skills. Therefore, having different teams for each layer creates friction and slows down the momentum of the cloud-first strategy. A cross-functional team is better equipped to drive adoption and align the cloud offering to business outcomes.

- **Mindset**
  New technologies require a new way of thinking, especially for the cloud. Provisioning

a new system doesn't take weeks, and you don't pay for the server when you're not using it. Agility and flexibility are cloud ways to infrastructure rather than upfront investment and limited scalability.

Creating a cloud operating model is important in the successful transition to a cloud-first world where the business model and profits are often accelerated by how easily you can adapt the new technologies. Figure 12.1 highlights the essential elements of creating a successful cloud operating model.

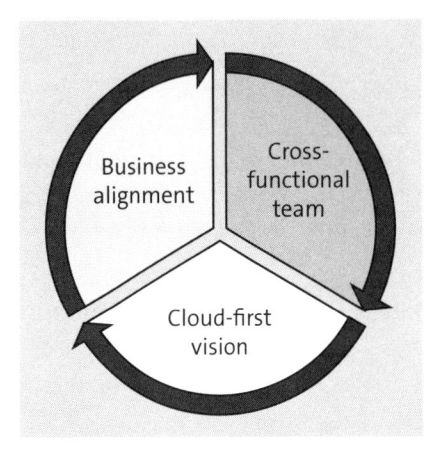

Figure 12.1 Essential Elements of a Cloud Operating Model

12.2 Operational Efficiency

Now that all the SAP systems are migrated to Microsoft Azure, the excitement is dwindling down, but not so fast—managing (or operating) systems in Microsoft Azure is more fun than the migration itself. We've already talked about how you can shut down the virtual machine (VM) when not in use to save money and resize to increase or lower the capacity. This section will explore how SAP operational scenarios make use of Microsoft Azure's flexibility and scalability.

12.2.1 SAP Snoozing

With the pay-as-you-go model, Microsoft Azure has per second billing, meaning if you shut down (deallocate) the VM when not in use, you don't get billed. So, shutting down sandbox and other nonproduction systems when not in use is a good way to optimize cost. This sounds like a no-brainer until you realize that just shutting down the VM would crash SAP, and bringing it up doesn't necessarily start the application.

You need to orchestrate the SAP shutdown and startup sequence using other scripts. Figure 12.2 shows the SAP snoozing workflow with dependency among the SAP application, database, and VM. It can be implemented using several methods, such as automation accounts, Power Apps, DevOps tools, and so on, depending on whether it's administrator driven or self-service (for developers).

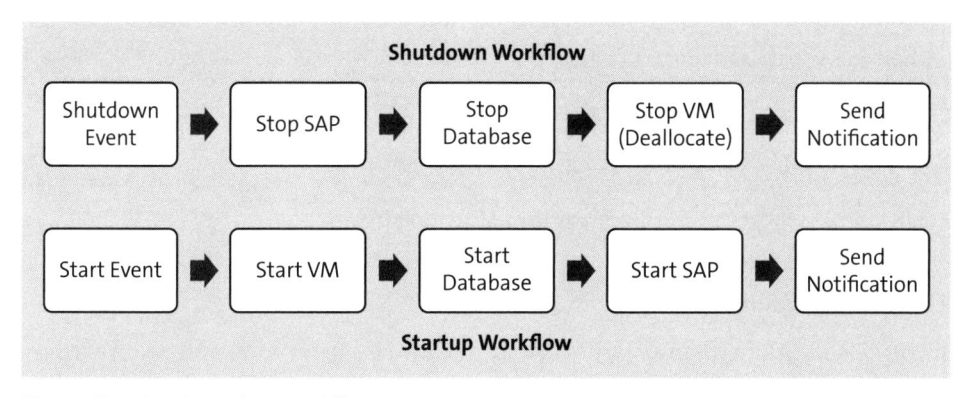

Shutdown Workflow

Shutdown Event → Stop SAP → Stop Database → Stop VM (Deallocate) → Send Notification

Start Event → Start VM → Start Database → Start SAP → Send Notification

Startup Workflow

Figure 12.2 SAP Snoozing Workflow

> **Note**
> When you buy reserved instances, you pay for the VM regardless of whether it's up, so snoozing doesn't save money for reserved instances.

Shutdown and startup can either be schedule based (every night), trigger based (don't bring it up unless someone needs to use it), or machine learning-driven (recommends a downtime window based on historical usage and user activity), and you can add more intelligence to the process by checking for active users and jobs before shutting the application down.

So, how much money does snoozing save? The exact savings depends on several factors, such as duration of snoozing, VM stock-keeping unit (SKU), region, and so on. Table 12.1 shows savings for a sample SAP landscape using mostly DS series VMs, and shutting down nonproduction VMs during the weekend achieves a savings of 17%.

SAP Landscape	Input	Comment
SAP landscape	Three-system landscape	DEV, QA, PRD
Number of compute resources (servers)	170	
Number of production servers	67	
Number of nonproduction servers	103	
Weekly uptime for nonproduction (hours)	120	Shutting down for weekend
Weekly uptime for production (hours)	168	Total hours (7*24) = 168

Table 12.1 Sample SAP Landscape Snoozing Calculation

12 Operations

SAP Landscape	Input	Comment
Total weekly cost – Production ($)	13717.368	
Total weekly cost – Nonproduction ($)	20565.048	
Savings for nonproduction environment ($)	5875.728	
Percentage nonproduction cost saving	**17.13918879**	

Table 12.1 Sample SAP Landscape Snoozing Calculation (Cont.)

12.2.2 Autoscaling

If you've had SAP for many years, you may already be aware of the utilization pattern: the peak load window and events, such as year-end closing, holiday season (for retail), and so on. SAP EarlyWatch Alert also shows the historical data of usage, which is helpful in validating the assumptions and discovering anomalous patterns. Autoscaling is a great way to meet the higher demand while optimizing the environment for cost.

> **Note**
>
> The SAP architecture makes only the application server flexible enough to scale up and down quickly without impacting the system. SAP Central Services and database don't provide the same flexibility, so we'll discuss the automatic scale-up and scale-down for application servers only, as illustrated in Figure 12.3.

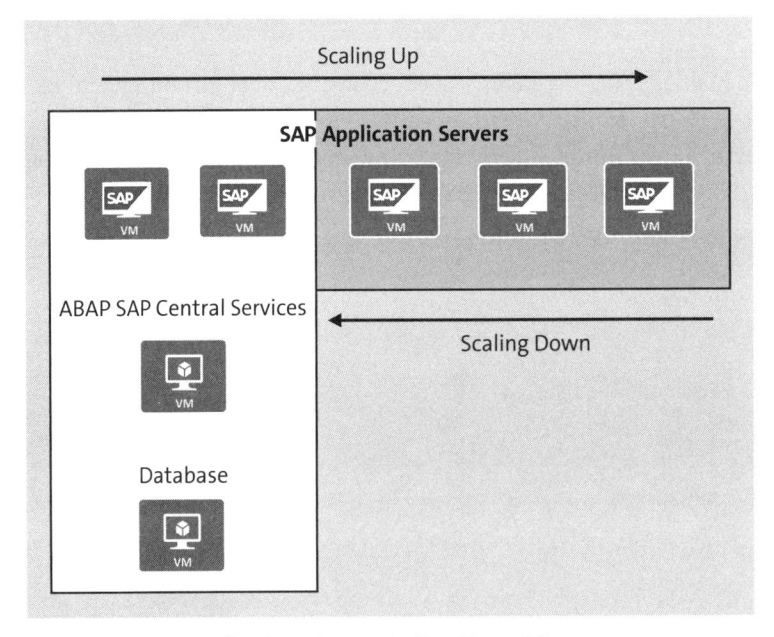

Figure 12.3 SAP Applications Server Scaling Up and Down

Autoscaling can either be load-based or schedule-based triggers and poses a similar challenge as snoozing; that is, creating more VMs doesn't create SAP application server out of the box. You have to add application logic to the automation in one of the following ways:

- Create the VM and install SAP application server, using automation, at the time of scaling, and then destroy when done.
- Install multiple applications servers ahead of time and keep them down (deallocated); bring those up when needed.
- Generalize an existing application server VM, and create an image to be deployed when scaling.

Each method has trade-offs in terms of orchestration complexity, time, effort, and cost (as highlighted in Table 12.2), and the right fit depends on your organization's skillset and automation maturity. Besides infrastructure consideration, you also need to account for monitoring using SAP Solution Manager and SAP logon groups. Without logon groups, load balancing wouldn't be optimal, and, without monitoring, you wouldn't be able to identify problems with new application servers, which is crucial for operations.

Scaling Method	Time	Complexity	Effort	Integration with SAP Solution Manager and Logon Groups	Cost When Not in Use
Install new	High	Low	Low	No	None
Startup existing	Low	Low	Medium	Yes	Storage cost for VMs
Create from image	Medium	High	High	No	Storage cost for image

Table 12.2 Comparison of Various Scaling Mechanisms

VM Scale Sets

Microsoft Azure VM scale sets, which have orchestration capabilities out of the box, aren't supported for SAP at the time of publication.

Autoscaling (up or down) of application servers can have several types of triggers, as shown in Figure 12.4:

- **Load-based triggers**
  These can be CPU, memory, or any other custom metric that can be monitored. The complexity also lies in detecting the metric and triggering the autoscaling -up and keep monitoring the metric so you can scale down.

12 Operations

- **Schedule-based triggers**
  These are easier to implement, especially if you're trying to do it every day or weekly. The downside is that if there is an unexpected load, it wouldn't be considered. You can minimize this scenario by reviewing the SAP EarlyWatch Alert report regularly, but you can't completely eliminate random events.

- **SAP event-based triggers**
  These can be implemented using the SAP external command feature from Transaction SM69.

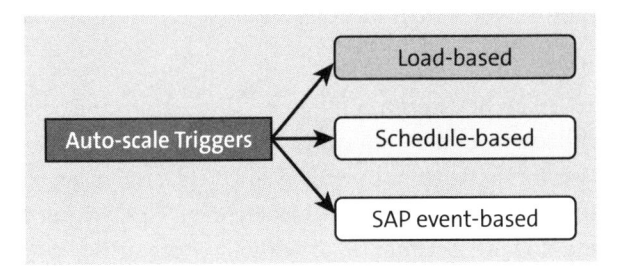

Figure 12.4 Type of Triggers for Autoscaling

You can get more granular by implementing different application servers for background jobs versus dialog (user load). That would optimize the implementation by just creating an application server for jobs during month end and dialog server during peak user load. You can also use SAP's operation mode feature to switch between dialog and background work processes.

> **Scaling Down**
>
> Remember that scaling down is an important part of autoscaling, without which, you'll be running peak capacity. In addition, when scaling down, you need to account for logged-in users and running jobs, which can be more involved than just simply shutting down. You can use SAP's *soft-shutdown* mechanism that waits for the transaction to end before shutting down the application.

12.2.3 Operating System and SAP Patching

Patching is a common operational activity (both OS and SAP kernel), and the requirements can be as often as monthly. Besides some exceptions (e.g., live patching compatible use cases), OS patching requires a VM restart, and SAP kernel patching requires an application restart.

The following sections will describe how you can use the flexibility of the cloud to minimize the downtime for patching.

12.2 Operational Efficiency

Rolling Patches

Patching one server at a time in a rolling manner (either though automation or manually) is a good way to minimize downtime. This is straightforward for application servers because they don't contain any transaction data but require HA configuration for SAP Central Services and database. Non-HA systems will incur downtime when patching SAP Central Services and database servers.

Figure 12.5 illustrates how rolling OS patching can be achieved for SAP NetWeaver and ABAP platform.

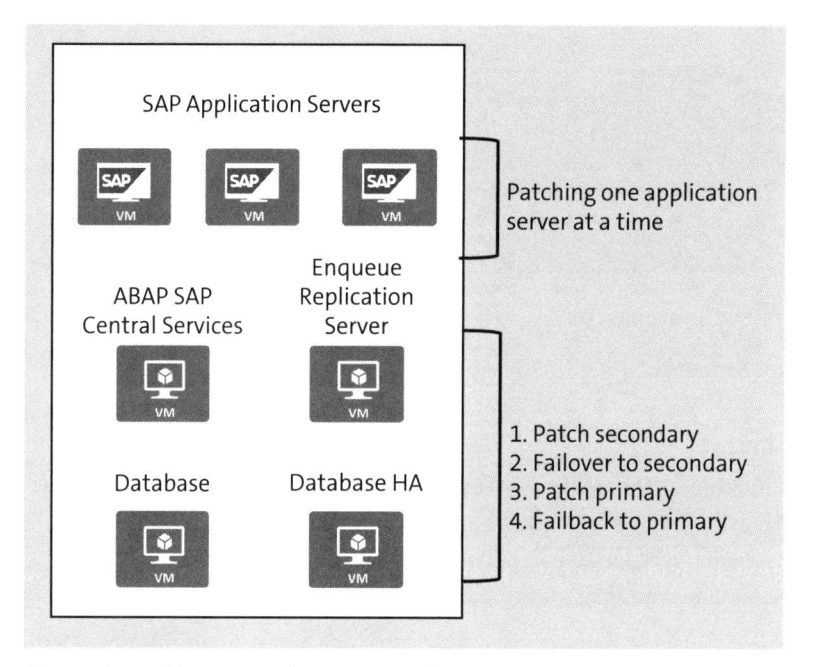

Figure 12.5 Rolling OS Patching Process Illustration

SAP Rolling Kernel Switch

The rolling kernel switch (RKS) process allows the kernel update for ABAP-based systems without overall system downtime; as a by-product, you can also change SAP static profile parameters during RKS.

The system designates an application server as a monitor that is restarted last; ABAP SAP Central Services also acts as a monitor for its own restart. The restart sequence is illustrated in Figure 12.6 and described as follows:

- Enqueue replication server (ERS) is restarted first ❶.
- ABAP SAP Central Services is restarted second (and it monitors itself) ❷.
- Application servers are restarted in the sequence defined by the system ❸–❺.

245

12 Operations

In Figure 12.6, the third application server, designated as ❺, is the monitor and is restarted in the end

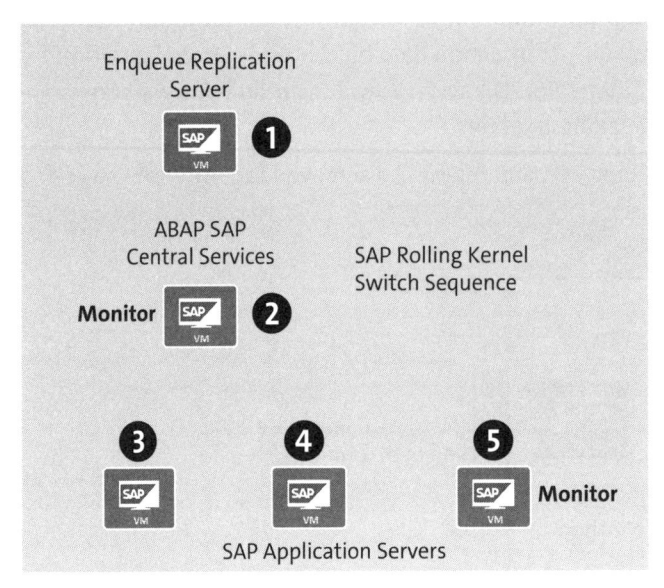

Figure 12.6 SAP RKS Sequence

Immutable Architecture

Another way of looking at the cloud infrastructure is as an immutable architecture; that is, servers aren't changed or updated, in place, after the initial deployment. If something needs to be upgraded or patched at the OS level, a new server with the same configuration is created that replaces the current one.

Because it's easy and fast to build new servers in Microsoft Azure, an immutable architecture can contribute to the efficiency in terms of patching and maintaining VMs. As usual, SAP architecture introduces additional complexities. We'll discuss the details one component at a time, that is, application servers, SAP Central Services, and database servers.

Application Servers

You deploy a new server with updated patches, install the SAP application with a virtual host name, and then replace the current ones with new instances. Figure 12.7 illustrates this concept. At the infrastructure layer, you need to ensure that the new servers use the same resiliency configuration, such as availability sets, availability zones, proximity placement groups, and so on. At the application layer, these new servers should be added to logon, batch, and remote function call (RFC) groups.

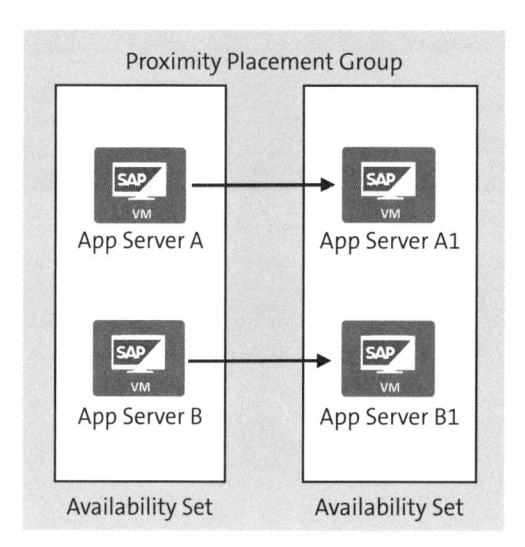

Figure 12.7 SAP Application Server Maintenance Using Immutable Architecture

SAP Central Services

Deploy new servers with SAP Central Services and switch the configuration to point to the new ones. Similar to rolling patching, HA configuration is required to avoid system downtime. Figure 12.8 highlights this concept, and the switch sequence is as follows:

- Deploy the new ERS with updated patches
- Reconfigure clustering to add the new ERS and remove the current one
- Failover to the new ERS
- Deploy the new ABAP SAP Central Services server
- Reconfigure clustering with the new ABAP SAP Central Services and ERS
- Failback to the new ABAP SAP Central Services
- Decommission the old ABAP SAP Central Services and ERS servers

This process also requires reconfiguration of Microsoft Azure Load Balancer to include the new servers during the switch.

> **Standalone Enqueue Server 2**
>
> If you're using standalone enqueue server 2 (ENSA2) configuration with more than two SAP Central Services VMs, the immutable process is similar; you just need to do it for all the servers.

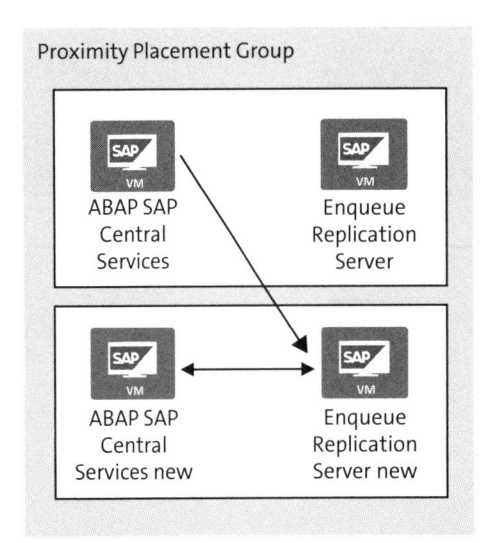

Figure 12.8 SAP Central Services Maintenance Using Immutable Architecture

Database Servers

Database server maintenance using immutable architecture is the most complex and time-consuming among all components because it requires data replication to the new server, which becomes impractical to do frequently for larger databases.

Figure 12.9 and the following steps illustrate how the SAP HANA multitarget replication feature (introduced in SAP HANA 2.0 SP 3) can be used to move a database to a new set of servers. SAP HANA versions are backward compatible, so the new servers can have a newer patch of database as well.

❶ Current setup includes primary server A replicating to B in HA configuration. Deploy C and D with the same or higher SAP HANA patch.

❷ Register C with A and D with B for replication.

❸ Failover B to D, and then register D with C.

❹ Failover A to C with C being the new primary and D being the new secondary in HA configuration (at this point, you can decommission A and B).

Immutable architecture doesn't leave any server in an inconsistent state because there is no patching error or rollback required. The backout plan includes reverting to the original configuration and deleting newly deployed servers. Immutable maintenance is recommended when your organization's automation capabilities are mature, so all of this can be done using the no-touch approach. Manual methods introduce delays and are error prone. In addition, it's not an all-or-nothing approach, so you can still choose to go this route for application servers and perform rolling maintenance for database servers.

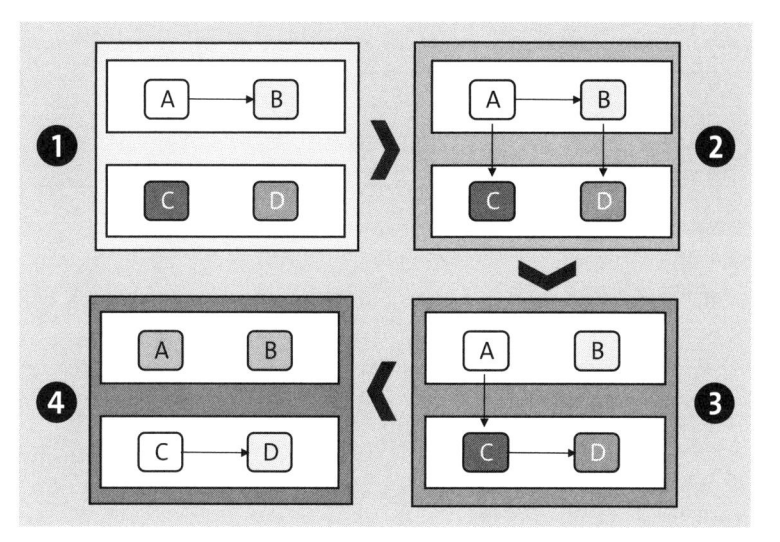

Figure 12.9 SAP HANA Server Maintenance Using Immutable Architecture

> **Impact to DR Configuration**
> With the introduction to new servers, the DR configuration needs to be revisited, which is also true for in-place upgrades and patching because they may break during the transition.

12.2.4 Rightsizing and Virtual Machine Resizing

Unlike traditional environments where you size for growth, and it may take weeks to get more resources, Microsoft Azure's flexibility enables you to rightsize the systems. Rightsizing is more important in the cloud for two reasons:

- Smaller sizing means lower cost.
- You can increase or decrease the size on short notice.

It may be an iterative exercise to figure out what size works best for your systems (as illustrated in Figure 12.10) and the SAP EarlyWatch Alert report is a good place to review the utilization. As far as resizing the VM goes, you need to ensure the application is gracefully shut down and brought up—the process and automation is similar to what we discussed for rolling patches. After the new size VMs are up, ensure that all the extensions (especially the enhanced monitoring extension) and HA/DR are working as expected. When you're resizing the VM, you can use the opportunity to resize disks as well, if needed.

12   Operations

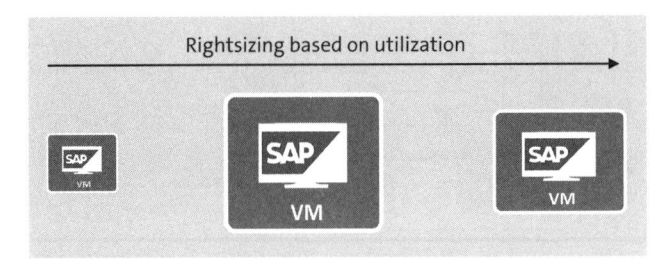

Figure 12.10 VM Resizing to Get to the Right Size

Size Flexibility for Reserved Instances

Microsoft Azure provides instance size flexibility for reserved instances, which lets you use the discount on any VM in the defined size flexibility group; for example, if you buy DSv2, the discount applies to DS1v2 – DS4v2.

Gen1 to Gen2 VM

At the time of publication, Microsoft Azure doesn't allow resizing from one generation to another, meaning you'll have to create a new VM and migrate the application/database if you choose to go to Gen2 from a Gen1 VM.

12.2.5   System Clone, Copy, and Refresh

System clone, copy, and refresh are some of the common operational use cases, and Figure 12.11 explains the differences and their use cases (ABP, ABS, ABT, and ABQ are SAP system IDs representing different installations). More often than not, database copy is the long pole in the tent for these options. In Microsoft Azure, you can simplify the process and cut down the database copy time; this section discusses some of those tools and techniques.

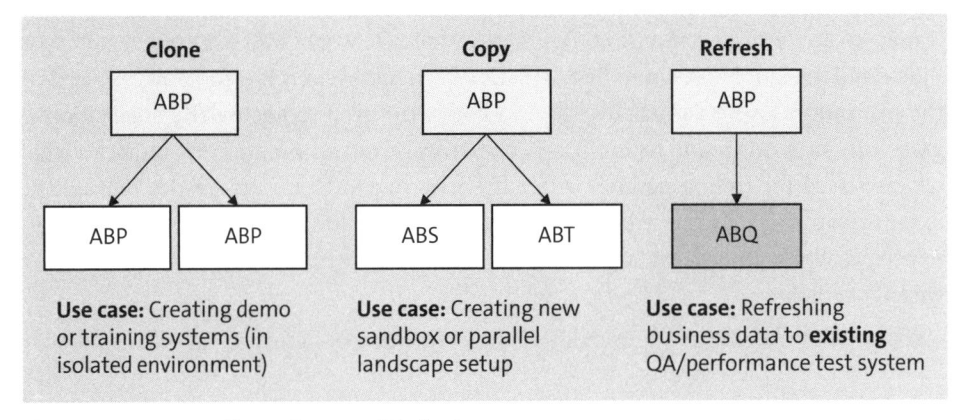

Figure 12.11 System Clone, Copy, and Refresh

12.2.6 Microsoft Azure Backup

If you're using Microsoft Azure Backup, the restore options include alternate VM as well as files (besides the same server), as shown in Figure 12.12, for SAP HANA, making it easier to build a new system (alternate location) as well as refresh.

Restore

Where and how to Restore?

| Alternate Location | Overwrite DB | Restore as files |

Figure 12.12 Restore Options for Microsoft Azure Backup for SAP HANA

12.2.7 Microsoft Azure NetApp Files and Disks Snapshot

Both Microsoft Azure managed disks and Microsoft Azure NetApp Files provide snapshot capabilities at the disk layer, which is great for large databases because snapshot times are in seconds compared to hours for a backup.

We've discussed the details in Chapter 8, and snapshot is a lightning fast way to restore the database for system copy, clone, and refresh processes. Third-party systems such as Commvault also integrate the same way and can create and restore snapshots.

12.2.8 SAP Landscape Management Integration

Microsoft Azure connector for SAP Landscape Management (Microsoft Azure LaMa 3.0 onwards) can make your SAP Landscape Management system much more productive in Microsoft Azure. Operational activities such as system relocate, copy, clone, refresh, and even VM provisioning are built-in to the framework (with some restrictions as highlighted in SAP Note: 2343511).

The Commvault backup management tool integrates with SAP Landscape Management to achieve automated database copy as well.

12.2.9 SAP HANA on Azure (Large Instances) to Virtual Machine Migration

If you were an early adopter of Microsoft Azure, before large-memory VMs were released, you may have chosen to go with SAP HANA on Azure (Large Instances) for SAP HANA databases. Now that VMs go up to 12 TB in memory (at the time of publication), it may make sense to move to VMs for the flexibility.

Because you'll be moving from bare metal to VM, there is no option of changing the SKU that exists for VMs; instead, you need to migrate the SAP HANA database as follows:

12 Operations

- If you'll be using Microsoft Azure premium or ultra disk in the target system (VM), setting up SAP HANA system replication is the least-downtime migration method.
- If you're planning to use Microsoft Azure NetApp Files for data and log files (in the VM), copying the data at the OS level using Linux tools is an option as well.

Figure 12.13 illustrates the source (SAP HANA on Azure [Large Instances]) and target (VM) setup for SAP HANA.

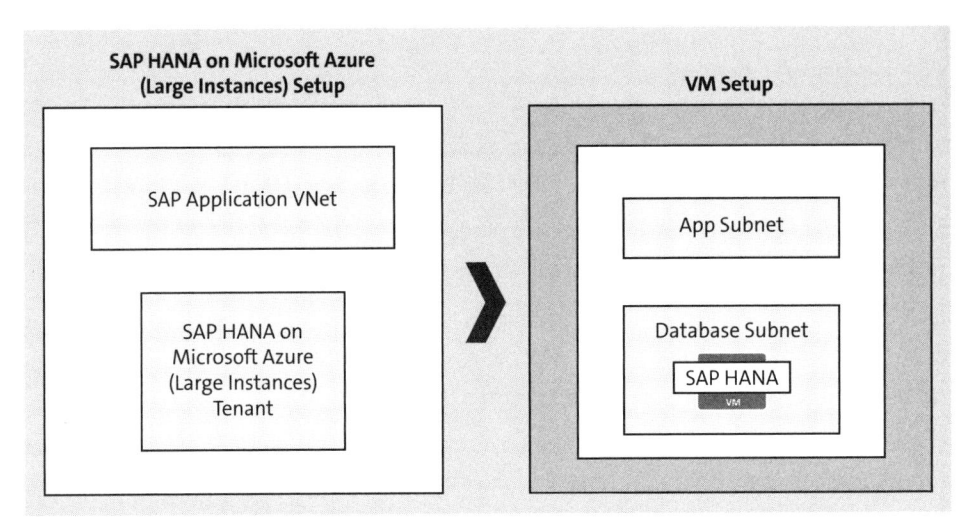

Figure 12.13 SAP HANA on Azure (Large Instances) to VM Migration for SAP HANA

Besides the obvious changes of hardware and network setup, there are several other differences between running SAP HANA on Azure (Large Instances) and VM, and those need to be considered during the migration:

- **License generation**
  A new SAP HANA license needs to be generated for the target VM.
- **HA and SLA**
  SAP HANA on Azure (Large Instances) HA is set up as a 99.99% SLA; to get the same SLA, you'll need to deploy the VMs in an availability zone (consider the proximity placement groups setup as well). Availability sets deployment has a 99.95% SLA.
- **Updates in OS and SAP HANA**
  Minor updates in the OS (as long as the target is supported, and all the patches and packages are compatible) and SAP HANA (as supported by SAP) are possible with the SAP HANA on Azure (Large Instances) to VM migration.
- **Source and target host name**
  If domain name service (DNS) redirection is used, there is no change; otherwise, configuration needs to reflect the new host name for connectivity to SAP HANA.
- **Backup and DR**
  You may want to revisit the backup/DR strategies and align them with the rest of the

VMs and databases on the VM, such as SAP HANA system replication for DR instead of default storage replication in SAP HANA on Azure (Large Instances).

- **Decommission SAP HANA on Azure (Large Instances) specific setup**
  After the migration, you need to get rid of SAP HANA on Azure (Large Instances) servers, OS licenses, global reach/IPTables, and any other setup used specifically for SAP HANA on Azure (Large Instances).

> **Rightsizing**
>
> SAP HANA on Azure (Large Instances) to VM migration is also a good opportunity to review the utilization and rightsize the VM for optimal utilization.

12.2.10 SAP Licensing and Hardware Key

SAP implemented a new hardware key calculation mechanism for licensing in Microsoft Azure with the following kernel patches:

Linux OS:

- SAP kernel 7.21 EXT PL #622 or higher
- SAP kernel 7.22 EXT PL #112 or higher
- SAP kernel 7.42 PL #324 or higher
- SAP kernel 7.45 PL #111 or higher

Windows OS:

- SAP kernel 7.21 PL #332 or higher
- SAP kernel 7.38 PL #72 or higher
- SAP kernel 7.41 PL #210 or higher
- SAP kernel 7.42 PL #31 or higher

If you did a kernel update to any of the patches listed, the SAP license gets invalidated, and a temporary license is created, which may trigger the license expiration popup. The resolution is the apply for new licensing using the hardware key as shown in Transaction SLICENSE or in the output of `saplikey -get`.

The new calculation takes the Microsoft Azure VM unique ID into account, which is a 128-bit identifier in Microsoft Azure VMs. Figure 12.14 shows the trace of `saplicense` in Microsoft Azure VM showing the ID.

```
VirtPGetBiosValue: reading /sys/devices/virtual/dmi/id/board_asset_tag
VirtPGetBiosValue: /sys/devices/virtual/dmi/id/board_asset_tag = ''
SlicGetFullHwId: hwid 'AZURE_643B041F-0307-C84C-B90C-901D9BC13C91' found
SlicGetHwId: ID >AZURE_643B041F-0307-C84C-B90C-901D9BC13C91<
```

Figure 12.14 saplicense Trace Showing the Microsoft Azure ID

The following scenarios don't change the VM ID, so they don't require regenerating an SAP license:

- Shutdown or reboot
- Deallocate
- Redeploy

The following VM scenarios require generating a license for SAP:

- Creating from saved image
- Cloning for system copy
- Kernel update as mentioned earlier
- Bringing up the system at the DR site when using Microsoft Azure Site Recovery

12.2.11 Operational Learning

Over time, learning become recommendations and, to that extent, not only helps avoid the pitfalls but also helps shape the thought process for architecture in Microsoft Azure. This section discusses some of the common things to keep in mind when running SAP on Microsoft Azure.

SAP Certified versus SAP on Microsoft Azure Certified

We know that SAP certifies the configuration in Microsoft Azure, but it doesn't necessarily map 1:1 from on-premise to the cloud. Not everything that's certified by SAP is certified for Microsoft Azure. A few examples include Oracle database use cases, OSs (and specific versions), and certain database HA configurations.

So, it's important to find out what configuration is certified in Microsoft Azure, and Microsoft documentation is a good way to verify that. If you're looking into SAP Notes, look for configurations related to Microsoft Azure.

Microsoft Azure Services and Service-Level Agreements

While Microsoft Azure publishes SLAs for most of the services, not everything is governed by the SLA. Keep this in mind not only when architecting a solution but also during operations because that's where you'll notice it. Besides SLAs, you can look at benchmarks (e.g., for throughput) or normal runtimes for the services to get an idea of their efficiency.

Following are some examples:

- **VM deployment time**
  Microsoft Azure doesn't guarantee a certain time within which a VM will be deployed.
- **VM start or restart**
  There is no formal SLA for how long it takes to restart or start a VM after deallocation.

- **Backup/restore time**
  Backup and restore depend on several factors, so defining an SLA may not be possible.

- **Microsoft Azure Site Recovery RPO**
  At the time of publication, Microsoft Azure Site Recovery provides a recovery time objective (RTO) of two hours, but there is no recovery point objective (RPO) SLA because it's based on asynchronous replication and can be affected by many factors.

Sometimes, SLAs among services may not be easy to interpret to a business use case. For example, you configure VMs in an availability zone to get the SLA of 99.99% and Microsoft Azure Monitor, which guarantees alerts 99.9% of the time (at the time of publication), so how do we configure the monitoring dashboard to interpret the outage results!

Capacity Availability Guarantee

Never assume guaranteed capacity in Microsoft Azure. For instance, if you have a reserved instance or dedicated host in one Microsoft Azure region, it doesn't by default guarantee another host with the same configuration in the paired region.

Similarly, when you deallocate a VM to save cost, the capacity is released back to Microsoft Azure. Statistically you may get the VM back when you try to bring it up, but it's not bound by any SLA.

Modularizing Automation

Automation templates built during deployment and migrations are still valuable during operations. Be sure to have smaller modules so the code can be swapped or the modules reused in a different context. It may sound like a no-brainer, but modules with thousands of lines that group everything together aren't uncommon. In the SAP context, you can create modules as follows (for example):

- Infrastructure
- Database
- SAP Central Services
- HA configuration
- Application servers
- DR configuration

It also makes it easier to keep up with the latest version; for example, if you want the latest database version with the same application version, you just need to update the database module to know where to find the version in question.

Holistic View of Services

When you choose a service, VM, or OS, ensure that it works across the landscape architecture, for example:

- Because Gen1 and Gen2 VMs aren't portable, when you choose Gen1, ensure that you don't immediately need or want to move to Gen2.
- Some configurations don't support disk encryption, so if encryption for everything is a policy, you want to avoid that setup.
- When SLES 15 was first certified for SAP, it didn't support Microsoft Azure Site Recovery.
- When proximity placement groups was introduced, it wasn't compatible with Microsoft Azure Site Recovery.

These examples highlight the importance of looking at the bigger picture to ensure that the particular service isn't only the best for one use case but also compatible with a broader set of services.

Automation versus Portal

Making another case for automation is the fact that services in Microsoft Azure are released for application programming interfaces (APIs) before finding a place in the portal. Therefore, be automation ready to get your hands on the latest feature that you've been waiting for. Proximity placement groups compatibility with Microsoft Azure Site Recovery is an example of a feature that you may have wanted and could use with automation prior to portal.

Heterogenous Operating System Configuration

SAP supports heterogenous OS configuration such as SAP HANA on Linux (only option for SAP HANA) and Windows for application and SAP Central Services or even different Linux flavors for SAP HANA system replication (as long as both are in the supported list). However, just because something is supported doesn't mean it would work well with your organizational operational processes.

Mixing different OSs creates challenges such as compatibility problems with patches, file sharing, parameter optimization, and day-zero vulnerabilities. If you decide to go this route, be aware of issues and plan for potential conflicts, such as the Linux application server is supported with Windows central instance but not if you're using SQL Server as the database (SAP Note: 2369910).

Microsoft Azure NetApp Files Configurations

We've discussed that you need a minimum 4 TiB pool to use Microsoft Azure NetApp Files, which can be stretched sometimes when you're trying to use it for HA configuration of SAP Central Services and need only a fraction of that. In those cases, you need to do a cost-benefit analysis of the features you're going to use in Microsoft Azure NetApp Files and what alternatives are available. For example, if you're going to set up Network File System (NFS) servers for SAP HA, the cost may be the same with added maintenance responsibility. If the snapshot capability is worth the extra cost to you, then it's a good fit for purpose.

Another way to look at Microsoft Azure NetApp Files is as a dynamic performance provider. Because the pool and volume sizes can be increased or decreased online, you'll be able to adjust throughput on demand, which has some use cases as well.

At the time of publication, Microsoft Azure NetApp Files doesn't enforce a volume quota, so what you created as 100 GiB initially can grow automatically, which may end up extending the pool size beyond 4 TiB, eventually costing more than planned. Automatic growth and not reflecting true volume size make it difficult to predict cost and create file system percentage-based alerts. You can still create Microsoft Azure-based alerts, but if you're using SAP Solution Manager or any other tool to get the space stats from the VM, there would be an additional layer of complexity.

As far as Microsoft Azure NetApp Files pools go, behind the scenes, Microsoft takes care of HA and performance, so you don't need to create separate pools for production and nonproduction just to get better performance and/or availability.

> **Tip**
> Microsoft Azure NetApp Files allows dynamic changes to service levels, meaning you can change from standard to premium to ultra as needed. This has an interesting use case for DR: when using Microsoft Azure NetApp Files cross-region replication for DR, you can use the standard service level at the DR site to optimize costs, which can be upgraded to premium at go time.

> **Note**
> Upgrading the service level (standard -> premium -> ultra) is immediate, whereas downgrade has a cool down period of seven days. In other words, after you change the service level, you can't downgrade for seven days.

Microsoft Azure NetApp Files is evolving fast, and new features release frequently specifically for SAP use cases. To keep up to date with new features, you can use this link: *https://docs.microsoft.com/en-us/azure/azure-netapp-files/whats-new*.

12.3 Monitoring

Monitoring and alerting is an important part of managing operations, and what you monitor is as important, if not more, as how you do it.

12 Operations

During migration planning, you should also discover all the services and metrics that are currently being monitored and captured. This is especially important if you're looking to optimize the monitoring setup after migrating to Microsoft Azure. Different tools have their own features and limitations, so it's not easy to map an on-premise tool to a Microsoft Azure tool for all monitoring. After you know what needs monitoring, then the discussion changes from tool specifics to requirement specifics, which is a better starting point.

Figure 12.15 illustrate a way of looking at layers of services and processes that you'll need to address for monitoring that ranges from infrastructure to business processes.

	Business Process	
SAP and third party	Application	Database
IaaS	Infrastructure	PaaS

Figure 12.15 Service and Process Categories to Be Monitored

After you have the areas pinned down, you need to look at the items that need monitoring and the metrics, such as VM availability, storage performance, and storage percentage used. You should also think about how you'd like to combine different views in a single dashboard and integrate with alerting and ticketing systems. After you get the complete picture of "what," then you can explore the "how" part with tools, scripts, or out-of-the-box solutions, as illustrated in Figure 12.16. The risk with starting with a tool earlier in a process is missing important items that may not be available with the tool, such as HA cluster or PaaS solutions monitoring.

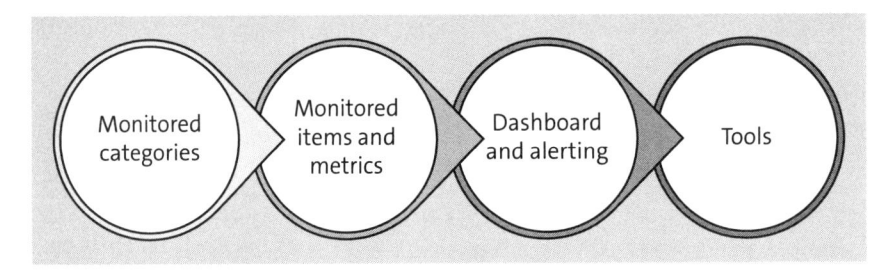

Figure 12.16 Monitoring Categories to Tools Flow of Decision

12.3.1 SAP Solution Manager

SAP Solution Manager and *SAP Focused Run*, being SAP products, are used by a lot of organizations to monitor business processes and application availability/performance monitoring, and they are better integrated with the SAP ecosystem. We'll discuss how

Microsoft Azure native solutions such as Microsoft Azure Monitor and Microsoft Azure Monitor for SAP Solutions can complement those tools. SAP Solution Manager is cloud independent so it's a good tool to have, especially if you're looking for hybrid SAP environments. However, you should also consider the bigger picture of a single dashboard and the fact that SAP Solution Manager must be installed on Infrastructure as a Service (IaaS), must be monitored, and needs resiliency configuration (HA) to be effective.

12.3.2 Microsoft Azure Monitor

Microsoft Azure services provide some basic metrics out of the box, such as CPU, disk, and availability for VMs, which internally use Microsoft Azure Monitor. To get better insights into performance and dependencies, additional configuration and feature enablement in Microsoft Azure Monitor can be used.

You can analyze, visualize, and act on telemetry from Microsoft Azure services and on-premise environments. It also shows insights and provides integration options, as illustrated in Figure 12.17.

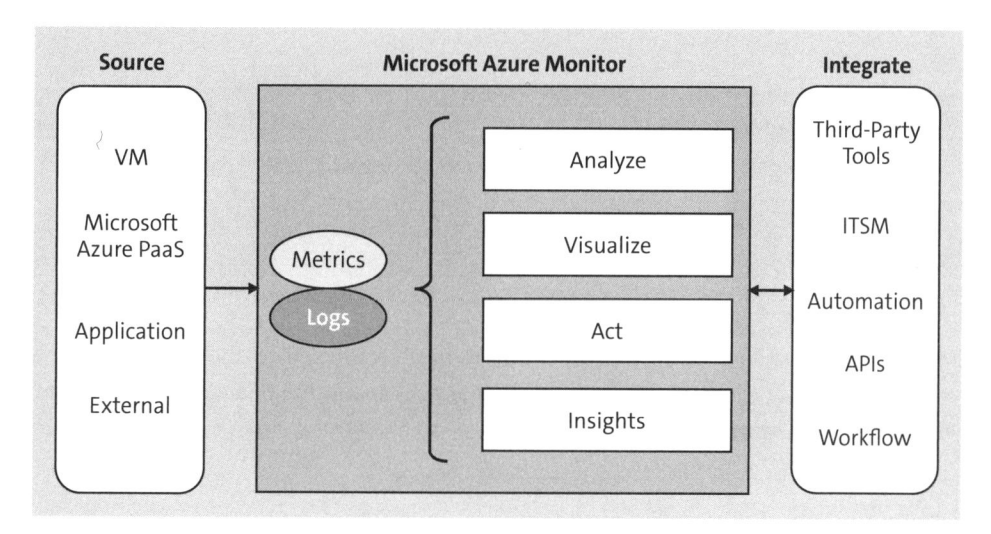

Figure 12.17 Microsoft Azure Monitor Data Ingestion and Actions

All the data collected is categorized into metrics, such as CPU utilization, disk input/output operations per second (IOPS), and logs (e.g., event logs and traces); from there, the monitoring tool combines the data to analyze and generate actionable insights. It can also collect data from external sources using APIs and applications, although SAP-related application data collection is limited at the time of publication. Figure 12.18 show an example of insights available using Microsoft Azure Monitor for a VM. You can access this information either by going to the Microsoft Azure Monitor service or directly from the VM by selecting the metrics and insights blade under the **Monitoring** section.

259

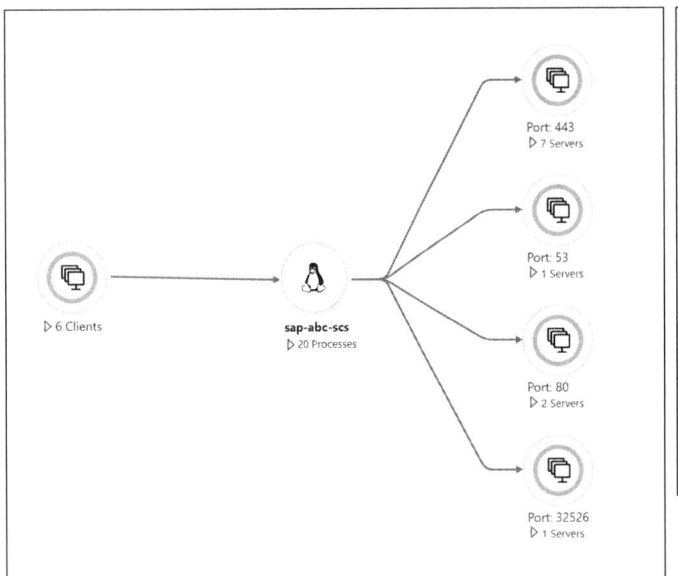

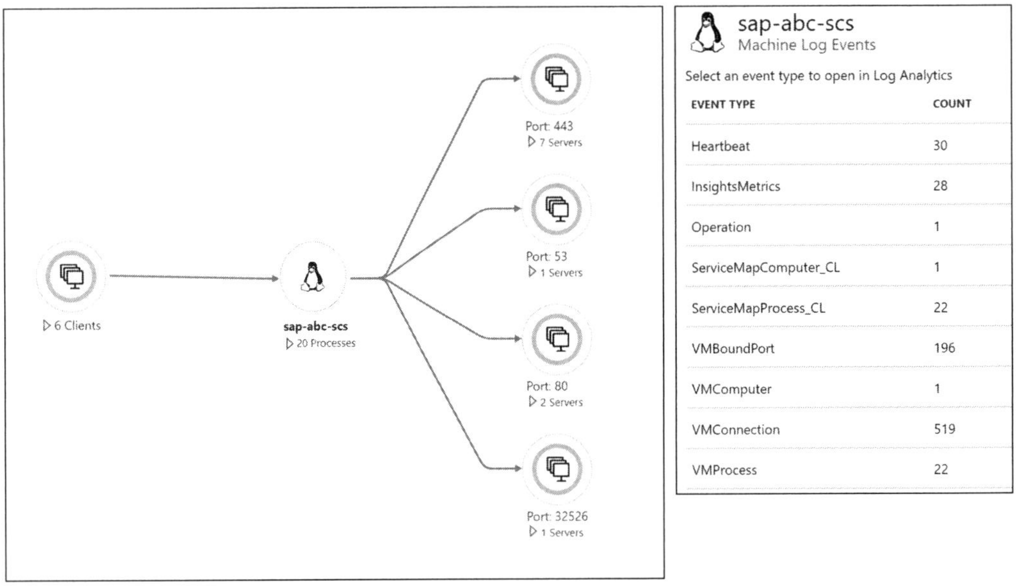

12 Operations

Figure 12.18 Microsoft Azure Monitor Insights Example

> **PaaS Solutions Monitoring**
> Services such as Microsoft Azure NetApp Files and Microsoft Azure Load Balancer provide performance metrics that are integrated with Microsoft Azure Monitor as well.

Metrics and Logs

Metrics are quantitative values that are periodically collected to show an aspect of a resource, such as CPU utilization, at a particular peak-load time or a graph showing the variation, as illustrated in Figure 12.19.

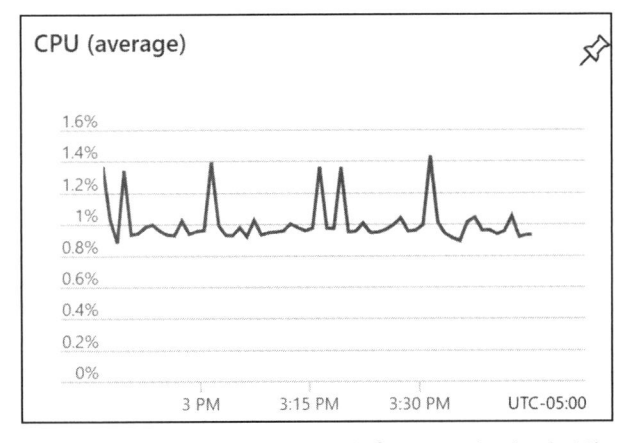

Figure 12.19 CPU Utilization Metric from Monitoring in Microsoft Azure

12.3 Monitoring

Logs can be divided into resource logs and activity logs:

- Resource logs (previously called diagnostic logs) capture the operation performed at a resource level (data plane), such as making a database request.
- Activity logs act at the management plane and show what, when, and who data in the subscription, such as concerning starting a VM.

Figure 12.20 shows examples of logs generated as viewed from the Microsoft Azure portal.

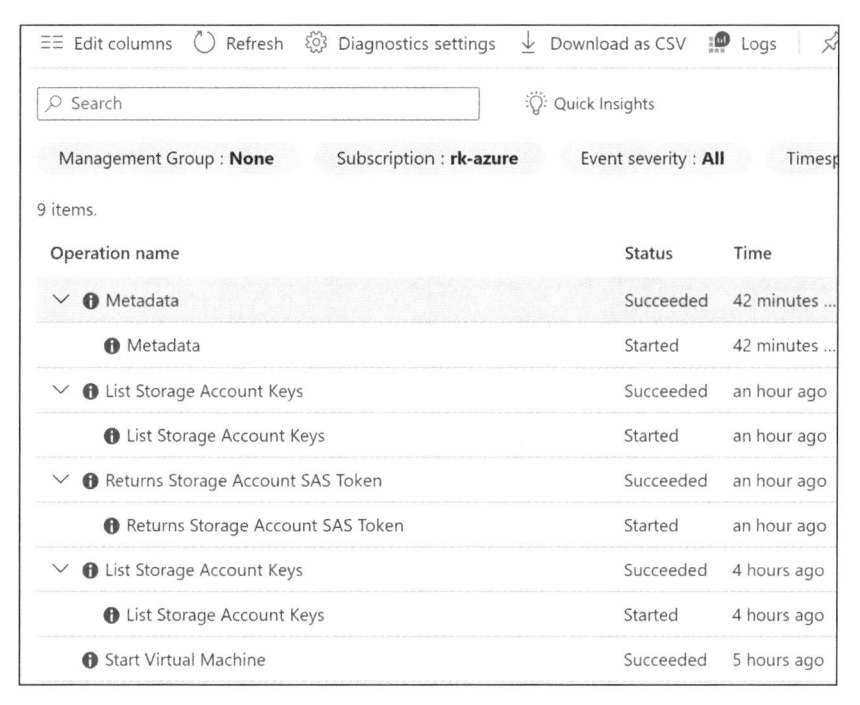

Operation name	Status	Time
⌄ ⓘ Metadata	Succeeded	42 minutes …
ⓘ Metadata	Started	42 minutes …
⌄ ⓘ List Storage Account Keys	Succeeded	an hour ago
ⓘ List Storage Account Keys	Started	an hour ago
⌄ ⓘ Returns Storage Account SAS Token	Succeeded	an hour ago
ⓘ Returns Storage Account SAS Token	Started	an hour ago
⌄ ⓘ List Storage Account Keys	Succeeded	4 hours ago
ⓘ List Storage Account Keys	Started	4 hours ago
ⓘ Start Virtual Machine	Succeeded	5 hours ago

Figure 12.20 Example of Logs from the Microsoft Azure Portal

Log Destination

The data that's collected can be stored in several ways depending on how you're planning to analyze and integrate. Diagnostic settings configurations allow you to set a destination such as log analytics workspace, event hubs, and storage account.

> **Microsoft Azure Monitor versus Microsoft Azure Service Health**
>
> Microsoft Azure Service Health compliments Microsoft Azure Monitor and together help you troubleshoot an issue. Let's say users are having issues accessing a particular system, and you don't know where the issue is; the first place to look is Microsoft Azure Service Health to determine whether it's a Microsoft Azure platform issue. If it's not a platform issue, then you can dig deeper into Microsoft Azure Monitor logs to figure out where the problem lies.

12   Operations

12.3.3 Dashboards

After all the data is collected, you probably don't want to see each piece of information individually, and that's were dashboards are useful: you can collate multiple resources, customize views, and share with others (role based). It's also helpful in data correlation across multiple resources. Monitoring dashboards can be built using Microsoft Azure's out-of-the-box dashboard option, using third-party tools such as Grafana, or the more involved option of building a custom application. We'll discuss some of these methods in this section.

Microsoft Azure Dashboard

Microsoft Azure portal provides a dashboard capability where you can view metrics, log analytics, and insights from multiple resources. You can create one in Microsoft Azure portal, with auto-refresh, as shown in Figure 12.21.

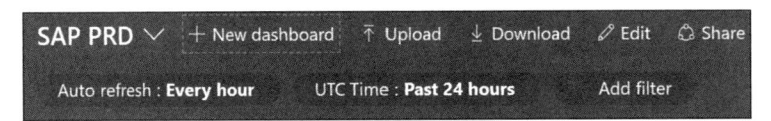

Figure 12.21 Microsoft Azure Dashboard Options from the Portal

You can add dashboard elements directly from there using the **Edit** option, but it's often easier to use the **Pin to Dashboard** button from the view you're looking at, as shown in Figure 12.22. You can add different aspects, such as infrastructure, security, network, and so on, making it easier to correlate across different layers to analyze a problem or look for optimization.

Figure 12.22 Pin to Dashboard Directly from the View

Because the Microsoft Azure dashboard is integrated with the platform, it makes dashboarding easier across different views and can add role-based access control to shared views. However, limitations such as no interaction option with dashboard data, limited drill down, lack of custom parameter support, and so on provide minimal use cases for complex landscapes.

Power BI

Power BI is a Microsoft product that can also be configured in the portal in embedded mode, which provides better reporting capabilities by analyzing long-term data and trends. Combining multiple sources is a powerful feature that comes with Power BI.

Besides rich visualizations, Power BI has filtering capabilities, and reports can be shared across the organization. It limits refreshes to eight times per day (at the time of publication) and needs to import query results into the model, which may have limitations on size and refresh.

> **Licensing**
> Power BI licensing is required, which has a separate model from Microsoft Azure services.

Third-Party and Custom-Built Dashboards

Because all the data from Microsoft Azure Monitor is accessible using APIs, you can also use third-party tools (e.g., Grafana) or build your own.

> **Trade-Offs**
> Third-party and custom tools have trade-offs with the cost and effort required to get it going, but they provide flexibility with customizations and interactivity.

Microsoft Azure Advisor

Microsoft Azure Advisor is a built-in dashboard that provides *personalized* recommendations along the following areas (see Figure 12.23) and can also be further customized based on your preferences:

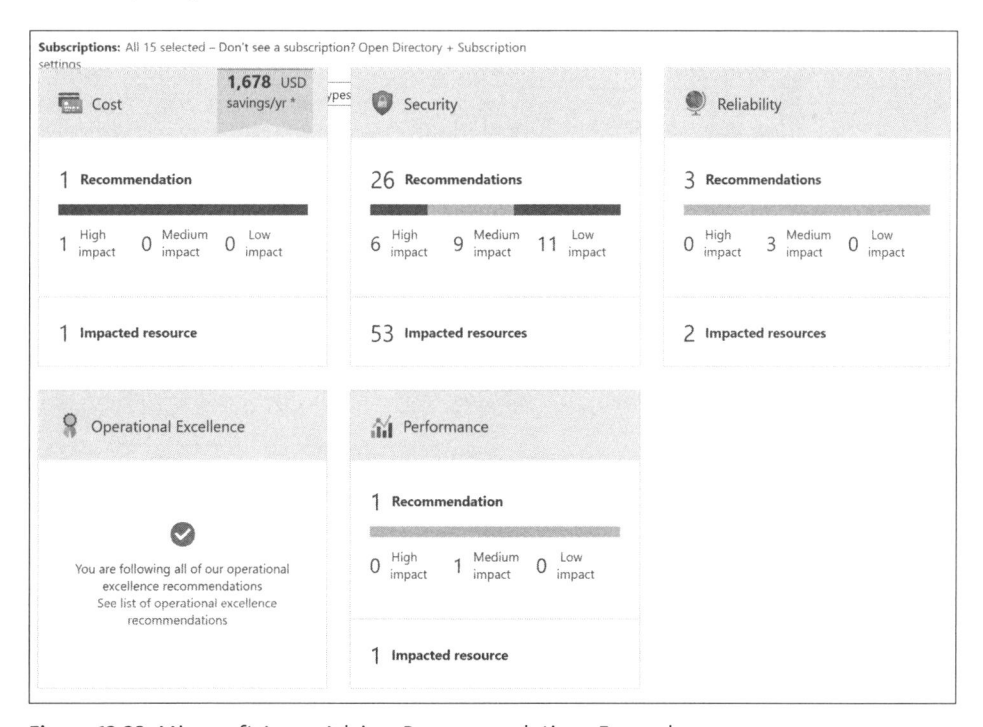

Figure 12.23 Microsoft Azure Advisor Recommendations Example

12 Operations

- Cost
- Security
- Reliability
- Operational Excellence
- Performance

Microsoft Azure Advisor recommendations can be exported in PDF or Microsoft Excel for offline analysis and sharing. Figure 12.23 shows an example of the dashboard from Microsoft Azure portal.

12.3.4 Alerts

Alerts are notifications based on set conditions and can be configured either directly from a resource, such as VM, or from Microsoft Azure Monitor **Alerts** blade.

Figure 12.24 illustrates the alert flow in Microsoft Azure. Alerts also have their status as **Enabled** or **Disabled**, and they trigger only when enabled. This is useful when you're performing maintenance and don't want to trigger unnecessary notifications.

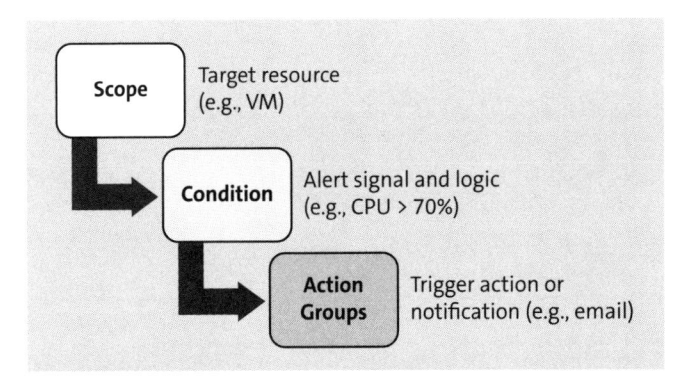

Figure 12.24 Microsoft Azure Alerts Flow

Action groups are helpful when triggering multiple alerts with the same action. Figure 12.25 shows the type of actions that can be defined, including an email alert, a ticket in IT Service Management (ITSM), a Microsoft Azure logic app workflow, or automation runbook.

> **Tip**
> You can also use action rules to supress alerts for maintenance activities.

You can also view alerts from the portal, as shown in Figure 12.26. Smart groups contain alerts that are grouped together based on machine learning algorithms, which use historical patterns to reduce the noise.

12.3 Monitoring

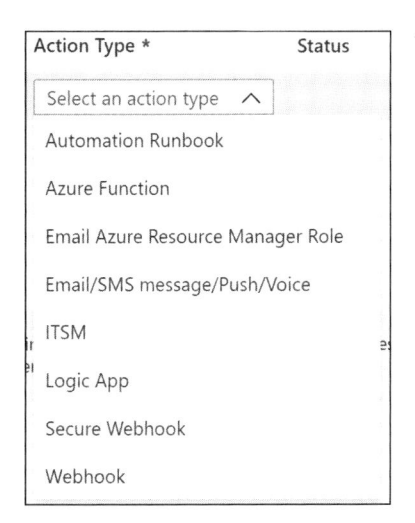

Figure 12.25 Types of Actions for an Alert

Figure 12.26 Alert View from the Portal

12.3.5 Microsoft Azure Monitor for SAP Solutions

Microsoft Azure Monitor for SAP Solutions is an open-source solution created by Microsoft to extend Microsoft Azure Monitor capabilities to SAP. It's a Microsoft Azure native solution available in the marketplace, as shown in Figure 12.27.

Figure 12.27 Microsoft Azure Monitor for SAP Solutions in the Marketplace

It connects to databases using credentials and uses the Prometheus exporter to monitor Pacemaker HA clusters. Under the hood, it uses a collector VM (with Ubuntu Linux OS and user-assigned managed identity), which hosts the monitoring payload, Microsoft Azure Key Vault to store the database credentials and provider information, and log analytics workspace, as illustrated in Figure 12.28.

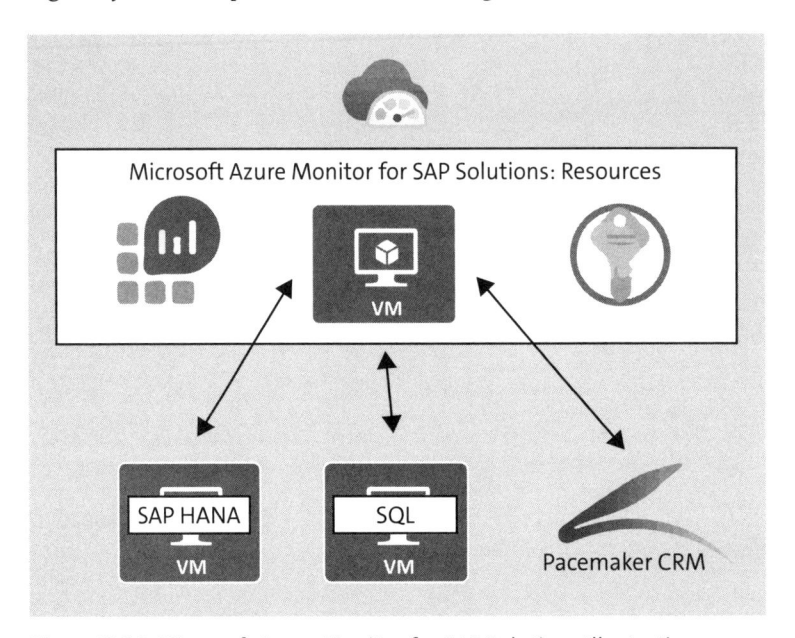

Figure 12.28 Microsoft Azure Monitor for SAP Solutions Illustration

Figure 12.29 shows the resources created in your Microsoft Azure subscription as part of enabling SAP monitoring use cases.

Name ↑↓	Type ↑↓
sapmon-osdisk-372cea3e86b677	Disk
sapmon-kv-372cea3e86b677	Key vault
sapmon-log-372cea3e86b677	Log Analytics workspace
sapmon-msi-372cea3e86b677	Managed Identity
sapmon-nic-372cea3e86b677	Network interface
sapmon-nsg-372cea3e86b677	Network security group
sapmonsto372cea3e86b677	Storage account
sapmon-vm-372cea3e86b677	Virtual machine

Figure 12.29 Resources Created in the Microsoft Azure Subscription

12.3 Monitoring

> **Cost Structure**
>
> Microsoft Azure Monitor for SAP Solutions setup incurs charges only for the infrastructure that is created to support it; there is no charge for monitoring or providers.

At the time of publication, it supports the following use cases (components, also known as providers, in the solution) for VM as well as SAP HANA on Azure (Large Instances):

- **SAP HANA**
  - Host status and metrics such as memory, disk, CPU, and network utilization
  - Database replication (SAP HANA system replication)
  - Database backup
  - SAP HANA services such as index and name server
- **Pacemaker HA cluster**
  - Pacemaker
  - Corosync
  - Storage-based death
  - Distributed Replicated Block Device (DRBD)
- **Microsoft SQL Server**
  - Host metrics such as memory, disk, and CPU utilization
  - Batch requests
  - Top expensive SQL statements
  - Largest tables
  - SQL wait stats and error logs

> **Microsoft Azure Monitor for SAP Solutions versus SAP Solution Manager**
>
> SAP Solution Manager collects and monitors a wider variety of metrics and logs than that of Microsoft Azure Monitor for SAP Solutions, so you can't replace SAP Solution Manager with the Microsoft Azure solution.

> **Tip**
>
> If you have another monitoring tool used organization wide, want to use an open-source monitoring tool, or even want to develop your own, all of that is still possible with Microsoft Azure. You need to do a cost and effort benefit analysis to determine which solution works best for your SAP landscape.

12 Operations

12.4 Cost Management

Because it's easy to deploy resources in Microsoft Azure, it's also easy to lose track of cost. Controlling and optimizing cost should be in the priority list right from the planning phase.

Cost management has several aspects to it such as understanding the cost, planning with a cost-focused approach, and optimizing on an ongoing basis (see Figure 12.30). It's also an *iterative process* given that things change in the cloud frequently.

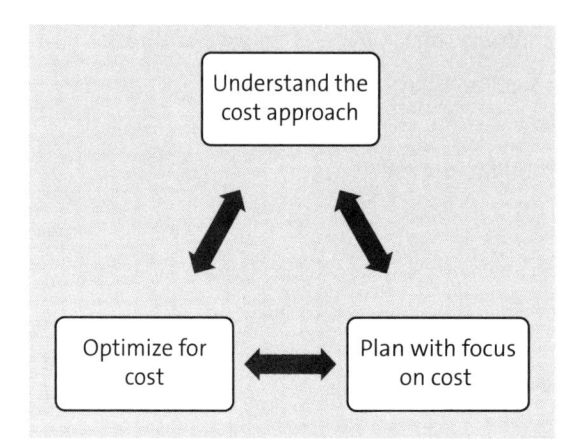

Figure 12.30 Approach to Managing Cost in Microsoft Azure

12.4.1 Understand the Cost Structure

As the saying goes, you can't fix what you don't understand. You should pay attention to the what and how of each service that you're using. Here are a few examples:

- Many services have tiered pricing for standard versus premium; there may not be a way to switch between the tiers, so switching can be an extensive exercise.
- Ingress/egress cost refers to the data transfer cost that applies between different virtual networks Starting in 2021, Microsoft Azure will also charge for data transfer between availability zones impacting the availability zone HA architecture cost.
- Storage that charges less to store the data, such as cool or archival tiers, has a data retrieval charge, making cost estimation more involved.
- Microsoft Azure Load Balancer is billed by the number of rules and data processed.
- The Microsoft Azure automation account is billed by the job runtime.
- VM is billed per second (pay-as-you-go).

> **Free versus Included in Price**
> Microsoft Azure has an à la carte pricing model, so it's safe to assume that there is a charge for everything unless mentioned otherwise. Some services are marked as free,

such as Microsoft Azure Policy; a good way to look at those is that it's included in the bill that you're paying. For example, when you get a charger with your phone, does it mean the charger is free or it's included in the price?

12.4.2 Plan with Focus on Cost

It's easier to plan something right rather than changing it later, so the initial architecture should reflect the cost versus performance versus complexity decision. This doesn't mean you go with the cheapest solution, but rather the decisions you made were more of a conscious approach.

You may decide to go with a cost-optimized DR setup and reserved instances to save costs but still decide to use availability zones for HA even though it may cost more. The idea here is to manage the cost while meeting the business goals. In addition, ensure that the business alignment is the guiding principle; for example, if a system's DR RPO is four hours, don't try to beat it by going overboard with complex solutions. Your target is to meet the business goal not necessarily beat it by a wide margin.

Tip

Use the Microsoft Azure pricing calculator to get a cost estimate for the setup you'll be deploying.

12.4.3 Optimize for Cost Regularly

After the systems are live on Microsoft Azure, review the performance of the systems and look at the SAP EarlyWatch Alert reports to find optimization opportunities. Review that against the recommendations from Microsoft Azure to get actionable insights.

12.4.4 Microsoft Azure Cost Management

Several tools are available to manage cloud costs along with the Microsoft Azure native tool called Microsoft Azure Cost Management + Billing, which can be accessed from the Microsoft Azure portal. Microsoft acquired a company called Cloudyn back in 2017, which is now a part of Microsoft Azure Cost Management. The Billing part of the tool deals with monthly invoicing for Microsoft Azure services, while Cost Management shows the level of details that can be analyzed further to make cost-related decisions.

Microsoft Azure Cost Management aims to help by providing visibility, drive accountability, and recommend optimizations, as illustrated in Figure 12.31.

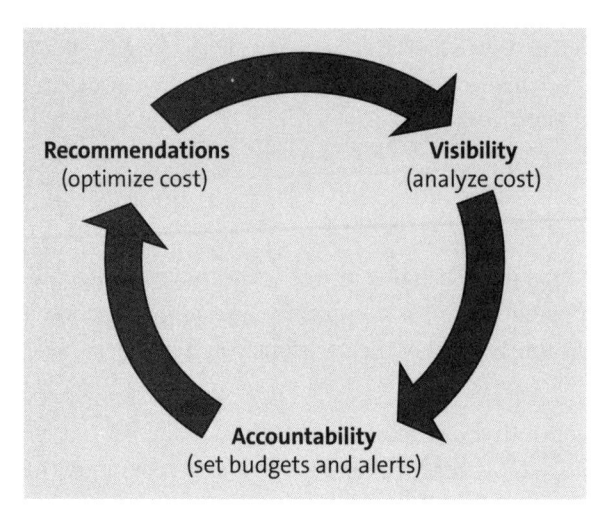

Figure 12.31 Microsoft Azure Cost Management Goals

Cost Analysis

The cost view can be scoped to the management group, subscription, or resource group level using the scope option in the **Cost Management** overview, as shown in Figure 12.32. This is the first thing to do in the cost analysis section to ensure you're looking at the right data.

Figure 12.32 Selecting the Scope for Cost Analysis

If you have multiple subscriptions for your SAP landscape, selecting the management group is a way to see the cost for the whole landscape across subscriptions.

The Microsoft Azure Cost Management initial view is intuitive and customizable to adapt to your preferences, as shown in Figure 12.33; customization options are highlighted in red.

12.4   Cost Management

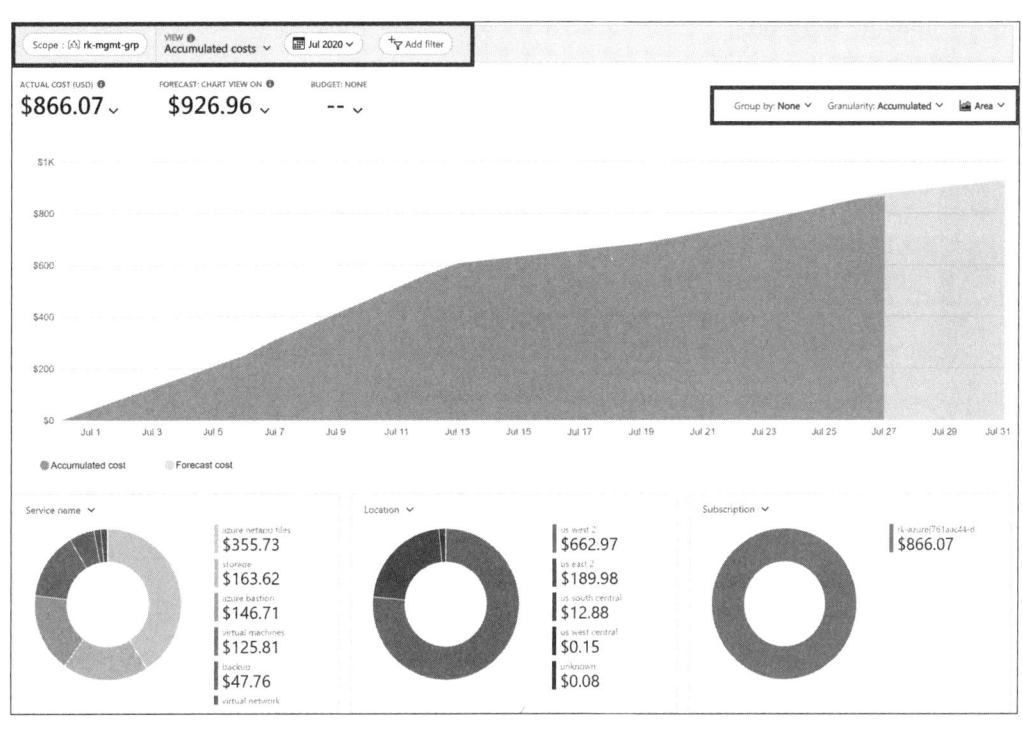

Figure 12.33   Microsoft Azure Cost Management Initial View and Customization Options

You can either select one of the built-in views or filter by several available options. **Service name** and **Location** cost views are helpful to understand the spend allocation, as shown in Figure 12.34.

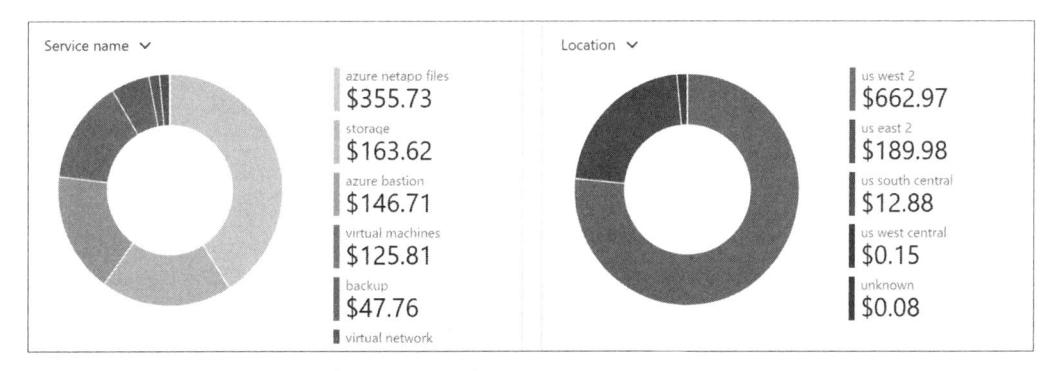

Figure 12.34   Cost Distribution by Service and Location

You can drill down on may factors to see a detailed view. When you've found a view that works for you, it can be saved and shared with others with role-based access control; it can also be pinned to the Microsoft Azure dashboard. If you're looking to use another visualization tool, such as Power BI, the data can be extracted using the **Exports** option or through billing and consumption APIs.

12 Operations

Budgets and Alerts

Setting budgets drives team accountability by nudging and helping them plan. Similar to cost analysis, you can also choose the scope, such as management groups, subscriptions, or resource groups, and then set filters, as illustrated in Figure 12.35.

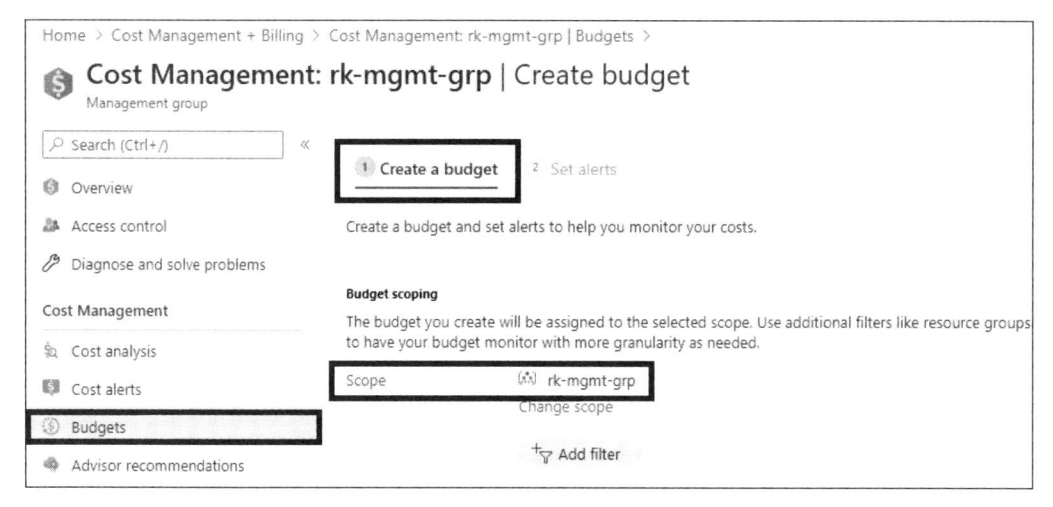

Figure 12.35 Creating Budgets and Setting Alerts in Microsoft Azure

> **Note**
> Budget calculation considers the cost for reserved instances based on actual cost rather than amortized cost.

Along with creating alerts that sends notification emails, you can also use action groups (as shown in Figure 12.36) to enforce the budget by triggering an automation runbook that shuts down the server, for example (in a sandbox environment).

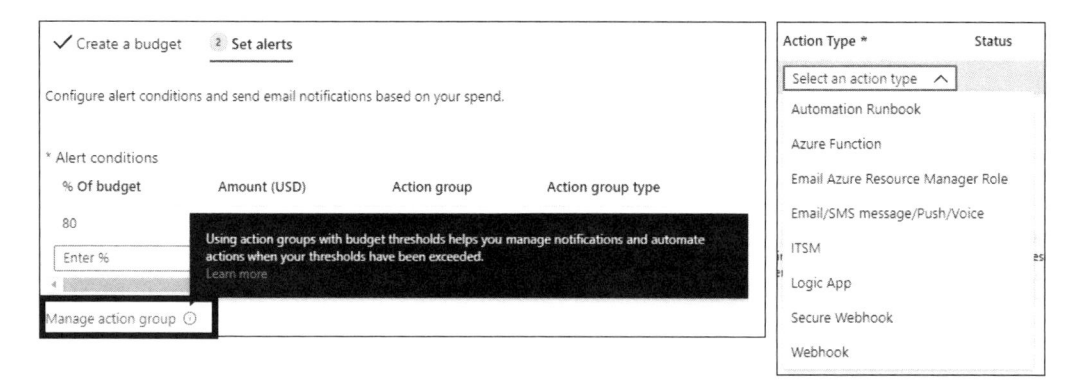

Figure 12.36 Action Groups in Budgets

12.4 Cost Management

Recommendations and Optimizations

The cost recommendations part of Microsoft Azure Advisor identifies things such as underutilized VMs and reservation savings potential by analyzing the last 30 days of usage. Figure 12.37 shows an example in which you can dig deeper to find the VM details. These recommendations are more tangible than a general approach because they point to the exact resource and also calculate tentative potential annual savings.

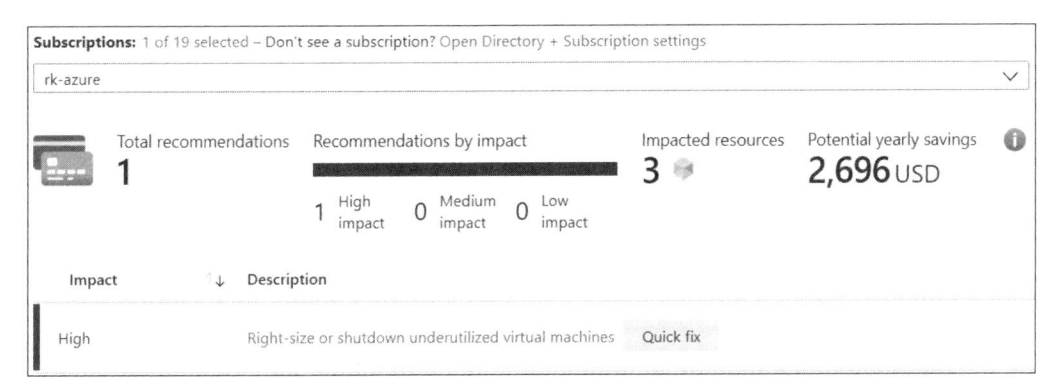

Subscriptions:	1 of 19 selected – Don't see a subscription? Open Directory + Subscription settings			
rk-azure				
Total recommendations	Recommendations by impact		Impacted resources	Potential yearly savings
1	1 High impact 0 Medium impact 0 Low impact		3	2,696 USD
Impact ↓	Description			
High	Right-size or shutdown underutilized virtual machines	Quick fix		

Figure 12.37 Microsoft Azure Cost Optimization Recommendations

Following are some other recommendations for cost optimization:

- **Resource versus effort and skill cost**
  Many times, it comes down to Microsoft Azure resource cost savings by optimizing versus a team member's effort (cost associated with learning and time spent) to achieve it. In the long run, cost savings is higher than effort cost when automation is used. When things start to happen in the background without much intervention, team members can focus on other high-value tasks to lock in the continuous savings.

- **Storage review**
  Often forgotten, the storage review reveals not only the percentage free in storage but also what kind of data it's storing. Premium storage follows a pay-what-you-provision model, so ongoing cleanup is a good way to keep unnecessary costs in check.

- **Look at cost from all sources**
  Similar to investments in financial markets, IT investment costs should be reviewed by looking at all sources together, such as other cloud estate, on-premise data centers, and so on. That gives you a comparative perspective and could mean moving something from one location or cloud to another to optimize cost.

- **Use tags to analyze and optimize cost**
  Tagging provides you with a custom way to filter (as shown in Figure 12.38) the cost and optimization, including chargeback. Make sure the tags are up to date when things change, and review them periodically if there is an email or owner assigned to systems.

12   Operations

Figure 12.38 Using Tags to Filter for Cost Analysis and Optimization

> **Note**
> Microsoft Azure Cost Management provides a multi-cloud analysis feature as well, and at the time of publication, it has an Amazon Web Services (AWS) connector to help simplify the aggregation.

12.4.5 Cost Projections

The cost management aspects we've discussed so far are retrospective; given that organizations have a yearly budget, let's discuss how you can predict the cost a quarter or a year out and how to deal with unexpected charges.

Microsoft Azure Cost Management doesn't provide an out-of-the-box capability, at the time of publication, because the cost projection exercise requires a lot of assumptions. Here's how you can create your own model:

1. Export the data set from Microsoft Azure so you can integrate with a visualization tool such as Power BI (Power BI provides an out-of-the-box connector for Microsoft Azure Cost Management, as shown in Figure 12.39).

2. Use the Microsoft Azure pricing calculator to estimate the cost of new services that will be deployed for a project during the year. You can use assumptions here for the tentative month of deployment, approximate size and number of VMs, and so on.

3. Adjust the cost to reflect any optimization savings that will be achieved as a part of planning.

4. For the unforeseen or difficult-to-calculate cost items such as load balancer rules, data transfer cost, and so on, evaluate the percentage deviation, and apply it to the new project cost.

5. You can also specify the cost from the model in terms of confidence interval.

> **Tip**
> Don't try to predict cost too far in the future because anything beyond a year adds more unknowns such as Microsoft Azure pricing, service lifecycle, new services availability, system decommission, and so on.

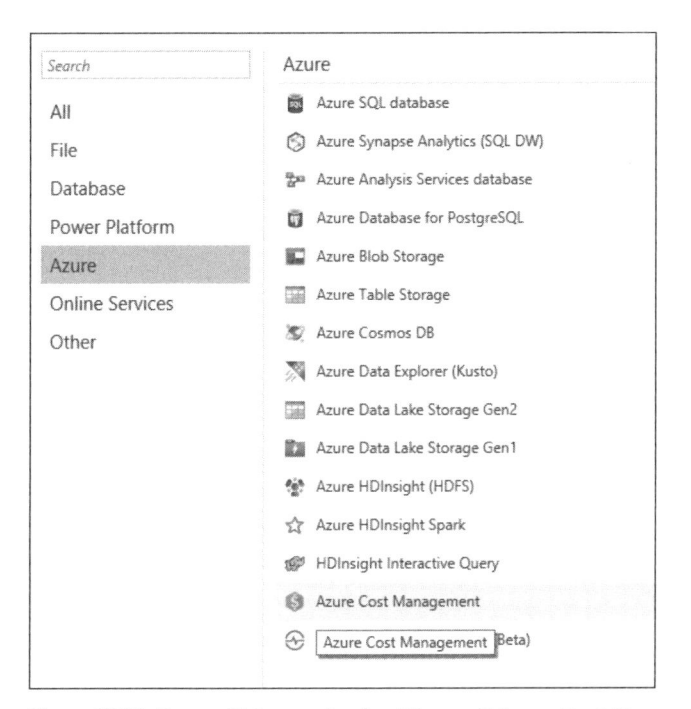

Figure 12.39 Power BI Connector for Microsoft Azure Cost Management

12.5 Summary

Infrastructure operations include a wide variety of topics and requires a multidisciplinary team approach. We discussed the aspects of cost, monitoring, and efficiency for SAP landscapes in this chapter. We also talked about things to be aware of when doing certain tasks, such as how SAP licensing is impacted by a hardware change.

In the next chapter, we'll discuss architecture and use cases using a case-study approach for migrations and new implementations.

Chapter 13
Case Study

So far, we've discussed concepts and examples about how to do certain things for a use case; in this chapter we'll tie it all together and walk through KashWebb (KW) LLC's journey to SAP on Microsoft Azure.

KashWebb (KW) is a global manufacturing company headquartered in the United States that is looking to implement SAP S/4HANA in Microsoft Azure. A subsidiary of KW (a company acquired last year) already has the SAP landscape on-premise, and after the initial deployment of SAP S/4HANA, the subsidiary will also migrate the existing landscape. The company followed the cloud adoption framework to formulate an outline, with detailed planning to follow after the initial design workshops.

Let's look at KW's decision-making process for deployment, how it aligns with requirements, and the kind of trade-offs the team comes across.

13.1 New Implementation Planning

One of the first items the KW technical team was tasked with was determining the cost of deploying the landscape on Microsoft Azure and the run rate for three to five years. Exploring via the Microsoft Azure pricing and total cost of ownership (TCO) calculator to project the financial figures, the team soon realized they needed to go through a sizing exercise because the calculators require information about the virtual machine (VM) stock-keeping units, storage, and all other components that will be used.

13.1.1 Milestone #1: Sizing and Total Cost of Ownership Calculation

The KW team went through the sizing exercise and created a bill of materials (BOM) they needed for the SAP deployment. They referred to SAP application and SAP HANA-certified VMs (the SAP HANA database wasn't large enough to warrant SAP HANA on Azure [Large Instances]) to ensure the correct stock-keeping units were chosen and SAP on Microsoft Azure reference architecture for SAP S/4HANA to understand all other required components, such as shared storage, load balancer, and so on.

Because the cost is region dependent as well, the team looked at the Microsoft Azure Product Availability Matrix and chose a region closer to their headquarters locations (data residency was considered, and there wasn't a strict legal requirement). All the services they were looking for were also available in the Microsoft Azure paired region, so it was chosen as the disaster recovery (DR) region. Because they expect the production systems to be up all the time, the reserved instance discount was used for VMs, and, based on the other available information, a tentative cost projection was derived for the first three years.

13.1.2 Milestone #2: Architecture Components

The next step was to gather a cross-functional team to discuss the architectural components in Microsoft Azure and finalize a design. During a workshop, the team validated that the information gathered so far was on the right track and discussed other components as covered in the following subsections. In addition, the decision was made to use only one subscription because the subscription limits were high enough to accommodate all services for the next few years.

Connectivity and Network

The team determined that ExpressRoute will be provisioned in the long run, but to get started, a site-to-site virtual private network (VPN) will be deployed as a stopgap. On the Microsoft Azure side, the hub-spoke network structure was chosen with shared services and identity components in the hub, along with central security components such as a perimeter network. The spoke virtual network (VNet) will follow micro segmentation with different subnets for applications and databases with SAP HANA, following the SAP recommendation of client, internode, and storage subnets.

Security

The discussion focused on identity management, Microsoft Azure Active Directory (Microsoft Azure AD), network security groups, application security groups, network virtual appliances, and encryption. Decisions evolved to using the enterprise cybersecurity software as the network virtual appliance in the hub subscription, using network security groups and application security groups for all networks and applications, and enforcing using Microsoft Azure Policy where possible. SAP systems would use their own user master with no single sign-on (SSO) with Microsoft Azure AD. KW also has a motto of "encrypt everything," so a decision was made to apply it for all components. In addition, just-in-time access was enabled for all VMs and, wherever applicable, user-assigned managed identities were used.

Operating System Flavor and Hardening

The KW team uses SUSE Linux Enterprise Server (SLES) for other applications so that was the obvious choice for the SAP environment as well, given that it's certified for SAP and also has an SAP flavor called SLES for SAP. In addition, because SAP HANA only supports Linux, the team didn't want to use the Windows OS for applications to ensure operational efficiency. The team decided to use Packer to harden the OS images with enterprise policies combined with SAP and SLES recommendations for SAP environments. As they already had licensing contracts with SUSE, bring your own subscription on Microsoft Azure was chosen.

High Availability

The uptime requirement from business was high enough to opt for high availability (HA) configuration, but they weren't sure whether to opt for an availability set or availability zone configuration (both options meet the uptime service-level agreement [SLA]). There were also discussions around infrastructure versus application HA and skillsets required to configure Pacemaker and SAP HANA system replication. To optimize cost, the multi-SID ABAP SAP Central Services cluster configuration was discussed to be tested. For the Network File System (NFS) share, the team didn't like the overhead of managing servers, so they were leaning toward using the Microsoft Azure NetApp Files platform as a service (PaaS) solution.

Disaster Recovery

KW's technical team gathered some information from the business about how long it can sustain SAP downtime (recovery time objective [RTO]) and how much data loss it can afford (recovery point objective [RPO]). They were also keen on understanding the business processes so that those can be mapped to SAP solutions to understand the DR strategy at the SAP SID level, or if there is another backup mechanism available, for example, manual processing for specific business processes, that can be used in a disaster scenario.

The team didn't have all the answers at the onset, and more information was to come; meanwhile, they reviewed the standard reference architecture for SAP DR to get familiar with technologies and components to be deployed.

Governance

Governance discussions revolved around the following:

- Role-based access control for least privilege
- Tagging strategy for cost and operational management
- Using Microsoft Azure policies for compliance
- Using resource groups per SID
- Resource locking for production
- Management group structure for Microsoft Azure subscription scaling management in the future
- Microsoft Azure services and VM naming conventions
- Logs management and auditing compliance

Not all decisions were finalized, but the overall consensus was for each team to perform more due diligence and come up with recommendations.

Performance

Performance is a key consideration, but given that the team doesn't have a current benchmark to compare against, the decision was made to follow SAP and Microsoft recommendations in terms of sizing, storage, and network configurations, keeping in mind that if there are performance issues, testing will highlight that, and the issues can be remediated before going live with business users.

The proximity placement group structure is to be adopted to ensure database and application VMs land in the same data center for each SID.

Backups

Options for backup were discussed, and their first thought was to use their on-premise enterprise backup tool on Microsoft Azure as well; however, Microsoft Azure integration and licensing costs were also discussed, and the team decided to do an in-depth analysis of features and costs for the current tool versus Microsoft Azure Backup. Features such as retention management, compression, time to backup and restore, integration with SAP processes, and so on were mapped out to use cases for comparison.

Monitoring

Discussion about monitoring started with the list of metrics and other items that should be covered by monitoring across components such as the OS, database, and application. Different tools were discussed, such as Microsoft Azure Monitor, SAP Solution Manager, and so on. The overall purpose was to start with items to be monitored and see what tools are required, ensuring the same item isn't monitored by multiple systems.

Tying the alerts to a ticketing system was discussed too, and, depending on the alert severity, notification methods such as email, phone call, and so on to the respective teams is to be determined.

Operations

Because this was the first landscape in Microsoft Azure for KW, they were still trying to understand the difference between OSs on-premise versus Microsoft Azure. They were considering what skills would be required given the shared responsibility between Microsoft and KW. They also wanted the cross-functional team to not only manage the Microsoft Azure infrastructure but also think about improvements and adapt to the evolution of Microsoft Azure services.

The team understood that they needed to rethink how activities such as patching, system maintenance, and so on are managed in Microsoft Azure and were eager to use

DevOps and the immutable architecture. The vision also was to have the same team manage the project and operations, so they would get familiar with all the processes and technologies being used.

13.1.3 Milestone #3: Infrastructure and SAP Deployment

Now it's time for action. The KW team was overwhelmed with everything so far and didn't see a way to go with the big-bang approach. Let's see how they proceeded with the deployment.

Automation

The KW team had attended sessions about automation and were familiar with infrastructure as code (IaC) concepts but didn't have the capability in-house. There was a plan to train folks and use publicly available scripts to hit the ground running. To get started, the team wanted to create some resources using Microsoft Azure portal so they can get familiar with the process and portal navigation.

Combining SAP deployment with infrastructure and orchestrating everything from the DevOps pipeline is the north star, but they recognized the importance of getting things started small.

Proof of Concept

By the end of the initial workshops, the KW team had a better grasp of the number of decisions to be made and known unknowns. To that extent, the team realized they needed to learn more, and instead of deploying everything at the same time, a pilot or proof of concept (POC) would be a better way to go.

The team created an architecture diagram and design documents based on the information they had and made a list of items they needed to test and put on a decision matrix.

> **Technical and Organizational Complexity**
>
> The narrative highlights the complexity of the SAP on Microsoft Azure implementation not only from a technical point of view, such as what services and configuration to use, but also from the organizational alignment in terms of the skillset required and multiple teams working together to make decisions.
>
> It's not uncommon for organizations to go through the exploration process and realize that they need a POC first. It's a good way to achieve risk mitigation and learn Microsoft Azure in a controlled, low-pressure environment.

After the POC, the KW team solidified more decisions such as using ASs for HA configuration, using database replication, and using Microsoft Azure Site Recovery for DR configuration. They also created a deployment timeline based on semi-automated provisioning and were able to get partial automation going but not to the end-to-end automation.

They did performance testing in QA systems, which was acceptable to business users, so production systems used the same specifications. After the successful go-live, they wanted to understand the operations aspects better before undertaking the migration project.

13.2 Migration Planning

The KW team documented, for the SAP S/4HANA deployment, the lessons learned and all the design elements so it would be a reusable asset. They realized things in Microsoft Azure change quick, but the concepts and informed decision-making would transfer to migration efforts too. After the business go-live of the SAP S/4HANA project, talks of migrating existing systems (from the subsidiary) started and planning meetings were triggered.

Migration has its own challenges, and they wanted to document the important metrics that would determine the success of the project:

- Downtime meets business expectations
- Cost optimization
- Operational downtime reduction
- Flexibility in getting more resources during special events

Having the goals defined early in the process not only helps measure the impact but also gets you thinking in that direction; every design decision you make aligns to the goals. The team also started the inventory of current systems, which had a dual purpose: decommission systems not using important business processes (potentially replacing with something else) and define the migration scope. Table 13.1 illustrates parts of inventory showing the SAP system landscape with OS and database flavors.

The inventory highlights a couple of important items:

- Three different databases and OSs are being used; in the spirit of streamlining operations, this needed to be consolidated.
- While most of the databases were smaller in size so downtime would be smaller, SAP Business Warehouse (SAP BW) and SAP ERP databases would be in the critical path.
- Not everything could be migrated together; the team needed to devise a phased migration approach.

SAP Product	Dev	QA	PRD	SBX	DB	OS	DB Size
SAP ERP	X	X	X	X	Oracle	Unix	6 TB
SAP BW	X	X	X	X	SAP HANA	SLES	8 TB
SAP Portal	X	X	X		Oracle	Windows	< 1 TB
SAP Web Dispatcher	X		X		N/A	Windows	
SAP Solution Manager	X		X		SQL Server	Windows	< 1 TB
SAP Global Trade Services (SAP GTS)	X	X	X	X	Oracle	Windows	< 1 TB

Table 13.1 Part of SAP System Inventory at KW

There were also discussions about an SAP ERP to SAP S/4HANA migration and consolidating the number of SAP systems by combining business processes.

13.2.1 Shared Architecture on Microsoft Azure

A lot of decisions that were made during the new implementation project (of SAP S/4HANA), such as governance, network, security, and backups, could be easily mapped to the new systems. It made some aspects easier, but the team still needed to plan other migration aspects such as migration method, downtime optimization, and so on. They chose the same region as earlier but decided to have a different subscription for migrated systems both governed by Microsoft Azure management groups.

As far as the OS and database on Microsoft Azure goes, the decision was made to consolidate to SQL Server and SAP HANA for database and Windows and SLES for the OS. This also meant that SAP ERP would have heterogenous migration and, given the size, downtime would be a big item to test and optimize. Other systems such as SAP Portal and SAP Global Trade Services (SAP GTS) (on Oracle) would be heterogenous as well, but those are smaller and not as critical as SAP ERP.

13.2.2 Resiliency Design (High Availability/Disaster Recovery)

Currently, on-premise HA isn't configured, and off-site backups act as the DR mechanism. The KW team started with uptime requirements on Microsoft Azure and decided to go with HA configuration (using Microsoft Azure availability set construct). For DR, they needed better RTO/RPO in Azure which led them to a design that makes use of database replication and Microsoft Azure Site Recovery.

13.2.3 Migration Methodology and Sequence

Both heterogeneous and homogeneous migration methods were part of the migration plan, depending on whether the new database/OS combination was changing. To get a baseline, sandbox systems would be migrated first (these were copies of production as of a few weeks ago and representative of the data and size of production systems) as pilots.

During the pilot, items such as data transfer rate, parallel export/import mechanism, HA/DR requirements, and performance would be baselined. The whole landscape was divided into migration groups and would go in separate waves with lower impact systems first in the earlier wave and SAP ERP/SAP BW in the last wave. The team would be using SAP-provided tools and technologies for migration (no third-party tools). The sequence of landscapes for migration within each wave looked like the following:

- Pilot (as sandbox systems)
- Development systems
- Production rehearsal
- Production cutover (and go-live)
- System copy from production to quality systems

Downtime optimization techniques, such as configuring SAP HANA system replication for SAP BW/4HANA, parallel exporting/importing for SAP ERP, using larger size VMs during migration, increasing ExpressRoute bandwidth, optimizing parameters, and so on, may need an additional round of testing for best results.

13.2.4 Phased Go-Live and Hybrid System Maintenance

With the phased go-live approach, as the systems move to Microsoft Azure, the on-premise hardware will be decommissioned; therefore, for the duration of the migration, there would be some kind of hybrid landscape: with some systems in Microsoft Azure while others are on-premise. During the transition period, the team would have to consider operational stability, monitoring, and transparency for business users.

Decisions such as when to migrate SAP Solution Manager (used for monitoring) and printing solutions become important as well. Because SAP systems are all interconnected, a hybrid setup may have performance impacts, which need to be considered.

13.2.5 Data Center Exit and Future Optimizations

After the whole SAP landscape is in Microsoft Azure, the KW team will evaluate other non-SAP infrastructures as well to decide what absolutely needs to be on-premise and plan for others to move to Microsoft Azure (or any other cloud). For SAP landscapes, the KW team will focus on further innovations in automation and operational excellence areas.

13.3 Summary

Moving SAP systems to the cloud is a big decision and is often much more involved than a mere lift-and-shift process. Project phases such as planning and iteration are as important as the final migration, if not more. This chapter highlights the importance of planning and decision-making; it also shows how concepts and methodologies highlighted earlier in the book are implemented during new deployments and migrations of SAP systems.

In the next chapter, we'll discuss the outlook of SAP on Microsoft Azure going forward. As both Microsoft Azure services and SAP products evolve, how will it shape the infrastructure, and how will we use these new paradigms?

Chapter 14
Outlook

We often don't know what's possible until someone has a crazy idea and path to make it happen; there are unintended effects during the journey as well, creating new opportunities and spin-off features. This is where the outlook comes into play and imagines the possible.

Now that the SAP landscape is in Microsoft Azure, the mission is accomplished! Where do you go from here? There are optimizations and new integration use cases for Microsoft Azure; both SAP and Microsoft also update documents frequently with new recommendations that should be a part of your periodic review.

In this chapter, we'll talk about the evolution of SAP on Microsoft Azure and some of the features and collaborations we'd like to see.

> **Note**
> The discussions about new features and evolutions are the author's own point of view or wish list; they may not be materialized by SAP and/or Microsoft.

14.1 Marching towards SAP S/4HANA

If you migrated existing non-SAP S/4HANA systems to Microsoft Azure, given the 2027 deadline for end of mainstream maintenance for SAP Business Suite 7, moving to SAP S/4HANA would be the next focus. Besides all the functional benefits and simplifications, one of the biggest architectural advantages is the introduction of standalone enqueue server 2 (default installation starting with ABAP platform 1809) for high availability (HA); it removes the restriction for SAP Central Services to follow enqueue replication server (ERS), thus the two-node cluster. Making use of Microsoft Azure's flexibility, imagine having a three- or four-node SAP Central Services cluster for critical business periods such as year-end, holidays sales, and so on.

14.2 Integration to Cloud Native Tools

We've discussed using cloud native tools for monitoring and backups, but it goes beyond that. Some of the common integrations include Microsoft Azure logic apps, power

14   Outlook

apps, data lakes, and so on, as illustrated in Figure 14.1. Microsoft has documented these scenarios as well.

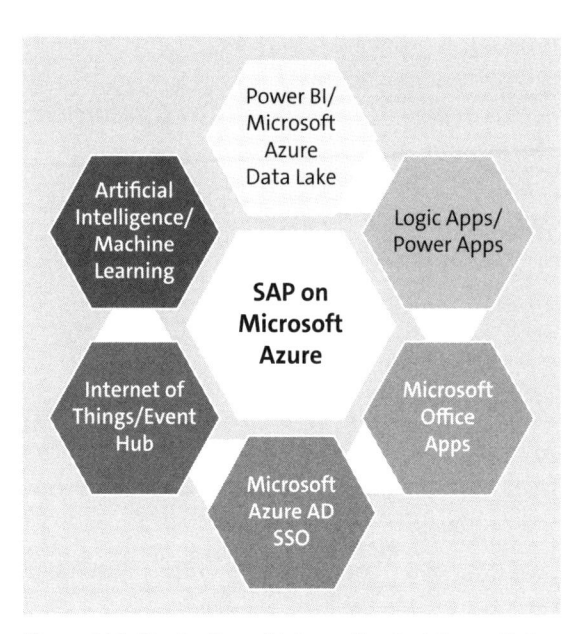

Figure 14.1 Illustration of Integration in Microsoft Azure for SAP

As your SAP landscape stabilizers, look for opportunities to integrate with these services to further strengthen your cloud strategy.

> **Tip**
> Whenever you're integrating SAP with external services, ensure that the licensing model your organization has allows the integration.

14.3   SAP Innovations

Recent SAP product innovations make those features even better in a cloud environment, and the trend will continue. Following are a couple of examples:

- **Evolution of enqueue replication server 2 with more than two-node cluster support**
  It's easy to spin up multiple servers during high-impact business events and shut down when not in use, so having three or five nodes for SAP Central Services/ERS is not as taxing as on-premise systems where you have upfront investment. Automation makes it an easy and low administrative task that can be a part of operations.
- **SAP HANA multitarget replication**
  Combining multitarget replication with immutable architecture provides a near-zero downtime SAP HANA and OS upgrade/patching mechanism.

- **Introduction of SAP Cloud Application Programming Model**
  This is a language framework that can be used to create cloud native applications

SAP Cloud Platform, which is a platform as a service (PaaS; integration and extension platform that supports multiple languages) offering, supports multiple clouds and runs on Cloud Foundry. It's a great example of how SAP is adopting cloud standards not only for its integration capabilities with traditional applications but also for build extensions and keeping the core clean. SAP Cloud Platform Extension Suite provides SAP Ariba, SAP S/4HANA, and SAP SuccessFactors solutions to name a few. You can integrate SAP solutions on Microsoft Azure with SAP Cloud Platform as well.

Something that SAP may streamline, which would be very useful for cloud deployments, is the unattended install process (install database and application using configuration file) and up-to-date installation, which triggers Software Updated Manager (SUM) after the installation is completed using software provisioning manager (SWPM). Currently, there are different types of configuration files (XML versus parameter file) and different tools that don't necessarily work well together from an end-to-end deployment experience perspective. The use case is new deployments that go through the upgrade process just after the base install. Combining up-to-date install with infrastructure automation will reduce both effort and time, along with manual intervention, which is where mistakes happen.

14.4 Evolution of Microsoft Azure

Microsoft Azure has come a long way since its first certification for SAP as an Infrastructure as a Service (IaaS) platform. SAP offerings have evolved as well, and Microsoft Azure has been good about adapting based on feedback such as SAP HANA on Azure (Large Instances) revision 4, which deploys bare metal servers to Microsoft Azure data centers to provide better network latency between the database and application. As more features get added, we like to evaluate use cases periodically to see what can be done better; for example, when Microsoft Azure NetApp Files came as a Network File System (NFS) solution, that became a better choice for shared storage than creating your own NFS HA solution using virtual machines (VMs).

Following are some more things we'd like to see going forward:

- **Automation integration to Microsoft Azure portal**
  Creating your own automation capability is great, but given the time and effort it takes, it may not be worth investing in for everyone. Some of the GitHub scripts let you deploy to Microsoft Azure directly but aren't as flexible and don't do end-to-end deployment. In addition, if it's integrated with Microsoft Azure portal, you won't necessarily need to know what language the automation uses and how to maintain it as long as it asks for inputs to customize the landscape you're creating. The use cases for this would range from doing pilot deployments to small landscapes or even new SAP deployments after the original migration is done.

- **SAP application server autoscaling**
  VM scale sets aren't supported for SAP, so if you're looking to scale up or down application servers for, say, a holiday event or other business-critical milestone, you have to create your own scripts and tools. While that may work because application server scaling is a common use case with a wide variety of applications, integrating that in Microsoft Azure portal with prebaked runbooks would be a great addition!

- **Making it easier to use immutable architecture**
  We've discussed immutable architecture and how it can be used for operational efficiency. Given that it can be integrated with DevOps tools such as Microsoft Azure DevOps, creating tools and workflows that make it easier and better integrated with the portal would be a value addition.

- **Adapting new features faster to use cases**
  Whenever a new feature is added for an SAP use case, it should be adapted quickly for all OS/database combinations or other infrastructures for consistent experience and faster adoption. A few examples include the following:
    - When Microsoft Azure SAP HANA backup was introduced, it was restricted only to SUSE Linux Enterprise Server (SLES). Red Hat Enterprise Linux (RHEL) was added later instead of being in the support list either from the beginning or shortly after.
    - Microsoft Azure shared file started support for HA with SAP acting as a shared file system for Windows; even though it supported NFS, the road map for the Linux HA use case wasn't clear. Releasing features such as this for all use cases promotes consistency in the SAP landscape and drives better adoption.
    - Putting VMs in an availability zone is a well-used feature for HA, however, at the time of publication, Microsoft Azure NetApp Files is not zone aware. Given that Microsoft Azure NetApp Files (or Microsoft Azure shared files once supported for all platforms) is a better way to go for HA shared file systems, zone awareness should be brought to these so availability zones can be included in automation scripts.

14.5 Containers for SAP?

Containers have become popular (popular may be an understatement) in the last couple of years, but the majority of SAP applications such as those based on SAP NetWeaver and ABAP platform aren't supported on containers *yet*—probably for a good reason. Putting everything in a docker image may be a complicated task, and managing lifecycles may be difficult with dependencies given the SAP architecture.

Having said that, SAP Cloud Platform runs on Cloud Foundry, and SAP's project Gardner is based on Kubernetes. It would be great even if it starts small, such as SAP application server in containers that can be scaled up and down based on load.

14.6 Summary

The ever-changing nature of software and the cloud is good and bad at the same time—good because it brings optimizations and new features, and bad because you have to continuously adapt to these new things to efficiently manage the infrastructure.

SAP on the cloud started as an IaaS, but now, there are a lot more PaaS and SaaS components; all of this is to ensure that IT fulfills its mission statement of enabling the business. This book serves the same purpose—to enable your learning! As you explore more, you'll appreciate different components, decisions, and experimentations that go into designing a solution that appears simple once put in a Microsoft Visio diagram.

The Author

Ravi Kashyap is a certified Microsoft Azure architect and currently works at Microsoft as an architect and customer advocate for SAP systems on Microsoft Azure. Ravi has worked with SAP systems throughout his career as SAP cloud architect, SAP migration lead, and SAP managed services lead for a variety of clients across multiple industries. He believes that to be a trusted advisor, along with possessing subject matter expertise, you also need to ask the right questions.

Index

A

ABAP platform 41, 145–146
ABAP SAP Central Services 41, 245
Access management 90
Active Directory 82, 87, 208, 278
   sign-in 89
Activity logs 261
Address spaces 71
Advanced encryption standard (AES) 208
Alerts 264, 272
AlwaysOn for SQL Server 219
Application deployment 196
Application programming interface
   (API) 194
Application security group 72, 90
Application server 224, 246
Application splitting 37
Authorized access 212
Automation 112, 193, 201, 230, 256, 281
   benefits 193
   disadvantages 204
   modularizing 255
   recommended practices 205
   tools 197
   use cases 195
Autoscaling 242–243
Availability sets 102–104, 144–145, 148
Availability zones 103–104, 145, 237, 290
Azure NetApp Files 75

B

BACKINT 181
Backups 175, 280
   classification 177
   database 180
   differential 177
   disk-based database 183
   frequency 176
   full vs. incremental 177
   online and offline 177
   overview 175
   policy 179, 186
   shared disk 185
   third-party tools 185
   VM 178

BitLocker 209
Bring your own subscription 76
Budgets 272
Bursting 97
Business process mapping 46
Business-critical systems 35

C

Caching 98
Capacity Availability Guarantee 255
Case study 277
Center for Internet Security (CIS) 91
Certification requirement 36
Classless inter-domain routing
   (CIDR) 71, 132
Cloud adoption framework 26, 214
   categories 26
   feedback loop 28
Cloud first strategy 236
Cloud Foundry 290
Cloud migration 85
Cloud native tools 287
Cloud operating model 239
Cloud rationalization 45–46
   decision flow 47
   replace 47
   retain 46
   retire 47
Cloud services 22
   pillars 23
   vs. on-premise 24
Cloud Solution Provider 60
Cloudyn 269
Cluster resource manager 153
Clustered shared disk 143
Clustering solutions 149
Command-line interface (CLI) 197–198
Commvault 186, 251
Compliance 115
   regulatory 126
Compute offering 64
   constraints 66
   cost 65
   other 67
   performance 66
Compute operations 94, 136

295

Confidential computing 91
Configuration management 201
Connectivity 60, 131, 236
Consistent environment 125
Containers 290
Continuous integration and continuous delivery
 (CI/CD) 203
Corosync 153
Cost management 268
Cost optimization 112
Cost structures 268
Cross-region restore 107, 130
Custom roles 87, 119
Customer-managed keys (CMKs) ... 92, 207, 210

D

Dashboards 262
Data center exit 284
Data encryption key 92, 208
Data Guard for Oracle 219
Data Migration Option (DMO) 221
 downtime 230
 system move 223
Data scrambling 210
Data transfer 238
Database app connectivity 135
Database as a service (DBaaS) 26
Database parameter tuning 228
Database replication 164
Database server maintenance 248
Declarative approach 198
Demilitarized zone (DMZ) 135
Deployment models 43
 all SAP on Microsoft Azure 43
 hybrid 44
 multi-cloud 44
DevOps 88
DevOps integration 203
Diagnostic setting 126
Disaster recovery (DR) ... 22, 129, 162, 165, 219,
 278–279
 failover 165
 shared storage 169
 tests 170
Disk benchmarking 98
Distributed denial of service (DDoS)
 protection 90
Distributed Replicated Block Device
 (DRBD) 142
Distributed systems 40
Domain name service (DNS) 219

Downtime 226
 optimization 227
DR as a device (DRaaS) 106
Dual stack 41

E

Encryption 207
 at rest 207–208
 backup 210
 database 209
 database and disk 140
 disk 209
 in transit 211
 key areas 207
 storage service 209
Encryption in transit 93
Enqueue replication server (ERS) 144, 161,
 245, 288
Enqueue server 144, 161
Enqueue Server 2 .... 144, 160–161
Enrollment hierarchy 59
Enterprise Agreement 59
Enterprise infrastructure 32
Event-based triggers 33
Export directory 228
ExpressRoute 61, 98, 131, 278, 284
ExpressRoute encryption 211
ExpressRoute Global Reach 61, 82
ExpressRoute Premium 61

F

Fast start failover 158
Fault domains 102
Federal Information Processing Standard Publi-
 cation (FIPS) 210
Fencing 153
File share 152
File transfer protocol (FTP) 72

G

Gartner's five Rs of migration 45
General Data Protection Regulation
 (GDPR) 115
Geo-redundant storage 108, 164, 185
Geo-zone-redundant storage 108
GitHub 203
GlusterFS 142
Governance 111, 115, 279

H

Hard disk drive	68
Hardware benchmarking	94
Hardware keys	253
Hardware security module	210
HashiCorp Packer	91, 202
Health Insurance Portability and Accountability Act (HIPPA)	208
High availability	25, 129, 141, 219, 279, 287
disaster recovery	165
IBM DB2	158
linux	153
multi-SID	161–162
SAP application server	143
SAP Central Services and database	144
SAP HANA	157
shared storage	140, 142
VM with shared disk	149
Hot patching	77
Hybrid cloud	22

I

IBM DB2	158
Idempotence	194
Identity management	87
Immutable architecture	246, 248
Imperative approach	198
Infrastructure architecture	129
Infrastructure as a service (IaaS)	23, 25, 39
Infrastructure as code (IaC)	33, 194, 281
Infrastructure foundation	64
compute	64
network	70
storage	68
Infrastructure groups	195
Input/output operations per second (IOPS)	67, 96, 139, 259
Internet Assigned Numbers Authority (IANA)	132
Internet Small Computer Systems Interface (iSCSI)	154
IP security	62, 211
IPTables	82
IT Service Management (ITSM)	264

J

Java Enterprise Edition	41
JavaScript Object Notation (JSON)	198

K

Key encryption key (KEK)	208
Key management	212
Key Vault	82, 88, 92, 266

L

Landing zones	82, 125
Licenses	75
Licensing	253
Lifecycle management	91, 197
Lift-and-shift	215
Linux	153
Live migration	77
Load balancer	144
Locally redundant storage	108, 178
Logs	126, 260
destination	261

M

M Series Virtual Machine (VM)	130
MACsec	211
Managed disks	68
Managed identity	88
Management groups	117
Management network	135
Metrics	260
Micro segmentation strategy	132
Microsoft Azure	
benefits	32
connectivity	131
data centers	211
disks	69
enhanced monitoring extension	37
enterprise enrollment hierarchy	59
infrastructure offerings	59
initiative	117
licenses	75
overview	21
paired regions	163
paths	45
platform maintenance	77
premium disk	184
reference architecture	42, 171–172
regions	129
SAP architecture	35
service previews	29
services	24, 42, 254
shared architecture	283
shared disk	152

Microsoft Azure (Cont.)
 storage 211
 storage accounts 69
 storage resiliency 107
 subscription 55
 support prerequisites 36
 supported databases 38
 supported operating systems 38
 supported SAP products 38
Microsoft Azure Advisor 128, 263
 cost recommendations 273
Microsoft Azure Backup 107, 178, 188,
 209–210, 251, 280
 limitations 182
 management 190
 retention management 186
 SAP HANA 181
 SQL Server 180
Microsoft Azure Blueprint 124
 use cases 125
Microsoft Azure Cloud Shell 197–198
Microsoft Azure compute units
 (ACUs) 94–95
Microsoft Azure Cost Management ... 269–270,
 274
Microsoft Azure Data Box 218
Microsoft Azure Dedicated Host 67, 78
 available capacity 79
 cost 80
 group 78
 maintenance control 80
 VM provisioning 78
Microsoft Azure Diagnostics 139
Microsoft Azure Disk Encryption ... 92, 140, 209
Microsoft Azure Firewall 90
Microsoft Azure Front Door 90
Microsoft Azure Image Builder 202
Microsoft Azure Key Vault 208, 212
Microsoft Azure Load Balancer 108, 260
Microsoft Azure Monitor 128, 190, 259
 alerts 264
Microsoft Azure Monitor for
 SAP Solutions 265
 cost structure 267
Microsoft Azure NetApp Files 74–75, 110,
 143, 155, 157, 210, 251, 279, 290
 configurations 256
 SAP HANA backup 183
 storage-level snapshots 184
Microsoft Azure Policy 116–117, 278
Microsoft Azure portal 59–60, 90
 dashboard 262

Microsoft Azure portal (Cont.)
 SQL Server backup 180
 templates 199
Microsoft Azure Resource Manager
 (ARM) 87, 193, 198
 API 200
 template 198
Microsoft Azure Security Center 93, 126
Microsoft Azure Service Health 128
Microsoft Azure Site Recovery 105, 112, 137,
 166, 171, 212, 219–220, 224
 enable replication 168
 infrastructure 168
 use cases 106
 zone-to-zone 167
Microsoft Customer Agreement 60
Microsoft Windows
 licensing 77
Migration 213, 284
 archiving and cleanup 215
 backup/restore 218
 choose strategy 225
 cutover 234
 database 217
 database replication 219
 export/import 220
 heterogenous 220
 homogeneous 218
 large database 226
 large landscape 235
 methodologies 215
 migration check 221
 nonproduction 233
 optimization 226
 paths 215
 phases 231
 pilot 232
 planning 213, 282
 production rehearsal 234
 readiness 213–214
 systems rationalization 214
 third-party solutions 225
 trade-offs 225
Monitoring 111, 257, 280
Multiple instances 138

N

Naming conventions 121
Near-zero downtime (nZDT) 230
Network design 131

Index

Network File System (NFS) 74, 140, 142, 185, 212, 279
Network operations 98
Network performance 35
Network scope 72
Network security group 72, 90
Network throughput 228
Network virtual appliance 90, 132, 136
Network Watcher 90
Network zones 134
Nonoverlapping IP ranges 72

O

Operational efficiency 109, 240
Operational learning 254
Operations 239, 280
Optimization 227
Oracle 158
Oracle Linux
  licensing 77
Orchestration 201
OS patching 110

P

Pacemaker 142, 150, 154
  HA clusters 266
Patching 244
Pay-as-you-go 22, 65, 76, 240
Payment Card Industry (PCI) 208
Peering 72
Performance 93, 280
  databae and applications 100
Perimeter network 135
Phased go-live 284
Platform as a service (PaaS) 23, 25, 185, 214
  shared storage 143
Platform-managed keys (PMKs) 207
Point-to-site VPN 62
Policies 116
  monitor compliance 117
Power BI 262
Pricing calculator 62
Pricing models 65
Private cloud 21
Proof of concept (POC) 281
Proximity placement groups 99, 104, 145, 147
Public cloud 21
  vs. private cloud 22

Q

Quickstart templates 203
Quotas 131

R

R3LOAD 227, 230
Ranges 132
Read-access geo-redundant storage 108
Recovery point object (RPO) .. 163, 165, 169, 279
Recovery services vault 178
Recovery time objective (RTO) 163, 165, 169, 279
Red Hat Enterprise Linux
  (RHEL) 153, 155, 290
  licensing 76
Redundancy 102
Reference architecture 42
Regional pairs 105
Regions 236
Reporting 127
Resiliency 101, 141, 283
  infrastructure-level 149
  platform 101
  region 105
Resiliency layers 105
Resilient File System (ReFS) 151
Resource groups 118
Resource locks 122
Resource logs 261
Resource providers 195
Restore 175
Retention policy 186
Rightsizing 249, 253
Role-based access control 82, 91, 119, 201, 212, 279
  scope 120
  use cases 119
  vs policy 120
Roles 87, 119
Rollback plan 238
Rolling kernel switch (RKS) 245
Rolling patches 245
Root cause analysis 128
Runbook types 201

S

SAP 17, 35
  architecture 40
  migration vs. new implementation 48

Index

SAP (Cont.)
- on Microsoft Azure 35
- reference architecture 42
- snoozing 240
- system copy 110
- technology stacks 40

SAP Adaptive Server Enterprise (SAP ASE) ... 49, 159, 222

SAP Application Performance Standard (SAPS) 66, 94

SAP Business Suite on SAP HANA 216

SAP Business Warehouse (SAP BW) 282

SAP BusinessObjects Business Intelligence 159

SAP BW/4HANA 284

SAP Central Services ... 31, 41, 74, 119, 138, 143, 160, 224, 287
- cluster 150
- cross-zone setup 146
- Linux 155
- nonzone deployment 146

SAP Cloud Appliance Library 49
- account details 50
- accounts 50
- connect to Microsoft Azure 50
- costs 53
- instance details 52
- instance operations 54
- SAP NetWeaver 51
- solution scheduling 53
- VM and storage selection 52

SAP Cloud Application Programming Model 289

SAP Cloud Platform 214, 289

SAP Cloud Platform Extension Suite 289

SAP Customer Experience 41

SAP EarlyWatch Alert 94, 242, 244, 249

SAP ERP 6.0 41

SAP ERP Human Capital Management (SAP ERP HCM) 47

SAP Focused Run 258

SAP Global Trade Services (SAP GTS) 283

SAP HANA 41, 205, 222, 267
- backup 181
- certified hardware directory 39
- Linux 156
- restore 189
- scale out 156
- system replication 156

SAP HANA Backup
- plug-in 182

SAP HANA Enterprise Cloud 45

SAP HANA Hardware Directory 136, 138

SAP HANA multitarget replication 288

SAP HANA on Azure (Large Instances) ... 42, 66, 80, 130, 137, 149, 277
- architecture 81
- deployment timelilne 81
- differences 252
- revision 4 81
- VM migration 251

SAP HANA system replication 219

SAP HANA tailored data center integration 139

SAP Landscape Management 202, 251

SAP MaxDB 229

SAP NetWeaver 41, 145–146, 176

SAP NetWeaver AS ABAP 42, 49

SAP Notes 56

SAP S/4HANA 42, 48, 215, 287

SAP Solution Manager 41, 111, 258

SAP SuccessFactors 47

SAP Support Portal 40, 56

SAP Web Dispatcher 73, 135, 143, 156

SAProuter 90

Sarbanes-Oxley Act (SOX) 125

Scalability 100

Scale-Out File Server (SOFS) 143, 151

Secondary Region 169

Security 85, 207, 236, 278
- application and data 92
- infrastructure 90
- network 89

Security Assertion Markup Language (SAML) 89

Security groups 72

Selective disk backup 183

Self-service notifications 78

Server-side encryption (SSE) 209

Service availability 28

Service level agreements (SLAs) 21, 29
- composite 31
- percentages 30
- unmet SLA 30

Service level objective (SLO) 101, 141

Service-level agreements (SLAs) 61, 95, 101, 109, 141, 254

Shared access signature 92

Shared disks 74

Shared storage 73

Simple Mail Transfer Protocol (SMTP) 49

Single computing unit 95

Single point of failure 104, 141

Single sign-on (SSO) 87, 278

SIOS DataKeeper 143
Site recovery 166
Site-to-site VPN 62
Small computer system interface persistent
   reservations (SCSI PR) 74
Snapshot 184, 251
   transfer 180
Soft delete 107
Software as a service (SaaS) 23, 26, 214
Software provisioning manager (SWPM) 220
Software Update Manager (SUM) 196, 221
Solid-state drive (SDD) 68
Spoke network 133
SQL Server 42, 152, 267
   backup 180
   restore 189
SQL Server AlwaysOn 152
Standard systems 40
STONITH fencing 154
Storage 96, 139, 273
   solutions 140
Storage snapshot 184
Storage Spaces Direct (S2D) 143
Striping 96
Subnets 70
   sizes 133
Subscription design 130
Support contract 36
SUSE Linux Enterprise Server (SLES) 153,
   155, 204, 278, 290
   licensing 76
System clone, copy, and refresh 250
System design framework 85

T

Table splitting 229
Tagging 123
Terraform 87, 200
Third-party systems 49
Total cost of ownership (TCO) 277
Total cost of ownership calculator 62
Transaction
   OS07 37
   SLICENSE 253
   SM69 244
   ST06 37
Transparent data encryption (TDE) 209

U

Unattended install 196
   workflow 196
Unsorted export 229
Update domains 102

V

Virtual central processing unit (vCPU) 66–67
Virtual machines (VMs) ... 21, 59, 137, 141, 176,
   209–210, 277
   backup 178
   backup without database file system 183
   multiple instances 138
   resizing 249
   restore 187–188
   scale sets 243
   upsizing 230
Virtual network (VNET) 70
Virtual private network (VPN) 211, 278
Virtual wide area network (WAN) 62
VNets 90, 119, 131, 164, 198, 278
   peering 132
Vormetric 210

W

Wide area network (WAN) connectivity 95
Windows Server failover cluster 150

Y

YAML 200

Z

Zonal services 103
Zone-redundant services 103
Zone-redundant storage 108, 185

- Understand the technical foundation of SAP S/4HANA
- Explore the architecture of key application areas, including finance, logistics, procurement, and sales
- Learn about SAP S/4HANA Cloud's unique cloud architecture

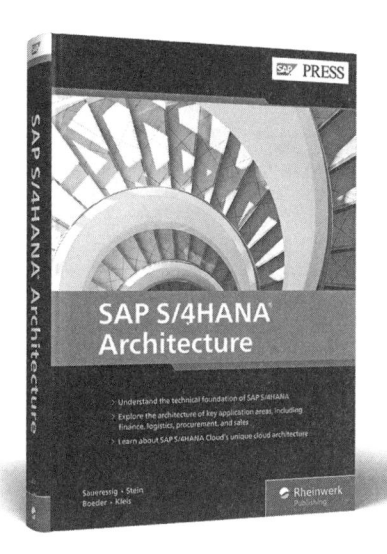

Saueressig, Stein, Boeder, Kleis

SAP S/4HANA Architecture

Pop the hood on SAP S/4HANA with this guide to its technical and application architecture! Understand the new data and programming models that underpin SAP S/4HANA and see how they differ from SAP ERP. Learn about technology components, like embedded analytics and integration. Then walk through the architecture of individual application areas like finance and logistics to see how they work and interact. Considering SAP S/4HANA Cloud? Explore scoping, compliance, performance, and more. Get the complete blueprint to SAP S/4HANA!

520 pages, pub. 11/2020
E-Book: $69.99 | **Print:** $79.95 | **Bundle:** $89.99

www.sap-press.com/5189

- Plan and prepare for your migration from SAP ERP to SAP S/4HANA
- Perform the technical conversion and adapt custom code and business functions for SAP S/4HANA
- Explore functional conversion steps for finance, logistics, and more

Mark Mergaerts, Bert Vanstechelman

SAP S/4HANA System Conversion Guide

If you're performing a brownfield migration from an existing SAP ERP system, this is the technical guide for you! From planning the project and preparing your system to adjusting custom code and executing the conversion, you'll get step-by-step instructions for all stages of your implementation. Troubleshooting tips and extensive coverage of the functional conversion will help you ensure that all your data makes it to where it needs to be. The time to move to SAP S/4HANA is here!

537 pages, pub. 07/2020
E-Book: $79.99 | **Print:** $89.95 | **Bundle:** $99.99

www.sap-press.com/5035

www.sap-press.com

Interested in reading more?

Please visit our website for all new book and e-book releases from SAP PRESS.

www.sap-press.com